W9-BYB-964

MAKING GLOBAL TRADE WORK FOR PEOPLE

M60U
MR927

MAKING GLOBAL TRADE WORK FOR PEOPLE

UN
DP

HEINRICH BÖLL FOUNDATION

ROCKEFELLER BROTHERS FUND

WALLACE
GLOBAL FUND
For a sustainable future

Université d'Ottawa
BIBLIOTHEQUES

LIBRARIES
University of Ottawa

London and Sterling, Virginia

b25362008

First published in the UK and USA in 2003
by Earthscan Publications Ltd

Reprinted 2004

Copyright © 2003
United Nations Development Programme
One United Nations Plaza
New York, NY 10017

All rights reserved

A catalogue record for this book is available from the British Library

ISBN: 1 85383 982 5 paperback
1 85383 981 7 hardback

DISCLAIMER
The responsibility for opinions in this book rests solely with its authors. Publication does not constitute an endorsement by the United Nations Development Programme or the institutions of the United Nations system or the Heinrich Böll Foundation, Rockefeller Brothers Fund, Rockefeller Foundation, or Wallace Global Fund.

UN2
DP
2003M13

Design and layout by Communications Development, Washington, DC
Printed in the UK by CPI Bath
Cover by Yvonne Booth based on a design by Karin Hug
Cover photographs: floating market, hands and camel train © Panos Pictures

Earthscan
8-12 Camden High Street, London, N1 OJH
Tel: +44 (0)20 7387 8558 Fax: +44 (0)20 7387 8998
Email: earthinfo@earthscan.co.uk
Web: www.earthscan.co.uk

22883 Quicksilver Drive, Sterling, VA 20166-2012, USA

Earthscan publishes in association with WWF-UK and the International Institute
for Environment and Development

This book is printed on elemental chlorine-free paper

CONTENTS

CONTENTS

BOXES

CONTENTS

FIGURES

TABLES

ANNEX TABLES

PREFACE

Trade has been an indispensable engine for economic growth across the world throughout human history. But while that growth has in many instances been translated into sustained poverty reduction, the connection is not automatic. Amidst the street riots of Seattle in 1999, the question of whether the international trading system as currently structured helps or hinders the progress of developing countries was called into question.

Almost immediately, that meeting became a kind of Rorschach test for how different constituencies view globalisation. Supporters of open markets and free trade claimed progress was held back by the inaction of some governments and misunderstanding or obstruction by some civil society organisations. Opponents, pointing to the fact that 60 countries from all parts of the world got poorer over the last decade, declared that the combination of unfettered capitalism and rigged trade rules was in practice leaving developing countries further and further behind. They also criticized the double standards of some industrialized countries that preach free trade but do not practice it themselves.

And with big business, civil society, labour, and rich and poor governments alike all noisily blaming each other for the failure to agree on a new trade round, the general public was left confused about the details but—as was clearly evidenced in a raft of opinion polls across both the developing and industrialized world—increasingly convinced that something was going wrong with the great globalisation experiment.

Trade can, and must, be made to work as an engine of growth and indeed of human development. What is needed to enable this is a serious, systematic effort to apply the lessons of history, which show that, with very few exceptions, today's rich countries in the past enjoyed many of the protections they now seek to deny developing countries, only dismantling them after growing wealthier and more powerful. It is also important to ensure that the multilateral trade regime is better aligned with broader objectives of human development: helping poor people everywhere gain the tools, opportunities and choices to build a better life for themselves, their families and their communities. This is the only way to reverse the current disaffection with globalisation.

With this goal firmly in mind, the United Nations Development Programme (UNDP), the Rockefeller Brothers Fund and the Rockefeller Foundation commissioned the Trade and Sustainable Human Development Project in mid-2000 to help flesh out exactly what this might mean in practice. The Ford Foundation, Heinrich Böll Foundation and Wallace Global Fund joined this effort in subsequent months. And while this book is the product of that initiative, the process of preparing it has in many ways been as important as the final result.

The Project was divided into five main phases. First was to commission papers by respected independent scholars and experts from academia and civil society. Second, to convene an advisory team of concerned and internationally respected experts to critically assess the background paper outlines and advise on overall project strategy. Third, to prepare the draft and final background papers. Fourth, to use the draft papers as inputs into a series of consultations with developing country governments and civil society organisations in the Asia, Africa, Latin America and the Arab States region in the lead-up to the World Trade Organization (WTO) Ministerial Conference in Doha in November 2001, to obtain their feedback and understand their concerns more fully. And last, to draw on all of these and other inputs to prepare and finalize this book.

By engaging with a very wide range of experts across government, academia and civil society, the Project has provided a platform for a wide range of views and recommendations—ranging from issues of intellectual property to agricultural reform to capacity building to helping developing countries participate more effectively in trade negotiations—on how to make the multilateral trade regime work more effectively for poor people and for human development. As a result, it is important to stress that the recommendations in the book are not necessarily a reflection of the policy of its sponsors. While we hope and believe that many of the recommendations will have direct relevance for the work of the Project's sponsors, the main aim of this book has been to provide a substantive basis for refocusing discussion and debate around the broad issue of how trade can best contribute to human development.

Our hope is that this book will provide policymakers, practitioners, civil society groups and others engaged in trade issues with some concrete ideas on how to move forward. This is important because unless we can give developing countries the means and voice to participate as full partners in a more inclusive global trade system, the world has little prospect of meeting its shared agenda of the Millennium Development Goals.

Team for the preparation of

Making Global Trade Work for People

Coordinator and lead author
Kamal Malhotra

Core research and writing team
Chandrika Bahadur
Selim Jahan
Mümtaz Keklik
Kamal Malhotra

*Principal consultants for
background papers*
Nilüfer Çağatay
Dani Rodrik
Third World Network

Contributors
Özlem Altýok, Susan Benjamin, Janine Berg, Murray Gibbs, Taisuke Ito,
Abdelaziz Megzari, William Milberg, Bonapas Onguglo, Andreas Pfeil, Moeed
Pirzada, Marina Ponti, Bharati Sadasivam, Swarnim Wagle, Jake Werksman

Principal editor
Bruce Ross-Larson

ACKNOWLEDGEMENTS

The initial co-sponsors of the Trade and Sustainable Human Development Project and this book were the United Nations Development Programme, the Rockefeller Brothers Fund and the Rockefeller Foundation. The Ford Foundation, Heinrich Böll Foundation, and Wallace Global Fund joined the effort in subsequent months. The generous contributions of many other individuals and organizations—contributions that took the form of intense consultations and the preparation and sharing of policy research papers and other inputs have played an equally important role.

EMINENT PERSONS GROUP

The book has benefited enormously from the overall guidance of a group of eminent experts in global economic policies, governance, trade and human development. The group comprised: Gerald Helleiner, Professor, Department of Economics and Distinguished Research Fellow, Munk Centre for International Studies, University of Toronto; Noeleen Heyzer, Executive Director, United Nations Development Fund for Women (UNIFEM); Vice-Minister Yong-Tu Long, Ministry of Trade and Economic Cooperation, People's Republic of China; Ambassador Ali Said Mchumo, Deputy Secretary General, East African Community, and ambassador and permanent representative of the United Republic of Tanzania to the UN and other offices in Geneva and Vienna and WTO Ambassador till recently, and chair of the WTO General Council between February 1999 and February 2000; Deepak Nayyar, Vice-Chancellor, University of Delhi; and Jose Antonio Ocampo, Executive Secretary, UN Economic Commission for Latin America and the Caribbean (ECLAC).

PEER REVIEW GROUP

The book has also benefited greatly from intellectual advice and guidance from a peer review group of experts on trade, governance and human development. This group comprised: Yilmaz Akyüz, Georges Chapelier, Sakiko Fukuda-Parr, Murray Gibbs, Gerald Helleiner, Rashid Kaukab, Inge Kaul, Carlos Lopes, Deepak Nayyar and Jan Vandemoortele.

EXPERT REVIEWERS AND ADVISERS

Other expert reviewers and advisers either provided valuable advice or commented on the complete draft, specific chapters or on issues in the first, intermediate or final drafts, making valuable contributions: Munir Ahmad, Anne-Birgitte Albrectsen, Safiatou Ba-N'Daw, Debapriya Bhattacharya, Henk-Jan Brinkman, Stephen Browne, Patrice Chiwota, Carlos M. Correa, Carolyn Deere, Biswajit Dhar, Graham Dutfield, Georgina Fekete, Duncan Green, James Greishaber-Otto, Yonita Grigorova, Rima Khalaf Hunaidi, Abdoulie Janneh, Bruce Jenks, Hande Keklik, Mohan Kumar, Thierry Lemaresquier, Joseph Anthony Lim, David Luke, Elena Martinez, Mina Mashayekhi, Ronald Mendoza, Saraswathi Menon, William Milberg, Kalman Mizsei, Mehrnaz Mostafavi, Sophia Murphy, John Ohiorhenuan, Hafiz Pasha, Robert Pollin, Ravi Rajan, Dani Rodrik, Pedro Roffe, Anwar Shaik, Miho Shirotori, Scott Sinclair, Ajit Singh, Mark Suzman, Jake Werksman, Caitlin Wiesen and Ngaire Woods.

SPECIFIC CONTRIBUTIONS

Specific contributions were made by Status of Women Canada, Janet VanGrasstek, Ricardo Melendez-Ortiz, Ronald Mendoza, Sophia Murphy, Jonathan Rose, Xiaobing Tang, Aster Zaoude and Simonetta Zarilli.

BRAINSTORMING MEETING

A brainstorming meeting was organized in October 2000 in Tarrytown, New York. The opening address was given by Mark Malloch Brown, Administrator, UNDP, while closing remarks were provided by Eimi Watanabe, then Assistant Administrator and Director, Bureau for Development Policy, UNDP. The participants were Barbara Adams, Yilmaz Akyüz, Chandrika Bahadur, Stephen Browne, Nilüfer Çağatay, Ambassador Federico Alberto Cuello Camilo, Qiang Cui, Bhagirath Lal Das, Carolyn Deere, Luis Gomez-Echeverri, Sakiko Fukuda-Parr, Murray Gibbs, Yao Graham, Evelyn Hampstead, Gerald Helleiner, Bruce Jenks, Susan Joekes, Ambassador Tichaona J.B. Jokonya, Mbaya Kankwenda, Rashid Kaukab, Inge Kaul, Dot Keet, Mümtaz Keklik, Martin Khor, Aileen Kwa, Radhika Lal, Thierry Lemaresquier, Carlos Lopes, Kamal Malhotra, Ambassador Ali Said Mchumo, Robert McIntyre, Terry McKinley, Ronald Mendoza, Manuel Montes, Bruno Moro, Deepak Nayyar, Michael Northrop, Leo Palma, Ernestos Panayiotou, Alejandra Pero, Minh H. Pham, Geoff Prewitt, Chakravarthi Raghavan, Dani Rodrik, Gita Sen, Anuradha Seth, Rehman Sobhan, Mounir Tabet, Yash Tandon, Ambassador Juan Gabriel Valdes, Alejandro Villamar, Caitlin Wiesen, Kanni Wignaraja, Mariama Williams and Aster Zaoude.

CONSULTATIONS

The book gained considerably from a series of consultations with representatives from governments and civil society organizations. Approximately 400 people participated in nine consultations that took place prior to the Fourth WTO Ministerial Conference in November 2001 in Doha, Qatar. Three were regional government consultations held in Mongolia, Zimbabwe and Chile. One took place in Switzerland, led by the G-77 New York Secretariat in collaboration with its Geneva chapter and supported by UNCTAD's Secretariat. Four regional meetings with civil society organizations were held in Malaysia, Lebanon, Ghana and Brazil. A Round Table Meeting was organised in Canada at the request of Canadian policy researchers.

While the participants in these consultations were too numerous to name individually, their valuable insights, critical comments and the preparations and logistical support of the lead organisations are gratefully acknowledged. Special thanks are due to UNDP staff Zena Ali-Ahmad, Victor Angelo, Safiatou Ba N'Daw, Jesimen Chipika, Thierry Lemaresquier, Saraswathi Menon, Bernard Mokam, Nada al-Nashif, Hikwa Nkuleko, Yves de San, Arusha Stanislaus, Kanni Wignaraja and Yiping Zhou; to Ricardo Ffrench-Davis, Jose Antonio Ocampo and Vivianne Ventura at ECLAC; to Juanita Chacon, the organizer of the regional consultation in Chile; to Ambassador Bagher Asadi, chairman of the G-77 in New York in 2001; to Mourad Ahmia of the G-77 Secretariat in New York; to Awni Benham of UNCTAD; to Yao Graham of the Africa Trade Network; to Ziad Abdel-Samad of the Arab NGO Network for Development; to Alejandro Villamar of the Inter-Hemispheric Social Alliance; to Martin Khor of the Third World Network; to Yash Tandon of the Southern and Eastern African Trade Information, and Negotiations Initiative (SEA-TINI) and to John Foster of the North-South Institute in Canada.

PROJECT MANAGEMENT AND STAFF SUPPORT

Efficient and timely support for project management is gratefully acknowledged from Daniela Costantino, Michele Jack and Martha Mai of the UN Office of Project Services. Equally critical administrative support for the project and the book's preparation was provided by Evelyn Hampstead, Clarice A. King and Kale Yideg.

EDITING, PRODUCTION AND PUBLISHING

The book benefited from the team at Communications Development Inc. In addition to Bruce Ross-Larson, principal editor and team leader, thanks are due to editors Meta de Coquereaumont, Paul Holtz and Alison Strong; Stephanie Rostron, project manager; and Elaine Wilson, layout artist. Editing of earlier drafts benefited from Shawna Tropp and Anita Malhotra, while Karen Judd edited the three Background Papers.

The book's cover was designed by Yvonne Booth, with important inputs from Karin Hug and Anita Malhotra. Advice on production and related matters is gratefully acknowledged from Elizabeth Scott Andrews, Gillian Chalmers, Fe Conway, Rajeswary Iruthayanathan, Maureen Lynch and Judith Puyat-Magnaye. Thanks are also due to Earthscan London, especially to Victoria Burrows, Frances MacDermott and Jonathan Sinclair-Wilson.

* * * *

The team expresses its thanks to Eimi Watanabe and Siba Kumar Das for their support for the project in its early stages and to Shoji Nishimoto for his support in its most recent stage. Special and sincere appreciation is due to Carlos Lopes and Jan Vandemoortele for their consistent and committed support throughout, especially during the period when this book was being written and was in the process of publication.

The team is also especially grateful to Mark Malloch Brown, Administrator, UNDP; Stephen Heintz, President, Rockefeller Brothers Fund; Gordon Conway, President, Rockefeller Foundation; Ralf Fücks and Barbara Unmüßig, Co-Presidents, Heinrich Böll Foundation; Susan V. Berresford, President, Ford Foundation; and Catherine Cameron, Executive Director, Wallace Global Fund for their vision, leadership and support without which this book would not have been possible.

While thankful for the support they have received, the core research and writing team, especially its coordinator and lead author, assumes full responsibility for the opinions expressed in the book.

ABBREVIATIONS

ACP	African, Caribbean and Pacific
AMS	Aggregate Measure of Support
APEC	Asia-Pacific Economic Cooperation
ASCM	Agreement on Subsidies and Countervailing Measures
ASEAN	Association of Southeast Asian Nations
ATC	Agreement on Textiles and Clothing
BSE	bovine spongiform encephalopathy
CGE	computable general equilibrium
COMESA	Common Market for Eastern and Southern Africa
CTE	Committee on Trade and Environment (World Trade Organization)
EU	European Union
FAO	Food and Agriculture Organization (of the United Nations)
FDI	foreign direct investment
GATS	General Agreement on Trade in Services
GATT	General Agreement on Tariffs and Trade
GDP	gross domestic product
GNP	gross national product
GPA	Government Procurement Agreement
GSP	Generalized System of Preferences
HIPC	heavily indebted poor countries
IMF	International Monetary Fund
ISO	International Organization for Standardization
ITO	International Trade Organization
JITAP	Joint Integrated Technical Assistance Programme to Selected Least Developed and Other African Countries
LDCs	least developed countries
LTA	Long-Term Arrangement
Mercosur	Mercado Comun del Sur (Common Market of the South)
MFA	Multifibre Arrangement
MFN	most-favoured nation
MITI	Ministry of International Trade and Industry (of Japan)

MTBE	methyl tertiary butyl ether
NAFTA	North American Free Trade Agreement
NGO	non-governmental organization
OECD	Organisation for Economic Co-operation and Development
OPEC	Organization of Petroleum Exporting Countries
PPM	process and production method
PRSP	Poverty Reduction Strategy Paper
R&D	research and development
SPS	Sanitary and Phytosanitary Standards
TBT	Technical Barriers to Trade
TRIMs	Trade-Related Investment Measures
TRIPS	Trade-Related Aspects of Intellectual Property Rights
UN	United Nations
UNCTAD	United Nations Conference on Trade and Development
UNDP	United Nations Development Programme
WCO	World Customs Organization
WIPO	World Intellectual Property Rights Organization
WTO	World Trade Organization

GLOSSARY

absolute advantage: The ability of one country compared with another to produce a good at lower cost in real resources.

African, Caribbean and Pacific (ACP) countries: Group of African, Caribbean and Pacific countries whose partnership with the EU has been defined in a series of agreements, from the Lomé Convention to the Cotonou Agreement.

ad valorem tariff: Duty (tariff or charge) calculated as a percentage of the value of the dutiable item. Contrast with *specific tariff.*

Aggregate Measure of Support: An index that measures the monetary value of government support to a sector. The Agreement on Agriculture's Aggregate Measure of Support includes direct payments to producers, input subsidies (such as for irrigation water), programmes that distort market prices to consumers (market price supports) and interest subsidies on commodity loan programmes.

Agreement on Agriculture. WTO agreement commiting member governments to improve *market access* and reduce trade-distorting *domestic support payments* and *export subsidies* in agriculture.

amber box: All domestic support measures considered to distort production and trade (with a few exceptions) fall into the amber box. These subsidies are subject to reduction under the Agreement on Agriculture.

anti-dumping duties: These duties may be imposed if export *dumping* causes injury to producers of competing products in an importing country. The duties should equal the difference between the export price and the normal value of the dumped good.

Appellate Body: The WTO body that hears appeals to the findings of dispute settlement panels.

blue box: Comprises measures regarded as exceptions to the general rule that all subsidies linked to production must be reduced or kept within defined minimal levels. Covers payments directly linked to land size or livestock as long as the activity being supported limits production.

Bretton Woods: Town in New Hampshire (US) where a 1944 conference led to the creation of the International Monetary Fund and the World Bank. These two institutions are known as the Bretton Woods institutions.

built-in agenda: Many of the accords agreed in the Uruguay Round specify future dates for continuing review or negotiations of specific sectors or subject areas—for example, in agriculture and services. Together such reviews or negotiations comprise the built-in agenda.

Cairns Group: Comprises 18 developing and industrial countries with similar, though not identical, views on agricultural liberalization: Argentina, Australia, Bolivia, Brazil, Canada, Chile, Colombia, Costa Rica, Fiji, Guatemala, Indonesia, Malaysia, New Zealand, Paraguay, Philippines, South Africa, Thailand and Uruguay.

cartelization: The formation of a group of firms that seek to raise the price of a good by restricting its supply. The term is usually used for international groups, especially involving governments or state-owned firms.

ceiling binding: Commitment by countries not to raise certain tariffs above specific or bound levels.

Codex Alimentarius: This is the 'food code', consisting of standards, codes of practice, guidelines and recommendations for producing and processing food. The Codex Alimentarius Commission is responsible for compiling the standards.

collusion: Cooperation among firms to raise prices and increase profits.

comparative advantage: The ability of one country compared with another to produce a good at lower cost relative to other goods. Under conditions of perfect competition and undistorted markets, countries tend to export goods in which they have comparative advantage.

commodity: Total primary commodities comprise total non-fuel primary commodities—the sum of agricultural primary and mineral commodities.

competition policy: Policies designed to protect and stimulate competition in markets by outlawing anticompetitive business practices such as cartels, market sharing or price fixing.

compulsory license: Authorization by a government for a government or company to make and sell a product (such as a drug) without the permission of the patent holder. Compulsory licenses are generally issued on the basis of public interest, such as for reasons of public health or defence.

Cotonou Agreement: Agreement between EU and African, Caribbean and Pacific countries signed in June 2000 in Cotonou, Benin. Replaces the Lomé Convention.

countervailing duty: Duty levied on imports of goods that have benefited from subsidies. The duty is intended to offset the effects of the subsidies.

customs union: Group of countries forming a single customs territory in which tariffs and other barriers are eliminated on most or all trade for products originating in these countries, and a common external trade policy (common external tariff) is applied to non-members.

de minimis: The level of domestic support below which subsidies are exempt from reduction commitments, quantified in monetary terms on a product-specific basis and, for sector-wide measures, a non-product-specific basis. De minimis levels are 5 per cent of the value of production for specific products (or the total value of agricultural production for non-product-specific measures) for industrial country members and 10 per cent for developing country members.

development box: Measures proposed to give developing countries the flexibility needed to enhance domestic agricultural production for home consumption and to take other measures needed to ensure food security, protect farmer livelihoods and reduce poverty.

Dispute Settlement Body: The General Council of the WTO, composed of representatives of all member countries, convenes as the Dispute Settlement Body to administer rules and procedures established in various agreements. It has the authority to establish panels, oversee implementation of rulings and recommendations and authorize suspension of concessions or other obligations under various agreements.

domestic content requirement: A requirement that goods produced in a country contain a certain proportion of domestic inputs. Same as local content requirement.

dumping: Occurs when goods are exported at a price less than their normal value, generally meaning they are exported for less than they are sold in the domestic market or third-country markets, or at less than production cost.

dumping margin: The amount by which the normal value exceeds the export price or constructed export price of the subject merchandise.

economic needs test: Requirements that need to be met in order for a non-national to obtain a work permit for a specific period to fill a particular post. To ensure that suitable nationals are given an opportunity to fill the vacancy first, a key requirement is that qualified nationals be unavailable.

effective rate of protection: Measures the protection provided to an industry through *tariffs* and other trade barriers on both inputs and outputs.

enabling clause: The 1979 decision of the GATT to give developing countries 'differential and more favorable treatment, reciprocity and fuller participation'. One of the so-called framework agreements, it enables WTO members to accord such treatment to developing countries without giving it to other contracting parties.

escape clause: Clause in a legal text allowing temporary derogation from its provisions under specified emergency conditions.

EUROMED: An agreement on bilateral, multilateral and regional cooperation signed in Barcelona, Spain, in 1995 between the 15 members of the EU and 12 Mediterranean partners.

Europe Agreement: An agreement between the EU and each of 10 Eastern European countries (starting with Hungary and Poland in 1994) creating free trade areas and establishing additional forms of political and economic cooperation in preparation for these countries' eventual membership in the EU.

Everything but Arms: The name given by the EU to the package it offered to the least developed countries in 2001, which is expected to eliminate quotas and tariffs on all of their exports—except arms.

exchange control: Restrictions imposed by a government or central bank on the holding, sale or purchase of foreign currency.

exhaustion: The legal principle that once a company has sold its product in one country, its patent is exhausted and it no longer has any rights over what happens to that product. Applies to the agreement on *Trade-Related Aspects of Intellectual Property Rights*. This agreement does not explicitly address the issue of international exhaustion of property rights, leaving individual member countries to decide whether to recognize that the right to patent is exhausted at sale.

export processing zone (EPZ): Designated area or region where firms can import duty-free as long as the imports are used as inputs into the production of exports.

export promotion: A strategy for economic development that stresses expanding exports, often through policies to assist them such as export subsidies.

externality: The action of one agent (person, firm, government) that directly affects other agents, making them better or worse off. Beneficial effects are called positive externalities; harmful ones, negative externalities.

fallacy of composition: The erroneous view that what is good for one country is necessarily good for all countries.

fast-track negotiating authority: Authority granted to the US president by Congress to negotiate trade agreements. Under fast track, Congress can accept or reject an agreement but cannot alter any negotiated agreement. Introduced in the 1974 Trade Act.

foreign direct investment (FDI): A corporation's acquisition abroad of physical assets such as plants and equipment, with operating control residing in the parent corporation outside the country where the acquisition occurs. Also includes mergers and acquisitions of corporations in one country with or by those in another country.

foreign trade zone: Area in a country where imported goods can be stored or processed without being subject to import duty. Also called a 'free zone', 'free port' or 'bonded warehouse'.

free trade area: A group of countries that adopt free trade (zero tariffs and no other trade restrictions) among themselves, without necessarily changing the trade barriers that each member has for countries outside the group.

Friends of the Chair: People selected by the conference chair to lead working groups during the November 2001 WTO ministerial conference in Doha, Qatar.

G-7: A group of seven major industrial countries—Canada, France, Germany, Italy, Japan, the UK and the US—whose heads of state have met every year since 1976 for economic and political summits.

G-8: The G-7 plus the Russian Federation, whose heads of state have met every year since 1998 for economic and political summits.

G-24: Established in 1971, a group of 24 developing countries that seeks to promote the position of developing countries on monetary and development finance issues. The only formal developing country group within the International Monetary Fund and World Bank, it meets twice a year—preceding the spring and autumn meetings of the two financial institutions.

G-77: A group of developing countries within the UN established in 1964 to articulate and promote the collective economic interests of its members and enhance their negotiating capacity. Founded by 77 developing countries, by 2002 it had 133 members.

General Agreement on Tariffs and Trade (GATT): A multilateral forum for trade discussion and negotiation aimed at encouraging trade between its members through the reduction of trade barriers. It led to a series of trade agreements, the first of which was in 1947. The *Uruguay Round,* completed in 1994, created the World Trade Organization which superseeded the GATT in 1995. GATT 1994 contains some of the WTO's underlying principles and its initial agreements.

General Agreement on Trade in Services (GATS): WTO agreement concluded at the end of the *Uruguay Round*. It provides a legal framework for trade in services and the negotiated, progressive liberalization of regulations that impede this. It covers areas such as transport, investment, education, communications, financial services, energy and water services and the movement of persons.

Generalized System of Preferences (GSP): System through which high-income countries grant preferential access to their markets to developing countries.

geographic indication: Measure aimed to protect the reputation of goods originating in particular geographic locations by limiting the use of distinctive place names and regional appellations to goods actually produced in those locations.

government procurement: Purchase of goods and services by governments and state-owned enterprises.

graduation: Generally used in the context of preferential treatment of low-income countries as a mechanism or set of criteria to determine when countries cease to be eligible for preferences.

grandfather clause: A provision in an agreement—including the GATT but not the WTO—that allows signatories to retain certain laws that otherwise would violate the agreement.

green box: Contains income support and subsidies that are expected to cause little or no trade distortion. The subsidies have to be funded by governments but must not involve price support. Environmental protection subsidies are included. No limits or reductions are required for such income support or subsidies.

greenfield investment: Productive investments, such as new factories and power plants, that are located on new sites rather than on sites with existing facilities.

green room: The meeting of a limited number of (often self-selected) countries to work out an agreement among themselves is referred to in WTO jargon as the green room process—named after the colour of the room of the GATT director-general where many such meetings took place during the *Uruguay Round*. In the WTO era the green room process has taken place especially in the intense negotiations prior to and at ministerial conferences, including in Seattle and Doha.

grey area measures: Trade barriers that were in a legally murky area before the *Uruguay Round*. Voluntary export restraints, for example, were grey area measures because they violated the *most-favoured-nation* principle and the principle of protection by *tariff*, and because they were applied without sanction by the GATT.

gross domestic product (GDP): Total value of new goods and services produced in a given year within the borders of a country, regardless of by whom.

gross national product (GNP): Total value of new goods and services produced in a given year by a country's domestically owned factors of production, regardless of where.

immiserizing growth: When an increase in export production not absorbed by world markets leads to severe deterioration in a country's terms of trade, imposing a loss in real income that outweighs the primary gain in real income due to the growth in production.

import quota: The maximum quantity or value of a commodity allowed to enter a country during a specified period.

import substitution: Policies aimed at reducing imports by substituting domestically produced goods and services.

infant industry protection: Protection of a newly established domestic industry.

intra-industry trade: Trade through which a country both exports and imports goods classified in the same industry.

Like-minded Group: An informal group of 13 developing country WTO members that includes Cuba, the Dominican Republic, Egypt, Honduras, India, Indonesia, Jamaica, Kenya, Malaysia, Pakistan, Sri Lanka, Tanzania, Uganda and Zimbabwe. Jamaica and China are special invitees, and Mauritius is an observer.

maquiladora: An export processing factory, usually foreign-owned, that assembles goods for duty-free export, mainly to the US. The word originated in Mexico in the 1960s.

market access: The extent to which a country permits imports. A variety of *tariff* and *non-tariff* trade *barriers* can be used to limit the entry of products from other countries.

market failure: The inability of the market to deliver certain public goods or services and to allocate resources efficiently, therefore requiring state intervention.

markup: The amount (percentage) by which price exceeds marginal cost.

matching grant: A subsidy that is conditional on a co-payment or contribution by an industry or enterprise.

maximum (minimum) price system: Specification of the highest (lowest) price permitted for an import.

Mercosur: Common market among Argentina, Brazil, Paraguay and Uruguay, known as the Common Market of the South (Mercado Comun del Sur), created by the Treaty of Asunción on 26 March 1991. Chile and Bolivia were added as associate members in 1996 and 1997.

Millennium Development Goals: At the UN General Assembly in 2000, governments committed to achieving the following goals by 2015: eradicating extreme poverty and hunger, achieving universal primary education, promoting gender equality and empowering women, reducing child mortality, improving maternal health, combating HIV/AIDS, malaria, and other diseases, ensuring environmental sustainability and developing a global partnership for development.

minimum access: The minimum quantity of imports allowed access to a market.

mixing regulation: Specification of the proportion of domestically produced content in products sold on the domestic market or specification of the amount of domestically produced goods that must be bought by an exporter for given quantities of imports.

mode of supply: WTO term to identify how a service is provided by a supplier to a buyer.

most-favoured-nation (MFN): A commitment that a country will extend to another country the lowest tariff rates it applies to any other country. All WTO contracting parties undertake to apply such treatment to one another under article I of the GATT. When a country agrees to cut tariffs on a particular product imported from one country, the tariff reduction automatically applies to imports of that product from any other country eligible for most-favoured-nation treatment.

multifunctionality: A term indicating that agriculture plays non-commodity roles in addition to providing food and fibre, including the provision of landscape and open space amenities, rural economic viability, cultural heritage, domestic food security, prevention of natural hazards and preservation of biodiversity.

mutual recognition: The acceptance by one country of another country's certification that a satisfactory standard has been met for ability, performance, safety and the like.

national treatment: Commitment to treat foreign producers and sellers the same as domestic firms.

necessity test: Procedure to determine whether a policy restricting trade is necessary to achieve its intended objective.

negative list: In an international agreement, a list of items, entities, products and the like to which the agreement will not apply, on the understanding that the agreement applies to everything else. Contrast with *positive* list.

nominal tariff: The nominal protection provided by a tariff—that is, the stated tariff amount. Contrast with *effective rate of protection*.

non-actionable subsidy: A type of subsidy not prohibited under WTO rules. However, a member country may respond to non-actionable subsidies by imposing *tariffs* on imports that are subsidized in exporting countries.

non-tariff barriers (NTBs): A catch-all phrase describing barriers to international trade other than *tariffs*.

non-tariff measure: Any government action with a potential effect on the value, volume or direction of trade.

normal value: Price charged by an exporting firm in its home market.

offset requirement: As a condition for importing into a country, a requirement that foreign exporters purchase domestic products or invest in the importing country.

opt-out: A country's withdrawal from an international agreement.

Organisation for Economic Co-operation and Development (OECD): Group of industrial countries that 'provides governments a setting in which to discuss, develop and perfect economic and social policy'. In July 2002 it had 30 members.

origin rule: Criterion for establishing the country of origin of a product. Often based on whether production (processing) leads to a change in tariff heading (classification) or in the level of value added in the country where the good was last processed.

parallel imports: Products made and marketed by the *patent* owner (or trademark or copyright owner) in one country and imported into another country without the approval of the patent owner.

Pareto efficiency: The criterion that stipulates that for change in an economy to be viewed as socially beneficial, it should make no one worse off while making at least one person better off.

patent: The legal right to proceeds from and control over the use of an invented product or process, granted for a fixed period of time—usually 20 years.

peace clause: A provision in article 13 of the Agreement on Agriculture designed to reduce the threat of trade disputes during the period of agricultural trade reform, especially in industrial countries. It stipulates that agricultural subsidies permitted by the agreement cannot be challenged under other WTO agreements. Expires at the end of 2003. Unless renewed, its expiry will subject agricultural subsidies to the same disciplines as industrial subsidies.

plurilateral agreement: Plurilateral WTO agreements contrast with multilateral agreements in that plurilateral agreements are signed only by member countries that choose to do so, while all members are party to multilateral agreements.

portfolio investment: The acquisition of financial assets, including stocks, bonds, deposits and currencies. Usually refers to such transactions across national borders or across currencies.

positive agenda: An initiative introduced by the secretary-general of the United Nations Conference on Trade and Development. Based on the perception that in the preparations leading to the 1996 WTO ministerial conference in Singapore, developing countries had focused on opposing the inclusion of certain issues (such as investment) in the WTO work programme, without formulating proposals or counter-proposals on issues of interest to them.

positive list: In an international agreement, a list of items, entities, products and the like to which the agreement will apply, with no commitment to apply the agreement to anything else. Contrast with *negative list*.

Poverty Reduction Strategy Paper (PRSP): Initiated by the boards of the World Bank and International Monetary Fund (IMF), this is a document describing a country's macroeconomic, structural and social policies and programmes to promote growth and reduce poverty, as well as associated external financing needs. PRSPs are expected to be prepared by governments through a participatory process involving civil society and development partners, including the World Bank and IMF, and are required for countries seeking to obtain concessional lending and debt relief under the enhanced Heavily Indebted Poor Countries (HIPC) initiative.

precautionary principle: The view that when science has not yet determined whether a new product or process is safe or unsafe, policy should prohibit or restrict its use until it is known to be safe. Applied to trade, this has, for example, been used as the basis for prohibiting imports of genetically modified organisms.

predatory pricing: Action by a firm to lower prices so much that rival firms are driven out of business, after which the firm raises prices to exploit its resulting monopoly power.

pre-shipment inspection: Certification of the value, quality or identity of traded goods in the exporting country by specialized agencies or firms on behalf of the importing country. Traditionally used as a means to prevent over- or under-invoicing, it is now also being used as a security measure.

price discrimination: The sale by a firm to different buyers at different prices. When it occurs internationally and the lower price is charged for export, it is called *dumping*.

price undertaking: A commitment by an exporting firm to raise its price in an importing country market, as a means of settling an anti-dumping suit and preventing an *anti-dumping duty*.

principal-supplier rule: Rule in bilateral negotiating procedures whereby an import concession on a specific product is to be negotiated only with the country that is actually or potentially the principal supplier of that product. Note that the WTO *most-favoured-nation* rule requires that the concessions be extended to all other members.

process and production method (PPM): Used when trade policy action by a country is motivated by a desire to ensure that imports have been produced in a way that satisfies a national or international production or process norm. The norms are often environmental.

producer support estimate: A measure of the aggregate value of the gross transfers from consumers and taxpayers to farmers resulting from policy measures. Also called *producer subsidy* equivalent.

production subsidy: A payment by government, perhaps implicit, to producers encouraging and assisting their activities and allowing them to produce at lower cost or to sell at a price lower than the market price.

protocol of accession: Legal document recording the conditions and obligations under which a country accedes to an international agreement or organization.

Quad (group of countries): The participants in the Quadrilateral meetings: Canada, the EU, Japan and the US.

quantitative restriction or quota: Measure restricting the quantity of a good imported or exported. Quantitative restrictions include quotas, non-automatic licensing, mixing regulations, voluntary export restraints and prohibitions or embargos.

quota rent: The amounts paid by traders or producers that need quotas to holders of quotas in an exporting country for specific textile and clothing products destined for specific importing countries. To the extent that the quota rents remain in exporting countries, they represent the amount of income transferred to such countries from importing countries. The quota rent equals the domestic price of the imported good, net of any *tariff*, minus the world price, times the quantity of imports.

rent-seeking: Economic rents that arise from policies that impose an extra cost to society (the loss of income due to the diversion of resources away from productive activities towards rent-seeking ones) beyond the distortionary costs associated with the measures that give rise to the rents.

request-offer procedure: Negotiating procedure based on the tabling, by each party, of a list of concessions requested of other parties, followed by an offer list of the concessions that could be granted in response to such requests.

restrictive business practice: Practice of business enterprises aimed at limiting access to markets and restraining competition (such as the formation of cartels).

retaliation: An action taken by one country against another for imposing a tariff or other trade barrier. Forms of retaliation include raising tariffs, imposing import restrictions or withdrawing a previously agreed trade concession. Under the WTO, restrictive trade action by one country entitles the harmed nation to take counter-action.

rules-based trade policy: Policy that adheres to accepted international rules and agreements on trade such as those embodied in GATT 1947 and the WTO.

safeguard action or measure: Emergency protection to safeguard domestic producers of a specific good from an unforeseen surge in imports.

sanitary and phytosanitary measures: Border control measures necessary to protect human, animal or plant life or health.

second-best argument for protection: An argument for protection to partially correct an existing distortion in the economy when the first-best policy for that purpose is not available.

selectivity: Application of a rule, regulation or trade action on a discriminatory basis to certain countries.

Singapore issues: The four issues on which it was agreed at the 1996 WTO Singapore Ministerial Conference to form working groups: trade and investment, competition policy, transparency in government procurement and trade facilitation.

single undertaking: Provision that requires countries to accept all the agreements reached during the *Uruguay Round* negotiations as a single package, rather than on a case-by-case basis.

special and differential treatment: The principle in the WTO that developing countries be accorded special privileges, either exempting them from some WTO rules or granting them preferential treatment in the application of WTO rules.

specific commitment: Under the *General Agreement on Trade in Services*, technical term describing the commitments made by WTO members on national treatment and market access for service sectors.

specific tariff: Duty (tariff or charge) expressed in terms of a fixed amount per unit of the dutiable item. For example, $1,000 on each imported vehicle or $50 on each ton of wheat. Contrast with *ad valorem tariff*.

standard: Rule, regulation or procedure specifying characteristics that must be met by a product (such as dimensions, quality, performance or safety). When these put foreign producers at a disadvantage, they may constitute a *non-tariff barrier*. See also *technical barrier to trade*.

state trading enterprise: A government entity responsible for exporting or importing specified products.

sunset clause: A provision within a piece of legislation providing for its demise on a specified date unless deliberately renewed.

tariff: A government-imposed tax on imports.

tariff binding: Commitment not to increase a rate of duty beyond an agreed level. Once a rate of duty is bound, it may not be raised without compensating the affected parties.

tariff equivalent: The level of *tariff* that would be the same, in terms of its effect, as a given *non-tariff barrier*.

tariff escalation: An increase in *tariffs* as a good becomes more processed, with lower tariffs on raw materials and less processed goods than on more processed versions of the same or derivative goods. For example, low duties on fresh tomatoes, higher duties on canned tomatoes and higher yet on tomato ketchup.

tariffication: Conversion of *non-tariff barriers* to their *tariff equivalents*.

tariff peak: A single, particularly high tariff, often defined as more than three times the average nominal tariff.

tariff rate quotas (TRQs): The quantitative level of imports of agricultural products (quota) above which higher tariffs are applied.

technical barrier to trade: Trade-restrictive effect arising from the application of technical regulations or standards such as testing requirements, labelling requirements, packaging requirements, marketing standards, certification requirements, origin marking requirements, health and safety regulations and sanitary and phytosanitary regulations.

technical regulation: Mandatory requirement or standard specifying the characteristics that an imported product must meet. Usually intended to protect public health or safety.

temporary admission: Permission to import a good duty-free for use as an input in production for export.

terms of trade: The price of a country's exports relative to its imports.

trade diversion: Trade displacement, as a result of trade policies that discriminate among trading partners, of more efficient (lower-cost) sources by less efficient (higher-cost) sources. Can arise when some preferred suppliers are freed from barriers but others are not.

trade integration: Process of reducing barriers to trade and increasing participation in the international economy through trade.

trade liberalization: Reduction of *tariffs* and removal or relaxation of *non-tariff barriers*.

trademark: Distinctive mark or name to identify a product, service or company.

trade policy review mechanism: WTO mechanism for periodic review of the trade policies and practices of members.

Trade-Related Aspects of Intellectual Property Rights (TRIPS). WTO agreement aimed at establishing minimum standards of intellectual property rights protection for all products and services, covering copyrights, trademarks, geographical indications, industrial designs, integrated circuits, patents and trade secrets.

Trade-Related Investment Measures (TRIMs). WTO agreement aimed at eliminating the trade-distorting effects of investment measures taken by members. It does not introduce any new obligations, but merely prohibits TRIMs considered inconsistent with the provisions of GATT 1994 for both agricultural and industrial goods.

trade-related technical assistance: Services financed or provided by donors and development agencies to strengthen trade-related institutions and build trade capacity in developing countries.

trade-weighted average tariff: A country's average tariff, weighted by the value of its imports. Easily calculated as the ratio of total tariff revenue to total value of imports.

transaction value: The actual price of a product, paid or payable, used for customs valuation purposes.

Uruguay Round. The last round under the GATT, which began in Uruguay in 1986 and was completed in 1994 after nearly eight years of negotiations. Included agreements in trade-related intellectual property rights and services for the first time, in addition to agreements in traditional trade areas such as agriculture and textiles and clothing. Its conclusion led to the creation of the World Trade Organization.

value added: The value of output minus the value of all inputs used in production.

variable levy: A tax on imports that varies over time to stabilize the domestic prices of imported goods. Essentially, the tax is set equal to the difference between the target domestic price and the world price.

voluntary export restraint: An agreement between importing and exporting countries in which the exporting country restrains exports of a certain product to an agreed maximum within a certain period.

waiver: An authorized deviation from the terms of a previously negotiated and legally binding agreement. Many countries have sought and obtained waivers from particular obligations of the GATT and WTO.

WTO panel: Group composed of neutral representatives that may be established by the WTO Secretariat under dispute settlement provisions to review the facts of a dispute and render findings and recommendations.

WTO plus: Trade agreements that contain more stringent obligations than the WTO multilateral trade regime requires. Regional trade agreements sometimes contain WTO plus elements.

OVERVIEW
MAKING GLOBAL TRADE WORK FOR PEOPLE

Human development is a process of expanding people's choices, allowing them to live secure lives with full freedoms and rights. Human development requires equitable, sustainable economic growth. It also requires promoting gender equality and fostering people's participation in decisions that affect their lives.

By expediting economic growth, creating jobs and raising incomes, globalization has the potential to advance human development around the world. But globalization has also increased vulnerability and insecurity. Multilateral institutions can play a major role in maximizing the potential benefits of trade and globalization while minimizing their risks. But the evolution of these institutions has not kept pace with the challenges of the 21st century.

By expanding markets, facilitating competition and disseminating knowledge, international trade can create opportunities for growth and promote human development. Trade can also increase aggregate productivity and exposure to new technologies, which can spur growth. Indeed, the regions that have grown the fastest over the past 20 years have also had the highest export growth.

But liberalizing trade does not automatically ensure human development, and increasing trade does not always have a positive impact on human development. The expansion of trade guarantees neither immediate economic growth nor long-term economic or human development. Internal and external institutional and social conditions play a significant role in determining whether and to what extent a country or group of people reaps the benefits of trade (Rodrik, 2001).

Pervasive gender discrimination in economic life causes trade policy to have very different effects on women and men. Trade liberalization has also had mixed results for gender outcomes. It is particularly troublesome from a human development perspective if export growth comes at the expense of exploiting female workers, neglecting care work[1] and increasing gender inequalities in opportunities and benefits (Çağatay, 2001).

A key message of this book is that an evaluation of the multilateral trade regime should be based on whether it maximizes possibilities for human development—especially in developing countries. To achieve that goal, the regime needs to shift its focus from promoting liberalization and market access to fostering development

(Rodrik, 2001). The regime should provide developing countries with policy space, giving them the flexibility they need to make institutional and other innovations—while still recognizing that trade liberalization and market access can make important contributions to human development in specific situations and certain sectors.

While the evidence on trade and human development shows that the links between them run in both directions, trade theories do not offer clear or unequivocal conclusions about the direction or dynamics of the relationship. But while the debate about the relationship between trade liberalization, economic growth and poverty reduction continues, evidence shows that trade liberalization is not a reliable mechanism for generating self-sustaining growth and poverty reduction—let alone human development (Rodrik, 2001).

Conventional wisdom holds that trade is linked to human development through economic growth. Though there is no automatic relationship between growth and human development, growth can contribute to human development if increased incomes and higher government revenue translate into social and productive spending that positively influences human development indicators (UNDP, 1996). Meanwhile, the absence of growth makes it extremely difficult to achieve human development objectives.

But what does the evidence reveal about the links between trade liberalization and economic growth? A close study of the empirical literature finds no compelling evidence that trade liberalization is systematically associated with higher growth (see chapter 1). Some leading researchers argue that the only systematic relationship between trade liberalization and growth is that countries dismantle trade barriers as they grow richer. Moreover, the experiences of industrial countries and successful developing countries provide two other important lessons. First, economic integration with the global economy is a result of successful growth and development—not a prerequisite for it. Second, domestic institutional innovations—many of them unorthodox and requiring considerable policy space and flexibility—have been integral to most successful development strategies.

Thus multilateral trade rules need to seek peaceful co-existence among national practices, not harmonization. This point has obvious implications for the governance of global trade, not least because of the need to permit asymmetric rules that favour the weakest members—especially the least developed countries. In the long run such rules will benefit both industrial and developing countries.

THE WORLD TRADE ORGANIZATION—A MAJOR SHIFT IN MULTILATERAL TRADE RULES

Few observers question the potential advantages of trade for human development, and most developing countries support the idea of multilateral trade negotiations. But many people, organizations and developing country governments across the political spectrum have concerns about World Trade Organization (WTO) agreements and how they are negotiated.

This is partly because of how the institutional framework for the multilateral trade regime has evolved over the past 50 or so years. The transformation of the General Agreement on Tariffs and Trade (GATT) into the WTO in 1995 marked a paradigm shift, resulting in significant differences between the two regimes. The GATT system was primarily about negotiating market access for traded goods. But the WTO's extension into new substantive areas, intrusiveness into domestic policy-making, 'single undertaking' mandate, explicit linkage of trade with protection of investment and intellectual property rights, and strict enforcement of disputes and cross-retaliation have extended its authority into areas of domestic regulation, legislation, governance and policy-making central to the development process.

Recent agreements under the trade regime commit members not just to liberalizing trade in goods but also to making specific policy choices on services, investment and intellectual property. These choices can affect human development through their effects on employment, education, public health, movements of capital and labour and ownership of and access to technology. Many believe that these changes link global trade under the WTO much more closely to human development than did the GATT.

The journey from the triumph of the 1994 Marrakesh Agreement, which led to the creation of the WTO in 1995, to the debacle of the 1999 WTO conference in Seattle spanned just five years. Although those consulted gave many reasons for the breakdown of multilateral trade negotiations in Seattle, an important one was different governments' very different perceptions and expectations of the global trade regime. These differences were particularly marked between the majority of developing countries and most industrial nations.

Though some parts of the negotiating process leading up to the 2001 WTO conference in Doha were handled better, basic differences in expectations remain. Some believe that the Doha Round should simply be a continuation of the Uruguay Round, aimed at tightening existing obligations and extending multilateral trade disciplines into new, policy areas that are currently in the domestic domain. Others—including most developing countries and many civil society organizations in both industrial and developing countries—believe that future multilateral trade negotiations should be corrective, making the system more supportive of human development.

MAKING TRADE A MEANS FOR HUMAN DEVELOPMENT

Since its inception the WTO has faced criticism from many quarters for failing to deliver the promised gains from trade integration. As a result a wide range of international experts, policy-makers and civil society organizations have called for an independent review of the global trade regime from a human development perspective.

Efforts to dissect this dissatisfaction must separate the role of domestic policy-making from the role of the international trade regime. Countries are responsible for the extent to which they take advantage of increased trade for long-term development. But the multilateral system can and should be held accountable for influencing the environment in which government choices are made. While the need for a fair, rules-based multilateral trade system is indisputable, the central question is: does the current regime enable developing countries to design policies that promote human development?

This book is the product of considerable policy research by academics and international experts and extensive consultations with developing country governments and civil society organizations. Based on these contributions, it suggests a framework in which trade is viewed neither as a means only for economic growth nor as an end in itself. Instead, trade should be seen as a means for human development.

Those consulted made it clear that a number of reforms are required to put human development at the centre of the multilateral trade regime. This book identifies and explores the main concerns raised by developing country governments and civil society organizations in terms of their human development implications and impacts. It makes proposals for reform that could help ensure that the global trade regime consistently works for people and human development.

KEY REFORMS IN THE GLOBAL GOVERNANCE OF TRADE

There is widespread hope that a multilateral trade regime governed by a relatively young, one-country, one-vote, member-driven organization with a majority of developing country members has enormous potential for serious governance reform. What should such reform involve?

The single undertaking

The WTO's single undertaking mandate, which compels governments to accept agreements as a complete package rather than on an individual basis, is unique among multilateral organizations. The single undertaking appears to have provided some benefits to developing countries by more effectively subjecting agriculture and textiles and clothing to multilateral trade disciplines. But many developing countries argue that the single undertaking has also sharply reduced their flexibility in choosing which agreements to sign, limiting their options for domestic development policies to those compatible with the new rules and agreements of the global trade regime (TWN, 2001).

Many developing countries argue that the single undertaking's human development impact would be maximized if it ensured that all countries' interests were reflected in the trade regime's rules and agreements. Thus a major challenge for the international trade regime is to incorporate human development objectives as positive obligations in its rules and agreements. Many developing country governments and trade policy specialists argue that special and differential treatment can help achieve this goal.

Special and differential treatment

To ensure progress in crafting trade agreements that support human development, the September 2003 WTO conference in Cancun, Mexico, must reach clear consensus on the importance of special and differential treatment. A conference declaration on special and differential treatment and human development would show a concrete ministerial commitment to achieving the universally agreed Millennium Development Goals.

In terms of human development, possible areas that such a declaration could cover include education, energy, health care, technology transfers, gender equality, environmental protection, cultural integrity and diversity, and the right to use traditional knowledge to promote human development.

Governance structure and decision-making

Formally, the WTO is the most democratic of all intergovernmental organizations with a global mandate. Its one-country, one-vote system of governance makes it far more democratic than many other multilateral institutions. The WTO is also a member-driven organization, with its members involved in day-to-day activities through its general council. In keeping with this status, the WTO's secretariat is relatively small and has limited power and autonomy.

These features suggest that the WTO's formal governance structure provides developing countries with unique opportunities in a global forum for economic governance—especially when they have a clear majority. But such opportunities may be difficult to realize, because informal consensus building has had a far greater influence on WTO decision-making than its formal processes.

Some governance experts and developing country governments have suggested changes to the consensus-building process, including increasing the size of the quorum required to make decisions and allowing countries without representatives in Geneva to participate through videoconferencing or other arrangements. Some developing countries have also encouraged voting for certain decisions, such as those related to the trade regime's governance, budget, management and administration. Such voting could occur by mail or electronically to ensure the participation of members without Geneva representation. This approach would lead to better-informed decisions that are more genuinely owned by the majority of members and be more sustainable in the long run. There is widespread agreement that the least developed countries and small island developing countries require support to bolster their representation and capacity in Geneva.

Academics, policy experts and veterans of trade negotiations have also suggested that the WTO's governance structure allow for more effective organization and participation of coalitions of developing countries as well as developing and industrial countries. Some informal groups of developing countries have already emerged, among them the Like-Minded Group. Another example is the Cairns Group, which brings together industrial and developing countries to discuss market access for agriculture. Such coalitions should be encouraged and supported.

Dispute settlement

The WTO's dispute settlement mechanism, central to the governance of the trade system, is in many ways a marked improvement over its predecessor under the GATT. The new mechanism is more time-bound, predictable, consistent and binding on all members. As a result developing countries are participating more in the dispute settlement process.

Still, many international experts and developing country governments have argued for important changes in the mechanism's rules and functions. Changes are partly needed because of the perception that trade sanctions are an acceptable way—indeed, to some the only effective way—of enforcing international commitments. This perception has fuelled initiatives to extend the WTO's agenda to cover areas of international economic interaction far beyond cross-border trade in goods.

Given the importance of trade sanctions and retaliation in the dispute settlement process, developing countries are in a weak position relative to industrial countries because their threat of retaliation is less credible. Proposals have been made to rectify this imbalance, and there is a need for mechanisms to ensure that all countries honour WTO rulings. Such mechanisms could include requiring financial compensation and levying penalty payments on countries that delay implementation of dispute settlement rulings. Some experts have also suggested that in certain cases a collective action clause be used against powerful members that refuse to implement dispute rulings.

Agenda

Most developing country members believe that the WTO's agenda is already full. A growing number of these countries, especially the least developed, also believe that they lack the capacity to deal with such a large, diverse and complex agenda in international trade negotiations. Similarly, the Doha declaration recognizes that the WTO's enhanced agenda has led to problems of policy coherence among multilateral organizations and agreements (multilateral environment agreements, regional trade agreements).

Moreover, many parliamentarians and civil society organizations believe that the way the agenda is determined and negotiated has diminished the influence of national legislative processes on economic and social issues of domestic concern. This makes it even more important to develop governance processes in a genuinely democratic, participatory and inclusive way.

Relationship with regional trade agreements

Though there is considerable overlap in coverage between regional and multilateral trade agreements, some regional agreements are considered more development-friendly by their members. However, a growing number of regional trade agreements incorporate 'WTO plus' elements. Many analysts have argued that WTO rules should provide the overall boundaries for regional agreements—but that WTO rules should first be made more flexible and friendly to human development.

In addition, many developing countries believe that WTO rules on regional agreements must be clarified to ensure that the agreements reflect human development criteria and countries enjoy the same special and differential treatment at the regional level as at the multilateral level. The Doha declaration and current negotiations on a number of regional trade agreements (such as the Cotonou Agreement between African, Caribbean and Pacific countries and the EU) provide opportunities to achieve these goals.

Accountability and external transparency

The global trade regime's mechanisms for accountability and transparency to outsiders are considered inadequate by a wide range of policy-makers, academics and civil society activists. As a result there are growing demands for increased public accountability and transparency in the WTO's functioning.

Although the WTO has responded by sharing more information and documents, developing countries and civil society organizations do not consider these valid substitutes for more transparency—much less for their actual participation in meetings. But member states have had great difficulty in agreeing to more formal roles for civil society organizations within the WTO and its dispute settlement process. Some industrial countries have argued for opening the dispute process to private lawyers, but this move has been strongly opposed by many civil society organizations and governments from developing countries.

Broad national ownership

Global governance of trade not only needs to be made more fair, it also needs to give greater voice to vulnerable populations not being represented by their governments at the national and international levels. Thus widespread participation in national dialogues involving multiple stakeholders—including parliamentarians, civil society organizations, community groups and the private sector—should be encouraged and supported. Broad, equitable ownership of such discussions can significantly contribute to long-term human development. In addition, trade ministries should be encouraged to develop an institutional ethos conducive to gender-sensitive trade policies.

PROPOSALS ON SPECIFIC AGREEMENTS AND ISSUES

WTO agreements, and issues planned for or under negotiation, can affect human development directly and indirectly. They can affect income, equity, employment, public health, food security, gender outcomes and ownership of and access to technology. By prohibiting or limiting the use of certain policy instruments or reducing market access, they can constrain flexibility in efforts to enhance human development. They can also impose significant opportunity costs if they lead to forgone growth or income that could potentially have been translated into human development. This overview focuses on the agreements and issues with the most significant potential or actual impacts on human development.

Agriculture

Agriculture remains the economic mainstay for the world's poorest people, providing employment for more than 70 per cent of the population in developing countries. Thus the WTO's Agreement on Agriculture has a pivotal influence on human development.

MARKET ACCESS. Although the Agreement on Agriculture eliminated many nontariff barriers to agricultural trade, agricultural tariffs remain significantly higher than industrial tariffs. Average tariffs on industrial goods fell from 40 per cent in 1945 to 4 per cent in 1995, yet agricultural tariffs still average 62 per cent. Nearly all the sources consulted for this book believe that this disparity persists because many industrial countries have lowered average tariffs in a way that fulfils the agriculture agreement's technical requirements—but that violates its spirit and intent.

Moreover, tariff peaks and escalation remain pronounced in many industrial countries. For some agricultural exports of interest to developing countries (sugar, rice, dairy products) the major economic powers maintain tariffs of 350–900 per cent. In contrast, many developing countries have been compelled to cut their tariffs and non-tariff barriers as conditions for World Bank and International Monetary Fund (IMF) loans.

FOOD SECURITY, FARMER LIVELIHOODS AND EMPLOYMENT. OECD members provide about $1 billion a day in domestic agricultural subsidies—more than six times what they spend on official development assistance for developing countries. Moreover, since 1997 such subsidies have increased by over a quarter.

Many food policy experts, developing country governments and civil society organizations believe that these subsidies—and the related dumping of agricultural exports by industrial countries—have serious implications for developing countries. For example, rapid growth in international trade has made developing countries much more dependent on food imports, with potentially enormous effects on gender and distribution outcomes. In South and Southeast Asia women perform 60 per cent of food cultivation and production tasks. Rural African women produce, process and store up to 80 per cent of food. The erosion of domestic food production has numerous repercussions for food security, social cohesion in rural communities and women's income, employment and status.

To correct this situation, many developing countries believe that they must have greater flexibility in developing their agricultural policies, to ensure that they achieve food security and other human development objectives. They also require increased market access, especially in EU and North American markets—where reductions in domestic support and export subsidies and the elimination of export dumping are long overdue.

The proposals embodied in the 'development box'—developed by civil society organizations and presented in WTO negotiations by a group of developing countries—are important because of their significance for human development.[2] If agreed, these proposals should apply only to developing countries and include a revised special safeguard mechanism. Some civil society organizations and developing countries have also argued for a 'positive list' approach to the development box, with illustrative criteria to ensure that this approach is not abused.[3] Many believe that the development box, especially if made operational through a positive list approach, could put human development at the heart of negotiations on agriculture.

Commodities

Unlike other agricultural and industrial products, trade in most commodities continues to occur outside the GATT and WTO framework. Yet many if not most commodities are subject to tariff peaks and escalation—especially in industrial countries. In addition, the potential benefits of liberalization in the minerals and metals sector are being nullified by anti-dumping actions and even by the resurgence of voluntary export restraints.

Since the mid-1990s markets have collapsed for several major commodities of export interest to developing countries. In response there have been calls by producer associations of developing countries for the adoption of supply management schemes aimed at raising the dismally low prices of many commodity exports. Collapsing terms of trade have had dramatic implications for human development through reduced employment, wages, incomes, livelihood security and social well-being.

Many analysts have indicated a pressing need for future multilateral trade negotiations to address the problems facing commodity exports—especially given their direct effects on human development, particularly for the poorest countries and people. An umbrella agreement on commodities could cover supply, financing and market access issues. Resource allocations should focus on enhancing developing countries' research and development capacity as well as their competitiveness in supplying and marketing dynamic new exports. In addition, compensatory financing is needed to help bridge shortfalls in export earnings. This issue is especially urgent for the least developed countries.

Textiles and clothing

Because of its labour intensity and large share of female workers, the textiles and clothing sector has enormous implications for human development in developing countries. Increased market access for these products in industrial countries can also improve human development outcomes in developing countries.

Under the WTO Agreement on Textiles and Clothing, the Multifibre Arrangement is to be phased out and quotas are to be eliminated. The liberalization is final and binding, with an outer deadline of December 2004 for all categories of textiles and clothing.

Developing countries have several concerns about the Agreement on Textiles and Clothing. Most believe that it liberalizes trade in a much wider range of textile and clothing products than was originally intended. They are also concerned that, through recourse to anti-dumping measures and technical barriers to trade, major importing countries may not fulfil the letter and the spirit of the agreement.

There is also widespread apprehension about what the elimination of the Multifibre Arrangement will mean for some developing countries—especially least developed countries such as Bangladesh. China's accession to the WTO will also have important implications for trade in textiles and clothing, particularly for some least developed countries. Among the anticipated problems are excess supply and falling prices.

Given the sector's enormous implications for human development, it is crucial that the Agreement on Textiles and Clothing be fully implemented as agreed during the Uruguay Round. The elimination of quotas and the phase-out of the Multifibre Arrangement should significantly reduce protection in large North American and EU markets, giving the most competitive developing countries better access to those markets. (To ensure such access, the phase-out of the Multifibre Arrangement should not be replaced by an increase in anti-dumping actions.) At the same time, negatively affected countries, sectors and groups in both developing and industrial countries—especially women—will require assistance.

Trade-Related Aspects of Intellectual Property Rights (TRIPS)

Many trade policy experts, developing country governments and civil society organizations have concluded that the WTO's mutual bargaining framework is not suited to intellectual property rights, because low-income countries have little to bargain with.

The Doha declaration on TRIPS and public health affirms developing countries' right to interpret the TRIPS agreement from a public health perspective. The declaration also explicitly recognizes countries' ability to grant compulsory licenses and determine the criteria for their issuance. Thus the Doha declaration is an important milestone in the international debate on intellectual property rights. By recognizing that these rights are subservient to public health concerns, it paves the way for interpretations of the TRIPS agreement that are more supportive of public health concerns. And though a political rather than a legal statement, it could be valuable if disputes arise on interpretations of the TRIPS agreement.

Developing country governments and civil society organizations have identified—and should take advantage of—several other ways to use the TRIPS agreement

in a more development-friendly manner. Many developing countries have also lobbied for protection of traditional knowledge and biological resources under intellectual property rights regimes.

Recent debates and proposals have triggered considerable rethinking of the
TRIPS agreement. Academics and policy experts have argued that WTO members
should explore alternative mechanisms for protecting intellectual property rights.
New mechanisms could encourage innovation in both developing and industrial
countries and support technology transfers to developing countries. Ultimately,
the international community should settle on a way to protect intellectual property that does not involve trade sanctions. Possible reforms suggested include intellectual property 'ladders', a 'TRIPS minus' model, an intellectual property regime
with specific opt-out clauses and separate intellectual property regimes for collective and individual rights.

In the meantime there is an urgent need to interpret and implement the TRIPS
agreement in a more development-friendly manner—especially when efforts to do
so are challenged under the dispute settlement mechanism. The Doha declaration
on TRIPS and public health is a step in the right direction. But concrete action at
the international level will need to be supplemented by national legislation that
gives full weight to human development concerns.

Trade-Related Investment Measures (TRIMs)

The agreement on TRIMs is intended to eliminate trade-distorting investment
measures among WTO members. Introducing no new obligations, it merely prohibits TRIMs considered inconsistent with the 1994 GATT for both agricultural
and industrial goods.

Many developing countries have argued that they should be allowed to maintain
TRIMs for development purposes. They believe that certain TRIMs can enable small
firms to expand to full competitive scale or channel foreign direct investment to bring
infant industries to maturity, increasing domestic employment and valued added.

Implementation of the TRIMs agreement has also created problems for developing countries by limiting their flexibility in using performance requirements for
foreign investors. Some developing countries consider these requirements—such
as those for local content and export-import balancing—essential to their development. Such policy instruments made important contributions to human development in several East and Southeast Asian countries. TRIMs were also crucial to
several of today's industrial countries in the early stages of their development.
Developing countries worry that because the TRIMs agreement limits important
policy choices and instruments, it is not in their best interests or in those of human
development.

The WTO Council for Trade in Goods responded to some of these concerns
in July 2001 by extending the transition period for notification of TRIMs by an
additional two years retroactively from 1 January 2000, in addition to leaving open

the possibility of a further extension of two years if certain conditions were met. Though useful in the short run, this fails to address the basic concerns of developing countries.

General Agreement on Trade in Services (GATS)

The GATS provides a legal framework for trade in services, defined to cover a range of areas including investment, financial services, communications, transportation, education, energy, water and movement of persons. It also calls for negotiating the progressive liberalization of regulations that impede trade and investment in services.

The GATS provides two types of benefits for developing countries: the potential flexibility provided through its 'positive list' approach and through the provisions for human development incorporated in several of its articles.

Still, civil society organizations and some developing countries have found problems with the GATS. These arise from the agreement's actual application and from developing countries' inability to fully benefit from its flexibility and beneficial articles. Moreover, a lack of credible data on the impact of services liberalization has made it difficult for developing countries to determine which areas to liberalize and what limitations to include in country schedules. In addition, many civil society organizations have argued that the GATS could facilitate the commercialisation of public services to the detriment of poor women and children.

It is widely held that one of the main shortcomings of the GATS is its lack of progress on the movement of natural persons—an area that offers significant potential benefits for developing countries and human development. Significant barriers impede the temporary movement of skilled and unskilled workers in the services sector, and industrial countries have made few commercially meaningful commitments in this area.

Though many countries support the agreement's positive list approach, they believe that it should be improved through the adoption of such modalities as the 'conditional offer approach'.[4] They also believe that the agreement's development-friendly articles should be operationalized. To enable that, developing countries should negotiate service modes of greatest interest to themselves in the exchange of offers and requests in a manner that ensures that these articles are effectively implemented at the sectoral level.

The extent to which public services are open to GATS rules will ultimately depend on how the agreement's text is interpreted by the WTO's dispute settlement body. In the interests of human development, many governments and civil society organizations are calling for exemptions from progressive liberalization for basic public services such as water, health, education and social protection.

Many countries and trade experts have also proposed concrete measures and timeframes for improving commitments on the movement of natural persons, especially unskilled workers. Such measures could have enormous benefits for human development.

Environment

The relationship between trade, capital flows and environmental standards is unclear. Available data say little about whether increased trade and capital flows adversely affect the environment or whether high environmental standards discourage trade and capital flows.

Some observers have argued that human development goals should guide the trade-offs between trade-related environment measures (such as environment taxes or subsides, technical standards, trade bans and quarantines) and trade policy. Every country should be free to manage its environmental problems in a way that is consistent with its human development priorities and international environmental (rather than trade) obligations. Trade measures designed to protect a country's consumers and environment from hazardous products are legitimate aspects of a human development strategy. But trade measures designed to coerce another country to harmonize its environmental standards are protectionist and inappropriate. Many developing countries believe that some international efforts to harmonize environmental standards are driven by protectionist rather than development concerns.

The WTO Committee on Trade and Environment has focused on fitting environmental concerns within the existing trade regime rather than on finding synergies between environment and trade as equally legitimate policy objectives. The WTO's post-Doha work programme gives the committee a new, more focused mandate. Negotiations will move ahead on the relationship between WTO rules and specific trade obligations in multilateral environmental agreements and on the reduction or elimination of tariffs and non-tariff barriers to environmental goods and services. Developing countries are seeking solutions to their environmental challenges—and want the flexibility to design appropriate solutions without fear of trade sanctions from countries with different environmental priorities.

Singapore issues

The four Singapore issues (so called because they were introduced at the Singapore Ministerial Conference in 1996) on which working groups exist are investment, competition policy, trade facilitation and transparency in government procurement. Crucial decisions on whether there will be trade negotiations on them are expected at the Fifth WTO Ministerial Conference in Cancun, Mexico, in September 2003. But as noted, there is widespread belief among developing country policy-makers and trade negotiators that the WTO's agenda is already full and that many reforms are needed in the global governance of trade and on agreements that have already been negotiated. So, regardless of their merit, it would be wise not to overburden the WTO's agenda with new issues at this time. The main issues surrounding discussions of investment and competition policy in the WTO are summarized below.

INVESTMENT. In the wake of recent financial crises around the developing world, most developing countries have argued that any discussions of investment should focus on foreign direct investment rather than include portfolio or other more volatile capital flows. Many forms of foreign direct investment have longer terms and can contribute to the creation of new productive assets, aiding human development. Overall, however, such investment has had a mixed impact on human development.

Though there are no firm proposals, some WTO members are seeking a definition of investment that includes portfolio and other capital flows as well as foreign direct investment. In addition, some industrial countries are seeking agreement on issues such as the right of establishment for foreign investors, most-favoured-nation treatment, national treatment, investment incentives and protection, abolition of the performance requirements allowed under TRIMs and binding dispute settlement. Many developing countries and international experts argue that agreements in these areas would be premature and overly ambitious.

Many developing countries believe that any attempt to bring investment under multilateral trade disciplines should be approached with caution and subject to further study, keeping in mind the WTO's experience with the TRIMs agreement and the commercial presence and investment aspects of the GATS. They also believe that any multilateral investment agreement will need to provide developing countries with greater flexibility (relative to current bilateral investment agreements) to choose policies that allow foreign direct investment to contribute to human development.

COMPETITION POLICY. Competition policy refers to laws and regulations aimed at maintaining fair competition by eliminating restrictive business practices among private enterprises. Thus it aims at limiting monopolies to encourage competition and its benefits. Competition policy covers a range of issues, many of which are unrelated to trade.

While most developing countries recognize the need for competition policies, even the most effective domestic policies will not be able to deal effectively with the current global situation. The global context will, it is argued, require the cooperation of industrial countries. As such, it will require an appropriate framework for international cooperation on competition issues.

Many experts argue that developing countries should continue to develop their competition policies, both to regulate domestic monopolies and to control the possible anticompetitive behaviour of transnational corporations. There is also evidence that human development interests will be served if such policies encourage the development of strategic and genuine infant industries, managerial and marketing capacity and efficient public utilities, services and technologies.

The domestic experiences of industrial countries suggest that competition policies should be flexible in their sectoral application. But even if effective, such policies are unlikely to be able to deal with the increased volume and complexity of transnational business activity over the past two decades. So, governments will also need to coordinate national competition policies to minimize the possibility of abuse.

Strengthening capacities

A global trade system based on mutual bargaining cannot deliver fair and desirable human development outcomes unless all members have the capacity to negotiate and extract benefits from international trade. Strengthening the capacities of developing and especially the least developed countries is thus a crucial, cross-cutting issue that should be viewed as integral to a human development-oriented multilateral trade regime.

Most developing countries lack the capacity to influence the agenda and pace of multilateral trade negotiations, negotiate effectively on issues of concern to them and fulfil their commitments to the trade regime. Many of the reforms proposed in this book seek to enhance such capacities.

Many experts have argued for stronger trade policy research and analysis capacity for developing countries—serving them collectively but existing independently and financed by their governments. This could be a significant input into enhanced trade negotiations capacity in developing country capitals and in Geneva. Moreover, while the need for technical assistance has been recognized in the WTO (and was reaffirmed in Doha), its volume and quality need to be considerably enhanced. New technical assistance programs should be designed in a way that makes it clear they are driven by human development needs and goals.

VISION FOR THE FUTURE

The vision that emerges from the discussion above can be summarized in four basic principles that should be accepted and operationalized:

- Trade is a means to an end—not an end in itself.
- Trade rules should allow for diversity in national institutions and standards.
- Countries should have the right to protect their institutions and development priorities.
- No country has the right to impose its institutional preferences on others.

A human development–oriented trade regime would give governments the space to design policies that embody these principles. Ideally, the regime would also help developing countries build their capacity to gain from trade. Among the elements that such a regime would need to emphasize are regular human development assessments of trade agreements and issues, policy space for the coexistence of diverse development strategies, and asymmetric rules for industrial and developing countries.

Market access is important for enabling developing countries to reach a level of development at which they can compete on an equal basis. But it is not enough. Developing countries gain less from trade than do industrial countries, partly because of falling commodity prices and specialization in exports with low value added. Developing countries also lack capacity to compensate those adversely affected by trade liberalization. Industrial countries, by contrast, gain much more from trade and have developed mechanisms to help cope with the vulnerabilities induced by liberalization. If it is to consistently serve the needs of human development, the global trade regime must reflect these differences more seriously and effectively than at present.

*   *   *   *

By expanding markets, facilitating competition, disseminating knowledge, increasing exposure to new technology and stimulating gains in productivity, trade can spur economic growth, reduce poverty and support better human development outcomes. Moreover, higher levels of human development increase the likelihood that countries and communities will gain from trade.

Today, however, the global governance of trade is generating inequitable outcomes. Though not surprising in a world of unequal players, this set-up makes it difficult for developing countries—especially the poorest and weakest—to formulate policies that promote human development. Thus policy-makers in both developing and industrial countries face an urgent challenge: to ensure that the multilateral trade regime allows people to fully benefit from the potential contributions that trade can make to human development.

NOTES

1. *Care work* refers to services that nurture other people, that are costly in time and energy, and that are undertaken as contractual or social obligations.

2. The *development box* includes a set of measures that would allow developing countries the flexibility they need to enhance domestic agricultural production for home consumption and to take other measures necessary to protect the livelihoods of farmers and reduce poverty.

3. A *positive list* is the list of items, entities, products, and the like to which an international agreement will apply, with no commitment to apply the agreement to anything else.

4. Under the conditional offer approach developing countries would indicate a willingness to undertake liberalization commitments if industrial countries undertake to implement certain provisions or make additional implementation commitments regarding the increasing participation of developing countries. The conditional offer approach would recognize differences in capacity and levels of development.

REFERENCES

Çağatay, Nilüfer. 2001. 'Trade, Gender, and Poverty'. Background paper for Trade and Sustainable Human Development Project. United Nations Development Programme, New York.

Rodrik, Dani. 2001. 'The Global Governance of Trade As If Development Really Mattered'. Background paper for Trade and Sustainable Human Development Project. United Nations Development Programme, New York.

TWN (Third World Network). 2001. 'The Multilateral Trading System: A Development Perspective'. Background paper for Trade and Sustainable Human Development Project. United Nations Development Programme, New York.

UNDP (United Nations Development Programme). 1996. *Human Development Report 1996.* New York: Oxford University Press.

PART 1

TRADE FOR HUMAN DEVELOPMENT

CHAPTER 1
HUMAN DEVELOPMENT AND TRADE

Trade and human development have a complex relationship. Understanding their interaction requires understanding the complexity of trade policy and human development as part of broader development policy.

Though the relationship between trade and development is the subject of contentious debate in the literature, there is little doubt that trade can be a powerful source of economic growth. But while broadly based economic growth is necessary for human development, it is not enough. Human development also requires enlarging people's choices and opportunities—especially poor people's.

International trade can expand markets, facilitate competition and disseminate knowledge, creating opportunities for growth and human development. Trade can also raise productivity and increase exposure to new technologies, which can also spur growth. Indeed, over the past 20 years the fastest-growing regions have also had the highest export growth.[1]

But liberalizing trade does not ensure human development, and expanding trade does not always have a positive or neutral effect on human development. Trade expansion neither guarantees immediate economic growth nor longer-run economic or human development. Internal and external institutional and social pre-conditions largely determine whether and to what extent a country or population group benefits from trade.

This chapter begins by discussing the many dimensions of human development. It then identifies how trade is linked, directly or indirectly, to human development. After that it discusses important policy questions: the relationship between trade liberalization, economic growth and human development, and the role of trade in broader industrialization and development strategies. The chapter concludes with a few key messages that provide the framework for the rest of the book.

HUMAN DEVELOPMENT—THE CONCEPT AND ITS IMPLICATIONS

People are the real wealth of nations, and the main goal of development is to create an enabling environment for people to enjoy long, healthy, creative lives. This may appear to be a simple truth. But for too long, development efforts have focused on creating financial wealth and improving material well-being. Forgotten in such pursuits is that development is about people. The preoccupation with economic growth has pushed people to the periphery of development discussions.

The first *Human Development Report*, published by the United Nations Development Programme (UNDP) in 1990, tried to reverse that trend. With its concept of human development, construction of a measure for it and discussion of the policy implications, the report changed how the world looked at development.

Defining human development

People constantly make choices—economic, social, political, cultural. The ultimate aim of development is not to create more wealth or to achieve higher growth. It is to expand the range of choices for every human being. Thus human development is concerned with enlarging choices and enhancing their outcomes—and with advancing basic human freedoms and rights. Defined in this way, human development is a simple notion with far-reaching implications.

- People's choices are enlarged if they acquire more capabilities and have more opportunities to use them.

- Choices are important for current as well as future generations. For human development to be sustainable, today's generations must enlarge their choices without reducing those of future generations.

- Though important, economic growth is a means of development—not the ultimate goal (box 1.1). Higher income makes an important contribution if it improves people's lives. But income growth is not an end. Development must be focused on people, and economic growth must be equitable if its benefits are to be felt in people's lives.

- Gender equality is at the core of human development. A development process that bypasses half of humanity—or discriminates against it—limits women's choices.

- By focusing on choices, the human development concept implies that people must participate in the processes that shape their lives. They must help make and implement decisions and monitor their outcomes.

- Human security is distinct from but contributes to human development (UNDP, 1994). Security means safety from chronic hunger, disease and repression. It also means protection from sudden, harmful disruptions in the patterns of daily life. In an economic context, it protects people from threats to their incomes, food security and livelihoods.

Looking at development through a human development lens is not new. The idea that social arrangements must be judged by how much they promote human goods dates back to at least Aristotle, who said: 'Wealth is evidently not the good we are seeking, for it is merely useful and for the sake of something else.' He argued for seeing the 'difference between a good political arrangement and a bad one' in its successes and failures in facilitating people's ability to lead 'flourishing lives'

BOX 1.1 ECONOMIC GROWTH AND HUMAN DEVELOPMENT

Economic growth is necessary but insufficient for human development. And the quality of growth, not just its quantity, is crucial for human well-being. Growth can be jobless, rather than job creating; ruthless, rather than poverty reducing; voiceless, rather than participatory; rootless, rather than culturally enshrined; and futureless, rather than environmentally friendly. Growth that is jobless, ruthless, voiceless, rootless and futureless is not conducive to human development.

Source: Jahan, 2000.

(cited in UNDP, 1990). Seeing people as the real end of all activities was a recurring theme in the writings of most early philosophers.

The same concern can be found in the writings of the early leaders on quantification in economics: William Petty, Gregory King, Francois Quesnay, Antoine Lavoisier and Joseph Lagrange, the grandparent of the concepts of gross national product (GNP) and gross domestic product (GDP). It is also clear in the writings of the leading political economists: Adam Smith, David Ricardo, Robert Malthus, Karl Marx and John Stuart Mill.

The human development concept is an extension of that long tradition, and is broader than other people-oriented approaches to development. The human resource approach emphasizes human capital and treats human beings as inputs into the production process, not as its beneficiaries. The basic needs approach focuses on people's minimum requirements, not their choices. The human welfare approach looks at people as recipients, not as active participants in the processes that shape their lives.

Human development treats people as the subject of development, not the object. It is both distinct from and more holistic than other approaches to development. Development of the people builds human capabilities. Development for the people translates the benefits of growth into people's lives. And development by the people emphasizes that people must actively participate in the processes that shape their lives.

As a holistic concept, human development is broader than any of its measures, such as the human development index. In principle, human choices can be infinite and change over time. But three essential choices are those that allow people to lead long and healthy lives, to acquire knowledge and to have access to resources for a decent standard of living. The human development index measures these three basic dimensions of human development.[2] Though not comprehensive, it is better than other economic measures—such as per capita income—in assessing human well-being.[3]

The objectives of human development were recently codified in the Millennium Development Goals (UN, 2000). The goals set numerical, time-bound targets for advancing human development in developing countries, including halving extreme income poverty and hunger, achieving universal primary education and gender equality in primary education, reducing under-5 mortality by two-thirds and maternal mortality by three-quarters, reversing the spread of HIV/AIDS and other major diseases, and halving the portion of people without access to safe water. These targets are to be achieved by 2015, with reductions based on levels in 1990.

Human poverty

If income is not the sum total of human development, lack of it cannot be the sum total of human deprivation. So, from a human development perspective, poverty is also multidimensional. Beyond lack of income, people can be deprived if they lead short and unhealthy lives, are illiterate, feel personal insecurity or are not allowed to participate. Thus human poverty is larger than income poverty.

Human poverty is more than just a state: it is a process. People living in poverty deploy whatever assets they have to cope with it. A dynamic phenomenon reproduced over time and across generations, poverty is also the result of structural inequalities and discrimination—based on class, race, gender and other characteristics—within and between countries.

Gender is among the most important determinants of power in society.[4] This is reflected in institutions, including markets and the state, which transmit gender biases into economic outcomes. In most societies women work more than men, earn less, receive less schooling and face greater obstacles to accessing wealth, credit, information and knowledge.[5] Thus gender inequalities are a fundamental obstacle to human development (Çağatay, Elson and Grown, 1995; Grown, Elson and Çağatay, 2000). Gender influences economic behaviour, and gender relations influence the distribution of output, work, income, wealth and power.

The relationship between gender and poverty goes both ways. Gender inequalities influence the relationship between macro-economic and trade policies and their outcomes. Gender also affects growth performance and so poverty. Labour is poor people's most abundant asset. But women have less control than men over their labour and income. Moreover, labour remains partly invisible as long as unpaid household work, performed mostly by women, is not considered part of economic activity.[6]

In some cases men may forbid their wives from working outside the home.[7] In others men may extract labour from women through actual or threatened violence, as with unpaid female family workers. During crises men are generally able to mobilize women's labour, but women lack the reciprocal ability to mobilize men's. For these reasons and others it is harder for women to transform their capabilities into income and well-being (Kabeer, 1996).

LINKING TRADE AND HUMAN DEVELOPMENT

Trade can generate significant static welfare gains by increasing allocative efficiency, raising capacity use, achieving scale economies in production and making a wider variety of products available for consumption (box 1.2). But none of these

Box 1.2 Trade theory

Few branches of the literature on economics are richer or more controversial than that on international trade. There has been little consensus on the relationship between trade and short- to medium-term economic growth—and even less on its role in long-term economic development.

The principle of comparative advantage, first described by David Ricardo, forms the theoretical basis for traditional trade theory and provides the rationale for free trade. The principle states that even if a country produced all goods more cheaply than other countries, it would benefit by specializing in the export of its relatively cheapest good (or the good in which it has a comparative advantage).

Some classical economists believed that comparative advantage was driven by differences in production techniques. Later theoretical developments identified differences in factor endowments as the principal basis for comparative advantage. Traditional trade analysis acknowledged the argument for policy intervention (protectionism) if market failures created a need for temporary protection of infant industries—though direct subsidies were still considered preferable. Intervention was also justifiable, though still discouraged, if it could improve a nation's terms of trade by deploying market power. But these were exceptions to the general principle that free trade is best.

Traditional trade theory has been challenged because it often cannot explain actual trade patterns. Careful empirical investigations show that many of the theory's basic assumptions—perfect competition, full employment, perfect factor mobility within countries, immobile factors between countries—are unrealistic and do not conform to theoretical predictions. When these assumptions are relaxed, welfare and other outcomes are less clear. Moreover, the introduction of assumptions on differential learning effects, positive externalities and technical changes associated with different economic activities creates the theoretical possibility of weak (if any) gains from trade for countries that specialize in low value-added, labour-intensive products.

Several analysts have tried to modify, expand or reject some of the conclusions of traditional trade theory. New trade theorists cite the role of scale economies and imperfectly competitive markets in determining intra-industry trade patterns among industrial countries. This view led strategic trade theorists to argue for subsidizing certain industries, to give them strategic advantage in oligopolistic international markets. The recent literature on trade and growth also emphasizes that, in dynamic terms, comparative advantage can be created based on human capital, learning, technology and productivity. It can also change over time based on economic policy.

Other responses come from theorists who question the validity of the comparative advantage principle, arguing that absolute or competitive advantage is a more reliable determinant of trade outcomes. One such response is a macro-level analysis that looks at trade in the context of low aggregate demand, structural unemployment and inflexible wage adjustments. Another argues that international industrial competitiveness is determined by the technology gaps between nations.

The common thread in these different theories is that trade can contribute to growth by expanding markets, facilitating competition and disseminating knowledge. Controversy continues to surround the efficacy of growth-promoting policy intervention. And the trade literature says little about how trade and trade policy relate to human development over time.

Source: UNDP, 2002.

benefits are guaranteed, and trade can impose hefty adjustment costs for certain segments of the population and, in some cases, for the economy as a whole. Trade also has dynamic effects, but it is less clear how trade affects economic growth and growth then affects human development.

Links between growth and human development

Conventional wisdom holds that economic growth links trade to human development. But there is no automatic relationship between growth and human development. While 'economic growth expands the material base for fulfilling human needs' (UNDP, 1996, p. 66), the extent to which those needs are met depends on resource allocations and on the creation of opportunities for all parts of the population.

Still, in the long run, economic growth and human development tend to move together and be mutually reinforcing. Growth can contribute to human development in two ways (figure 1.1). First, employment-led growth raises household income. Depending on how it is spent, the additional income can be used to improve nutrition, augment children's education or increase skills—all of which enhance human capabilities. The extent to which household income is spent on human development partly depends on who controls it. If women control it, it is more likely to be spent on health, nutrition and education.

Second, growth can contribute to human development through government policies and spending. Growth can increase government revenue—which, if used to reduce income inequality and enhance health and education, benefits human development.

FIGURE 1.1

From human development to growth—and back

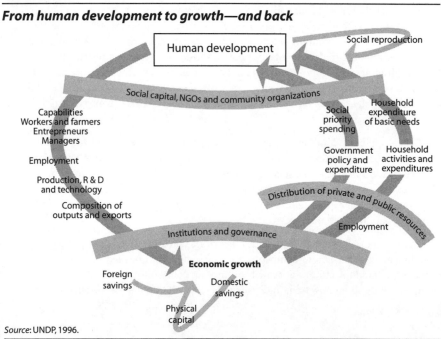

Source: UNDP, 1996.

Other links between trade and human development

Beyond its direct benefits for human development through economic growth, trade can enlarge people's choices by expanding markets for goods and services and by providing stable incomes for households. In addition, increased employment leads to higher incomes that, if spent on health and education, enhance people's capabilities.

Although trade has an ambiguous effect on the distribution of wealth, governments can harness trade's economic benefits to increase equity among different groups. In many developing countries large parts of the population do not participate in the formal economy and markets. Without mechanisms to distribute the gains from trade, poor and vulnerable people are unlikely to benefit. Ownership patterns will be reinforced, leaving few opportunities for widespread gains.

Trade policies also reflect and affect gender relations. Similarly, trade's effects on women and men vary, depending in part on gender relations: increased trade can expand female employment but does not automatically lead to higher wages or more secure jobs. Indeed, trade can increase women's work burden.

Trade also affects other aspects of human development. Deeper integration with the global economy can make developing countries more vulnerable to external shocks. In many developing countries trade liberalization has resulted in deteriorating terms of trade—and in some even immiserizing growth, where increased export production is not absorbed in world markets, causing severe damage to terms of trade and a loss in real income. In many developing countries trade liberalization has also increased volatility, threatening the security of livelihoods and incomes. But trade can also increase people's economic participation by providing jobs as well as access to credit and markets for goods. Such developments empower people and so can foster political participation.

The two-way relationship between human development and trade

The links running the other way—from human development to growth, and its relationship with trade—are just as important. Better human development outcomes, in the form of improved capabilities as the result of a healthier, better-educated and more skilled work force, with a strong focus on knowledge creation, contribute to higher economic growth and better trade outcomes.

But countries with low social and economic indicators are generally compelled to export primary or low value-added products. Over the long run such exports often fail to raise skill levels and productivity and seldom stimulate technological change. Thus, unlike wealthier countries, poor countries with low literacy, weak infrastructure and other supply-side constraints may have limited capacity to benefit from trade. On the other hand, countries that invest in building people's capabilities can engage in production and trade that raise productivity, which can generate a virtuous cycle of better human development and trade.

This potential for a mutually reinforcing relationship makes trade an important means of achieving better human development outcomes. As a result trade's effect on growth—and the converse—is often a useful proxy for its effect on human development.

IS TRADE LIBERALIZATION GOOD FOR GROWTH AND HUMAN DEVELOPMENT?

Trade liberalization is the common policy prescription for increasing trade flows. The voluminous literature in this area forms the basis for often-heard claims about the benefits of trade openness. But that literature is far from unequivocal. There is no convincing evidence that trade liberalization is always associated with economic growth.[8] Thus there is no evidence that trade liberalization is inevitably good for human development.

Consider Viet Nam and Haiti. Since the mid-1980s Viet Nam has taken a gradual approach to economic reform, following a two-track programme. It engages in state trading, maintains import monopolies, retains quantitative restrictions and high tariffs (30–50 per cent) on agricultural and industrial imports and is not a member of the World Trade Organization (WTO). Yet it has been phenomenally successful, achieving GDP growth of more than 8 per cent a year since the mid-1980s, sharply reducing poverty, expanding trade at double-digit rates and attracting considerable foreign investment. And despite high trade barriers, it has rapidly integrated with the global economy.

Haiti, meanwhile, undertook comprehensive trade liberalization in 1994–95, has slashed import tariffs to a maximum of 15 per cent and has removed all quantitative restrictions (US Department of State, 1999). Yet its economy has gone nowhere, and its social indicators are deteriorating. And despite being a WTO member, it has made little progress in integrating with the global economy.

These countries' contrasting experiences highlight two points. First, leadership committed to development and supporting a coherent growth strategy counts for a lot more than trade liberalization—even when the strategy departs sharply from the 'enlightened' standard view on reform.[9] Second, integration with the world economy is an outcome, not a prerequisite, of a successful growth strategy. Protected Viet Nam is integrating with the global economy much faster than open Haiti, because Viet Nam is growing and Haiti is not.

This comparison illustrates a common misdiagnosis. A typical World Bank exercise consists of classifying developing countries into 'globalizers' and 'non-globalizers' based on their rates of growth in trade volumes. The analyst asks whether globalizers (those with the highest rates of trade growth) have faster income growth, greater poverty reduction and worsening income distribution (see Dollar and Kraay, 2000). The answers tend to be yes, yes and no. But as Viet Nam and Haiti show, this approach is misleading. Trade volumes are the outcome of

FIGURE 1.2

Low import tariffs are good for growth? Think again

Annual average per-capita GDP growth rate during the 1990s
(unexplained part, per cent) vs. average import tariff rate (per cent)

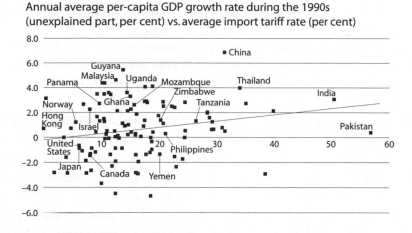

Note: All data are averages for the 1990s. Specifications are based on Dollar and Kraay (2000), replacing trade–GDP ratios with tariff levels and controlling separately for inflation, initial income and government consumption as a share of GDP.
Source: Dollar and Kraay, 2000.

many things—including, most important, an economy's overall performance. They are not something that governments control directly. What governments control are trade policies: levels of tariff and non-tariff barriers, membership in the WTO, compliance with its agreements and so on. The relevant question is, do open trade policies reliably produce higher economic growth, greater poverty reduction and more human development?

Cross-national comparisons reveal no systematic relationship between countries' average levels of tariffs and non-tariff barriers and their subsequent economic growth. If anything, evidence for the 1990s indicates a positive (but statistically insignificant) relationship between tariffs and economic growth (figure 1.2). The only systematic relationship is that countries dismantle trade barriers as they get richer. That accounts for the fact that with few exceptions, today's rich countries embarked on economic growth behind protective barriers but now have low barriers.

The absence of a robust positive relationship between open trade policies and economic growth may come as a surprise given the ubiquitous claim that trade liberalization promotes higher growth. Indeed, the literature is replete with cross-country studies concluding that growth and economic dynamism are strongly linked to more liberal trade policies. For example, an influential study by Sachs and Warner (1995) found that economies that were open (by the authors' definition) grew 2.4 percentage points a year faster than economies that were not—an enormous difference. Without such studies, organizations such as the World Bank, International Monetary Fund and WTO could not have been so vociferous in their promotion of trade-centred development strategies.

But such studies are flawed. The classification of countries as 'open' or 'closed' in the Sachs-Warner study, for example, is not based on actual trade policies but largely on indicators related to exchange rate policy and location in Sub-Saharan Africa. The authors' classification of countries conflates macroeconomics, geography and institutions with trade policy. The classification is so correlated with plausible alternative explanatory variables—macroeconomic instability, poor institutions, location in Africa—that one cannot draw from the empirical analysis any strong inferences about the effects of openness on growth (Rodriguez and Rodrik, 2001).

This problem is widespread. In a review of the best-known literature (Dollar, 1992; Ben-David, 1993; Edwards, 1998; Frankel and Romer, 1999; Sachs and Warner, 1995), Rodriguez and Rodrik (2001) found major gaps between the policy conclusions drawn and what the research actually showed. A common shortcoming is the misattribution of macroeconomic phenomena (overvalued currencies or macroeconomic instability) or geographic location (in the tropical zone) to trade policies. Once these problems are corrected, any meaningful cross-country relationship between trade barriers and economic growth evaporates (Helleiner, 1994).

In reality, the relationship between trade openness and growth is likely to be contingent on a host of internal and external factors. That nearly all of today's industrial countries embarked on their growth behind tariff barriers, and reduced protection only subsequently, surely offers a clue. Moreover, the modern theory of endogenous growth yields an ambiguous answer to the question of whether trade liberalization promotes growth—one that depends on whether the forces of comparative advantage push an economy's resources towards activities that generate long-run growth (conducting research and development, expanding product variety, upgrading product quality and so on) or divert them from such activities.

No country has developed successfully by turning its back on international trade and long-term capital flows. And few have grown over long periods without experiencing an increase in the share of foreign trade in their national product. The most compelling mechanism linking trade to growth in developing countries is that imported capital goods are likely to be much cheaper than those manufactured at home. Policies that restrict imports of capital equipment and raise the prices of capital goods at home—and so reduce real investment—must be viewed as undesirable on the face of it (though this does not rule out the possibility of selective 'infant' industry protection in certain segments of capital goods industries). Exports, in turn, are important because they permit purchases of imported capital equipment.

But it is also true that no country has developed simply by opening itself to foreign trade and investment. The trick has been to combine the opportunities offered by global markets with strategies for domestic investment and institution building, to stimulate domestic entrepreneurs. Nearly all the cases of development

FIGURE 1.3

Tariffs did not impede growth in India

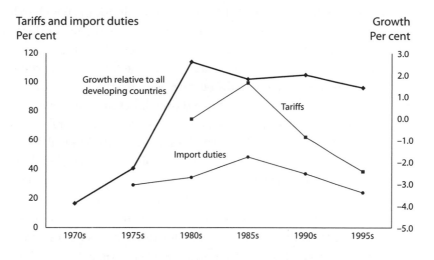

Tariffs and import duties
Per cent

Growth
Per cent

Source: Rodrik, 2001, using data in Dollar and Kraay, 2000 and World Bank, *World Development Indicators 2000*, 2000.

in recent decades—East Asia since the 1960s, China and India since the early 1980s—have involved partial, gradual opening to imports and foreign investment.

China and India are particularly noteworthy. Both countries are huge, have done extremely well economically, and are often cited as examples of what openness can achieve (see Stern, 2000, p. 3). But again, the reality is more complicated. China and India implemented their main trade reforms about a decade after the onset of higher growth. Moreover, their trade restrictions remain among the highest in the world. The increase in China's growth started in the late 1970s. Trade liberalization did not start in earnest until much later, in the second half of the 1980s and especially in the 1990s—once the trend growth rate had already increased substantially.

India's growth rate increased substantially in the early 1980s, while serious trade reform did not start until 1991–93. Tariffs were actually higher in the higher-growth period of the 1980s than in the low-growth 1970s (figure 1.3). Although tariffs are hardly the most serious trade restrictions in India, they reflect trends in its trade policy fairly accurately.

Both China and India participated in international trade during the 1980s and 1990s, so by that measure they are both globalizers. But the relevant question for policy-makers is not whether trade is good or bad: countries that achieve rapid growth also see trade accounting for a growing share of GDP. The question is the correct sequence of policies and how much priority deep trade liberalization should receive early in the reform process. China and India suggest the benefits of a gradual, sequenced approach.

The point here is not that trade protection is inherently preferable to trade liberalization. Certainly, there is scant evidence from the past 50 years that inward-looking economies experience faster growth than open ones. But the benefits of trade openness have been greatly oversold. Deep trade liberalization cannot be relied on to deliver high economic growth and so does not deserve the high priority it receives in the development strategies pushed by leading multilateral institutions.[10]

As Helleiner (2000, p. 3) puts it, there are 'few reputable developing country analysts or governments who question the positive potential roles of international trade or capital inflow in economic growth and overall development. How *could* they question the inevitable need for participation in, indeed a considerable degree of integration with, the global economy?' (emphasis in original). The real debate is not over whether integration is good or bad, but over policies and priorities: 'It isn't at all obvious *either* (1) that further external liberalization ('open-ness') is now in every country's interest and in all dimensions *or* (2) that in the over-arching sweep of global economic history what the world now *most* requires is a set of global rules that promote or ease the path to greater freedom for global market actors, and are universal in application' (Helleiner, 2000, p. 4, emphasis in original).

DOES TRADE LIBERALIZATION IMPROVE GENDER OUTCOMES?

Trade liberalization has had mixed results for gender outcomes, especially in developing countries.[11] Increased female employment is the main benefit that open trade provides for women. But there are others, including higher consumption and legislative improvements (Gammage and Fernandez, 2002). In addition to altering the gender composition of the work force (composition effect), trade policy and performance change working conditions (compensation effect).

Trade liberalization may increase female employment in two ways. First, female workers tend to be concentrated in certain industries and sectors—and increased international competition causes female-intensive sectors to expand and male-intensive sectors to decline (Elson, 1996). Second, intensified competition and supply-side macroeconomics and deregulation push employers to look for more flexible sources of labour. Because women's wages and other working standards (such as unionization) tend to be lower than men's, female labour is substituted for male labour—increasing employment for women (Standing, 1989; Standing, 1999).

Over the past two decades the share of women in the work force has risen steadily around the world. In Africa, Asia and Latin America more than 900 million women are economically active, accounting for 39 per cent of the economically active population (ILO, 2001). Women's paid employment due to liberalization seems to have increased—with mixed results. Employment increases women's autonomy and negotiating power (Çağatay, 2001). But export-oriented jobs for women often pay low wages and involve poor working conditions, so the net effect has not necessarily been positive.

Institutional structures, coupled with patriarchal gender norms and stereo-types, limit women's bargaining power and generate the large (and growing) gen-der-based wage gap (Seguino, 2000). Weakening rights for workers in general and for women in particular—often due to labour market deregulation—also affect areas other than low wages and unfavourable working conditions. Employment has become increasingly insecure (due to unstable, unpredictable world markets), increasingly intense and increasingly hazardous (with both health and safety risks). It also shows increasing disregard for labour required in the household, especially child care.

Repetitive, low-skill work locks women into dead-end jobs. And when pro-duction calls for higher skills or technological sophistication, women are replaced by men. Employment in the electronics industry in the Republic of Korea and in the *maquiladoras* in Mexico, for example, has shifted in favour of men (UN, 1999).

Although trade liberalization and export-oriented policies have increased women's paid employment in developing countries, there has not been a corre-sponding decrease in their household and care responsibilities, contributing to their 'triple burden'. In Bangladesh increased women's employment has been accompanied by reduced leisure time (Fontana and Wood, 2000). This pattern implies that liberalization has also adversely affected care, jeopardizing long-term human development (UNDP, 1999).

Governments can influence how trade liberalization affects women's well-being. For example, some countries have cut spending on social services in part because of lower revenue from trade taxes. Such cuts hurt women disproportion-ately because they must make up for the reduction in health care, safe water and the like by increasing their (unpaid) household work and care.

How do gender inequalities affect trade performance?

Evidence from Asia suggests that the fastest-growing economies have had the widest gender-based wage gaps (Seguino, 2000). While most dimensions of gender inequality (health, education, skills training) constrain productivity and growth, wage inequality appears to have aided growth by increasing international compet-itiveness. Indeed, in some export-oriented semi-industrial countries, gender inequalities in manufacturing wages have stimulated investment and exports. Lower labour costs free resources to purchase capital and intermediate goods and advanced technology, leading to higher growth.

If used extensively, however, a competition strategy based on lower wages for women could cause steady deterioration in the terms of trade of developing relative to industrial countries—especially in female-intensive manufactured exports—if export prices reflect the true cost of such wages.[12] On the other hand, Joekes (1999, p. 55) points out that 'low wages paid to women workers have allowed the final prod-uct prices to be lower than what they would otherwise have been without compro-

---

Box 1.3 Trade, poverty and growth in the least developed countries

The world's 49 least developed countries suffer from extreme poverty and underdevelopment. During 1995–99 half of the people in these countries lived on less than $1 a day, and four-fifths lived on less than $2 a day. International trade plays a crucial role in these countries' economies. In 22 of the 39 for which data are available, trade accounts for more than half of GDP—a larger share than in high-income OECD countries.

In 1997–98 imports equalled 26 per cent of GDP in the least developed countries, considerably more than the 17 per cent for exports. This imbalance is reflected in the group's trade deficit, which is much higher than the deficits for other groups of countries. Among the least developed countries, trade varies greatly depending on whether countries export primary products, non-oil primary products, or manufactured goods. Primary product exporters have the highest poverty; with more than 80 per cent of the people in mineral-exporting countries living on less than $1 a day at the end of the 1990s, compared with 43 per cent in service exporters and 25 per cent in manufactured goods exporters (excluding Bangladesh).

There is little correlation between trade liberalization and poverty reduction: poverty appears to be increasing unambiguously in the least developed countries with the most open and the most closed trade regimes. But between those extremes poverty is also increasing in countries that have liberalized trade more. While these findings do not prove that liberalization increases poverty, they do show that liberalization does not automatically reduce poverty.

The least developed countries that experienced economic growth in the 1990s also became more export oriented. But that does not mean that increased export orientation was associated with growth: GDP per capita declined or stagnated in 8 of the 22 least developed countries with increasing export orientation between 1987 and 1999. And in 10 of these countries poverty increased. Sustained economic growth is the key to reducing poverty in the least developed countries: 14 with rising GDP per capita saw poverty fall. So, unless accompanied by sustained growth, greater export orientation was not associated with reduced poverty.

Source: UNCTAD, 2002a, ch 3.

---

mising the profit share'. Developing and industrial countries export different kinds of manufactured goods, with developing countries oriented towards standardized commodities that require fewer skills (UNCTAD, 2002b). Manufactured exports also differ in the gender composition of the workers who produce them, with developing country exports more female-intensive than industrial country exports. Osterreich (2002) finds that gender-based wage gaps are associated with worse terms of trade in semi-industrial countries than in industrial countries.

What really matters for trade as part of a broader industrialization and development strategy

Should governments pursue economic growth first and foremost? Or should they focus on reducing poverty? Recent debate on this issue has become embroiled in broader political controversies on globalization and its impact on developing economies.[13] Critics of the WTO accuse it of being overly concerned about economic

TABLE 1.1

The Washington Consensus

The original Washington Consensus

Fiscal discipline	*Trade liberalization*
Reorientation of public spending	*Openness to foreign direct investment*
Tax reform	*Privatization*
Financial liberalization	*Deregulation*
Unified and competitive exchange rates	*Secure property rights*

The augmented Washington Consensus

The original list plus:

Legal and political reform	*Financial codes and standards*
Regulatory institutions	*'Prudent' capital account opening*
Anti-corruption efforts	*Non-intermediate exchange rate regimes*
Labour market flexibility	*Social safety nets*
World Trade Organization agreements	*Poverty reduction*

Source: Rodrik, 2001.

activity and growth at the expense of poverty reduction. Supporters argue that expanded trade and higher growth are the best ways to reduce poverty. But this largely sterile debate diverts attention from the real issues.

The real question is (or should be) whether open trade policies are a reliable way of generating self-sustaining growth *and* poverty reduction—evidence for which is far from convincing. Despite a voluminous literature, almost nothing is known about which kinds of trade policies are conducive to growth. In the least developed countries, for example, standard policy prescriptions over the past two decades have advocated trade liberalization as a way out of poverty. But there is little evidence to back that claim (box 1.3).

Today's enlightened standard view of development policy emerged from dissatisfaction with the limited results yielded by the Washington Consensus policies of the 1980s and 1990s. Disappointing growth and increasing economic volatility in Latin America (the region that went furthest with privatization, liberalization and openness), failures in the former Soviet Union and the East Asian financial crisis of 1997–98 contributed to a refashioning, resulting in the augmented Washington Consensus (table 1.1). This new approach goes beyond liberalization and privatization to emphasize the need to create the institutional underpinnings of market economies. Reforms now include labour market flexibility, social safety nets, financial sector regulation and prudential supervision, and governance, corruption, legal and administrative measures.

These institutional reforms are heavily influenced by an Anglo-American conception of what constitutes desirable institutions, as with the preference for arm's-length finance over 'development banking' and for flexible over institutionalized labour markets. The reforms are also driven by the requirements of integration

35

with the global economy. Hence their emphasis on international harmonization of regulation, as with financial codes and standards and through WTO agreements.

Market economies rely on a wide array of non-market institutions that perform regulatory, stabilizing and legitimizing functions (Rodrik, 2000). The quality of a country's public institutions is a crucial—perhaps the most important—determinant of its long-term development (Acemoglu, Johnson and Robinson, 2000). Thus the recent emphasis on institutions is highly welcome. But there is no universal institutional foundation for a market economy: that is, no single form defines the non-market institutions required to sustain a well-functioning market, as is clear from the wide variety of regulatory, stabilizing and legitimizing institutions in today's advanced industrial countries. US capitalism is very different from Japanese capitalism, and both differ from the European style. And even in Europe, there are big differences between the institutional arrangements in, say, Germany and Sweden. Yet over the long term, all have performed well.[14]

This point about institutional diversity has a more fundamental implication. As Roberto Unger (1998) argues, today's varied institutional arrangements are merely a subset of the full range of institutional possibilities. There is no reason to believe that modern societies have exhausted all the institutional variations that could underpin healthy, vibrant economies. Analysts must avoid thinking that a specific type of institution—whether, for example, a mode of corporate governance, system for social security or legislation for the labour market—is the only one compatible with a well-functioning market economy.

Leaving aside the issue of choice on institutional forms, the 'enlightened' standard view, as a model for stimulating economic growth, suffers from a fatal flaw: it identifies no priorities among a long and demanding list of institutional prerequisites. This all-encompassing approach to development strategy is at odds with the historical experiences of today's advanced industrial countries. What are today considered key institutional reforms in such areas as corporate governance, financial supervision, trade law and social safety nets did not occur in Europe or North America until late in the economic development process (Chang, 2000). Indeed, many items on the augmented Washington Consensus agenda should be seen as outcomes of successful development, not prerequisites.

The factors underpinning economic growth are driven by an initially narrow set of policy and institutional initiatives that can be called 'investment strategies' (Rodrik, 1999). Adequate human resources, public infrastructure, social peace and political and economic stability are key elements of such strategies. But the critical factor is often targeted policy interventions that motivate domestic investors. Investment strategies set off a period of economic growth that facilitates institutional development and further growth. The initiating reforms are rarely replicas of each other, and they bear only partial resemblance to the requirements highlighted by the 'enlightened' standard view of development policy. Typically, they mix orthodox approaches with unconventional domestic innovations.

Analysis of three investment strategies elucidates this central point and high-lights different paths to industrialization and prosperity: import substitution, East Asian–style outward orientation and two-track strategies. This list is by no means exhaustive, and future successful strategies will likely differ from all three.

Import-substituting industrialization

Import-substituting industrialization is based on the idea that domestic investment and technological capabilities can be spurred by providing domestic producers with (temporary) protection against imports. Although this approach has fallen into disgrace since the 1980s, it worked quite well for a long time in scores of developing nations. Until the oil shock in 1973, at least 42 developing countries had experienced per capita growth of more than 2.5 per cent a year since 1960 (see Rodrik, 1999, ch 4). At that rate per capita incomes would double at least every 28 years. Most of these countries used import-substituting industrialization policies, including 15 in sub-Saharan Africa, 12 in South America and 6 in the Middle East and North Africa. Until 1973, in fact, 6 sub-Saharan countries were among the world's 20 fastest-growing developing countries.[15]

Import-substituting industrialization catalysed growth by creating protected—and so profitable—home markets for domestic entrepreneurs to invest in. Contrary to received wisdom, this approach did not produce technological lags and large inefficiencies in economies of scale. Indeed, compared with today the productivity of many Latin American and Middle Eastern countries was exemplary. According to Collins and Bosworth (1996), during the period preceding the first oil shock total factor productivity growth was quite high in the Middle East (2.3 per cent a year) and Latin America (1.8 per cent)—and significantly higher than in East Asia (1.3 per cent).[16]

The dismal reputation of import substitution is partly due to the subsequent economic collapse (in the 1980s) in many of the countries that pursued it and partly to the influential studies of Little, Scitovsky and Scott (1970) and Balassa (1971). Those studies documented some of the static economic inefficiencies generated by high and extremely dispersed effective rates of protection in the manufacturing sectors of the countries under study. The discovery of cases of negative value added at world prices—that is, cases where countries would have been better off throwing away inputs rather than processing them in highly protected plants—was particularly shocking.

But neither study showed that countries that had followed outward-oriented strategies were immune from such inefficiencies. In fact, there was no clear difference between the performance of outward-oriented and import-substituting countries.[17] In addition, the data above on growth in total factor productivity show that it is wrong to assume that inward orientation produced more dynamic inefficiency than did outward orientation.

So, as an industrialization strategy intended to raise domestic investment and enhance productivity, import substitution worked fairly well in a broad range of countries until at least the mid-1970s. But starting in the second half of the 1970s, disaster struck in most of the economies that had been doing well. Only 12 of the 42 developing countries with growth rates above 2.5 per cent between 1960–73 were able to maintain them over the next decade (1973–84). The Middle East and Latin America, which had led the developing world in total factor productivity growth until 1973, began to experience negative average growth in productivity. East Asia held steady, while South Asia improved its performance (Collins and Bosworth, 1996).

Did worsening economic performance result from the 'exhaustion' of import substitution policies? Probably not. As argued elsewhere (Rodrik, 1999), the common timing of the downturns implicates the turbulence in the global economy after 1973, including the abandonment of the Bretton Woods system of fixed exchange rates, two major oil shocks, various other commodity booms and busts, and the U.S. Federal Reserve interest rate shock of the early 1980s. That some of South Asia's most ardent followers of import substitution policies—especially India and Pakistan—managed to maintain (Pakistan) or increase (India) growth after 1973 also suggests that mechanisms other than import substitution contributed to the economic collapse.[18]

Macroeconomic policies were among the most important of these other mechanisms. Many countries were unable to properly adjust macroeconomic policies in the wake of external shocks, leading to high or repressed inflation, scarce foreign exchange and large black market premiums for it, debt crises and external payment imbalances—greatly magnifying the real costs of the shocks. The countries that suffered the most were those with the largest increases in inflation and the highest black market premiums for foreign exchange. The culprits were poor monetary and fiscal policies and inadequate adjustments in exchange rate policies, sometimes aggravated by short-sighted policies of creditors and the Bretton Woods institutions (the World Bank and the International Monetary Fund). The bottom line for countries that experienced debt crises: the crises were the product of monetary and fiscal policies that were incompatible with sustainable external balances. Trade and industrial policies had little to do with them.

Outward-oriented industrialization

The East Asian 'tiger' economies are often presented as examples of export-led growth, where opening to the world economy unleashed powerful industrial diversification and technological advancement. But this conventional account overlooks the active role played by the governments of the Republic of Korea and Taiwan, province of China (and Japan before them) in shaping the allocation of resources. Neither economy undertook significant import liberalization early in the growth process. Most of their trade liberalization occurred in the 1980s, after high growth was already firmly established.

Key to the success of these and other East Asian economies was a coherent strategy of raising the returns to private investment through a range of policies that included credit subsidies, tax incentives, education promotion, establishment of public enterprises, export inducements, duty-free access to inputs and capital goods and government coordination of investment plans. In the Republic of Korea the main investment subsidy was the extension of credit to large business groups at negative real interest rates. Banks were nationalized after the military coup of 1961, giving the government exclusive control over the allocation of investible funds in the economy. Investment was also subsidized through the socialization of investment risk in selected sectors. This approach emerged because the government implicitly guaranteed that the state would bail out entrepreneurs investing in 'desirable' activities if circumstances later threatened the profitability of those investments. In Taiwan, province of China investment subsidies took the form of tax incentives.

In both Korea and Taiwan public enterprises played important roles in enhancing the profitability of private investment by ensuring that key inputs were available for private producers. Public enterprises accounted for a large share of manufacturing output and investment in both economies, and their importance increased during the critical take-off years of the 1960s. Singapore also heavily subsidized investment, but it differed from Korea and Taiwan in that its investment incentives focused on foreign investors.

Although trade policies that spurred exports were part of the arsenal of incentives in all the East Asian tiger economies, investment and its promotion were the primary goals. To that end, the governments of Korea and Taiwan resorted to unorthodox strategies: they protected domestic markets to raise profits, provided generous export subsidies, encouraged firms to reverse engineer foreign-patented products and imposed requirements on foreign investors (when they were allowed in) such as export-import balance requirements and domestic content requirements. All these strategies are now severely restricted under WTO agreements.

Two-track strategy

Relatively minimal reforms in China in the late 1970s set the stage for phenomenal economic performance that has been the envy of every developing country since. Initial reforms were fairly simple: loosening the communal farming system and allowing farmers to sell their crops in free markets once they had fulfilled their obligations to the state. Subsequent reforms created township and village enterprises, extended the 'market track' to the urban and industrial sectors, and created special economic zones to attract foreign investment. What stands out about these reforms is that they are based on two tracks (state and market), gradualism and experimentation.

Chinese-style gradualism can be interpreted in two ways. One perspective, represented forcefully by Sachs and Woo (2000), minimizes the relevance of China's particularism by arguing that its economic success is not due to any special aspects of its transition to a market economy, but largely to convergence between Chinese institutions and those in non-socialist economies. In this view the faster is the convergence, the better are the outcomes: 'favorable outcomes have emerged not because of gradualism, but *despite* gradualism' (Sachs and Woo, 2000, p. 3). The policy message is that countries looking to China for lessons should focus not on institutional experimentation but on harmonizing their institutions with those abroad.

The alternative perspective, perhaps best developed by Yingi Qian and Gerard Roland, is that the peculiarities of the Chinese model represent responses to specific political and informational problems for which there is no universal solution. Lau, Qian and Roland (1997) interpret the two-track approach to liberalization as a way of implementing Pareto-efficient reforms: an alteration in the planned economy that improves incentives at the margin, enhances efficiency in resource allocation and yet leaves none of the plan beneficiaries worse off. Qian, Roland and Xu (1999) see Chinese-style decentralization as a way of allowing the development of superior institutions for coordination: when economic activity requires products with matched attributes, local experimentation is a more effective way of processing and using local knowledge. These analysts find much to praise in the Chinese model because they believe that the system generates the right incentives for developing the knowledge required to build and sustain a market economy. Thus they are not overly bothered by some of the economic inefficiencies that may be generated along the way.

A less-known example of a successful two-track strategy is Mauritius, where superior economic performance has been built on a unique combination of orthodox and heterodox strategies. During the 1970s an export processing zone, operating under free trade principles, enabled a boom in garment exports to European markets and an accompanying boom in investment at home. Yet the export processing zone was combined with a domestic sector that was highly protected until the mid-1980s. In the early 1990s the International Monetary Fund still considered Mauritius the world's most 'policy restrictive' economy, and even by the late 1990s viewed it as one of the world's most protected economies (Subramanian, 2001). Mauritius has followed a two-track strategy not unlike China's, but underpinned by social and political arrangements that encourage participation, representation and coalition building.

The circumstances under which the Mauritian export processing zone was set up in 1970 are instructive, highlighting how participatory political systems help develop creative strategies for building locally adapted institutions. Given the small home market, it was evident that Mauritius would benefit from an outward-oriented strategy. But as in other developing countries, policy-makers had to contend with import-substituting industrialists who had been propped up by the restrictive commercial policies of the early 1960s—and who were naturally opposed to relaxing the trade regime.

A traditional World Bank or International Monetary Fund economist would have advocated across-the-board liberalization, without regard to what that might do to the island's precarious ethnic and political balance. The export processing zone provided a neat way around the political difficulties. The zone created trade and employment opportunities without removing protection from import-substituting industries and from the male workers who dominated established industries. The new employment and profit opportunities paved the way for more substantial liberalizations in the mid-1980s and 1990s. By the 1990s the female-male earning ratio was higher in the export processing zone than in the rest of the economy (ILO, 2001). Able to devise a strategy that was unorthodox but effective, Mauritius found its own path to economic and human development.

KEY MESSAGES

Trade should be seen as a means to development rather than an end. Though there is a two-way relationship between trade and human development, trade theories do not offer unequivocal conclusions about the direction or dynamics of the relationship. Moreover, trade liberalization policies should not be viewed as a reliable mechanism for generating self-sustaining growth and reducing poverty, let alone achieving other positive human development outcomes.

Gender inequalities, an important but often neglected aspect of human development, mediate the relationship between trade policies and trade performance. Because of pervasive gender discrimination in economic life, men and women are generally affected by trade policies differently. Gender inequalities sometimes constrain countries' ability to increase exports—but they can also be used as an instrument of international competition. That is troublesome from a human development perspective because it can mean that export growth comes at the expense of gender equality, child care and family well-being.

The only systematic relationship between countries' average tariffs and non-tariff restrictions and their subsequent economic growth is that countries dismantle trade restrictions as they get richer. With few exceptions, today's rich countries embarked on modern economic growth behind protective trade barriers but now have low barriers. The experiences of industrial and successful developing countries also provide two other lessons. First, economic integration with the world economy is an outcome of growth and development, not a prerequisite. Second, institutional innovations—many of them unorthodox and requiring considerable domestic policy space and flexibility—have been crucial for successful development strategies and outcomes.

The design of the multilateral trade regime needs to shift from one based on a market access perspective to one based on a human development perspective. It should also be evaluated not on the basis of whether it maximizes the flow of goods and services but on whether trade arrangements—current and proposed—maximize possibilities for human development, especially in developing countries. A world trade regime friendly to human development would provide domestic policy space and give developing countries flexibility to make institutional and other innovations. Such policy space should take precedence over market access considerations, even as the trade regime continues to recognize that market access can make an important contribution to human development in specific situations and for specific sectors and issues.

NOTES

1. During 1980–2000 average GDP growth was highest in East Asia and the Pacific (7.3 per cent a year), followed by South Asia (5.5 per cent), Latin America and the Caribbean (2.5 per cent) and Africa (2.2 per cent). This pattern was mirrored in the regions' export growth, which was 11.1 per cent, 7.9 per cent, 6.9 per cent and 2.8 per cent, respectively (World Bank, 2002).

2. The human development index is based on four indicators: life expectancy at birth, to reflect the dimension of a long and healthy life; the adult literacy rate and combined enrolment rate at the primary, secondary and tertiary levels, to represent the knowledge dimension; and real GDP per capita—measured using purchasing power parity (PPP)—to proxy for the resources required for a decent standard of living.

3. First, the human development index is not a comprehensive measure of human development: it ignores several important dimensions. Second, the index is composed of long-term human development indicators and does not reflect policy inputs or short-term human development achievements. Third, it is an average measure and so masks disparities and inequalities within countries. Disaggregating the index in terms of gender, region, race and ethnicity gives human development accounting much-needed breadth.

4. Gender refers to the social meanings constructed around sex differences; gender relations refer to the social norms and practices that regulate the relationships between men and women in a given society at a given time. Gender relations are not immutable; they change over time and vary across societies.

5. For example, formal credit institutions discriminate against women even though they are more reliable borrowers.

6. For economic analysis to be accurate and complete, unpaid work needs to be made visible and the economic meaning of work redefined to include unpaid household labour. For example, what may appear to be efficient from a market-focused perspective may be socially inefficient once full labour accounting and time use are considered.

7. Research in rural Tanzania found that even men in the poorest households forbid their wives from taking up wage labour (cited in Kabeer, 1996).

8. This discussion is drawn from Rodrik (2001).

9. The 'enlightened' standard view of development policy argues that to succeed, economic openness in developing countries requires both market access in advanced industrial countries and institutional reforms at home—ranging from legal and administrative reforms to safety nets. This view is 'enlightened' because it recognizes that there is more to economic integration than lowering tariffs and non-tariff barriers to trade, and standard because it represents the prevailing conventional wisdom (see World Bank and IMF, 2000).

10. The same is true of the promotion and subsidization of inward foreign direct investment (see Hanson, 2001).

11. This section and the next one are modified versions of the discussion in Çağatay (2001).

12. See UNCTAD (2002b) for a discussion of the fallacy of composition in global trade of labour-intensive manufactures.

13. This section is a modified version of the discussion in Rodrik (2001).

14. The supposition that one set of institutional arrangements must dominate has produced the fads of various decades. Europe, with its low unemployment, high growth and thriving culture, was the continent to emulate throughout much of the 1970s. During the trade-conscious 1980s Japan became the exemplar of choice. And the 1990s were the decade of US-style freewheeling capitalism.

15. The six countries were Swaziland, Botswana, Côte d'Ivoire, Gabon and Togo, with Kenya ranking 21st.

16. Countries such as Brazil, the Dominican Republic and Ecuador in Latin America; Iran, Morocco and Tunisia in the Middle East; and Côte d'Ivoire and Kenya in Africa all experienced more rapid TFP growth than any of the East Asian countries in this early period (with the possible exception of Hong Kong, for which comparable data are not available). Mexico, Bolivia, Panama, Egypt, Algeria, Tanzania and Zaire experienced higher TFP growth than all but Taiwan (Province of China). Of course, not all countries that pursued import-substituting industrialization did well. In Argentina growth in total factor productivity averaged just 0.2 per cent a year in 1960–73.

17. For example, although Mexico and Taiwan (province of China) are commonly seen as following diametrically opposed development paths, Little, Scitovsky and Scott (1970, pp 174–90) show that long after introducing trade reforms, Taiwan had a higher average effective rate of protection in manufacturing and greater variations in effective rates of protection than did Mexico.

18. Although India gradually liberalized its trade regime after 1991, its performance began to improve in the early 1980s—a decade before those reforms went into effect.

REFERENCES

Acemoglu, Daron, Simon Johnson and James A. Robinson. 2000. 'The Colonial Origins of Comparative Development: An Empirical Investigation'. Massachusetts Institute of Technology, Cambridge, Mass.

Balassa, Bela. 1971. *The Structure of Protection in Developing Countries*. Baltimore, Md: The Johns Hopkins University Press.

Ben-David, Dan. 1993. 'Equalizing Exchange: Trade Liberalization and Income Convergence'. *Quarterly Journal of Economics* 108 (3).

Benería, L., and Amy Lind. 1994. 'Engendering International Trade: Concepts, Policy and Action'. International Federation of Institutes for Advanced Study and United Nations Development Fund for Women, Gender Science and Development Programme, New York.

Bhagwati, Jagdish. 1968. 'Distortions and Immiserizing Growth: A Generalization'. *Review of Economic Studies* 35 (4): 481–85.

———. 1958. 'Immiserizing Growth: A Geometric Note'. *Review of Economic Studies* 25 (3): 201–05.

Çağatay, Nilufer. 2001. 'Trade, Gender and Poverty'. Background paper for Trade and Sustainable Human Development Project. United Nations Development Programme, New York.

Çağatay, Nilufer, Diane Elson and Caren Grown, eds. 1995. *World Development* 23 (8). Special issue on gender, adjustment and macroeconomics.

Chang, Ha-Joon. 2000. 'Institutional Development in Developing Countries in a Historical Perspective'. Cambridge University, Faculty of Economics and Politics.

Chipman, John. 1965a. 'A Survey of the Theory of International Trade: Part I, The Classical Theory'. *Econometrica* 33 (3): 477–519.

———. 1965b. 'A Survey of the Theory of International Trade: Part II, The Neo-Classical Theory'. *Econometrica* 33 (4): 685–760.

———. 1965c. 'A Survey of the Theory of International Trade: Part III, The Modern Theory'. *Econometrica* 34 (1): 18–76.

Collins, Susan, and Barry Bosworth. 1996. 'Economic Growth in East Asia: Accumulation vs. Assimilation'. *Brookings Papers on Economic Activity* 2: 135–91. Washington, DC: Brookings Institution.

Dollar, David. 1992. 'Outward-Oriented Developing Economies Really Do Grow More Rapidly: Evidence from 95 LDCs, 1976–85'. *Economic Development and Cultural Change* 40: 523–44.

Dollar, David, and Aart Kraay. 2000. 'Trade, Growth and Poverty'. Policy Research Working Paper 2615. World Bank, Washington, DC.

Dornbusch, Rudiger, Stanley Fischer and Paul Samuelson. 1977. 'Comparative Advantage, Trade and Payments in a Ricardian Model with a Continuum of Goods'. *American Economic Review* 67 (5): 823–39.

Dosi, Giovanni., K. Pavitt and L. Soete. 1990. *The Economics of Technical Change and International Trade.* New York: New York University Press.

Edwards, Sebastian. 1998. 'Openness, Productivity and Growth: What Do We Really Know?' *Economic Journal* 108 (447): 383–98.

Elson, Diane. 1996. 'Appraising Recent Developments in the World Market for Nimble Fingers: Accumulation, Regulation, Organization'. In A. Chaachi and R. Putin, eds., *Confronting State, Capital and Patriarchy: Women Organizing in the Process of Industrialization.* Basingstoke, UK: Macmillan and Institute of Social Studies.

Fontana, Marzia, and Adrian Wood. 2000. 'Modeling the Effects of Trade on Women at Work and at Home'. *World Development* 28 (7): 1173–90.

Frankel, Jeffrey, and David Romer. 1999. 'Does Trade Cause Growth?' *American Economic Review* 89 (3): 379–99.

Gammage, S., and J. Fernandez. 2000. 'Gender, Conflict and Reintegration: Household Survey Evidence from El Salvador'. Working Paper 25. United Nations High Commissioner for Refugees, Geneva.

Gomory, Ralph E., and William Baumol. 2000. *Global Trade and Conflicting National Interests.* Cambridge, Mass: Massachusetts Institute of Technology Press.

Grossman, Gene, and Elhahan Helpman. 1990. 'Comparative Advantage and Long Run Growth'. *American Economic Review* 80 (4): 796–815.

———. 1991. 'Quality Ladders and Product Cycles'. *Quarterly Journal of Economics* 106 (2): 557–86.

Grown, Caren, Diane Elson and Nilufer Cagatay, eds. 2000. *World Development* 28 (7). Special issue on growth, trade, finance and gender inequality.

Hanson, Gordon. 2001. 'Should Countries Promote Foreign Direct Investment?' Discussion Paper 9. Group of 24. United Nations Conference on Trade and Development, New York and Geneva, and Harvard University, Center for International Development, Cambridge, Mass.

Harrod, R. F. 1939. 'An Essay in Dynamic Theory'. *Economic Journal* 49: 14–33.

Helleiner, Gerald K. 1994. *Trade Policy and Industrialization in Turbulent Times.* New York: Routledge.

———. 2000. 'Markets, Politics and the Global Economy: Can the Global Economy Be Civilized?' Tenth Raul Prebisch lecture, United Nations Conference on Trade and Development, 11 December, Geneva.

ILO (International Labour Organization). 1993. *World Labor Report.* Geneva: International Labour Office.

———. 2001. 'Women, Gender and Work'. International Labour Office, Geneva.

Jahan, Selim. 2000. 'Economic Growth and Human Development: Issues Revisited'. Keynote speech at a conference hosted by the St. Mary's University Institute for International Development, Halifax, Canada.

Joekes, Susan. 1983. 'New Theories of Trade among Industrial Countries'. *American Economic Review* 73 (2): 343–47.

———. 1987. 'Is Free Trade Passe?' *Journal of Economic Perspectives* 1 (2): 131–44.

———. 1999. 'A Gender-Analytical Perspective on Trade and Sustainable Development'. In *Trade, Sustainable Development and Gender.* New York and Geneva: United Nations Conference on Trade and Development.

Jones, Ronald. 2000. *Globalization and the Theory of Input Trade.* Cambridge, Mass: Massachusetts Institute of Technology Press.

Kabeer, Naila. 1996. 'Agency, Well-being and Inequality: Reflections on Gender Dimensions of Poverty'. *IDS Bulletin* 27 (1): 11–21.

Krugman, Paul. 1981. 'Intraindustry Specialization and the Gains from Trade'. *Journal of Political Economy* 89 (5): 959–73.

Lau, Lawrence J., Yingyi Qian and Gerard Roland. 1997. 'Pareto-Improving Economic Reforms through Dual-Track Liberalization'. *Economics Letters* 55: 285–92.

Little, Ian, Tibor Scitovsky and Maurice Scott. 1970. *Industry and Trade in Some Developing Countries.* London and New York: Oxford University Press.

Lucas, Robert E. 1993. 'Making a Miracle'. *Econometrica* 61 (2): 251–72.

Milberg, William. 1993. 'Is Absolute Advantage Passe? Towards a Post-Keynesian/ Marxian Theory of International Trade'. In Mark Glick, ed., *Competition,*

Technology and Money: Classical and Post-Keynesian Perspectives. Aldershot, UK: Edward Elgar.

———. 2002. 'Says Law in the Open Economy: Keynes's Rejection of the Theory of Comparative Advantage'. In Sheila Don and John Hillard, eds., *Keynes, Uncertainty and the Global Economy.* Aldershot, UK: Edward Elgar.

Mill, John Stuart. 1909. *Principles of Political Economy with Some of Their Applications to Social Philosophy.* London: Longmans, Green and Co. (Based on the 7th edition.1st edition published in 1848; 7th edition first published in 1870.)

Osterreich-Warner, Shaianne. 2002. 'Engendering International Wage Differentials: Women, Export Promotion and Trade'. PhD diss. University of Utah, Department of Economics, Salt Lake City.

Prescott, Edward, and John Boyd. 1987. 'Dynamic Coalitions: Engines of Growth'. *American Economic Review* 77 (2): 63–67.

Qian, Yingi, Gerard Roland and Chenggang Xu. 1999. 'Coordinating Changes in M-form and U-form Organizations'. Paper prepared for the Nobel symposium, April, Oslo.

Redding, Stephen. 1997. 'Dynamic Comparative Advantage and the Welfare Effects of Trade'. Centre for Economic Policy Research, London.

Rodriguez, Francisco, and Dani Rodrik. 2001. 'Trade Policy and Economic Growth: A Sceptic's Guide to Cross-National Literature'. In Ben Bernanke and Kenneth Rogoff, eds., *National Bureau for Economic Research Macro Annual 2000,* Cambridge, Mass: Massachusetts Institute for Technology Press.

Rodrik, Dani. 1999. *The New Global Economy and the Developing Countries: Making Openness Work.* Washington, DC: Overseas Development Council.

———. 2000. 'Institutions for High-Quality Growth: What They Are and How to Acquire Them'. *Studies in Comparative International Development* 35 (3).

———. 2001. 'The Global Governance of Trade As If Development Really Mattered'. Background paper for Trade and Sustainable Human Development Project. United Nations Development Programme, New York.

Romer, Paul. 1986. 'Increasing Returns and Long-run Growth'. *Journal of Political Economy* 95 (5): 1002–37.

Sachs, Jeffrey, and Andrew Warner. 1995. 'Economic Reform and the Process of Global Integration'. *Brookings Papers on Economic Activity* 1: 1–118. Washington, DC: Brookings Institution.

Sachs, Jeffrey, and Wing Thye Woo. 2000. 'Understanding China's Economic Performance'. *Journal of Policy Reform* 4 (1).

Seguino, Stephanie. 2000. 'Gender Inequality and Economic Growth: A Cross-Country Analysis'. *World Development* 28 (7): 1211–30.

Sen, Amartya 1990. 'Gender and Cooperative Conflicts'. In I. Tinker, ed., *Persistent Inequalities: Women and World Development.* New York: Oxford University Press.

———. 1999. *Development As Freedom.* New York: Knopf.

Shaikh, Anwar. 1995. 'Free Trade, Unemployment and Economic Policy'. In John Eatwell, ed., *Global Unemployment.* Armonk, New York: M.E. Sharpe.

Standing, Guy. 1989. 'Global Feminization through Flexible Labor'. *World Development* 17 (7): 1077–95.

————. 1999. 'Global Feminization through Flexible Labor: A Theme Revisited'. *World Development* 27 (3): 583–602.

Stern, Nicholas. 2000. 'Globalization and Poverty'. Paper presented at a conference hosted by the University of Indonesia's Institute of Economic and Social Research, Faculty of Economics, 20 December, Depok.

Stokey, Nancy. 1988. 'Learning by Doing and the Introduction of New Goods'. *Journal of Political Economy* 96 (4): 701–17.

————. 1991a. 'Human Capital, Product Quality and Growth'. *Quarterly Journal of Economics* 106 (2): 587–616.

————. 1991b. 'The Volume and Composition of Trade between Rich and Poor Countries'. *Review of Economic Studies* 58 (1): 63–80.

Subramanian, Arvind. 2001. 'Mauritius Trade and Development Strategy: What Lessons Does it Offer?' Paper presented at the International Monetary Fund High-Level Seminar on Globalization and Africa, 5–6 April, Tunis.

UN (United Nations). 1999. *World Survey on the Role of Women in Development: Globalization, Gender and Work.* New York.

————. 2000. 'The Millennium Development Goals Declaration'. New York. [www.un.org/millennium/declaration/ares552e.htm].

UNCTAD (United Nations Conference on Trade and Development). 2002a. *The Least Developed Countries Report: Escaping the Poverty Trap.* Geneva.

————. 2002b. *Trade and Development Report.* Geneva.

UNDP (United Nations Development Programme). Various years. *Human Development Report.* New York: Oxford University Press.

Unger, Roberto Mangabeira. 1998. *Democracy Realized: The Progressive Alternative.* London and New York: Verso Books.

US Department of State. 1999. '1999 Country Report on Economic Policies and Trade Practices: Haiti'. Washington, DC. [www.state.gov/www/issues/economic/trade_reports/1999/haiti.pdf].

World Bank. Various years. *World Development Indicators.* Washington, DC

World Bank and IMF (International Monetary Fund). 2000. 'Trade, Development and Poverty Reduction'. Paper prepared for the Development Committee, Washington, DC.

Young, Alwyn. 1991. 'Learning by Doing and the Dynamic Effects of International Trade'. *Quarterly Journal of Economics* 106 (2): 369–405.

CHAPTER 2
THE GLOBAL TRADE REGIME

'Human development requires fair governance—a framework of institutions, rules and established practices that ensure fair processes and outcomes secured through participation of people and accountability of the powerful'.
                        —*Adapted from* Human Development Report 2002

The United Nations Development Programme's *Human Development Report 2002* views good democratic governance as integral to human development. In assessing whether governance is good or bad, the report highlights critical processes, including:

- How and by whom mandates, agendas and forums for discussions and decision-making are chosen and agreed. These activities determine what gets done—and what remains undone.
- Who establishes, elaborates and enforces rules.
- The transparency of the process.
- The effectiveness of representation.
- The participation of the weakest members.
- The fairness and consistency of dispute settlement and enforcement processes.

CAN THERE BE FAIR OUTCOMES WITHOUT FAIR PROCESSES?

These process-related concerns are highly relevant to the emerging international trade regime. Why? Because in the complex web of global governance, the trade system exemplifies some historical and structural inequities that continue to confound the global economic system. Process concerns took on greater urgency after the failure of the 1999 World Trade Organization (WTO) ministerial conference in Seattle, Washington (US). Through the 'single undertaking' that resulted from the Uruguay Round of trade negotiations (box 2.1), developing countries had assumed obligations similar to those of industrial countries and so demanded that equal importance be given to their proposals. But discussions broke down partly because many developing country representatives felt excluded from informal negotiating

Box 2.1 A BRIEF HISTORY OF THE GLOBAL TRADE REGIME

The General Agreement on Tariffs and Trade (GATT) involved seven rounds of negotiations before the Uruguay Round: Geneva (1947), Annecy (1948), Torquay (1950), Geneva (1956), Dhillon (1960–61), Kennedy (1964–67) and Tokyo (1973–79). The first six rounds focused on reducing tariffs. And in the first five, tariff negotiations were based on reciprocal tariff concessions, negotiated bilaterally between 'principal' and 'substantial' suppliers and extended to all contracting parties.

In contrast, the Kennedy and Tokyo rounds took a linear approach to tariff cuts. While a few major developing countries had participated in negotiations up to the Kennedy Round, few developing countries were contracting parties to the GATT. Indeed, many did not achieve independence from colonial regimes until the 1960s. In 1964, when the United Nations Conference on Trade and Development (UNCTAD) was created to reform the GATT, efforts were made to make the system more acceptable to developing countries, including by incorporating a clause on trade and development.

The Tokyo Round, launched in 1973, was not confined to GATT contracting parties. The round established more stringent codes for non-tariff measures, but they were binding only on countries that accepted them. In addition, the round resulted in the decision on differential and more favourable treatment, reciprocity and fuller participation of developing countries—known as the 'enabling clause'. For example, industrial countries did not expect reciprocity from developing countries for commitments made to them, and developing countries were not expected to make contributions inconsistent with their development, financial and trade needs. The clause also legitimized the Generalized System of Preferences and the application of differential and favourable treatment to developing countries, including special attention to the least developed countries.

Multilateral trade negotiations changed substantially with the start of the Uruguay Round in 1986. Industrial countries sought to extend the GATT system to cover additional areas of international economic relations, and on their initative it was urged to place negotiations on goods on one track and negotiations on services on another. The agreement was that developing countries would negotiate on the new issues of services, Trade-Related Aspects of Intellectual Property Rights (TRIPS) and Trade-Related Investment Measures (TRIMs). In return, they would get better market access for exports of goods.

By the end of the Uruguay Round the two tracks had merged. While the negotiating mandate on functioning of the GATT system (FOGS) did not envisage the creation of what would ultimately become the WTO, it became apparent that the GATT system could not accommodate a radical enhancement and extension of multilateral trade mechanisms. As a result the European Communities and Canada submitted proposals for a new multilateral trade agreement to be administered by a new multilateral trade organization. The idea was that the Uruguay Round agreements on goods, services and intellectual property would be treated as a single undertaking, all under the aegis of the new World Trade Organization (WTO) and all subject to its dispute settlement system—thus enabling cross-sectoral retaliation as part of the WTO enforcement mechanism.

Industrial countries suggested that the WTO should replace the GATT while incorporating its fundamental provisions. Developing countries were given the choice of continuing as contracting parties to the defunct GATT or joining the WTO. By taking the second course, they became full stakeholders in the WTO.

The collapse of the 1999 WTO Ministerial Conference in Seattle, Washington (US), caused more attention to be paid to the concerns of developing countries at the 2001 conference in Doha, Qatar. The conference produced three major documents: a ministerial declaration, a decision on implementation issues and concerns and a declaration on TRIPS and public health:

- The ministerial declaration put forward an ambitious agenda for post-Doha work, including new negotiations on market access for non-agriculture products, negotiations on aspects of trade and the environment, negotiations to clarify certain rules (on anti-dumping, subsidies and countervailing measures) and negotiations on dispute settlement.

- Also to be negotiated are the implementation issues and concerns that developing countries had put forward earlier, only a few of which have been resolved.

- The declaration on TRIPS and public health reaffirmed countries' right to prioritize public health concerns—an important milestone.

- Post-Doha work is also to include more focused discussions on the four 'Singapore' issues (investment, competition policy, transparency in government procurement and trade facilitation). But negotiations on these issues will occur only if 'explicit consensus' is obtained at the 2003 ministerial conference.

The Doha conference ended with an expanded negotiating agenda, to be concluded by January 2005, placing a tremendous negotiating and administrative burden on developing countries. But the conference also marked their emergence as effective negotiators, clearly articulating their development needs.

Source: TWN, 2001.

processes. As participation and content issues became intertwined, participation sometimes became the most important issue—overshadowing the content of the negotiations.

In an effort to avoid the problems experienced in Seattle, some parts of the negotiating process were handled better before and at the 2001 WTO Ministerial Conference in Doha, Qatar. There were fewer 'green rooms', and more parts of the conference were open to all delegations.[1] But serious and legitimate concerns remained. First was the draft agreement transmitted from Geneva (Switzerland) to Doha, which did not reflect the many areas of disagreement among WTO members. Second was the process for selecting 'friends of the chair' (leaders of different working groups chosen by the chair of the Doha conference). Third was the extension of the conference by a day without the formal consensus of all members. And fourth was the use of a green room for much of the crucial last day.

When it comes to human development, the links between processes and outcomes cannot be severed. Fairness, representativeness, transparency and participation have intrinsic value in international trade negotiations. They also have implications for the mandates, agendas and substance of negotiations—and so for human development. Whether and how trade negotiations deal with intellectual property rights, market access or the links between trade and environmental standards affect the health, education, economic growth and socio-cultural destinies of hundreds of millions of people and the communities and countries they live in.

Box 2.2 Underlying features of GATT 1947 and WTO 1995

Under the General Agreement on Tariffs and Trade (GATT), the multilateral trade regime was characterized by the following features:

- *Reciprocity.* The operating feature of the regime was reciprocity and mutual advantage: countries agreed to liberalize trade in return for similar commitments from other members of the regime. This arrangement meant that concessions granted by one country were matched by concessions received—giving member nations an incentive to increase their commitments.

- *Non-discrimination.* Members of the regime were not to discriminate between trading partners—all members were given unconditional most-favoured-nation (MFN) status—or between domestic and foreign goods, services or nationals once imported into their territories ('national treatment').

- *Objective of freer, more predictable trade.* The GATT recognized price-based measures—that is, tariffs—as the only legitimate tool for regulating trade. It sought to reduce and eliminate non-tariff barriers and encouraged contracting parties to bind their tariffs to make trade more predictable. The agreement also encouraged members to reduce tariffs through successive rounds of trade negotiations, with the expectation that trade volumes would increase under binding commitments.

- *Special provisions for developing countries.* The regime provided flexibility for developing countries by permitting them much greater flexibility in their trade policies. The Tokyo Round's 'enabling clause' gave industrial countries the option of providing preferences and other favourable conditions to imports from developing countries.

With the creation of the World Trade Organization (WTO) in 1995, the regime evolved into a more complex and intrusive framework. In addition to the GATT features, the WTO involves:

- *The single undertaking.* Member nations agreed to negotiate and sign all WTO agreements as part of a package deal—a 'single undertaking'. This meant finalizing the content of the agreements based on mutual bargaining (reflecting relative bargaining strengths) and the concept of 'overall reciprocity' rather than on the value of each agreement. This approach was seen as benefiting developing countries by including in the final package of agreements areas that had previously been effectively excluded (such as agriculture and textiles). But it also meant that all member countries would be covered by the same disciplines—both the enhanced versions of the Tokyo Round codes and the new agreements, including those that extended multilateral disciplines into new areas such as services and intellectual property rights. The single undertaking principle was retained in the declaration issued from the 2001 WTO ministerial conference in Doha, Qatar.

- *Binding implications for domestic policies.* The scope of global trade agreements has extended into areas (such as services and intellectual property rights) that until the creation of the WTO were in the domestic domain, while at the same time enhancing existing disciplines to make them more intrusive. Together these new features—extension into new areas, more intrusiveness into domestic policy-making and the single undertaking—extend the WTO's influence over domestic policy-making in areas critical to the development process. The agreements under the regime commit members not just to trade liberalization but also to specific policy choices on services, investment and intellectual property rights. The nature of these choices directly affects human development—linking the global trade regime under the WTO much more closely to human development outcomes than did the GATT.

• *Compliance mechanisms.* Today's trade regime has stronger compliance mechanisms than did the GATT. Non-compliance with agreements can be challenged under the WTO's integrated dispute settlement system, and no member can block such actions. Remedial action is mandated through compensatory trade action (retaliation) by trading partners affected by a member's failure to meet obligations. Retaliation can also cross agreements and sectors, in keeping with the single undertaking principle.

Source: UNDP, 2002.

Fair negotiating processes are more likely than unfair ones to generate workable, sustainable outcomes. Moreover, decision-making should be open to public scrutiny, and decisions should reflect the interests of all stakeholders—with special attention to the poorest people and least developed countries (Johnson, 2001). For the global trade regime, good governance at a minimum requires genuine multilateralism and active, equal participation by all members.

THE WORLD TRADE ORGANIZATION—A MAJOR SHIFT IN GLOBAL TRADE RULES

The WTO has been responsible for making and enforcing rules on global trade since 1995. Its predecessor, the General Agreement on Tariffs and Trade (GATT), mainly dealt with cross-border transactions involving goods. But during the Uruguay Round of trade negotiations, developing countries were presented with a 'take it or leave it' choice of becoming full members of the WTO (Ricupero, 1994; see also box 2.1). The Uruguay Round agreements that created the WTO committed its members to deep integration in a single undertaking through the inclusion of many areas traditionally considered outside the purview of bilateral, regional and multilateral trade rules. The single undertaking and the threat of sanctions through the WTO's global dispute settlement body give the organization a mandate different from all preceding intergovernmental forums (box 2.2).

The WTO's features and agenda extend beyond the GATT's in several ways. First, the single undertaking extends revised rules on non-tariff barriers to all countries. Second, some of these rules, such as those on subsidies and Trade-Related Investment Measures (TRIMs), are much more intrusive. And third, policies subject to multilateral trade rules now include areas traditionally in the domestic domain, such as trade in services and intellectual property (Woods and Narlikar, 2001). Although some of these new issues had been debated at the multilateral level before, this was the first time they were raised in the context of trade and linked specifically to trade agreements. It was also the first time that trade sanctions were seen as a way of enforcing property rights. Thus the international trade regime is starting to have a direct effect on national regulation and legislation, through rules and agreements that seek to harmonize different norms and standards of governance.

THE WORLD TRADE ORGANIZATION'S FORMAL GOVERNANCE STRUCTURE

Formally, the WTO is the most democratic of all the international institutions with a global mandate. Its one-country, one-vote system of governance makes it far more democratic than the Bretton Woods institutions—the World Bank and International Monetary Fund (IMF). That it lacks the equivalent of the Security Council makes it, in a structural sense, even more democratic than the UN (Evans, 2000), though its membership is not as broad.[2] But with the recent accession of China, all major countries and groups are WTO members except the Russian Federation, many least developed countries and Saudi Arabia and other Middle Eastern petroleum exporters, which are in the process of accession.

The WTO's highest decision-making body is the ministerial conference, which generally meets every two years. Below that is the general council, based in Geneva, which meets about once a month. The general council also meets as the trade policy review body and the dispute settlement body. Below the general council and reporting to it are councils for trade in goods, services and intellectual property, committees on trade and development and trade and the environment, and working groups established to study investment, competition policy, trade facilitation, trade and technology transfer, transparency in government procurement and trade, debt and finance. In addition, a work programme to examine the issues relating to the trade of small economies was agreed on in Doha. All these entities are made up of official representatives from WTO member states.

Ministers at the Doha conference approved the creation of a trade negotiations committee to supervise the conduct of negotiations. This committee includes two negotiating groups—one on market access (for non-agricultural products) and one on rules. But the committee and its negotiating groups are not parallel mechanisms to existing WTO bodies, and most negotiations will continue to occur within those bodies. Moreover, the decision-making role of the trade negotiations committee remains unclear, because formal decisions will continue to be made by the general council. After considerable debate, the trade negotiations committee appointed the WTO's director-general as its chair in an ex officio capacity until January 2005, when the Doha round of negotiations is scheduled to conclude. But this has been explicitly agreed as a unique and temporary arrangement—not a precedent. As a member-driven organization, appointments to WTO bodies should be filled only by representatives of WTO members.

The ministerial conference and general council formally make decisions by consensus. If consensus fails, decisions are determined by a simple majority based on one member, one vote. Developing countries account for more than three-quarters of WTO members and in the mid-1990s had 76 per cent of its votes—less than the 83 per cent they had in the UN General Assembly but much more than their 39 per cent in the World Bank's International Bank for Reconstruction and Development and International Development Association and 38 per cent in the International Monetary Fund (Woods, 1998, table 4). Yet there have been no cases of voting. So far, all decisions have been made by consensus. This is also true in the committees and specialized bodies that report to the general council.

The WTO is a membership-driven organization. It has no permanent executive board. Its members participate in its day-to-day activities through the general council. Its secretariat is small, and its management's autonomy and power are limited—especially relative to international financial institutions such as the World Bank and International Monetary Fund. But though most WTO members are developing countries, many have limited capacity to attend meetings of the general council and other meetings in Geneva. And even if present, many developing countries cannot participate effectively in ongoing WTO discussions.

The WTO's dispute settlement mechanism is one of its most noteworthy features. Many experts consider the mechanism a unique feature in international law—with a major impact on trade diplomacy (Jackson, 2000). The mechanism is made up of ad hoc panels of three to five trade specialists and a standing appellate body of seven expert trade lawyers, overseen by the dispute settlement body of all WTO members.

SPECIAL AND DIFFERENTIAL TREATMENT

Efforts have been made to redress international inequalities since the start of global trade negotiations. In 1979 the Tokyo Round of trade negotiations produced the enabling clause—allowing developing countries to benefit, in principle, from preferential market access and flexible trade mechanisms not enjoyed by industrial countries (see box 2.1). The clause legitimized the Generalized System of Preferences and provided more favourable treatment with respect to non-tariff barriers, preferential trade rules for developing countries and special treatment for the least developed countries. The enabling clause was voluntary and selective, not binding. In return, developing countries agreed to graduation—meaning that their commitments to the multilateral trade regime would increase with improvements in their economic status.

During the 1980s there was a move away from special and differential treatment for developing countries. (Moreover, as a condition of their loans the International Monetary Fund and World Bank required many developing countries to cut tariffs and non-tariff protection.) Opponents portrayed special and differential treatment as a crutch that hindered developing countries' ability to develop competitive industries. The prevailing ideology portrayed special and differential treatment as 'ideological baggage'. More significantly, developing countries believed that any special or preferential trade treatment from industrial countries was nullified by discriminatory trade-related measures of even greater significance—including the agricultural regimes of industrial countries, the Multifibre Arrangement (MFA) and the creeping tendency towards managed trade under MFA-inspired 'grey area' measures (trade barriers which were in a legally murky area before the Uruguay Round) such as voluntary export restraints. And it was those measures, given developing countries' interest in export-oriented growth, that required them to shift their attention towards setting more multilateral discipline over industrial countries' actions, rather than seeking more freedom for their own.

The sixth meeting of the United Nations Conference on Trade and Development (UNCTAD VI), held in 1983 as part of preparations for what became the Uruguay Round, represented a watershed in this regard. At that meeting developing countries came out in active support of the unconditional most-favoured-nation (MFN) principle. As a result, at the start of the Uruguay Round developing countries had considerable hope that mutual reciprocity and full participation in the trade regime would be more effective than differential treatment.

The Uruguay Round agreements contained some measures on special and differential treatment, in the form of specific criteria and numerical thresholds (as well as vague provisions on access to technology). But they also resulted in the single undertaking, which eliminated most of the flexibility enjoyed by developing countries. There are 97 provisions for special and differential treatment in the WTO agreements; some are mandatory but others are not.[3] The WTO defines provisions as mandatory if they contain the word 'shall'. Non-mandatory provisions use 'should'.[4] Some of these provisions are related to conduct, providing developing countries with policy space. Others are related to outcomes, aiming to correct imbalances in procedures and results.

Policy space provisions allow developing countries to violate some WTO rules without fear of retaliation by industrial countries. There are two main types of policy space provisions: longer transition periods to adjust to new commitments (many of which have expired) and greater flexibility to deviate from commitments. Transition periods are more common: the Agreements on Agriculture, Textiles and Clothing, Sanitary and Phytosanitary Measures, Trade-Related Investment Measures (TRIMs), Customs Valuation, Import Licensing Procedures, Safeguards, Services (GATS) and Trade-Related Aspects of Intellectual Property Rights (TRIPS) provide for longer transition periods for developing countries before they fully commit to the agreements. In addition, most of these periods are subject to extensions, like the one provided to the least developed countries under the TRIPS agreement at the 2001 ministerial conference in Doha. (WTO commitments and the exceptions provided to developing and least developed countries are described in annexes 2.1 and 2.2.)

The second type of provisions help developing countries integrate with the global trading structure. These include active steps to increase market access for developing countries more than for others (such as preferential schemes and the Generalized System of Preferences), safeguard options to prevent injury and the provision of special preferences to the least developed countries.

With the growth of the WTO, non-reciprocal trade preferences such as those covered by the Generalized System of Preferences have declined in use and importance and are mostly confined to the least developed countries. Under WTO article 9, preferential trading schemes between industrial and developing countries require members to request an annual waiver from WTO rules, which requires the approval of three-quarters of WTO members. Agreements currently in force through such waivers are the US–Caribbean Basin Economic Recovery Act, the CARIBCAN agreement between Caribbean countries and Canada, the US-Andean Trade Preference Act and the Cotonou Agreement between African, Caribbean and Pacific countries (ACP) and the EU.

After several years' experience with implementation of Uruguay Round agreements, developing countries began to perceive that provisions for special and differential treatment did not adequately address their practical trade problems. Nor were the time limits for the application of the agreements realistic, undermining development policies. A large percentage of the almost 150 proposals submitted by developing countries in the process leading up to the 1999 WTO conference in Seattle focused on specific aspects of special and differential treatment.

After the Seattle conference, the firm position of developing countries on these proposals kept them alive during negotiations on agreement implementation. Moreover, the agenda emanating from the 2001 Doha conference resurrected and reaffirmed special and differential treatment as a legitimate, integral principle of WTO agreements. Ministers at the Doha conference agreed to review all special and differential treatment provisions to make them more precise, effective and operational. Thus all the pre-Seattle proposals are now the subject of negotiations.

The key principles and elements of the trade regime, its formal governance structure and enlarged mandate and its provisions on special and differential treatment are aimed at balancing the diverse needs and interests of its member nations. Still, the regime is primarily geared towards increasing trade. Its underlying features need to be analysed in greater detail and modified if it is to focus on human development as its ultimate goal.

ANNEX 2.1

Exceptions from World Trade Organization commitments for developing countries

Agreement	Exceptions
Agreement on Agriculture	Allows for different rates of tariff reductions and levels of domestic support and export subsidies. (At the same time, the design of the agreement negated this concession. Subsidies most relevant to developing countries were prohibited, while those relevant to industrial countries were allowed—reflecting an inherent imbalance in the agreement in complete contradiction to the special and differential treatment principle and promoting reverse special and differential treatment in favour of industrial countries.)
Agreement on Anti-dumping	Requires that where anti-dumping measures would affect developing country interests, there should first be an attempt to explore constructive remedies provided for by the agreement (article 15).
Agreement on Safeguards	Ensures that safeguard measures shall not be applied against a product from a developing country member if that product's share of imports does not exceed 3 per cent and if developing country members with less than 3 per cent shares do not account for more than 9 per cent of total imports of that product.
Agreement on Sanitary and Phytosanitary Measures	Allows for specific, time-bound exceptions to its obligations, taking into account the development, financial and trade needs of developing countries (article 10.3).
Agreement on Subsidies and Countervailing Measures	Exempts countries with per capita incomes of less than $1,000 from the prohibition on export subsidies. For other developing countries the export subsidy prohibition takes effect eight years after the entry into force of the agreement establishing the WTO (that is, in 2003). In addition, countervailing investigations of products from developing-country members are terminated if overall subsidies do not exceed 2 per cent (and from certain developing countries, 3 per cent) of the product's value or if the subsidized imports represent less than 4 per cent of total imports of that product (article 27.10b).
Agreement on Technical Barriers to Trade	Requires that members take into account the development, financial and trade needs of developing countries to ensure that technical regulations do not create obstacles to their exports (article 12.2 and 12.3).
Agreement on Textiles and Clothing	Requires members to take special account of developing country exports when applying the transitional safeguard provision and to accord more favourable treatment when setting economic criteria for imports from these countries. Also prohibits the use of the safeguard provision for developing country exports of cottage industry handlooms, traditional folk art textiles and products certified as such (article 6.6).

Agreement on Trade-Related Investment Measures (TRIMs)	Allows developing countries to temporarily deviate from the requirement to eliminate TRIMs inconsistent with national treatment or quantitative restrictions, if done to protect infant industries or for balance of payments safeguard measures (article 4).
Dispute Settlement Mechanism	Requires that the problems and interests of developing countries receive special attention (articles 4.10 and 21.2).
General Agreement on Trade in Services (GATS)	Provides flexibility in accordance with a country's level of development and instructs that negotiations should recognize the role of subsidies in development (articles 5.3a, 15.1 and 19.2).

ANNEX 2.2

Special provisions for the least developed countries in World Trade Organization agreements

Agreement	Provisions
WTO Agreement	Specifies that for the least developed countries to become original members, they are required only to 'undertake commitments and concessions that are consistent with their development, financial and trade needs, or their administrative and institutional capacity'. The WTO Committee on Trade and Development is to periodically review special provisions in favour of the least developed countries and offer appropriate recommendations (articles 4.7 and 11.2).
Agreement on Agriculture	Requires industrial countries to take actions stipulated by the Measures Concerning the Possible Negative Effects of the Reform Programme on Least Developed and Net Food Importing Developing Countries. The least developed countries are exempt from reduction commitments in agricultural market access, domestic support and export subsidies.
Agreement on Sanitary and Phytosanitary Measures	Provides an additional five-year transition period.
Agreement on Subsidies and Countervailing Measures	Recognizes that subsidies can play an important role in economic development. The WTO committee stands ready to review specific export subsidies to ensure that they conform with that country's development needs and to review measures against specific developing countries if needed (article 27). The least developed countries are exempt from the prohibition of local content subsidies for eight years.
Agreement on Technical Barriers to Trade	Stipulates that the least developed countries are to receive priority in receiving advice and technical assistance.
Agreement on Textiles and Clothing	Accords significantly more favourable treatment in the application of the transitional safeguard (article 6.6).

Agreement on Trade-Related Aspects of Intellectual Property Rights (TRIPS)	The least developed countries are exempt from provisions for protection until 2006 (extended to the end of 2015 at the Doha conference). Industrial countries are to provide incentives for technology transfers to the least developed countries to enable them to create sound and viable technology bases.
Agreement on Trade-Related Investment Measures (TRIMs)	Provides a seven-year transition period from 1995, the year the WTO came into existence.
General Agreement on Trade in Services (GATS)	The least developed countries shall be given special priority for increasing their participation, and particular account shall be taken of their difficulties in meeting commitments given their special development needs. Members shall give special consideration to opportunities for the least developed countries in telecommunications services.

NOTES

1. In WTO jargon a green room is a meeting among a limited number of countries to work out an agreement. This process has been especially common in the intense negotiations prior to and at ministerial conferences, including those in Seattle and Doha (TWN, 2001).

2. With Switzerland joining the UN, its membership increased to 190 countries. With the accession of China and the customs territory of Taiwan (province of China) to the WTO, its membership increased to 144 states.

3. The WTO classifies these provisions in six categories: to enhance trade opportunities, safeguard the interests of developing countries, allow flexibility of commitments, extend transition periods, provide technical assistance and provide special assistance to the least developed countries.

4. The WTO also clarifies that non-mandatory special and differential treatment provisions can be made mandatory through amendment or authoritative interpretation. Despite the fact that authoritative interpretation is possible only through ministerial conferences and the general council, the appellate body has ruled that in some cases the use of 'should' can imply a duty, making a provision mandatory (article 9:2, GATT Agreement, 1994).

REFERENCES

Evans, Peter. 2000. 'Economic Governance Institutions in a Global Political Economy: Implications for Developing Countries'. Paper presented at the High-level Round Table on Trade and Development: Directions for the Twenty-first Century, United Nations Conference on Trade and Development X, February 12, Bangkok.

Jackson, John J. 2000. 'The Role and Effectiveness of the WTO Dispute Settlement Mechanism'. In Susan M. Collins and Dani Rodrik, eds., *Brookings Trade Forum.* Washington, DC: Brookings Institution.

Johnson, Robert C. 2001. 'Linking Transparency to Accountability in Economic Governance: Are We Asking the Right Questions?' Paper prepared for the Carnegie Endowment for International Peace workshop on transparency, 10–11 May, Washington, DC.

Malhotra, Kamal. 2002. 'Doha: Is It Really a Development Round?' Trade and Environment Policy Paper. Carnegie Endowment for International Peace, Washington, DC.

Ricupero, Rubens. 1994. 'Los paises en dessarollo y la Ronda Uruguay: Desencuentros de un amor no correspondido'. In Patricio Leiva, ed., *La Ronda Uruguay y el desarrollo de América Latina*. Santiago de Chile: CLEPI.

TWN (Third World Network). 2001. 'The Multilateral Trading System: A Development Perspective'. Background paper for Trade and Sustainable Human Development Project. United Nations Development Programme, New York.

UNDP (United Nations Development Programme). 2002. *Human Development Report 2002: Deepening Democracy in a Fragmented World*. New York: Oxford University Press.

Woods, Ngaire. 1998. 'Governance in International Organisations: The Case for Reform in the Bretton Woods Institutions'. International Financial and Monetary Issues. United Nations Conference on Trade and Development, Geneva.

Woods, Ngaire, and Amrita Narlikar. 2001. 'Governance and the Limits of Accountability: The WTO, the IMF and the World Bank'. *International Social Science Journal* 53 (4): 569–83.

CHAPTER 3

TOWARDS A HUMAN DEVELOPMENT–ORIENTED GLOBAL TRADE REGIME

The rules and procedures of the multilateral trade regime determine how countries benefit from it. This chapter examines the regime's governance principles and suggests approaches that give higher priority to human development.

THE MULTILATERAL TRADE REGIME AND ITS IMPLICATIONS FOR HUMAN DEVELOPMENT

The breadth and depth of issues discussed by the World Trade Organization (WTO) have increased, leading to complex negotiations involving multiple trade-offs and objectives. This complexity reflects the diverse economic conditions of member nations. It also highlights the problems of a regime that requires similar binding commitments from all its members.

A basic tension exists between setting universal rules for international trade and giving member nations space to design policies suited to their economic situations. The current trade regime takes a one-size-fits-all approach—one that invariably reflects the needs and demands of powerful industrial countries. This approach would work if all WTO members had similar needs from the system. But wide disparities make it difficult for some members to comply with many WTO agreements. As a result many developing countries are dissatisfied with the current system because the promised gains from trade have not materialized.

Analysis of this dissatisfaction must consider the separate roles of domestic policy-making and the international trade regime. Domestic policy-making determines how effectively countries use trade to support long-term development, while the international regime determines the opportunities available to countries to gain from trade. The international regime cannot and should not be blamed for government failures to design appropriate policies. But it can and should be held accountable for restricting government choices and opportunities—or for channelling them in inappropriate directions. While the need for a fair, rules based multilateral trade regime is indisputable, a central question is, does the regime enable developing countries to design policies that promote human development?

Part 2 of this book examines various trade agreements and issues, asking whether they restrict countries' policy space and whether they provide opportunities to further human development through trade. Two kinds of issues and agreements are discussed. The first are 'old' issues that were disciplined by the General Agreement on Tariffs and Trade (GATT) or subjects of extensive multilateral discussions during the GATT period. Most if not all of the discussions about these issues—including agriculture, commodities, textiles, anti-dumping, industrial tariffs, standards and subsidies—involved the volume and nature of cross-border trade.

The second group of 'new' issues are those on which there was little if any discussion before the Uruguay Round. These issues now either have agreements governed by the WTO or are being discussed in its working groups. Most have a much more direct impact on domestic policies than do the issues disciplined or discussed in the GATT period. The new issues include agreements on Trade-Related Aspects of Intellectual Property Rights (TRIPS), Trade-Related Investment Measures (TRIMs) and General Agreement on Trade in Services (GATS), new areas of negotiation (such as the environment) and new discussion areas (investment, competition policy, transparency in government procurement, trade facilitation).

GATT principles and features

The main purpose of the GATT was to ensure stable, non-discriminatory trade through the unconditional most-favoured-nation principle, the national treatment principle, reduced tariffs and the prohibition of quantitative restrictions on trade in goods (see box 2.2 in chapter 2). These principles were covered by the GATT's first three articles. Its remaining articles and the subsequent Tokyo Round codes, issued in 1979, were aimed at ensuring the integrity of these principles, providing for exceptions where necessary. In addition, contracting parties were encouraged to participate in multilateral negotiations to reduce tariffs and other trade barriers.

Acceptance of multilateral rules reduced uncertainty and transaction costs in the flow of goods and services. It also reduced the transaction costs of negotiating such rules since the cost of negotiating a multilateral agreement for a country was less than the cost of negotiating similar agreements with each trading partner. This meant that there were economies of scale in negotiations. And as more countries traded under the regime, being outside it became more costly. By specifying the rules of the game, the GATT precluded arbitrary changes and made trade more predictable and less volatile. But with the Tokyo Round, the GATT departed from uniform adherence to rules: that round's codes were accepted only by countries that chose to do so. This shift resulted in different obligations for different countries, fragmenting the GATT.

The GATT's guiding philosophy was reciprocity and mutual benefit, with a bias towards free trade. The unconditional most-favoured-nation principle ensured that, in a legal sense, all countries would benefit from the concessions granted by other countries. But there was no assurance that all countries' trade would increase.

The regime assumed that all countries were equally able to benefit from reciprocal concessions and to harness trade to advance human development. But because of highly unequal levels of development and capacity among members, the reciprocity principle was relaxed for developing countries. Developing countries were also exempted from many GATT obligations and binding commitments. As a result they were not considered full members of the regime: they simply benefited from the concessions that industrial countries granted each other.

In 1982 industrial countries called for a new round of multilateral trade negotiations, partly to enable their transnational corporations to expand operations at the global level. The corporations felt that trade expansion required the same trade obligations for all countries, better access to investment and communications opportunities for them and stronger protection of their technological advantages.

The GATT was essentially a club. Trade negotiations were conducted by small groups of officials—mainly from trade ministries, supplemented when required by delegations from finance, agriculture, foreign and other ministries. In addition, negotiations were closely observed by private enterprises with vested interest in the concessions exchanged. The Uruguay Round occurred in this secretive atmosphere and involved little public debate, particularly in developing countries. Only when the draft agreements were circulated did their wide-ranging implications become apparent. With few exceptions, there were no real opportunities for the agreements' human development implications to be examined or debated, even in industrial countries.

WTO agreements and domestic policy space

Several WTO agreements affect trade indirectly by changing specifications for domestic demand and supply. These include agreements on domestic subsidies, trade in services, trade-related investment measures and trade-related intellectual property rights. These agreements were reached through mutual bargaining, not through analyses of their implications for different population groups in different countries. The single undertaking provision—a result of the Uruguay Round— requires that WTO members accept all these agreements in addition to commitments to tariff cuts (see chapter 2, especially box 2.1).

Developing countries agreed to the single undertaking—and avoided the creation of a two-tier system—so that they could be considered equal shareholders in the international trade system. Under the single undertaking agreements were accepted on the promise of overall net projected benefits—not net projected benefits from individual agreements. In an analysis of the Uruguay Round (Ostry, 2000, p. 4) refers to this as the 'grand bargain', that is, the inclusion of agriculture and textiles which developing countries wanted and TRIPS and services which industrial countries wanted. The single undertaking clause has forced developing countries to commit to domestic policies with human development implications that have not been estimated, let alone analysed.

An internationally negotiated agreement cannot serve all the objectives of its member countries. It is by definition a compromise, brokered over long negotiations. Thus it is crucial that such agreements at the very least be benign, enabling countries to design policies that improve human development outcomes.

By intruding into the domestic domain of countries, the multilateral trade rules have reduced government autonomy in policy-making. Although better market access can sometimes create opportunities for economic growth and improved welfare, it is not sufficient for human development. In fact, this mercantilist mindset often runs counter to human development outcomes, either by compelling developing countries to adopt policies with real opportunity costs or by raising the cost of more appropriate policies (Malhotra, 2002). Certain institutional and economic prerequisites are needed to translate better market access into improved human development outcomes. Yet several WTO agreements limit governments' ability to provide these prerequisites.

Four basic principles for trade

Is it possible to preserve developing countries' autonomy in pursuing human development goals while respecting industrial countries' desire to maintain high labour, social and environmental standards? Could such arrangements avoid resulting in a world trade regime riddled with protectionism, bilateralism and regional trade blocs? And would such arrangements be development-friendly? The answer to all these questions is yes—if four basic principles are accepted and put into practice.[1]

TRADE IS A MEANS TO AN END—NOT AN END IN ITSELF. The first step is to stop attaching normative significance to trade itself. The scope of market access and the volume of trade generated by the international trade regime are poor measures of how well it functions. As the preamble to the WTO agreement emphasizes, trade is useful only to the extent that it serves broader social and development goals. Developing countries should not be concerned with increasing their access to foreign markets at the cost of jeopardizing or overlooking more fundamental development challenges at home. And industrial countries should balance the interests of their exporters and transnational corporations with those of their workers and consumers.

Advocates of globalization constantly harp on the policy and institutional changes that countries must make to expand international trade and become more attractive to foreign investors. But this is another instance of confusing means with ends. At best, trade is a tool for achieving societal goals: prosperity, stability, freedom, better quality of life. WTO opponents suspect—and are enraged by the possibility—that when push comes to shove, the existing system allows trade to trump the environment or human rights. Moreover, developing countries are right to resist a system that evaluates their needs from the perspective of expanding world trade rather than reducing poverty and advancing human development. Reversing these priorities would have a simple but powerful implication. Instead of asking what kind of multilateral trading system maximizes foreign trade and investment opportunities, analysts would ask what kind of multilateral system best enables all countries to pursue their own values and development objectives.

TRADE RULES MUST ALLOW FOR DIVERSE NATIONAL INSTITUTIONS AND STANDARDS. As chapter 1 emphasizes, there is no single recipe for economic growth. Although market incentives, clear property rights, competition and macroeconomic stability are universal requirements, these can and have been embodied in diverse institutional forms. The investment strategies needed to jump-start economies can also take different forms.

Moreover, citizens of different countries have different preferences for the role of government regulation or provision of social welfare, however imperfectly these preferences are articulated or determined. People differ over the nature and extent of regulation on new technologies (such as genetically modified organisms) or environmental protection, on policies to protect property rights or extend social safety nets and, more broadly, on the entire relationship between efficiency and equity.

Rich and poor nations also have different needs for environmental standards and patent protection. Poor countries need space to follow development policies that rich countries no longer require. When countries use the trade system to impose their institutional preferences on others, it erodes the system's legitimacy and efficacy. Trade rules should seek peaceful co-existence among national practices, not harmonization.

COUNTRIES HAVE THE RIGHT TO PROTECT THEIR INSTITUTIONS AND DEVELOPMENT PRIORITIES. Opponents of today's trade regime argue that trade leads to a race to the bottom, with nations converging towards the lowest levels of environmental, labour and consumer protection. Advocates counter that there is little evidence that trade erodes national standards. Developing nations complain that trade laws are too intrusive and leave little room for development-friendly policies. WTO advocates reply that its rules provide useful discipline to rein in harmful policies that would otherwise end up wasting resources and hampering development.

One way to cut through this impasse is to accept that countries can uphold national standards and policies in these areas by withholding market access or suspending WTO obligations if trade undermines domestic practices that have broad popular support. For example, poor nations might be allowed to subsidize industrial activities (and indirectly, their exports) if this is part of a broadly supported development strategy aimed at stimulating technological capabilities. In some cases advanced countries may seek temporary protection against imports from developing countries.

The WTO already has a safeguard system in place to protect firms from import surges. Extending this principle to protect development priorities—with appropriate procedural restraints against abuse—might make the world trade system more development-friendly and resilient. Allowing opt-outs in this manner would not be without risks. The possibility must be considered that the new procedures would be abused for protectionist ends and open the door to unilateral action on a broad front, despite the high threshold envisaged here.

But as argued, current arrangements also have risks. Absent creative thinking and novel institutional designs, narrowing the room for institutional divergence harms development prospects. It may also lead to new 'grey area' measures entirely outside multilateral discipline. These consequences are far worse than an expanded safeguard regime.

BUT COUNTRIES DO NOT HAVE THE RIGHT TO IMPOSE THEIR INSTITUTIONAL PREFERENCES ON OTHERS. The use of opt-outs to uphold a country's priorities must be sharply distinguished from their use to impose those priorities on other countries. Trade rules should not force Americans to eat shrimp caught in ways that most Americans find unacceptable—but neither should they allow the United States to use trade sanctions to change how foreign nations engage in fishing. Citizens of rich countries who are genuinely concerned about the state of the environment or of workers in developing countries can be more effective through channels other than trade—such as diplomacy or foreign aid. Trade sanctions to promote a country's preferences are rarely effective and have no moral legitimacy in most cases.

A TRADE REGIME FRIENDLY TO HUMAN DEVELOPMENT IS POSSIBLE

A human development–oriented trade regime would give governments space to design appropriate policies and preferably help developing countries build their capacity to gain from trade. To achieve those goals, the trade regime should:

- *Conduct a human development assessment.* A human development assessment should be conducted to analyze the current and future implications for human development of each WTO agreement in various countries, estimate the costs of implementing current and proposed agreements for all WTO members and present the implications of these agreements under different scenarios of increased technical assistance, phased implementation and greater market access. This assessment should be conducted by a credible, independent research programme established with the approval of all WTO members. While not binding, the assessment's results should inform future negotiations and ensure that trade agreements are friendlier to human development.

- *Support diverse development strategies.* The trade regime is a means of serving the national goals of its members and is useful only as long as they see value in being part of it. Thus the regime should not systematically benefit or harm any one set of countries or interests. This outcome is possible only if the trade regime facilitates the different development agendas of different countries—giving countries maximum space to design appropriate development policies. The regime should focus on facilitating trade within this larger development context, and should not try to unify national policies.

- *Increase market access for developing countries.* The multilateral trade regime was established to facilitate a greater flow of goods and services between countries in a predictable, fair, rules-based manner. If developing countries are to realize gains from trade, they must be given access to the markets of industrial countries.

- *Allow for asymmetric rules.* A one-size-fits-all approach to trade does not work. Applying identical rules to unequal members locks weaker countries into unsatisfactory trade relationships and fails to address their development challenges. If the trade regime is to foster rather than restrict development, its rules should reflect its members' varying economic conditions. For example, reciprocity and non-discrimination principles should be linked to countries' economic capacity. One possible way of doing this would be to apply these principles within groups of countries at similar levels of human development—to build into the regime a necessary asymmetry between different groups of developing and industrial countries. This approach would allow developing countries to make fewer commitments and to enjoy greater latitude in policy-making, while requiring industrial countries to open their markets to developing country imports.

- *Reconcile asymmetric rules with market access requirements.* Developing countries require increased market access to reach a level of development where they can compete on an equal footing. But market access is not enough. With falling commodity prices and their specialization in products with low value added, developing countries gain much less from trade than do industrial countries. And, again unlike industrial countries, developing countries lack mechanisms to compensate domestic actors hurt by increased openness (Mendoza, 2003). WTO rules should reflect this difference in capacity by allowing developing countries more flexibility in compliance.

- *Ensure its sustainability.* An asymmetric trade regime will benefit all its members if the short-term costs in industrial countries—through lost markets and increased competition from imports—are less than the general short- and long-term gains in efficiency and welfare. In the short term, industrial country consumers will benefit from cheaper, more varied imports and possibly from more efficient resource allocation. In the long term, faster growth in developing countries will raise people's purchasing power, increasing their demand for imports—especially for products with high value added—and leading to quality competition and potentially greater gains from trade. Moreover, many of trade's short- and long-term costs in both industrial and developing countries can be mitigated with well-designed economic policies (UNCTAD, 2002, p. xi). By balancing the costs and benefits and providing policy options that reflect the inequalities and different stages of development of its members, the multilateral trade regime can provide enough incentives for all countries to join and enjoy its benefits.

FROM A MARKET EXCHANGE TO A HUMAN DEVELOPMENT PERSPECTIVE

Economists view the WTO as an institution designed to expand free trade and so enhance consumer welfare—in developing as much as industrial countries. In reality, the WTO enables countries to negotiate over market access. Free trade is not the typical outcome of this process, and consumer welfare (much less development) is not the main focus of the negotiators. Instead, most multilateral trade negotiations have been shaped by battles between exporters and transnational corporations in industrial countries (which have had the upper hand) and competing interests in both developing and industrial countries (usually, but not solely, labour). The main textbook beneficiaries of free trade—consumers—are not in the picture.[2]

The WTO is best understood in this context, as a political process involving intense lobbying by US or European exporter groups or compromises between such groups and other domestic groups. The differential treatment of manufacturing and agriculture (or of textiles, clothing and other goods within manufacturing), the anti-dumping regime and the intellectual property rights regime, to pick some of the major anomalies, are all results of this process. Understanding this is essential because it underscores the fact that very little in the structure of multilateral trade negotiations ensures that their outcomes are consistent with human development goals.

There are at least three sources of divergence between what human development requires and what the WTO does. First, even if free trade were optimal for development in a broad sense, the WTO does not pursue free trade. Second, even if it did, there is no guarantee that free trade is the best trade policy for countries at low levels of development. Third, compliance with WTO rules, even when they are not harmful in themselves, crowds out a more complete development agenda—at both the national and international levels.

Shifting from a market access to a human development perspective means that the trade regime should stop being evaluated in terms of whether it maximizes trade in goods and services. Instead the question should be whether trade arrangements—current and proposed—maximize possibilities for human development at the national level. Making this shift requires that developing countries articulate their needs not primarily in terms of market access, but in terms of the policy autonomy that will allow them to implement institutional innovations.

The WTO should not be conceived as an institution devoted to harmonizing and reducing institutional differences between countries, but as one that manages the interaction between different national systems. The current design and implementation of WTO agreements is far from satisfactory in providing this policy autonomy.

NOTES

1. This section draws on Rodrik (2001).
2. This section draws on Rodrik (2001).

REFERENCES

Malhotra, Kamal. 2002. 'Doha: Is It Really a Development Round?' Trade and Environment Policy Paper. Carnegie Endowment for International Peace, Washington, DC.

Mendoza, Ronald U. 2003. 'The Multilateral Trade Regime: A Global Public Good for All?' In Inge Kaul, Pedro Conceicao, Katell Le Goulven and Ronald U. Mendoza, eds., *Providing Global Public Goods: Managing Globalization.* New York: Oxford University Press.

Narlikar, Amrita. 2001. 'WTO Decision Making and Developing Countries'. Trade Related Agenda, Development and Equity (T.R.A.D.E.) Working Paper 11. South Centre, Geneva.

Ostry, Sylvia. 2000. 'The Uruguay Round North-South Bargain: Implications for Future Negotiations'. Prepared for a conference on The Political Economy of International Trade Law, University of Minnesota, 15–16 September, Minneapolis.

———. 2002. 'The World Trading System: In Dire Need of Reform'. Paper presented at the Canadians in Europe Conference, Centre for European Policy Studies, August, Brussels.

Oxfam International. 2002. 'Rigged Rules and Double Standards: Trade, Globalization and the Fight against Poverty'. Oxford.

Rodrik, Dani. 2001. 'The Global Governance of Trade As If Development Really Mattered'. Background paper for Trade and Sustainable Human Development Project. United Nations Development Programme, New York.

TWN (Third World Network). 2001. 'The Multilateral Trading Regime: A Development Perspective'. Background paper for Trade and Sustainable Human Development Project. United Nations Development Programme, New York.

UNCTAD (United Nations Conference on Trade and Development). 2002. *Trade and Development Report. 2002: Developing Countries in World Trade.* Geneva.

WTO (World Trade Organization). 1999. *Trading into the Future.* Geneva.

CHAPTER 4
REFORMS TO THE GLOBAL GOVERNANCE OF TRADE

This chapter applies chapter 3's suggestions for human development–oriented trade to today's multilateral trade regime. The chapter analyses pressing issues and challenges for the global governance of trade and offers recommendations for improving it consistent with human development objectives. In addition, the chapter analyses regional trade agreements and makes suggestions for their evolving relationship with the multilateral trade regime.

CHANGES NEEDED IN THE GLOBAL TRADE REGIME

Widespread perceptions that the multilateral trade regime urgently requires reform have placed it under constant scrutiny since the 1999 WTO ministerial conference in Seattle, Washington (US). Because the regime is governed by a young, one-country one-vote, member-driven organization in which most members are developing countries, serious reform should be achievable. But what should it involve?

The 'single undertaking' mandate of the World Trade Organization (WTO) compels members to accept a wide range of agreements in one package—making it a unique mechanism among multilateral organizations (see chapters 2 and 3). Although the single undertaking has provided some benefits to developing countries, it could do far more for human development if it ensured that trade rules and obligations reflected all countries' interests and incorporated human development objectives. More effective and meaningful special and differential treatment could help achieve this goal.

Special and differential treatment

Special and differential treatment focused on human development should be driven by two assumptions. First, different countries have different initial conditions. Second, different countries have different capacities for effective integration with the global economy—and among countries with similar capacities, reciprocal trade liberalization can bring significant gains.

Effective special and differential treatment would give developing countries space to implement policies that promote human development. It would also provide secure, preferential market access to support policies aimed at deriving human development benefits from international trade. The principle of special and differential treatment was reaffirmed at the 2001 WTO Ministerial Conference in Doha, Qatar—giving the international community an opportunity to achieve these goals.

Still, clear consensus on special and differential treatment is needed to ensure that trade agreements support human development. Thus it is hoped that the next WTO Ministerial Conference, in September 2003 in Cancun, Mexico, will generate a declaration on special and differential treatment and human development. This declaration could cover policies related to education, technology transfer, environmental protection, gender equality, cultural integrity and diversity, universal health care, universal access to energy and the right to use traditional knowledge to promote human development.

Such a declaration would mean that special and differential treatment becomes accepted as a general rule rather than as an exception or special case—an extremely desirable outcome regardless of whether the declaration emerges. Special and differential treatment should also be made unconditional, binding and operational, with countries able to suspend certain WTO commitments if they can show that doing so is necessary to achieve human development goals. Acceptance of this approach will require greater flexibility in the practical workings of the single undertaking.

Countries should be grouped by their level of human development, with reciprocal commitments within groups and asymmetrical relationships between them. A country's graduation from one group to another should be based on clear, objective criteria such as comprehensive indicators of human and technological capabilities or the achievement of specific Millennium Development Goals. Commitments made at the Third UN Least Developed Countries Conference in 2001 should be given contractual status in the WTO as a way of helping these countries achieve these goals.

Governance structure

The WTO's formal governance structure is the most democratic of all multilateral organizations and so requires no major changes. But the structure should allow for more effective organization and participation by coalitions of developing countries. In addition to formal subregional groups of developing countries—such as the Association of South-East Asian Nations (ASEAN) and members of the Southern Common Market (Mercosur)—and broader regional groups—say, the African group—ad hoc alliances formed on the basis of common interests or development levels (or both) can be effective. Examples include the Like-Minded Group and Least Developed Countries Group, which bring together developing countries, and the Cairns Group, which brings together developing and industrial countries to discuss access to agriculture markets.

These and similar groups should be supported and allowed to participate more formally in WTO negotiations (see Schott and Watal, 2000; and Das, 2000).

Drawing on different groups for different negotiation areas would likely be the most appropriate and effective approach—and would leave open the possibility of alliances between developing countries as well as between developing and industrial countries. Such alliances would not substitute for individual country participation and voting in the general council or at ministerial meetings. They are proposed primarily to break the governance impasse increasingly generated by informal meetings on specific issues and agreements, where consensus is reached behind closed doors. This informal consensus process has become far more influential in WTO decision-making than formal processes.

Agenda

The global trade regime's agenda is full, and many reforms are needed in the global governance of trade and in specific agreements and issues on which negotiations have concluded or just begun. So, regardless of their merit, the regime's agenda should not be overburdened with new issues at this time.

Moreover, the regime's agenda should be limited to trade issues that are purely multilateral and that require multilateral agreement. It should not be used as a tool to force agreement on a much larger normative agenda and range of issues.

Dispute settlement

The WTO's dispute settlement mechanism is central to the trade regime's system of governance and is in many ways a marked improvement over the mechanism used under the General Agreement on Tariffs and Trade (GATT). The current mechanism is more time-bound, predictable, consistent and binding on all members. But it is also subject to narrower, more legalistic interpretations—though the Doha declaration on Trade-Related Aspects of Intellectual Property Rights (TRIPS) and public health provides a precedent to change that.

Despite the dispute settlement mechanism's positive features, important changes are required in its rules and functioning. This is partly because of the widespread perception that trade sanctions are an acceptable way—and the only effective way—to enforce international commitments. This perception has inspired initiatives to extend the trade regime's agenda to areas of international economic interaction far beyond cross-border trade in goods. Changes are vital in this context because an offended party's ultimate recourse in a dispute is trade retaliation against major trading powers—placing developing countries in a weak position because their threat of retaliation is rarely credible. Proposals have been made to correct this inherent imbalance.

In addition, mechanisms are needed to ensure that all countries honour WTO rulings. Such mechanisms could include requiring financial compensation from and levying penalties on countries that delay implementation of a dispute settlement ruling (until the offending measure has been removed). Consideration should also be given to a collective action clause, to be invoked when powerful members refuse to implement dispute rulings.

The proposal for a collective action clause would have to be examined carefully before being endorsed. But a less bold approach—requiring the defaulting country to pay by implementing additional concessions (lowering tariffs or otherwise opening markets) or providing cash compensation—would be much harder to enforce because it would require the cooperation of the defaulting country. Such cooperation is unlikely since its absence would trigger action in the first place.

Decision-making

Formal voting never occurs in the WTO: all decision-making is based on consensus. There is an urgent need to review the workings of the consensus principle, which was adopted mainly to prevent large economic powers from being outvoted on issues where they cannot accept the will of the majority. Important changes could include increasing the size of the quorum required for decisions and allowing countries without representation in Geneva to participate through video-conferencing or other arrangements.

In addition, voting could be encouraged for some types of decisions (governance, budget, management and administrative issues), including by mail or electronically, especially for members without Geneva representation. While such changes may delay some decisions, they should lead to better-informed decisions—more genuinely owned by the majority of members and so more sustainable.

In addition, developing countries should use the consensus principle more actively to reach agreement on issues important to them before entering into detailed negotiations involving reciprocal trade-offs. The Doha declaration on TRIPS and public health shows what is possible when this approach is taken.

Relationship with regional trade agreements

WTO rules should provide the limits and boundaries for the scope and nature of regional trade agreements. But first, WTO rules need to be made more flexible and more friendly to human development. In particular, WTO rules should provide sufficient scope for addressing the development concerns of its members as well as non-members that are members of regional trade agreements. When such agreements involve both developing and industrial countries, they should allow for less than full reciprocity in trade relations between the two. In addition, regional agreements that are or intend to become 'WTO plus'—that is, having obligations that are broader, more stringent and less flexible than the WTO's—should be made WTO compatible.

External transparency

Like all international organizations, including the UN, the WTO needs to increase its external transparency and public accountability—especially to civil society organizations and to small countries that do not have missions in Geneva. Its intergovernmental nature may preclude a formal decision-making role for civil society organizations and the private sector in its governance and dispute processes. Still, the UN, World Bank and other intergovernmental organizations offer lessons on how to promote participation by civil society organizations. Such participation would likely be beneficial for both human development and developing country concerns.

National ownership

In both industrial and developing countries, no amount of reform to the multilateral and regional trade regimes can substitute for increased national ownership and better national governance of trade policy-making. Thus the challenge is not only to make global governance fairer but also to give voice to vulnerable groups— including women—not effectively represented by their governments at the national and international levels. This lack of voice is inextricably linked to the issue of national ownership and actively undermines it. Broadly based participation and ownership at the national level, involving discussions among parliamentarians, civil society organizations, community groups and the private sector, should be encouraged and supported. Engendering such broadly based national ownership can contribute significantly to long-term human development.

BACKGROUND ANALYSIS AND ADDITIONAL ISSUES

The reform proposals above are based on detailed analysis of the issues and challenges confronting the global governance of trade. The rest of the chapter elaborates this analysis.

Mandate

Views differ on the future evolution of the multilateral trade regime. For some the next round of trade negotiations should simply be a continuation of the Uruguay Round, aimed at tightening its obligations and making them more intrusive—as well as extending them into new areas. For others the negotiations should be corrective, making the regime more supportive of development efforts.

As noted, the WTO's single undertaking obligates members to accept multiple agreements as one package, making it a unique mechanism among multilateral organizations. The International Monetary Fund (IMF), for example, does not require member countries to adopt a particular exchange rate system. Similarly, countries are allowed to sign human rights treaties and conventions separately and individually.

At the domestic level the single undertaking has considerably reduced developing countries' flexibility in choosing which agreements to sign—limiting their development policy options to those compatible with the rules and agreements of the global trade regime. From a human development standpoint this approach also increases the need for and urgency of designing and implementing governance processes in a genuinely democratic, participatory and inclusive manner, bearing in mind the realities of developing countries.

Yet it is only because of the single undertaking that developing countries have become major shareholders in the multilateral trade system (Delgado, 1994). The implications of this change are only beginning to be realized by the world's major powers. The single undertaking will likely increase developing countries' bargaining power in some traditional trade areas of great interest to many of them, such as agriculture and textiles and clothing. Still, to maximize human development possibilities, the mechanism must allow greater flexibility. This can be achieved if it allows a modified 'positive list' approach in future agreements—similar to that in the General Agreement on Trade in Services (GATS)—and, ideally, in some existing ones (such as the Agreement on Agriculture) as a result of ongoing reviews.

At the international level the extended coverage of multilateral trade rules has encroached on other international forums and organizations. For example, the TRIPS agreement has made the WTO an enforcer of instruments created by the World Intellectual Property Organization (WIPO). It has also created an undefined border with the Convention on Biodiversity. Similarly, the GATS threatened the cultural domain of the United Nations Educational, Scientific, and Cultural Organization (UNESCO), provoking a last-minute crisis in the Uruguay Round. The GATS also established disciplines in areas where the International Telecommunication Union (ITU) had been sovereign. So far attempts have failed to make the WTO the enforcer of International Labour Organization (ILO) conventions. And the International Civil Aviation Organization (ICAO) has been able to protect its territorial integrity largely because that set-up suited the major powers.

The WTO's mandate has also created problems of policy coherence between multilateral organizations. In some cases the WTO can be seen as an enforcer of IMF and World Bank loan conditions. But in other cases WTO rules (such as on tariff levels) are less stringent than IMF and World Bank loan conditions attached to structural adjustment programmes. There is also a lack of clarity between whether, in cases of conflict, WTO disciplines will prevail over those of multilateral environmental agreements and the Convention on Biodiversity.

The multilateral trade regime's broad mandate is a result not of trade's supremacy over other interests but of the view that trade sanctions are a credible enforcement mechanism. As a result the trade regime has a mandate to discipline much more than global trade. Indeed, it is becoming the main mechanism for global governance. Against this background the Doha declaration on TRIPS and public health is a major breakthrough, because for the first time the international community formally recognized that multilateral trade agreements could undermine human development and harm people's lives.

Special and differential treatment

Developing countries have been trying to make the international trade system more consistent with their needs and aspirations since the 1947–48 Havana Conference. Special and different treatment seeks to compensate developing countries for their inherent disadvantages relative to industrial countries in drawing equal benefits from the trade system. The Doha declaration resurrected the principle of special and differential treatment, and efforts are being made to establish an approach that addresses the real needs of developing countries. In addition, inspired by the flexibility built into the General Agreement on Trade in Services (GATS), developing countries are seeking to establish structures that bias multilateral trade agreements towards development. Rather than being seen as an (often temporary) exception, special and differential treatment should be considered an essential part of multilateral rights and obligations.

Few WTO provisions for special and differential treatment are phrased in contractual language, making them difficult to operationalize. (See annex 2.1 for exceptions from WTO commitments for developing countries and annex 2.2 for special WTO provisions for the least developed countries.) In most cases special and differential treatment is conditional on negotiations for extended transition periods and on industrial country discretion. Moreover, such treatment is subject to costly, time-consuming litigation. Developing countries have suggested that all non-contractual provisions for special and differential treatment be converted into binding obligations or deleted because there should be no non-contractual language in WTO agreements. Non-contractual language conveys the impression that multilateral agreements are development oriented—even if that is not the case.

For these and other reasons the design and implementation of provisions for special and differential treatment have been a matter of serious concern for developing countries. When measured against the elements needed for effective and meaningful special and differential treatment, the provisions fall short in several ways:

- WTO agreements state that governments can take action against imports that cause injury, prejudice or damage to domestic industries—regardless of whether or not it is the result of unfair practices by governments or traders. Such safeguards (often called 'trade remedies') strongly bias domestic investigations in favour of import-competing groups who petition for import relief and are its main beneficiaries. Thus such safeguards are vulnerable to misuse[1] and do not fulfil their purpose of providing policy space. Injury has to be established as a prerequisite for such action, but the criteria for injury have been designed to address the complaints of domestic producers. These criteria include such factors as profits, losses and changes in sales, and do not consider human development indicators. Such indicators should be included in the injury criteria or be used in parallel when resort is made to such 'trade remedies'.

- The policy space provided is primarily in the form of different tariff and subsidy targets, greater flexibility in meeting commitments and special provisions for the least developed countries. But all these mechanisms aim at increasing adherence to the specific policies implied by the agreements. They do not allow developing countries to design possibly more appropriate and relevant policies. As a result developing countries often give precedence to WTO commitments before important development priorities.

- The provisional aspects of measures for special and differential treatment imply that countries constantly need to renegotiate extensions. Extensions, if granted, are political decisions based on asymmetric bargaining power. They are not determined by any rigorous estimation, based on human development or economic criteria, of how long countries will need to be allowed to use a particular measure or how long it will take them to graduate from it. As a result developing countries often bargain away other important concessions to get extensions on transition periods or other measures that were inadequate to begin with.

- Since 1995 developing countries have faced increasingly tough conditions for WTO accession. Beyond specific concessions and commitments on goods and services, they have been forced to accept plurilateral agreements as well as less flexibility in the use of investment performance requirements.[2] In some cases entirely new obligations—such as on energy prices—are being sought. These 'WTO-plus' conditions often deny developing countries the special and differential treatment enjoyed by members that joined when the WTO was created. Given that many aspiring members are least developed countries, more stringent terms of accession are especially contrary to the principle of special and differential treatment (UNCTAD, 2002). Terms of accession should not deny new members the means of promoting human development, especially when such means are available to existing members.

- Regional trade agreements have proliferated since 1995. A growing number of these agreements include 'WTO plus' aspects—particularly recent agreements between industrial and developing countries. The major powers often see regional agreements as a way of setting precedents for negotiations of similar provisions at the multilateral level. Developing countries, meanwhile, are trying to ensure that regional agreements reflect the principle of special and differential treatment articulated at the multilateral level. WTO rules on regional trade agreements must be clarified to ensure that developing countries enjoy the same rights to special and differential treatment at the regional level as at the multilateral level and that such provisions draw on human development criteria.

There are also examples of areas where the major trading countries will likely try to further reduce the flexibility of developing countries through future trade negotiations. Thus it is essential that future multilateral and regional trade negotiations recognize the legitimacy of human development considerations.

A world trade system committed to addressing human development concerns would consider it legitimate to extend asymmetrical rights and obligations to developing country members through special and differential treatment. Such a system would also accept human development considerations as legitimate criteria for trade measures. Establishing special and differential treatment will contribute to a stable world trade system as well as create a larger, more effective market for goods and services, benefiting all people. Without such positive discrimination, economically poor and politically weak countries will never be able to compete fairly and equitably with industrial countries. Accepting this line of reasoning also requires much greater flexibility in the workings of the single undertaking.

Thus WTO members should build on the Doha affirmation of special and differential treatment, and use it to help achieve human development goals. Special and differential treatment should not be seen only as a compensating tool to help developing countries integrate with the global trade regime—it should also be seen as an input to countries' development.

- *Special and differential treatment as a rule.* When classifying countries and establishing their eligibility for special and differential treatment, WTO agreements should consider their human development indicators and human development index (HDI) rankings—and assess the gaps between their human development indicators and the indicators used to measure progress towards the Millennium Development Goals.[3]

- *Unconditional, binding and operational provisions for special and differential treatment.* Provisions for special and differential treatment should be unconditional and non-negotiable. In other words, the extension of transition periods and use of more binding commitments for special and differential treatment should be based on objective assessments of economic and human development needs—not on a bargaining process in the single undertaking framework. Non mandatory provisions should be made mandatory, and all provisions for special and differential treatment should be phrased in contractual language.[4]

- *Reactivation of provisions on government assistance for economic development.* Article XVIII should be revisited, and human development criteria should be incorporated. This move would give developing countries more flexibility to suspend WTO obligations if necessary to meet their development challenges. The right to exercise this option should be limited by the need for internal and external validation, based on an objective assessment of needs, and require widespread deliberation at the national level.[5]

- *Thresholds and incentives for graduation.* Thresholds to determine whether countries should lose eligibility for special and differential treatment should be based on comprehensive indicators of human and technological capabilities or on the achievement of specific Millennium Development Goals.[6] A credible, independent monitoring authority should assess these indicators periodically and report to member nations. Further, using several levels of gradation, countries should move from more to less comprehensive provisions for special and differential treatment—with an eventual phase-out if warranted by objective criteria.

- *Generalized System of Preferences and other preferential schemes as part of the WTO mandate:* Preferential schemes should be part of formal mechanisms for special and differential treatment, and their coverage, scope and duration should be determined through objective assessments rather than as a result of bargaining or unilateral decisions by the preference-giving country. Specifically, the Generalized System of

Preferences should be grandfathered, and commitments made at the third UN conference on least developed countries should be given contractual status in the WTO.

Governance structure

Governance of the global trade regime is often assumed to be synonymous with governance of the WTO. But this assumption does not take into account the large and growing number of regional trade agreements, forums, ongoing negotiations and arrangements. Some of these are inter-regional (the Asia-Pacific Economic Cooperation forum, the Free Trade Area of the Americas), and individually include almost all the world's major trading nations. A brief analysis of regional trade agreements, especially their governance dimensions and human development implications, is provided in annex 4.1.

Because there is considerable overlap between the coverage of regional trade agreements and the multilateral trade regime, there is an urgent need to ensure that their rules are compatible. But members of some regional agreements consider them more development-friendly than WTO agreements. So, to achieve compatibility, WTO rules will need to be made more flexible and human development friendly.

The WTO's governance structure provides developing countries with unique opportunities in a global forum for economic governance. Their potential leverage was most evident in the late 1990s contest for leadership of the WTO secretariat, when it was clear that if a vote were taken, the candidate supported by the majority of developing countries would win. This situation forced a compromise that entailed the selection of both finalists for three-year terms, rather than a single winner for four years.

Still, governance problems have arisen—mainly because informal consensus building has become much more influential in WTO decision-making than formal processes. As practised, the principle of consensus decision-making consistently works in favour of the main industrial countries (EU members, Canada, Japan, the US) rather than the overwhelming developing country majority.

Agenda

During the Uruguay Round developing countries agreed to include the TRIPS and GATS agreements under the single undertaking in exchange for commitments from industrial countries on increased market access for agricultural, textile and clothing products. This arrangement shows the extent of the paradigm shift in the global trade regime. Shukla (2000, p.31) put it succinctly when he wrote, 'while the WTO Agreement furnished the legal and institutional infrastructure of the paradigm shift, TRIPS and GATS provided its architecture, with the TRIMs [Trade-Related Investment Measures] Agreement the blueprint for its future structural expansion.'

The Uruguay Round agenda was shaped by the most powerful industrial countries, especially EU members and the US. And since the WTO's creation in 1995, this already ambitious agenda has expanded. The WTO work programme now includes working groups on investment, competition policy, trade facilitation and transparency in government procurement (at the behest of the most powerful industrial countries during the 1996 ministerial conference in Singapore), discussions on electronic commerce (resulting from the 1998 conference in Geneva) and working groups on trade, debt and finance; and trade and technology transfer and a work programme on the problems of small economies (resulting from the 2001 conference in Doha). As a result there is a danger that the global trade regime will become overloaded and non-functional (Nayyar, 2002)—undermining efforts to advance human development in developing countries.

Though the working groups created in Doha resulted from developing country demands, such a rapidly expanding agenda creates enormous challenges for developing countries, particularly the least developed ones and small ones. These countries lack the capacity to deal with such a large, diverse, complex agenda in international trade negotiations, particularly since many of the new issues have not traditionally been considered trade-related and many countries have not yet defined their stances on them.

This growing agenda has reduced national ownership of trade negotiations and outcomes, as illustrated by the much smaller role of most national legislative processes—and so legislators and citizens—in setting agendas and making rules on crucial economic and social issues. Legislative issues once decided exclusively in the domestic domain are increasingly influenced by the judicial rulings of WTO panels and its appellate and dispute settlement bodies.[7] To some extent this was the result desired by developing countries, because they wanted stronger multilateral discipline exerted over the leading industrial countries.

Dispute settlement
Fair dispute settlement rules that are multilaterally agreed, consistent and well-enforced are fundamental to good governance of the trade regime and so to human development. Judged by this yardstick, the GATT dispute settlement system does not appear to have worked well—or indeed, at all—for developing countries. This shortcoming appears to have resulted from how the consensus principle worked, though in this case it was not due to the passive consensus fostered by the processes of the general council. Instead, active consensus was the crux of GATT procedures for settling disputes.

Consensus among all members was required to establish the panels that adjudicated disputes and to adopt the reports issued by panels. Thus a party to a dispute could block panel formation or report adoption in much the same way that permanent members of the UN Security Council can block resolutions. This de facto veto power paralysed the GATT dispute resolution mechanism. Not surprisingly, efforts to change it—such as a 1965 joint proposal by Brazil and Uruguay—failed.

So, as noted, the WTO Dispute Settlement Understanding is considered a marked improvement in many ways. It is more time-bound, predictable, consistent and binding on all members, though it is also more narrowly legalistic than its predecessor. Still, the overall improvements help explain why developing countries that made little use of the GATT dispute settlement system actively participate in the WTO version.

Increased participation can also be attributed to the significance and potential costs of the issues at stake. Whatever the reason, developing countries' dramatically increased use of the Dispute Settlement Understanding indicates that they believe it can be made to work for them. More cases were subject to dispute settlement in the WTO's first 7 years (262 as of 9 September 2002) than in the GATT's 50 or so years (196 cases). Industrial countries still file the majority of cases, including many against developing countries (65 as of September 2002). But between 1995 and September 2002 developing countries filed 48 cases against industrial countries,[8] up from just 40 in the preceding five decades (South Centre, 1999).

Countries have used the dispute settlement mechanism in an attempt to resolve issues of greatest importance to them. For that reason, useful and interesting insights emerge from an analysis of trends in disputes between developing and industrial countries. Developing countries have initiated the most cases against industrial countries under the Agreements on Anti-dumping and Subsidies and Countervailing Measures—reflecting concerns about both market access and domestic policy space (table 4.1). Industrial countries, on the other hand, have initiated the most cases against developing countries under the agreements on Agriculture, Textiles and Clothing, TRIMs and TRIPS—reflecting the issues of greatest importance to them.

The dispute panels and appellate body interpret WTO rules and, given the ambiguity of many of these rules, have in effect been making law. These laws have

TABLE 4.1

WTO-mediated disputes between developing and industrial countries, by agreement category, January 1995–9 September 2002

Category	Initiated by developing countries	Initiated by industrial countries
Agriculture	4	13
Anti-dumping	10	5
Safeguards	5	2
Subsidies and Countervailing Measures	8	4
Textiles and Clothing	4	8
TRIMs	—	11
TRIPS	1	6

Note: Includes only a few of the categories covered or contemplated by the dispute settlement mechanism. In addition, covers only disputes between developing and industrial countries; does not cover disputes between developing and transition economies, between industrial and transition economies, among industrial countries or among developing countries. If a dispute covers more than one category, it is counted in each.

Source: Tang, 2002; WTO data (www.wto.org/english/tratop_e/dispu_e/dispu_status_e.htm).

defined the boundaries of domestic policy space and highlighted the intrusions of the dispute settlement system in national affairs (Ostry, 2000b). In this context the Doha ministerial declaration on TRIPS and public health offers useful guidance since it should provide more space for the appellate body to pursue legal interpretations consistent with human development. The declaration can set a precedent for similar approaches on other human development issues, particularly where international consensus has been expressed by a UN body.

Even if that were to happen, using the Dispute Settlement Understanding causes problems. Costs are extremely high for all countries—and prohibitively high for the poorest and least developed countries, which have neither the legal expertise required to initiate and sustain cases or the financial resources to pay foreign trade lawyers. The WTO secretariat's provision of legal expertise for countries in this situation suffers from at least two shortcomings: it is inadequate for the huge demand, and the mandated neutrality of its lawyers means that they cannot prepare or conduct cases as assertively as independent, private law teams. This leaves the least developed countries at a major disadvantage against middle-income developing countries as well as industrial ones.

Among other major implementation issues, the most important is the lack of retroactive compensation even if a developing country wins its case. This is particularly damaging to developing countries with low export diversification—most of which are among the poorest and least developed—and can devastate both their export earnings and their market share. A disputed case, even in the stricter and more predictable time boundaries of the WTO system, can take up to two and a half years to conclude. This is likely to have a potentially devastating human development opportunity cost for a small economy that depends on the disputed product—a shortcoming compounded by the lack of concrete or meaningful special and differential treatment in the Dispute Settlement Understanding.

Finally, the inherent power inequity of the system has meant that even when such cases have been launched and won, little in the Dispute Settlement Understanding compels countries to change their laws except the threat of retaliation. While such a threat may be real between roughly equal players, such as the US and EU, none of the least developed countries can be expected to retaliate against any of the major economic powers. But if a developing country loses a case and does not change its legislation, the threat of retaliation is real and often follows.

While the creation of the Advisory Centre on WTO Law—announced in 1999 at the Seattle ministerial conference—has been a positive step, it is extremely modest given the needs. Even if the centre were better resourced, the other problems would remain. Arguably, those problems are far more intractable than the problems the centre was established to tackle.

Notwithstanding procedural and other problems, the asymmetry in economic and political power between industrial and developing countries remains the crux of the problem. In the final analysis, it stands out as the main constraint to the effective functioning of the Dispute Settlement Understanding. But because this problem extends well beyond the dispute settlement system's functioning, it is unlikely to be dealt with except as part of a solution to the broader governance concerns raised in this chapter.

Decision-making

Transparency means revealing one's actions and decisions consciously, visibly and understandably (G-22 Working Group, 1998). It also implies being open to considering all relevant information. In addition, transparency entails the timely disclosure of all relevant information and supporting materials. Lack of transparency and participation are often symptoms of serious power imbalances between member countries. Taken seriously, transparency represents a profound shift in the distribution of power and the way it is exercised (Florini, 1998).

Since the 1960s developing countries have intensified their efforts to make the multilateral trade regime more consistent with their needs and aspirations. For two decades their efforts focused on the United Nations Conference on Trade and Development (UNCTAD), which was seen as an alternative to the GATT system. But in the 1980s, for a variety of reasons (some of which are described in chapter 2), developing countries shifted their approach to pursuing their interests more directly within the GATT—both through attempts to modify it and by addressing increasingly serious trade problems.

One of the biggest paradoxes, however, is that despite their more active participation in the negotiating process, developing countries remain largely ineffective in ensuring transparency and their effective participation in the world trade regime. In many cases developing countries are unable to maintain or follow up on negotiating successes. They may succeed in listing items of their interest in work programmes and negotiating agendas—only to find that these remain dead letters. In addition, they sometimes find themselves under pressure to forgo the rights they have succeeded in negotiating. For example, they are reluctant to raise applied tariffs to bound rates, though they would be within their rights in doing so.

The most striking example is the TRIPS agreement, through which many countries were placed under strong political pressure to pass legislation that would have impeded their future ability to use the many flexible features contained in the agreement. Most of these have a strong human development component. The declaration on TRIPS and public health was an important step in encouraging countries to avail themselves fully of the flexibility provided in the TRIPS agreement (WHO and WTO, 2002).

Many industrial country members of the WTO have found it difficult to adapt from the 'club' approach to the new scenario where developing countries are full shareholders. This was a major factor leading to the collapse of the Seattle ministerial conference in 1999. A major reason for this is that consensus, as practiced in the GATT, cannot accommodate an agenda as broad and detailed as that of the

WTO—with all its intrusions into the domestic policy realm and the economic and social costs that its agreements entail for developing countries. As a result the democratic deficit inherent in the consensus principle has taken on far greater gravity and urgency. In addition, its deficiencies have aroused public protest. This is due to both the perceived and real domestic impacts of WTO agreements and to the often frustrated efforts of developing country governments to participate more actively in the WTO than they did in the GATT.

The consensus-based decision-making norm is incorporated in article IX: 1 of the WTO. It states that, unlike a process based on formal voting, where the views of the majority are decisive, the WTO consensus approach requires only those present at a meeting (with a quorum, defined as 51 per cent of members) not to object to a decision. This effectively bars developing countries from making full use of their equal status with industrial countries through the one-country one-vote system. It also deprives them of the benefits of formal voting and can work against them even if they hold the majority view on an issue.

Consensus-based decision-making has a positive aspect in that it encourages a process in which members are consulted and their concerns heard before a decision is made. But for a decision to move ahead, it must allow the opportunity, should consensus fail, for the majority to make a decision by voting. If a vote is never taken, the value of the one-country one-vote system is seriously undermined. Under these circumstances consensus can become a means by which a powerful minority can persuade a less powerful majority to concede. When applied to the global governance of trade, this does not reflect a problem with the WTO's formal rules, which define consensus in the traditional manner and provide for voting to take place should it fail. Instead it highlights a problem with the WTO's informal processes and deeply ingrained culture of not voting. Consensus thus practiced also derives from passive rather than active choice and behaviour. The key criterion is a member's presence at a meeting rather then the member's active participation.

Many developing countries cannot satisfy even the fundamental participation criterion because they are not present in Geneva. According to Michalopoulos (2000), 64 developing countries maintain WTO missions in Geneva, 26 are represented by missions or embassies elsewhere in Europe and 7 rely on representatives based in their capitals. Of the 29 WTO members that are among the least developed countries, only 12 had missions in Geneva in 1997—all of which had to serve multiple international organizations (Blackhurst, 1997). Given how the consensus principle works, these shortcomings in representation imply exclusion from WTO decision-making and global trade agreement processes for many developing countries—especially the poorest and weakest.

Although the size of developing country delegations in Geneva has increased significantly since 1987, it has grown slower than that of industrial country delegations. Even in 1997 developing country delegations to the WTO averaged only 3.6 people, compared with 6.7 for industrial countries. Moreover, these averages

mask huge variations in the size of both developing and industrial country delegations. Many delegations from least developed countries and small developing
countries had just 1 member, compared with 10–15 for middle-income and larger
developing countries such as Brazil, Egypt, India, the Republic of Korea, and
Thailand.

Many developing countries present in Geneva cannot represent themselves
effectively because they have neither the policy research ability nor negotiating
capacity that would enable them to do so. Few developing countries can satisfy both
the presence and capacity requirements. And those that can will be increasingly
hard pressed on the latter given the WTO's expanding agenda and new human
resource capacity and presence requirements in Geneva.

Most developing countries—even those with relatively large delegations in
Geneva—were radically understaffed before the Doha ministerial meeting given
that each year about 1,200 formal and informal meetings occur in the WTO in
Geneva (Hoekman and Kostecki, 2001). Since the Doha meeting it is hard to speak
of effective Geneva representation even for some larger developing countries.
Indeed, given the ambitious agenda and short timeframe agreed for completion,
post-Doha negotiations threaten to draw scarce developing country expertise from
higher domestic development priorities. And within trade negotiations, the best
developing country negotiators will have to devote enormous energy to complex
new areas—including the 'Singapore issues' (investment, competition policy,
transparency in government procurement, trade facilitation)—reducing the time
spent on traditional issues, such as agriculture and textiles, where payoffs are most
likely to reduce poverty and advance human development (Winters, 2002).

Ironically, the need for formal consensus has increased the number of informal processes. In preparations for the Seattle conference and at the meeting itself,
this led to a multiplicity of now-infamous 'green room' meetings. While this practice dates back to GATT, it took on new meaning in the context of a developing
country membership that is trying to become more assertive in the world trade
regime. 'Green room' consultations have often substituted for full-fledged negotiating processes. Because these consultations have excluded all but the most sys-
temically important and more assertive developing countries—while including the
vast majority of industrial countries, individually or collectively—the involvement
of most developing countries has largely been confined to the beginning, when
proposals are first tabled, and the end, when the general council makes a formal
decision by consensus (Das, 2000). The failure of such consensus building in Seattle
was a major reason for that meeting's failure. Though a conscious effort has since
been made to avoid such 'green rooms', the 'friends of the chair' process in Doha
also suffered from significant shortcomings (Malhotra, 2002).

In addition, the growth of informal processes works against the formal participation of developing country coalitions and alliances in WTO negotiations, reinforcing power asymmetries. This dynamic discourages developing countries from

gathering the strength in numbers they will need to rectify the imbalances that work against them in trade negotiations (Narlikar, 2001; Helleiner and Oyijede, 1998). While capacity and procedural problems remain serious and numerous, the over-arching problem is significant asymmetries in the power of member countries and how this is exercised in the broader interests of development.

External transparency

This chapter has focused on the internal workings of the global trade regime, but external transparency has become equally important—especially given the enormous civil society and media attention since the Seattle ministerial meeting in 1999. External transparency has also become important because WTO decisions directly affect local communities and domestic politics. As a result many groups are clamouring for a voice and wish to be treated as stakeholders (Woods and Narlikar, 2001).

Ostry (2000b) argues that demands for democratization of the WTO, especially opening it to civil society organizations, are complex and contentious because of the organization's institutional design. While greater public accountability through information transparency and the sharing of WTO documents is possible—and is taking place through the WTO Web site and other means—developing countries and civil society organizations argue that the organization's procedures should be made more accessible and transparent. The argument is that the formal publication of documents is a poor substitute for actual participation and transparency in meetings (Woods and Narlikar, 2001). But member states find great difficulty in agreeing to more formal roles for civil society organizations within the WTO and its dispute settlement processes.

The US has been the strongest proponent of opening the WTO dispute process to private parties. Private lawyers and environmental, labour and human rights groups from industrial countries have argued that they should be able to present 'friend of the court' briefs and otherwise be party to WTO dispute settlement cases—a position that the US government has sometimes encouraged. But the environmental sensitivities of many disputes in which such private interventions have primarily occurred (such as the shrimp-turtle dispute)[9] have only strengthened developing countries' opposition to interventions by civil society organizations and private actors. These countries emphasize the WTO's intergovernmental nature and believe that its basic character and their role are undermined by such private participation. Given the nature of many of the cases in dispute, many civil society organizations from developing countries also oppose a role for non-state actors in the Dispute Settlement Understanding, though a few support such a role.

Beyond specific disputes, there is a need for the WTO to more actively involve civil society organizations—not least because most multilateral institutions, including the World Bank, increasingly recognize the need to involve such organizations much more actively in their formal processes. In the meantime, civil society organizations will likely continue to encounter opposition to their arguments that an increasingly interdependent world requires citizen participation mechanisms that transcend national borders, particularly when transnational issues are at stake—even though these organizations are only requesting formal observer status at the WTO.

Most governments will likely continue to argue that civil society organizations should participate in national processes and convey their views through these processes and their elected representatives rather than directly to the WTO. This argument is based on traditional arguments related to accountability, governance and representation. But as UNDP's *Human Development Report 2002* explains, there are good reasons to question the effectiveness and recognize the limits of traditional forms of democracy in ensuring good governance and human development. The interests of countries, as expressed by their negotiators, are not necessarily in accord with the needs of their people or of human development. Governments and political parties rarely win or lose elections on a single issue, and even more rarely on positions taken by their representatives in international economic organizations (Woods and Narlikar, 2001). Moreover, governments are almost always represented in such organizations by professional civil servants, many of whom are bureaucrats or technocrats far removed from the concerns of ordinary citizens.

National ownership

Thus the challenge is not only to make the global governance of trade more fair but also to give voice to vulnerable groups not being effectively represented by their governments at the national and international levels. There is a striking difference between industrial and developing countries in the legislature's involvement in domestic debates on trade. For example, the decision by industrial countries, particularly the US, to seek to extend GATT rules into areas such as services and intellectual property rights can be traced to well-organized lobbies in the financial, telecommunications, pharmaceutical and software sectors. The European Parliament has also been active on some trade issues, such as agriculture. Even so, the pattern of protection in industrial countries reflects the political power of interest groups supported by members of legislative bodies (Vangrasstek, 2001). In some cases where legislatures in developing countries have been alerted to the pressures being exerted by the executive branch to sign WTO agreements, they have responded in a determined manner.

In all countries the severe under-representation of women in decision-making structures and national legislatures probably helps explain why gender issues are rarely taken into account in policy-making on domestic trade issues and multilateral trade agreements.[10] Though a critical mass of senior female policy-makers could result in more systematic consideration of gender issues, a surer route would be to train men—as well as women—to become gender sensitive at all stages of policy design and implementation.

It is especially critical for human development that trade ministries foster the institutional ethos and attitudes conducive to developing gender-sensitive trade policies. It is difficult to develop such policies without having focal points that are responsible for mainstreaming gender within the ministry, reporting directly to the minister, and without an interdepartmental committee on gender that ensures the inclusion of women's concerns.[11]

Many other vulnerable groups in both industrial and developing countries suffer from their lack of an effective voice. As noted, this lack of voice is closely linked to the issue of national ownership. Benefits come from broadly based participation and ownership at the national level, involving legislators, civil society organizations, community groups and the private sector in structured, multistakeholder dialogues. Moreover, if civil society organizations and vulnerable groups believe that governments take their concerns seriously, they will ease their demands to participate in multilateral forums such as the WTO.

Such ownership should also strengthen the hand of developing countries in trade negotiations, because they will be able to show organized support at home for trade negotiating positions intended to foster human development. This will allow them to better withstand pressure to capitulate, leading to fairer trade agreements. So, engendering broadly based national ownership can contribute significantly to long-term human development outcomes.

An effective secretariat

Relative to members, secretariats of member-driven organizations generally have limited power because it is the members that run the organization. This feature has mainly positive implications. Despite being relatively small compared with their best resourced members, secretariats of member-driven organizations can be enabled to provide support to members who need it most, if the membership prioritizes and properly resources this objective. However, many observers suggest that the WTO secretariat is currently able to provide its members with little support for the costs of representation and policy research and analysis. As a result, the unequal policy research and analysis capacities of industrial and developing countries outside the WTO are replicated and reflected in its negotiations and decision-making process (Narlikar, 2001). The implications of this have become more important as the multilateral trade regime's agenda has expanded to cover increasingly complex and technical matters requiring highly skilled professionals.

Enhancing the role of the secretariat could increase its capacity to respond to the analysis and capacity development needs of developing countries. Many worry, however, that most technical assistance programs focus on integration with the world trade system and compliance with its agreements, with little attention paid to the agreements' development costs and benefits and to the opportunity and other costs of complying with them. Stronger mechanisms for evaluating and monitoring technical assistance programs could help solve part of this problem. But even if such mechanisms were improved and resulted in better designed technical assistance, a number of broader developments concerns would likely persist.

More work is needed to address such concerns, and the United Nations Conference on Trade and Development (UNCTAD) and the United Nations Development Programme (UNDP) should play major roles. Although UNCTAD (especially through its Positive Agenda), UNDP, the South Center and some non-governmental organizations (NGOs) have taken steps to strengthen developing countries' capacity in this crucial area, the gap far outstrips their technical capacity and financial ability to respond effectively.

Choice of forums

Helleiner and Oyejide (1998) show that the forum chosen for international economic discussions and negotiations plays a crucial role in their outcomes and subsequent agreements. The authors argue that in the 1970s, when negotiations on investment occurred in the UN system, efforts focused on developing a code of conduct for transnational corporations, rules and principles governing restrictive business practices and a code for technology transfers. These negotiations advanced the interests of developing countries, but the draft instruments they produced were abandoned because a few powerful industrial countries were reluctant to accept them.

In 1998, during discussions sponsored by the Organisation for Economic Co-operation and Development (OECD) on a proposed multilateral agreement on investment, the focus was completely different. The more recent discussions placed priority on protecting foreign investors and ensuring fair national treatment rather than on regulating transnational corporations.

The lesson from this and other examples is that developing countries need to seek negotiating forums that are unlikely to impose undesirable outcomes on them. Because the global political economy has worked against this in recent decades, developing countries need to join or form coalitions among themselves that are not necessarily regionally based. Transregional coalitions of developing countries will be essential in the effort to move choices on negotiating forums in a direction that consistently serves the interests of human development and of poor, vulnerable groups in developing countries.

*   *   *   *

A human development perspective implies that the importance of achieving certain outcomes outweighs the need for one-size-fits-all rules. Required are minimum, universally agreed rules that can be applied in a country-specific manner and tailored to different development circumstances. The WTO should not be focused on harmonizing trade rules (see chapter 1). Instead it should be concerned with managing the interaction between different national institutions and rules. To do so, all members must accept a minimum set of multilateral trade rules through which each country has the same rights—while its obligations are a function of its stage of development (Nayyar, 2002).

ANNEX 4.1 REGIONAL TRADE AGREEMENTS AND THE MULTILATERAL REGIME

Regional trade agreements provide benefits to their members through free trade areas, customs unions, common markets and other preferential arrangements. Regional integration is seen as a way for countries to benefit from and contribute to a region's development and for countries and regions to participate more effectively in the international trade system. Many policy-makers consider regional agreements an integral part of an overall development strategy for gradual, strategic integration with the global economy.

Since 1945 more than 300 regional trade agreements have been reported to the GATT and WTO—most (250 agreements) since 1995. About 200 of these agreements are currently in force. Thus regional trade agreements have become an important feature of the international trade system. Until 1980 Western Europe was the only example of successful regional integration. This changed when the GATT contracting parties failed to launch a round of multilateral trade negotiations in Geneva in 1982. Frustrated with the stalled multilateral process, the US started bilateral trade negotiations that included regional trade agreements with Israel (1985), Canada (1989) and Canada and Mexico (through the North American Free Trade Agreement, or NAFTA, in 1993).[12] At the same time, the EU continued its expansion, and in the 1990s a plethora of new regional trade agreements began emerging.

It is something of a paradox that regional trade agreements have been growing in number in an era of accelerating economic globalization and despite the creation of the WTO in 1995. A multitude of such agreements now exist. Although about 60 per cent of the regional agreements in force at the end of 2000 were between European countries, agreements involving developing countries accounted for about 15 per cent. Almost all developing countries are members of at least 1 or 2 regional agreements—and Chile is party to at least 11.

Compatibility with WTO disciplines

Compatibility with WTO disciplines is an important issue for many developing countries involved in regional trade agreements, whether the agreements are solely with other developing countries or also involve industrial countries. But the issue of compatibility requires care, because applicable WTO disciplines differ for the two types of agreements. The WTO's Enabling Clause applies to agreements between developing countries, providing them with more favourable conditions.

Compatibility is a bigger challenge in the context of regional trade agreements between developing and industrial countries. The applicable WTO discipline is GATT article 24—which, despite some flexibility, does not provide special and differential treatment for developing countries. Thus there is concern that the article does not provide adequate legal coverage for regional trade agreements such as those that might be negotiated between African, Caribbean and Pacific countries and the EU, where huge differences in development levels would legitimately call for greater flexibility and asymmetrical treatment. So, although WTO compatibility is recognized as the overriding principle in many regional trade agreements, a parallel concern is compatibility with new WTO rules that more adequately take into account human development and the interests of developing countries.

A policy of pragmatism has prevailed thus far, allowing regional trade agreements to operate without official endorsement from the WTO membership. But WTO disciplines applying to regional agreements could change, because the Doha negotiation agenda includes 'negotiations aimed at clarifying and improving disciplines and procedures applying to regional trade agreements'.[13] It is the primary responsibility of developing countries, supported by their industrial country partners in regional trade agreements, to ensure that any changes to WTO rules under the Doha work programme do not limit the potential for development afforded by these agreements or allow human development policy options to be constrained by agreements with 'WTO plus' provisions in areas of concern to developing countries—such as TRIPS, agriculture, textiles and clothing, investment, services, environment and labour.

The coincidence of the timing of the Doha negotiations and of several major negotiations on regional trade agreements presents a unique opportunity and major challenge to the international community. (For example, the agreement on the Free Trade Area of the Americas is scheduled for completion by 2005, and the free trade agreement between African, Caribbean and Pacific states and the EU is scheduled for completion by 2008.) Both industrial and developing countries must rise to the task of placing human development and poverty reduction at the centre of all trade negotiations, whether multilateral or regional.

Mercosur: An agreement between developing countries

The Mercado Comun del Sur (Southern Common Market, or Mercosur) is among the most widely cited examples of a successful trade pact, particularly among developing countries. The agreement and its original members—Argentina, Brazil, Paraguay and Uruguay—celebrated its 10th anniversary in 2001. Bolivia and Chile joined Mercosur as associate members in 1996. Mercosur was designed to start as a free trade area, then become a customs union and eventually a common market. Currently a customs union, it accounts for 70 per cent of Latin American trade. Its members have a combined GDP of nearly $1 trillion and are home to more than

230 million people, making Mercosur the world's third largest trading bloc after the EU and NAFTA.

In many ways Mercosur has been a success. It has provided significant economic benefits to its members: between 1990 and 1999 trade among its members grew by more than 200 per cent, and among the world's regions Latin America has experienced the sharpest increase in intra-regional trade. But income disparities in member countries remain largely unchanged, and more than 37 per cent of citizens in Mercosur countries still live below the poverty line. In addition, there has been little collaboration in non-economic areas, and members were not able to reach agreement in many areas—including on a common negotiating position for the Free Trade Area of the Americas—even before the recent Argentine crisis.

From a human development perspective, while some initial steps have been taken towards common education and drug policies, there is no cooperation on labour mobility, labour standards or the environment. Still, Mercosur may have had a positive effect on democratic governance in its member countries due to a 1996 amendment to its charter (after a planned coup attempt in Paraguay) formally excluding any country that 'abandons the full exercise of republican institutions'.

Some institutional steps have been taken to address the social impact of trade liberalization in Mercosur member countries, but the results have been mixed. Social issues associated with economic integration were largely ignored until organized labour in the region pushed for the creation of a working group to address labour relations, employment and social security. Geared towards studying the labour situation in the region, the group focused on issues of commercial interest and business competitiveness.

In 1994 a Forum for Economic and Social Consultations was formed to represent the private sector in Mercosur member states. The forum has since opened its doors to other actors, including labour organizations, consumer protection groups, universities and an environmental group (Espino, 2000). But it has not admitted women's organizations or government bodies that focus on women's development.

Women's advocates see the Forum for Economic and Social Consultations primarily as a tool of economic and commercial interests. Because most female workers are in sectors outside the scope of organized labour, they do not feel represented by it. Women's organizations rallied to address this shortcoming and in 1997 succeeded in setting up a Women's Commission under the Coordinating Authority for Southern Cone Confederations of Labour. Their demands to governments and organized labour included promoting the participation of female workers in Mercosur, speeding the ratification of International Labour Organization agreements specific to women and keeping all labour unions and women's departments informed.

A series of civil society meetings and forums, supported by the United Nations Development Fund for Women, also furthered activities to address women's concerns in government ministries responsible for them in Mercosur countries (Espino, 2000). In 1995 women in Uruguay set up an advocacy lobby called the Mercosur Women's

Forum, with branches in each member country. The Paraguay branch is the most active and has brought its concerns to the national chapter of Forum for Economic and Social Consultations. Despite these networking strategies across countries, the forum does not appear to have tangibly influenced the working or executive bodies of Mercosur.

The 1997 Mercosur declaration reflected some of these women's initiatives, calling for measures 'to guarantee equality of opportunities among women and men in the…various forums for negotiations which are part of Mercosur'. The declaration also recommended making the participation of women's organizations mandatory in the Forum for Economic and Social Consultations. As a result the Reunion Especializada de Mujeres came into being in 1998. This gender advisory unit seeks to ensure that gender issues are addressed in Mercosur's key decision-making bodies.

But according to some sections of civil society, the unit has not made much progress in analysing negotiations or creating mechanisms to ensure gender equality in the region (WIDE, 2001). Among the factors that have impeded the incorporation of a gender perspective in negotiations on an institutional structure in Mercosur are the low priority given to the social dimensions of economic integration and its lack of prominence in negotiations between employers and workers (WIDE, 2001).

Asia-Pacific Economic Cooperation: An agreement between industrial and developing countries

The 21 member countries of the Asia-Pacific Economic Cooperation (APEC) forum have agreed to form an Asia-Pacific regional trade agreement by 2010 for APEC's industrial economies and by 2020 for its developing economies.[14] APEC is not a free trade area in the formal sense of GATT article 24 because free trade and investment are being pursued voluntarily by each member rather than through an agreed tariff reduction plan. But if the regional trade agreement comes into existence, it will be the world's largest—with members accounting for 55 per cent of global GDP, about half of global exports and almost 40 per cent of the world's population.

Apart from its projected economic benefits, APEC is expected to practice 'open regionalism'—meaning that it will offer non-discriminatory trade treatment to non-members as well. But many observers question whether that will actually happen. APEC has made little progress on its tariff reduction goals precisely because of its open regionalism policy: members are unwilling to reduce tariffs for non-members and get nothing in return.

As a consultative forum, APEC cannot make decisions that are legally binding on its members. It is primarily a forum for discussing economic and trade policy and does not explicitly address social and development issues. Though it has links to several business groups and academic research organizations, there is no formal mechanism for consultations with other parts of civil society.

APEC's FRAMEWORK FOR GENDER INTEGRATION. In a 1996 statement APEC leaders acknowledged for the first time the importance of women and young people's participation in the economy. The statement was a victory for the Women Leaders' Network, which had drafted a call to action and presented it to APEC leaders. Launched that year as an informal network of female leaders from APEC members' public and private sectors, governments, civil society organizations and academia, the Women Leaders' Network has evolved into a policy forum and the main advocate for gender issues in APEC. The network has succeeded in getting the predominantly male leaders of APEC to recognize the gender implications of economic policies and has laid the ground for gender-based initiatives. The network is a completely voluntary organization that functions through country focal points. Although it lacks an institutional structure and funding, the network has held six annual meetings since its inception.

Advocacy by the Women Leaders' Network has had some encouraging results. For example, it led APEC to convene its first ministerial meeting on women in 1998. As a result of that event APEC agreed to develop a framework for integrating women into all its activities, and in 1999 the framework was endorsed. The meeting also led to the creation of an advisory group to implement the framework. In addition, the Women Leaders' Network influenced the creation of a women's science and technology group under APEC's industrial science and technology working group, initiated a gender information site on the APEC Web site and provided gender expertise in a number of APEC forums.

APEC's framework for integrating women consists of three inter-related elements: gender analysis, collection and use of sex-disaggregated data and involvement of women in APEC. The framework's advisory group has developed practical guides to facilitate implementation of the framework.

Members of the Women Leaders' Network say that it is too early to assess the framework's impact on APEC policies. Still, there have been some tangible results in individual countries. For example, Viet Nam has adapted the framework for its national programme on women. But overall within APEC, gender mainstreaming efforts are still at the level of raising awareness and building capacity through, for example, gender information sessions and the publication of best practices. Some APEC working groups—notably those on human resources development, industrial science and technology and small and medium-size enterprises—have been more active in incorporating gender criteria into project proposals and evaluation concerns.

As a group composed primarily of businesswomen, the Women Leaders' Network is focused on improving market access for female entrepreneurs. There are sound economic arguments for this approach: more than a third of the region's small and medium-size enterprises are owned by women, and 80 per cent of these are in the burgeoning services sector. But this business-oriented approach has prompted criticism that the Women Leaders' Network is a group of privileged professional women who use efficiency arguments to gain support for gender issues in APEC and subordinate human development to economic development. Conspicuous by its absence, both in the network and in APEC, is a gender focus on the social impact of trade liberalization.

Moreover, much of the integration of gender has occurred at the working group and technical cooperation levels, and has had no impact on the agendas for trade and investment liberalization and trade facilitation.

CHALLENGES AND RECOMMENDATIONS. The Women Leaders' Network faces three major challenges: organizing itself better to take on a monitoring role, ensuring that development and ethical issues are not eclipsed by the business agenda, and raising funds to ensure its survival. Not being a formal APEC mechanism limits the network's potential role in gender mainstreaming.

Among the main constraints to gender integration in APEC are a lack of data and information on women's economic roles, a lack of recognition of women's roles in the paid work force in APEC data and analysis, a lack of data on women's contributions in the informal sector and unpaid work, and under-representation of women in APEC forums and activities (Corner, 1999).

Thus APEC should encourage its members to collect more and better information on women's economic roles and on the effects that trade and investment liberalization have on them. It should also formally recognize gender as a cross-cutting issue and routinely undertake analysis to identify the different impacts of policies and programmes on women and men. Finally, APEC should collect data on women's participation in its activities and assess the impact that gender integration and women's participation have on achieving its goals.

The Women Leaders' Network, on the other hand, should ensure more balanced participation and representation at its annual meetings and address a broader range of the issues facing female workers in Asia and the Pacific—not just those of women in business.

A way forward for regional trade agreements

The surge in regional trade agreements has intensified concerns and debates on promoting national and local interests alongside international trade regimes. Efforts to include human development and poverty reduction objectives in regional (and multilateral) trade agreements have assumed even greater importance and support against the backdrop of a rapidly liberalizing global economy—particularly because of concerns about the agreements' inimical effects on human development.

Although new opportunities are being created by multilateral and regional trade liberalization, central aspects of globalization are limiting countries' development policy options. Moreover, many countries do not ensure active, regular consultations between governments and national stakeholders on development priorities in regional and other international trade agreements. As a result human development priorities and strategies to promote them are likely to be marginalized relative to business and political objectives.

If human development goals are to be achieved, parliamentarians and representatives of civil society must become engaged in the formulation of trade policy and in the negotiation and implementation of regional trade agreements. Some progress has been made in this area, but much more is needed. Consultations with key stakeholders were critical in the development of South Africa's free trade agreement with the EU. Similarly, the Cotonou Agreement between African, Caribbean and Pacific states and the EU requires that non-state actors and the business community be consulted on all aspects of the development partnership.

WTO compatibility should be a fundamental principle for regional trade agreements, but first WTO rules need to be made more flexible and human development friendly. Several recent regional agreements have included compliance with the WTO as a general principle, but this is not true of all. WTO rules should provide the overall boundaries for the scope and nature of regional agreements. As much as possible, these agreements should be non-discriminatory to non-members. To enable that, WTO rules should provide regional trade agreements with sufficient scope for addressing development concerns, and agreements between industrial and developing countries should allow for less than full reciprocity from the developing country partners.

Several other issues are important in updating and adapting regional trade agreements. First, flexibility in admitting members is needed to create the widest possible development space and to strengthen social and cultural ties. If useful, membership should be extended to countries beyond the standard geographic definition of a region. Widening membership to enlarge economic and social space is already an accepted objective in some regional trade agreements (though too wide a membership can become unwieldy and increase the size of the economic problems to be resolved). For example, the Common Market for Eastern and Southern Africa (COMESA) includes countries from North, East and Southern Africa and the Indian Ocean—while the African, Caribbean and Pacific Group of States includes countries from three continents.

This wider development space should be complemented by a policy of selectively stimulating growth in certain non-traditional subregions made up of two or more countries that are natural integration areas but that are in bordering regions unlikely to be covered by a formal regional trade agreement. Properly designed, such zones can help create a network of trade in an area—energizing regional integration within established groups and strengthening political solidarity between countries. Moreover, businesses and consumers in such zones can benefit considerably from the economic activities generated.

Many such selective free trade and economic complementarity agreements have been concluded in Latin America and the Caribbean outside the context of existing regional integration agreements. The Argentina-Brazil Programme of Economic Integration and Cooperation, adopted in 1986, is an example—and formed the basis for the creation of Mercosur in 1991. The Southern African Development Community is now pursing this philosophy in the form of 'development corridors' linking landlocked countries to countries with ports and access to the sea, or linking less developed to more developed areas. This form of regional integration deserves more support because it could foster development and reduce poverty in outlying regions of countries—regions normally overlooked by profit-focused economic activities and development funding.

Enormous human development benefits can come from regional trade agreements among developing countries when such agreements create regional or like-minded development space or link neglected outlying areas. These kinds of agreements can build solidarity and bring together countries at similar stages of development, allowing for more symmetrical power relationships than under agreements between industrial and developing countries. Such agreements often provide developing countries with the greatest potential for mutually beneficial human development gains, at least in the short run. And if strategically managed, they are also likely to increase the bargaining power of developing country coalitions in international trade negotiating forums such as the WTO. Developing countries are likely to obtain much greater human development benefits when they combine their efforts in such forums.

Regional trade agreements between industrial and developing countries can also be instrumental in promoting economic growth and generating resources for human development activities. But the benefits to developing countries in the early stages of such agreements will depend on the accompanying social and economic adjustment measures. Developing country partners must ensure that they benefit from non-reciprocal trade arrangements and should assume less stringent liberalization commitments than their industrial country partners.

Regional trade agreements are no panacea for human development. None of the existing or planned regional trade agreements include provisions that will automatically enhance human development. The gender framework in APEC, while promising, still needs to be implemented, while NAFTA's labour and environmental clauses have not changed the environmental situation or labour relations in US-Mexico border areas. Agreements among EU countries may be an exception. But it is hard to see how the positive aspects of EU agreements can be emulated by developing countries given the high incomes and human development indicators of EU members and their relative equality in terms of sustainable human development.

NOTES

1. Indeed, this is a key problem with hearings in anti-dumping proceedings, where testimony from groups other than the import-competing industry is typically not allowed.

2. Plurilateral agreements are signed by WTO members that choose to do so, while all members are party to multilateral agreements.

3. Income is a proxy for more relevant indicators such as composition of exports and imports, industrial structure, sectoral composition and human capital levels, and further classification may be necessary in some cases. A full description of the Millennium Development Goals can be found at http://www.undp.org/mdg/99-Millennium_Declaration_and_Follow_up_Resolution.pdf.

4. Several examples of ways of doing this come from developing country proposals such as the ones submitted to the special session of the WTO Committee on Trade and Development on 18 June 2002, with communications from the African group, Paraguay, India, the least developed countries group and the joint communication from Cuba, the Dominican Republic, Honduras, India, Indonesia, Kenya, Pakistan, Sri Lanka, Tanzania and Zimbabwe.

5. This requires that the investigative process in each case gather testimony and views from all relevant parties, including consumer and public interest groups, importers and exporters and civil society organizations, and determine whether there is sufficiently broad support among these groups for the exercise of the opt-out or safeguard in question. Requiring groups—importers and exporters—whose incomes might be adversely affected by the opt-out to testify and the investigative body to trade off competing interests in a transparent manner would help ensure that protectionist measures that benefit a small segment of an industry at a large cost to society would not have much chance of success. When the opt-out in question is part of a broader development strategy that has already been adopted after broad debate and participation, an additional investigative process need not be launched (Rodrik, 2001).

6. Sanjaya Lall's index on domestic capabilities, which includes industrial performance and technology effort indexes, is an example. This index, supplemented by a human development index, could provide one such mechanism.

7. Taken together, these rulings are regarded by some as creating a cumulative jurisprudence on trade issues, though legally each ruling is independent.

8. Data are from http://www.wto.org/english/tratop_e/dispu_e/dispu_status_e.htm.

9. India, Malaysia, Pakistan and Thailand used the WTO dispute settlement process to challenge US restrictions on shrimp imports caught using nets known to harm certain species of endangered sea turtles.

10. Women legislators, for instance, represent only 9 per cent of the seats in parliament in Latin America and the Caribbean (UNDP, 1995). The situation is not much better in some industrial countries: women hold only 12 per cent of the seats in the US Congress and 23 per cent of the seats in the Canadian parliament (Hemispheric Social Alliance, 2001).

11. This is the experience in making finance ministries more gender-aware (Sen, 1999). However, given the structural similarities between finance and trade ministries, especially in developing countries, similar institutional constraints are likely in trade ministries.

12. Members of regional trade agreements are often but not always located in the same geographic region.

13. Paragraph 29, Doha Ministerial Declaration adopted 14 November 2001 (WT/MIN(01)/DEC/1), 20 November 2001.

14. The members of APEC are Australia, Brunei Darussalam, Canada, Chile, China, Hong Kong (China, SAR), Indonesia, Japan, the Republic of Korea, Malaysia, Mexico, New Zealand, Papua New Guinea, Peru, the Philippines, the Russian Federation, Singapore, Taiwan (China), Thailand, the United States and Viet Nam.

REFERENCES

Blackhurst, Richard. 1997. 'The Capacity of the WTO to Fulfill Its Mandate'. In A. O. Kruger, ed., *The WTO as an International Organization.* University of Chicago Press.

Corner, Lorraine. 1999. 'Women and Economic Development and Cooperation in Asia-Pacific Economic Cooperation (APEC)'. Economic Empowerment Series. United Nations Development Fund for Women (UNIFEM), East and Southeast Asia Regional Office, Bangkok, Thailand, and UNFEM, New York.

Das, B. L. 2000. 'Trade: Full Participation and Efficiency in Negotiations'. Briefing paper. Third World Network, Penang, Malaysia.

Delgado, Sergio. 1994. 'Impacto de los resultados de la Ronda Uruguay'. In Patricio Leiva, ed., *La Ronda Uruguay y el desarrollo de América Latina.* Santiago de Chile: CLEPI.

Espino, Maria Alma. 2000. 'Mujer y Mercosur: Las dimensiones de genero de la integration economica en UNIFEM Mujeres: Empoderamento y justicia economica. United Nations Development Fund for Women, New York.

Florini, Ann M. 1998. 'The End of Secrecy'. *Foreign Policy* 111 (summer): 50–63.

Helliener, Gerald K. 2002. 'Developing Countries in Global Economic Governance and Negotiation Processes'. In Deepak Nayyar, ed., *Governing Globalisation: Issues and Institutions.* Oxford: Oxford University Press.

Helliener, Gerald K, and Ademola Oyejide. 1998. 'Global Economic Governance, Global Negotiations and the Developing Countries'. Background paper for *Human Development Report 1999.* United Nations Development Programme, New York.

Hemispheric Social Alliance. 2001. 'Alternatives for the Americas'. Discussion draft 3, an expanded and revised edition prepared for the 2nd People's Summit of the Americas, Quebec City, Canada, April 2001. [www.asc-hsa.org].

Hoekman, Bernard, and Michel Kostecki. 2001. *The Political Economy of the World Trading System: The WTO and Beyond.* Oxford: Oxford University Press.

IMF (International Monetary Fund). 1998. 'Report of the Working Group on Transparency and Accountability'. G-22 Working Group. Washington, DC.

Kohler, Horst. 2000. 'The IMF in a Changing World'. Remarks made at the National Press Club, 7 August, Washington, DC.

Malhotra, Kamal. 2002. 'Doha: Is It Really a Development Round?' Trade and Environment Policy Paper. Carnegie Endowment for International Peace, Washington, DC.

Michalopoulos, Constantine. 2000. 'The Participation of Developing Countries in the WTO'. Background paper for WTO Capacity Building Project. World Bank, Washington, DC.

Mohammed, Azizali. 2001. 'Governance Issues in Inter-Governmental Groupings of Developing Countries'. Background paper for Global Financial Governance Initiative. Working Group on Institutional Reform, Oxford University. [users.ox.ca.uk/~ntwoods/wg3.htm].

Narlikar, Amrita. 2001. 'WTO Decision Making and Developing Countries'. Trade Related Agenda, Development and Equity (T.R.A.D.E.) Working Paper 11. South Centre, Geneva.

Nayyar, Deepak. 2002. 'The Existing System and the Missing Institutions'. In Deepak Nayyar, ed., *Governing Globalisation: Issues and Institutions*. Oxford: Oxford University Press.

Ohiorhenuan, John. 1998. 'Capacity Building Implications of Enhanced African Participation in Global Trade Rules-Making and Arrangements.' WTO Working Paper CRC-3-11. African Economic Research Consortium, Nairobi, Kenya.

Onguglo, Bonapas, and Taisuke Ito. 2002. 'Human Development and Regional Trade Agreements in an Evolving Trading System'. Background note for Trade and Sustainable Human Development Project. United Nations Development Programme, New York.

Ostry, Sylvia. 2000a. 'The Uruguay Round North-South Bargain: Implications for Future Negotiations'. Prepared for a conference on The Political Economy of International Trade Law, University of Minnesota, Minneapolis, September 15–16, 2000.

———. 2000b. 'WTO: Institutional Design for Better Governance.' Paper presented at a conference hosted by Harvard University, Kennedy School of Government, 2–3 June, Cambridge, Mass.

Oyejide, T. A. 1998. 'Costs and Benefits of S and D Treatment for Developing Countries in the GATT/WTO: An African Perspective'. African Economic Research Consortium, Nairobi, Kenya.

Pfeil, Andreas. 2001. 'Can Regional Trade Integration Promote Sustainable Human Development?' Background note for Trade and Sustainable Human Development Project. United Nations Development Programme, New York.

Schott, Jeffrey J., and Jayashree Watal. 2000. 'Decision-making in the WTO'. In Jeffrey Schott, ed., *The WTO after Seattle*. Washington, DC: Institute for International Economics.

Shukla, S. P. 2000. 'GATT to WTO and Beyond'. Working Paper 195. United Nations University and World Institute for Development Economics Research, Helsinki.

South Centre. 1999. 'Issues Regarding the Review of the WTO Dispute Settlement Mechanism'. Geneva.

Tang, Xiaobing. 2002. 'Experience of Implementation of the WTO Agreement on Trade-Related Investment Measures: Difficulties and Challenges Faced by Developing Countries'. United Nations Conference on Trade and Development, Geneva.

UNCTAD (United Nations Conference on Trade and Development). 2002. *WTO Accessions and Development Policy*. Geneva.

UNDP (United Nations Development Programme). 1995. *Human Development Report 1995*. New York: Oxford University Press.

————. 2002. *Human Development Report 2002: Deepening Democracy in a Fragmented World*. New York: Oxford University Press.

Vangrasstek, Craig . 2001. 'The Political Economy of Residual Protection in the Trade Regime of the United States of America'. United Nations Conference on Trade and Development, Geneva.

White, Marceline A. 2002. 'Women and Trade: Investing in Women—FTAA Investment Policies and Women'. Coalition for Women's Economic Development and Global Equality, Washington, DC.

WHO (World Health Organization) and WTO (World Trade Organization). 2002. *WTO Agreements and Public Health*. Geneva.

WIDE (Women in Development Europe). 2001. 'Instruments for Gender Equality in Trade Agreements'. European Union, Brussels.

Winters, L. Alan. 2002. 'Doha and the World Poverty Targets'. Paper presented at the World Bank Annual Conference on Development Economics, April, Washington, DC.

Woods, Ngaire, and Amrita Narlikar. 2001. 'Governance and the Limits of Accountability: The WTO, the IMF and the World Bank'. *International Social Science Journal* 53 (4): 569–83.

WTO (World Trade Organization). 2001. 'Doha Ministerial Declaration'. [www.wto.org/english/thewto_e/inist_e/min01_e/mindecl_e.htm].

PART 2
AGREEMENTS AND ISSUES

The current focus on reducing global poverty has direct implications for discussions at the World Trade Organization (WTO). Indeed, the multilateral trade regime will be well governed if it is focused on the achievement of the Millennium Development Goals.

The multilateral trading system comprises several agreements in goods, services and intellectual property rights. Agreements on goods cover agriculture, sanitary and phytosanitary measures, textiles and clothing, technical barriers to trade and trade related investment measures (TRIMs). They also encompass rules on anti-dumping, subsidies and countervailing measures, safeguards, customs valuation, pre-shipment inspection and rules of origin. And there are plurilateral agreements on trade in civil aircraft, government procurement, the international dairy agreement and the international bovine meat agreement.[1]

In addition to these agreements are a number of issues under discussion and negotiation. At the Fourth WTO Ministerial Conference at Doha in 2001, countries agreed to negotiate on environment and industrial tariff issues and to discuss further the four Singapore issues—investment, competition policy, transparency in government procurement and trade facilitation. These issues, first raised in the WTO at its Ministerial Conference in Singapore in 1996, are now under active discussion. A final decision on whether to include them in the negotiation agenda is expected at the September 2003 Ministerial Conference in Cancun, Mexico. A decision to include them in the WTO's negotiation agenda can be agreed only by explicit consensus of all members.

Many agreements—and the issues agreed either for negotiation or for discussion—affect human development variables directly through their implications for income, equity, employment, food security, public health, gender outcomes and access to technology.

Beyond such impact, each of the agreements and issues also affects both the domestic policy space and the market access opportunities for countries. They can either facilitate or constrain the policy flexibility and autonomy of members. Constraints can take the form of multilateral trade rules prohibiting or restricting the use of specific policy instruments that, if adopted and effectively implemented, can contribute to human development. And trade rules and obligations can result in significant opportunity costs if they lead to forgone economic growth that might have been translated into human development gains.

A few examples illustrate these points.

DIRECT IMPLICATIONS AND IMPACTS

The Agreement on Agriculture directly affects rural livelihoods, food security and farmer incomes. The Agreement on Textiles and Clothing affects family incomes, especially the work burden and wage earnings of women. Commodities trade, while not currently subject to multilateral trade disciplines, is vital to the livelihoods of the poorest and most vulnerable population groups in many low-income developing countries. The Agreement on Trade-Related Aspects of Intellectual Property Rights (TRIPS) affects knowledge creation, ownership of biological resources and access to public health. The TRIMs Agreement impacts the growth and development of local industry. The agreements on standards affect public health concerns. Many new issues still under discussion or those agreed for negotiation in Doha directly relate to technological and industrial capabilities and capacity, employment, the provision of public services and environmental issues.

POLICY SPACE

Along with their mandated tariff commitments, many WTO agreements—such as the TRIMs Agreement, the Agreement on Agriculture, and the Agreement on Subsidies and Countervailing Measures—restrict the ability of member governments to use subsidies as a tool to encourage and direct domestic production in certain sectors of the economy. Subsidies have been particularly important as policy instruments for countries at low levels of development.

TRIPS requires countries to conform to minimum standards of intellectual property rights, thereby limiting policy options that could encourage adaptation and transfer of technology. The General Agreement on Trade in Services (GATS), by contrast, provides greater policy space to governments by allowing them to selectively liberalize specific sectors. Proposed future issues-such as investment, competition policy and transparency in government procurement-all have implications for the domestic policy space of member countries. While the specific impact is likely to vary depending on what might be covered, agreements in these areas could constrain the policy space in critical domestic economic and social policy areas.

MARKET ACCESS

Increasing market access across borders is one of the primary aims of the WTO. The 1947 General Agreement on Tariffs and Trade (GATT) was an attempt to commit all member nations to lower their barriers to trade and make them more transparent and easier to measure. Under the Agreement on Agriculture and the Agreement on Textiles and Clothing (from the Uruguay Round), countries agreed to commit themselves to greater and more effective market access in these areas. Despite some progress in implementation since the WTO's creation in 1995, significant trade barriers remain for exports of many products of importance to developing countries.

Other Agreements—such as TRIMs, GATS and the Agreement on Standards and Technical Barriers to Trade—also aim at substantially enhancing market access. The discussion on new issues also focuses on market access benefits for members.

Part 2 of this book focuses on agreements and issues that have the clearest or most significant direct or indirect implications for human development. It does not seek to be exhaustive in its coverage of the very broad range of trade agreements and issues in the ambit of the world trade regime. It does, however, seek to be comprehensive in its coverage. And in so doing, it discusses and analyses different ways in which specific WTO agreements and issues affect human development, going beyond economic growth and income to consider the implications for livelihoods, security, gender relations, health, education and technological capabilities and capacities.

NOTE

1. See http://www.wto.org/english/docs_e/legal_e/legal_e.htm.

CHAPTER 5
AGRICULTURE

Agriculture plays a central role in the economies of low-income countries, accounting for more than 70 per cent of employment—compared with 30 per cent in middle-income countries and just 4 per cent in high-income countries. Particularly in low-income African countries, agriculture is also a major source of foreign exchange earnings and supplies incomes, basic foods and subsistence livelihoods for most of the population (UN, 2002). Women in rural Africa produce, process and store up to 80 per cent of food, while in South and Southeast Asia women do 60 per cent of cultivation work and other food production (UNIFEM, 2000). In most developing countries achieving equitable, sustainable progress on human development requires increasing food security and agricultural productivity, incomes and employment.

Agriculture is also an important source of exports and foreign exchange earnings in Latin America (UNCTAD, 1999b). Indeed, for countries with agricultural surpluses, trade can generate revenue to finance human development needs including health care, education and social security. And in many developing countries, agriculture is the main source of potential domestic surplus for investment in sectors with higher value-added potential—including food processing and industrial production—that are crucial for human development. Thus what happens—or does not happen—in agriculture has an enormous effect on efforts to reduce poverty, improve gender relations and advance human development in a wide range of developing countries.

SHOULD AGRICULTURE BE TREATED DIFFERENTLY?

Agriculture has long been one of the most hotly debated issues in international trade forums (box 5.1). Arguments ranging from 'multifunctionality' (supported by the EU, Japan and others) to 'food security and development' (most developing countries) to 'food sovereignty' (several civil society organizations) are used to justify different approaches to the treatment of agriculture.

The EU, Japan and some other WTO members argue that agriculture is multifunctional, meaning that it performs various non-commodity roles in addition to pro-

---

BOX 5.1 THE AGREEMENT ON AGRICULTURE: HISTORY, PROMISE AND WHERE WE ARE NOW

History and promise

Though formally covered by the 1947 General Agreement on Tariffs and Trade (GATT), agriculture was exempted from its disciplines for nearly 50 years—largely because in the 1950s the US asked to be allowed to continue protecting sugar, dairy and other agricultural products. After the US was granted a very liberal waiver from GATT obligations in 1955, article XI was laxly enforced for other agricultural producers. (Article XI prohibited quantitative restrictions on imports and exports other than duties, taxes and other charges, whether through quotas, import or export licenses or other measures.) The EU was among those that benefited from this development, using export subsidies to transform itself from a net food importer to a net exporter between the 1950s and 1970s.

After World War II different countries supported agriculture using different forms of domestic support, export subsidies and market access. Some, like the EU, created systems with no limits on production and almost no limits on subsidy spending. This tendency accelerated in the 1980s, to the point where some countries generated surpluses that could be sold overseas only with export subsidies. Indeed, GATT rules were largely ineffective in regulating agricultural trade. Export and domestic subsidies dominated many agricultural trade flows, and stiffer import restrictions were often ignored.

That changed during the 1986–94 Uruguay Round of multilateral trade negotiations. Traditional agriculture-exporting countries, developing and industrial, insisted that the Uruguay Round reverse agricultural protection. Some developing countries, particularly those from Latin America, took forceful positions in the Uruguay Round to ensure that the final agreement included meaningful disciplines on agricultural trade. The Agreement on Agriculture emerged from these negotiations in 1994 with its three pillars of market access, domestic support and export subsidies. Though key aspects of the final agreement were influenced by the second EU-US Blair House bilateral accord, key elements of that deal were never reproduced in the agreement.

Where we are now

The Agreement on Agriculture stipulated that its review would commence by 2000, and the end-2003 expiration of its 'peace clause' provides a credible deadline for reaching at least a preliminary agreement. The first phase of this reform process, from March 2000–March 2001, generated 45 proposals from 126 countries—with almost half coming from developing countries. The second phase, from March 2001–February 2002, focused on technical elaborations of the proposals from the first phase and on questions about proposals submitted by others as 'non-papers'. Among the issues raised by developing countries were food security, food aid, special and differential treatment and the problems of single commodity producers and small island developing states.

The third phase, which began in March 2002, will be the most critical since the Uruguay Round because members are expected to agree on modalities for future negotiations by March 2003—though it is not entirely clear whether this means they will agree on the rules or on actual commitments. Key elements of the new Agreement on Agriculture, including prospects for a 'development box' (see box 5.8), will also be decided during this phase. It is expected that a new agreement will be reached before the September 2003 WTO ministerial conference in Cancun, Mexico.

Country positions still remain far apart, however. While the EU, Japan and Norway are keen on arguing for agriculture's multifunctionality, developing countries from Southeast Asia and elsewhere are pushing for meaningful market access in industrial countries, demanding across-the-board reductions in subsidies. Meanwhile, the Cairns Group (with members from both industrial and developing countries) and the US are pushing their own liberalization packages.

The July 2002 US proposal is noteworthy because it calls for significant cuts in 'trade-distorting' domestic support (that is, producer subsidies) for all products and trade partners, with a ceiling of 5 per cent of the value of agricultural production for industrial countries and 10 per cent for developing countries. The US proposal also calls for tariffs to be cut to a maximum of 25 per cent for all members (after a five-year phase-in period). Both recommendations are far-reaching and ambitious—especially the first one, given levels of agricultural subsidies in many countries, including the US. The proposal will not, however, require the US to make major changes to its farm support under current Agreement on Agriculture disciplines. This, despite the recent US Farm Security and Rural Investment Act, which implies $180 billion in subsidies to farms through 2011, with more than a third coming in the act's first three years.

In contrast to the liberalizing proposal of the US, countries such as India are demanding that food security and livelihoods be made the cornerstone of a revised Agreement on Agriculture, implying a greater role for non-trade concerns. And many other developing countries, while agreeing with India, want to take an even more holistic approach to agricultural development through their proposal for a 'development box'.

Source: Anderson, Hoekman and Strutt, 1999; WTO, 2001; Biswajit Dhar, 2002, 'Subsidising US Farmers under AoA', *The Economic Times* (India), 9 August.

viding food and fibre. These include the provision of food security, cultural heritage, rural economic viability, natural disaster prevention, landscape and open space amenities, biodiversity and other environmental preservation and continued employment of aging farmers. For these countries, agriculture's multifunctionality justifies their maintenance of high agricultural protection and domestic and export subsidies.

Most developing countries, however, see the multifunctionality concept as an excuse for agricultural protection. Though many recognize the non-trade aspects of agriculture, they do not believe that the situation in industrial countries is comparable to theirs. Thus most want strong, enforceable multilateral rules that reduce agricultural protection and eliminate export subsidies in industrial countries. Developing countries also want flexibility in designing policies to ensure their food security and the ability to pursue broader development goals. Moreover, countries with large populations dependent on subsistence agriculture argue that a significant portion of their agricultural activities should be exempt from multilateral disciplines, because most of their farmers have little capacity to distort agricultural trade. They also contend that their food needs and supply gaps are a development problem that cannot be left to the vagaries of the market.

Finally, many civil society organizations, such as La Via Campesina, have advanced the idea of food sovereignty as grounds for removing agriculture from the multilateral trade regime. Meanwhile, others favour a plurilateral structure, and still others advocate an opt-out clause until developing countries are ready to submit their agricultural sectors to the disciplines of the multilateral trade regime (Kwa, 2001).

Greater flexibility in the World Trade Organization (WTO) Agreement on Agriculture would enable developing countries facing food security threats to offer a 'positive list' of agricultural products that they would subject to the disciplines of the Uruguay Round (see box 5.1). Given the big differences in the agricultural situations of developing countries, such flexibility would also allow needed differentiation between developing countries that import food staples and those that export them, and between those that export staples and those that export commercial crops.

Increased flexibility would also allow industrial countries to address rural development needs and environmental concerns without hurting farmers in developing countries. This approach would likely also foster agricultural sustainability, because it would probably show greater sensitivity to biodiversity concerns.

TARIFFS AND MARKET ACCESS

In 2005, even after meeting its Uruguay Round commitments to the Agreement on Agriculture (see below), Western Europe's average tariff on agriculture and food processing is projected to be 30 per cent. The average tariff will be even higher in Japan and the Republic of Korea, at 57 per cent. In OECD countries as a whole the average tariff on agriculture and food processing will be 36 per cent—compared with 20 per cent in developing countries. Globally, the average tariff on agriculture and food processing, at 29 per cent, will be twice that on textiles and clothing—another heavily protected sector in many industrial countries—and almost four times that on other manufactures (Anderson, Hoekman and Strutt, 1999).

In 2000 the Australian Bureau of Agricultural and Resource Economics estimated that a 50 per cent reduction in agricultural support would increase global GDP by $53 billion a year by 2010 (relative to the reference case involving no policy change), with $40 billion going to industrial countries. The bureau considered these projections conservative because they do not take into account dynamic gains from increased competition, technological advances, innovation and the like—gains that many countries expect to be as large as if not larger than those from the base projections. While the overall projections were upbeat, the bureau expected adverse effects on terms of trade for Africa, China, India, Malaysia and the Philippines.

Global models of this type are not especially helpful for a human development assessment because they aggregate on a significant scale and are often too optimistic in their calculations. As a result they end up masking distributional impacts between rich and poor people, between countries and even between entire regions that in aggregate terms are predicted to be winners. Models that provide disaggregated estimates are much more useful because they differentiate between winners and losers. The few studies that provide disaggregated estimates of the effects of the Uruguay Round indicate that certain developing countries, especially those in Sub-Saharan Africa, will be net losers (Page and Davenport, 1994; Harrison, Rutherford and Tarr, 1996; Thomas and Whalley, 1998).

Though more useful, disaggregated models suffer from many of the same problems as those that aggregate at the global level. Benefits projected for winners often do not emerge because such models ignore the oligopolistic nature of the markets in question, assuming supply and demand relationships that do not hold in the real political economy of countries and regions.

For example, chemical companies—who have become dominant players in the seed business—are linked to grain traders and food processors in a production chain where prices become internal to the industry. In many cases the same transnational companies buy, ship and mill grain, then feed it to livestock or turn it into cereal, often crossing several national borders in the process. In the US, for example, 60 per cent of terminal grain handling facilities are owned by Cargill, Cenex, Harvest States, ADM and General Mills, 82 per cent of corn exporting is concentrated in Cargill, ADM and Zen Noh, 81 per cent of beef packing is held by ADM, ConAgra, Cargill and Farmland Nation, and 61 per cent of flour milling capacity is owned by ADM, ConAgra, Cargill and General Mills (Murphy, 2002).

State trading corporations also continue to play a major role in some developing and industrial countries. Developing countries, in the face of pressure to dismantle such operations, have argued that they are needed for both public policy reasons (such as food security) and as protection against the concentrated marketing power of transnational food and agricultural corporations.

For these and other reasons the optimistic projections made about the welfare benefits of the Uruguay Round Agreement on Agriculture have not been borne out. Murphy (2002, p. 3) argues that such projections 'were wrong about the direction prices would take, wrong about who would get the increased exports and wrong about how farmers would respond to changes in support programs'. Indeed, modelling-based projections of the benefits of multilateral trade rules are likely to remain of limited value for human development outcomes until the global trade regime takes into account the concentration of market power in transnational agricultural trade and the distribution of its benefits.

Tariffication, quotas and safeguards

The Uruguay Round Agreement on Agriculture converted all non-tariff barriers into bound tariffs that represented the ceiling to which they could be raised.[1] In industrial countries these new tariffs were subject to unweighted average reductions of 36 per cent over 1995–2000 (from the 1986–88 base period), with a minimum reduction of 15 per cent in each tariff line. In developing countries tariffs were to be cut by an unweighted average of 24 per cent, with a reduction of at least 10 per cent in each tariff line, to be implemented over 1995–2004. No reduction commitments were required of the least developed countries.[2]

It was recognized that despite these reductions, tariffs would remain high—often prohibitively so—in many sectors. So, to provide market access for products subject to tariffs, tariff rate quotas were established (box 5.2). The tariff quota system is the only mechanism that provided real improvements in market access under the agriculture agreement. Quotas fall into two categories:

- 'Current market access opportunities', which are allocated on a bilateral basis to enable exporting countries to maintain the access they enjoyed before non-tariff barriers were 'tariffied' (that is, the access allowed under import quotas or 'voluntary' export restraints). Current access opportunities are provided to products whose imports accounted for at least 3 per cent of domestic consumption in the base period (1986–88). The current access quantity should be at least the same as imports during the base period. This can be increased during the implementation period.

- 'Minimum access opportunities', applied on a most-favoured-nation basis, guarantee access for imports with a total value equivalent to at least 5 per cent of domestic consumption in the base period. These opportunities are provided to products whose imports accounted for less than 3 per cent of domestic consumption during the base period. The minimum access quantity—the absolute quantity that a member is bound to import—is 3 per cent of domestic consumption in the base period, rising to 5 per cent by 2000 (2004 for developing countries).

The concept of market access opportunities is intended to ensure that the tariffication process does not reduce existing import levels. Nearly 40 members of the World Trade Organization (WTO) maintain a total of about 1,400 tariff quotas (table 5.1). The introduction of tariff quotas has created a complex system that lends itself to bilateral deals. In addition, the administration of tariff quotas has been such that less than two-thirds of the quotas have been filled. The quotas do not provide duty-free access. Quota tariff rates reach as high as 30 per cent, which in the industrial sector would be considered a tariff peak.

A Special Safeguard mechanism was established for imports subject to tariff conversion and specifically identified as subject to safeguards in country schedules. This mechanism allows countries to impose an additional duty (but not quantity restrictions) on a product if its import growth exceeds a certain level or import

---

BOX 5.2 AN EXAMPLE OF A TARIFF RATE QUOTA

A tariff rate quota is a two-tier tariff system. While the bound most-favoured-nation tariff on a certain import may be set at a relatively high rate (due to tariffication), a certain amount of that import is allowed at a much lower rate. For example, in 1999 the EU offered a quota tariff rate for 2 million tonnes of corn imports at a price of 24.45 euros a tonne. The most-favoured-nation (above-quota) rate was 48.45 euros a tonne. The actual fill rate—the share of actual imports compared with the quota quantity—was 67 per cent.

TABLE 5.1

Examples of 1995 tariff quota rates

	EU		Japan		US	
	Within-quota tariff rate	*Above-quota tariff rate*	*Within-quota tariff rate*	*Above-quota tariff rate*	*Within-quota tariff rate*	*Above-quota tariff rate*
Milk	18.0	56.1	22.0 (0–35.0)	125.1 (25.1–309.6)	7.0 (1.1–17.5)	82.6 (34.8–275.6)
Butter	26.8 (24.5–28.0)	97.1 (87.5–106.8)	35.0	264.0 (245.5–282.6)	6.6 (3.3–10.0)	58.5 (48.4–68.6)
Wheat	0	167.7 (131.5–203.9)	6.7 (0–20.0)	352.7	(n/a)	(n/a)

Note: The simple averages of the tariff rates are provided when different rates exist within a product category. The range of tariff rates is given in parentheses.
Source: UNCTAD, TD/B/WG.8/2/Add.1, 26 July 1995, table I.1.

prices fall below a certain level.[3] No proof of injury is required, and the Special Safeguard may be invoked almost automatically—without reference to whether a rise in import quantity or fall in import price below the trigger level actually had an adverse impact on domestic consumers. So far this mechanism has been used by only 38 WTO members, almost all of them industrial countries (Ruffer, Jones and Akroyd, 2002). This is because, as a result of the conditions imposed by the structural adjustment programmes of international financial institutions, many developing countries have eliminated non-tariff barriers and so have nothing to 'tariffy'.

Tariff reductions, peaks and escalation

While the Agreement on Agriculture eliminated the myriad non-tariff barriers from the agricultural trade regime, agricultural tariffs remain significantly higher than those on industrial products, partly due to the tariffication process. The average tariff on industrial goods fell from 40 per cent in 1945 to 4 per cent in 1995, yet agricultural tariffs still average 62 per cent (Beierle, 2002)—largely because industrial countries have lowered their tariffs in a way that fulfils the Agreement on Agriculture's technical requirements but violates its spirit and intent. Tariffs have been eliminated on non-sensitive and infrequently traded products that already had low rates, while tariffs on sensitive products with very high rates have been cut by the minimum 15 per cent.[4]

Moreover, in industrial countries the tariffication process has often resulted in tariffs that exceed the effective protection previously provided by non-tariff barriers. For example, in 1995 average tariffs in OECD countries were 214 per cent for wheat, 197 per cent for barley and 154 per cent for corn (Konandreas and Greenfield, 1996). Tariffication has also caused industrial countries' tariffs on some products to be much higher in 2002 than before the Uruguay Round ('dirty tariffication')—despite compliance with the technical requirements of the

Agreement on Agriculture. Higher tariffs are especially common for sensitive products of particular export interest to developing countries.

Tariff peaks and escalation also remain pronounced in industrial countries.[5] A 1999 study by the United Nations Conference on Trade and Development (UNCTAD) and the WTO found that more than half of these countries' tariff peaks applied to agriculture (including food processing) and fisheries products. Major developing country exports (such as sugar, tobacco and cotton) and those of potential export interest (such as processed foods) are often taxed at some of the highest rates—more than 100 per cent (Shirotori, 2000). OECD members impose such rates on products such as meat, sugar, chocolate and milk and other dairy products (OECD, 2001b). Fruits and vegetables also face high tariffs. For example, above-quota bananas are subject to a tariff of 180 per cent in the EU, and the rate for shelled groundnuts is 550 per cent in Japan and 132 per cent in the US. In some OECD countries tariffs exceed 30 per cent for food products such as fruit juices, canned meats, peanut butter and confections. And Canada, the EU, Japan and the US maintain tariff peaks of 350–900 per cent on food products such as sugar, rice, dairy products, meat, fruits, vegetables and fish (Shirotori, 2000).

Similarly, tariff escalation occurs in product chains of particular interest to developing countries, such as coffee, cocoa, oilseeds, vegetables, fruits and nuts (Shirotori, 2000). After the Uruguay Round effective rates of protection reached 44 per cent for wheat flour and 25 per cent for orange juice in the EU, 30 per cent for refined sugar in Japan and 42 per cent for condensed milk in the US (Lindland, 1997). Tariff escalation is probably one of the main impediments to export diversification for developing countries—and a major constraint to vertical diversification of their agricultural exports (Supper, 2000). This partly explains why most developing country exports are concentrated in the first stage of food processing and why high value-added food products account for only 5 per cent of the agricultural exports of the least developed countries and 17 per cent for developing countries overall (compared with almost a third for industrial countries). But in some cases fundamental constraints in developing countries are more important than trade barriers in industrial countries.[6]

Tariffs in developing countries tell a completely different story. For example, a study by the Food and Agriculture Organization (FAO, 1999b) assessed the impact of the Agreement on Agriculture on trade flows in 16 developing countries.[7] The study found a significant unfair asymmetry between the high continuing tariffs of industrial countries and the relatively low tariffs of developing countries. Although the study may have covered too short a period to fully assess the long-term impact on the countries studied, several case studies reported relevant experiences:

- Most of the developing countries had unilaterally reduced both their non-tariff barriers and applied tariffs under World Bank and IMF structural adjustment programmes prior to the Agreement on Agriculture's existence. Those reductions had significant distributional implications and, as indicated above, prevented the countries from using the tariffication and Special Safeguard mechanisms.

- Political economy factors kept these countries from using the declared bound tariff measures under the Agreement on Agriculture. These factors included the loan conditions imposed by international financial institutions, the political necessity of maintaining low food prices for consumers and the fear of damaging their relationships with industrial countries that provided them with preferential market access and development aid.

- Exports did not improve much during the agricultural reform period in these countries. This could be attributed to many factors, including supply constraints in many developing countries (especially the least developed) and quality, health and sanitation requirements in importing countries. There continues to be a need for greater clarity on standards for 'identical and similar conditions', particularly in terms of animal diseases. (See chapter 17 for a discussion of standards and their human development implications and impacts.)

- High tariff peaks and tariff escalation were common in export markets, especially those of industrial countries, for products of greatest importance to these developing countries.

Another study highlights the impacts of unilaterally reduced tariffs in developing countries (White, 2001). It suggests that their slashing of tariffs has allowed cheap imports of low-cost fruits, vegetables and grains that compete with (and often dislodge) domestic products and destroy local livelihoods. Whether juice from France displaces domestic juices in Guyana or heavily subsidized basic grains from the US cut into native corn sales in Mexico, such imports can have disastrous income and consumption effects on poor families—especially for women and girls within them (White, 2001).

SUBSIDIES

Subsidies include both domestic support measures and export subsidies. Both have been the subject of intense, widespread debate and negotiation in the WTO, leading to calls for their reduction or even elimination. Such subsidies have also contributed to export dumping.

Domestic support measures

The Agreement on Agriculture's domestic support disciplines allow industrial country agribusinesses to buy and sell agricultural crops at prices below the cost of production, creating unfair competition for farmers in both developing and more efficient industrial countries (box 5.3). Indeed, many critics argue that by enabling the use of their preferred instruments for agricultural support, while cracking down on tariffs, quotas and subsidies in developing countries, the most powerful agriculture-exporting industrial countries engineered the Agreement on Agriculture so that its special and differential treatment works for them rather than for developing countries. This has had major negative consequences for food security, farmer livelihoods and employment in developing countries.

BOX 5.3 DOMESTIC SUPPORT MEASURES UNDER THE AGREEMENT ON AGRICULTURE

Most domestic support measures allowed under the Agreement on Agriculture fall into one of three categories: the 'amber box', 'blue box' or 'green box'. All measures considered distorting to production and trade (with a few exceptions) fall into the amber box. Such support is subject to reduction commitments measured through changes in the Aggregate Measure of Support, with reductions set at 20.0 per cent for industrial countries and 13.3 per cent for developing countries. But these targets are overall averages; the percentage change for specific products can be higher or lower. For countries not giving large subsidies to agriculture, the Agreement on Agriculture stipulates de minimis levels: 5 per cent for industrial countries and 10 per cent for developing countries.

The blue box, a last-minute concession to the EU that permitted the adoption of the Agreement on Agriculture, is an exception to the general rule that all subsidies linked to production must be reduced or kept within defined minimal (de minimis) levels. It covers payments directly linked to land size or livestock as long as the activity being supported limits production. Blue box proponents view its subsidies as less trade distorting than amber box subsidies. Although the blue box is a permanent provision of the Agreement on Agriculture, a number of countries—including most developing countries and the US—have called for its phase-out.

The green box covers subsidies that are expected to cause minimal or no trade distortion. Such subsidies have to be publicly funded but must not involve price support. Examples include the direct income support that the US provides its farmers, which is formally decoupled from production levels and prices, and environmental protection subsidies. No limits or reductions are placed on such support.

Other domestic support measures include the de minimis provision and the special and differential treatment provision. Special and differential treatment includes the right for developing countries—especially the least developed countries—to delay or opt out of certain liberalization commitments and to receive special market access for their exports to industrial countries.

Source: GATT, 1994; UNCTAD, 2000.

Implementation problems for developing countries include asymmetrical legal rights in the use of domestic support measures (in favour of industrial countries); lack of product specificity associated with Aggregate Measure of Support commitments, leading to the circumvention of tariff reductions on products of greatest interest to them; non-recognition of 'negative' Aggregate Measure of Support calculations;[8] and inflation and exchange rate fluctuations that can make it difficult to stay within the boundaries agreed under the Aggregate Measure of Support.[9]

The amount of domestic support provided in the base period (1986–88) was used to calculate reductions in the Aggregate Measure of Support for the 'amber box' (see box 5.3). The higher support was in the base period, the more it remained, even after compliance with the agreement. In most industrial countries declarations of such support exceeded 20 per cent of agricultural GDP, with almost half exceeding 50 per cent. Yet many developing countries claimed a zero value in the base period because they either could not provide such support fiscally or were politically constrained from doing so by IMF and World Bank structural adjustment programmes. This has restricted their ability to take advantage of the 'amber box', which many of them can use only within de minimis limits.

Similarly, because the Aggregate Measure of Support is presented in aggregate rather than product-specific terms, industrial countries have been able to increase their domestic support for sensitive products of export interest to developing countries (rice, sugar, dairy products) as long as they are able to meet their overall reduction commitments. By contrast, relatively high inflation in developing countries has led to a negative bias in comparisons and calculations under the Aggregate Measure of Support—a problem compounded by the fact that countries can be challenged by other WTO members if they offset 'negative' product-specific support against positive non-specific support when calculating the net sum of their subsidies. (India, for example, has been challenged by some WTO members for taking this approach.) Overall, the amber box has institutionalized a huge imbalance between the ability of industrial and developing countries to legally use domestic support measures.

There is also concern that blue box subsidies will be institutionalized rather than viewed as transitional, while different interpretations of permitted green box measures leave it open to the charge that it is too broadly defined and biased in favour of subsidies that only industrial countries can afford. Further, there are questions about whether many such subsides (especially direct income support to US farmers) do not distort trade—both because of their significant size and because there is widespread agreement that decoupling does not sterilize the impact of production levels and prices on export volumes. Some other measures allowed in this category, such as the provision of infrastructure services (including irrigation), could also have significant production-enhancing effects, especially when the initial base of such services is weak (Ruffer, Jones and Akroyd, 2002). The development argument can be made that investment in such production-enhancing measures should be allowed for developing countries but treated as part of a 'development box' (see below).

Export subsidies

The Agreement on Agriculture imposed the first meaningful disciplines on agricultural export subsidies. Countries maintaining such subsidies made commitments on their volume and value in specific product categories. These levels were subject to reductions of 36 per cent in value and 21 per cent in quantity for industrial countries over a 6-year period and 24 per cent in value and 14 per cent in quantity for developing countries over a 10-year period. Countries not maintaining export subsides were prohibited from introducing them in the future.

A major implementation problem with export subsidy reduction commitments is that only a few industrial countries have the right to use them. The EU accounts for 90 per cent of global export subsidies currently recognized under the Agreement on Agriculture.

Export credits, used primarily by the US, should be treated as export subsidies because of their similar trade impacts. They remain one of the main outstanding implementation issues and are to be negotiated under article 10 of the agreement on agriculture. Export credits are usually in the form of guaranteed bank loans at competitive interest rates and in some cases have the same effect as export subsidies in encouraging exports. They are one of the most popular means of circumventing export subsidy commitments. In 1998 the US export credit guarantee programme rose to $5.9 billion, nearly twice its amount in 1997 (UNCTAD, 1999).

These concerns meld with others, such as banning export controls and other export prohibition measures such as export taxes and restrictions—on food products, among others. These concerns have not been adequately dealt with in the Agreement on Agriculture. Josling (1998) proposes that export taxes be treated similarly to quantitative restrictions because it is inconsistent to leave in place the possibility of export taxes and quantitative restrictions that have immediate and harmful effects on developing country food importers.

In many developing countries export subsidies have had even more adverse effects on food security, livelihoods and employment than many domestic support measures. Export subsidies have allowed the continuing export of industrial countries' agriculture surpluses at prices below production costs, depressing world prices and causing import surges and agricultural dumping in developing countries. It has been estimated that the billions of dollars the EU and the US spend every year subsidizing their farmers—and protecting them from more efficient producers in developing and other industrial countries—allow them to export crops at prices more than a third lower than the cost of production. As a result 'some of the world's poorest countries are competing against its richest treasuries' (Oxfam International, 2002, p. 11). European dumping of milk powder in Jamaica vividly illustrates this point (box 5.4).

Indeed, subsidized agricultural output in industrial countries—through export subsidies and trade-distorting domestic support—leads to unfair competition in the markets of developing countries. It also obstructs imports from other developing countries, leading to significant income losses for efficient, low-cost, non-subsidized, agricultural exporters. So, for example, even though EU dairy producers have some of the world's highest production costs, they control half the world market (UNCTAD, 1999c).

Such subsidies offer potential short-term benefits only when they subsidize food imports for developing countries that are dependent on them or when they mitigate high international food prices for developing countries. But export subsidies rarely mitigate high international prices, because they are a support arrangement that results in the highest subsidies and food aid to developing countries when their needs are lowest—and the lowest subsidies and food aid when needs

> **BOX 5.4 EUROPEAN DUMPING OF MILK POWDER IN JAMAICA**
>
> Again and again, dairy farmers in Jamaica have to throw away fresh milk because they can no longer sell all the milk their cows produce. They are losing the battle against cheap dairy imports—especially subsidized milk powder from the EU.
>
> Aubrey Taylor, president of the St. Elizabeth dairy cooperative, explains: 'There is no market for fresh milk. No processor in Jamaica has any contract with any dairy farmer. It's a game of chance. Yes, milk powder is cheaper than our local milk. But what you must realize is that imports of milk powder have export subsidies on them. The Jamaican farmer has no subsidies whatsoever. Our production figures are true costs.'
>
> Until the early 1990s Jamaican dairy farmers were reasonably protected against imports, and the sector's output was growing fast. But then the Jamaican government liberalized the dairy market as part of adjustment policies mandated by the World Bank, and the country became increasingly flooded with foreign milk powder. Most imports originated in Europe, where an estimated 4 million euros a year were spent subsidizing exports for Jamaica. Jamaican dairy processors—the largest and most influential being Europe-based Nestlé—preferred cheap and easy European milk powder, and marketing opportunities for fresh milk became increasingly difficult. Nestlé had previously said that it would leave Jamaica if tariffs were increased, and in recent years has increasingly turned its back on local production.
>
> In 1999 the Jamaican dairy sector called on the European Commission and EU members to eliminate subsidies on EU dairy exports to Jamaica. But that plea fell on deaf ears, as did a recommendation to increase import duties on powdered milk. Despite its Uruguay Round commitment to reduce export subsidies, the EU still exports milk at prices well below production costs.
>
> *Source:* Oxfam International, 2002.

are highest (because subsidies are given most when international prices are lowest and least when international prices are highest). Moreover, such subsidies are rarely accompanied by technical assistance and financial support for agricultural research and development, with the goal of reducing developing countries' vulnerability and dependence on food imports. Thus such subsidies cannot be considered supportive of sustainable human development even if they result in lower food prices for poor consumers in the short term.

Although eliminating export subsidies is an important goal, doing so will not end export dumping. Export dumping is a wider problem and can be caused as much by domestic production subsidies as by export subsidies.

Export dumping

Export dumping is widespread.[10] It is the consequence of low-priced exports resulting from overproduction, even though such production has not benefited from export subsidies. Critics allege, for example, that export dumping is a structural feature of US agriculture. Combining data on producer costs and government support payments and estimates of transportation costs, Ritchie, Wisniewski and

Murphy (2000) estimate that US wheat and cotton have been dumped onto the world market for up to 30 per cent less than the cost of production.

Most of the benefits of such exports have accrued not to small US farmers but to giant US agribusinesses. Most farmers in both developing and industrial countries are price-takers who depend on large, often transnational corporations for their inputs and the sale of their products. Developing country farmers who depend on corn for their livelihoods typically do not compete with US farmers but with the giant companies that dominate the export of grain to their countries—companies that are the prime beneficiaries of US farm policy (Murphy, 2002). Farm-gate prices that do not capture the cost of production in the EU or US are transferred globally through transnational corporations' food production chains. This globalization of agricultural dumping requires multilateral rules, yet the Agreement on Agriculture has failed to address it. In fact, it can be seen as legitimizing it by encouraging decoupled payments, which have not been effective in controlling export volumes.

Some economists argue that such dumping should be welcomed because it is, in effect, a subsidy to developing country consumers. And some developing country governments appear to have internalized this argument. But this view is shortsighted, because cheap imports send the wrong message to the importing country's agricultural sector, reinforcing an existing bias against it. Dumping can have serious long-term consequences for agricultural production and for the livelihoods of the poor producers who make up a significant portion of the population in developing countries, sometimes outnumbering consumers. Dumping also reduces farm incomes, employment and food security—and so human development.

A far more preferable and sustainable approach to ensuring low food prices for consumers would be for developing countries, with technical and financial support from industrial countries, to invest in significant agricultural research and development for the production of their basic food staples. India, which spends more money on agriculture than any other Asian country, is testimony to this given the dramatic improvements in its food security since the mid-1960s (Fan, Hazell and Thorat, 1999). In India the efficacy of spending on agricultural research and extension was second only to that of roads (and greater than education, rural development, irrigation, power, soil and water and health). Every 100 billion rupees of investment in research and development increased agricultural productivity by 7 per cent.

Sustained investments in research and development would probably also allow developing countries to liberalize their agricultural sectors over the medium term by reducing protection for food staples. Yet in many developing countries spending on agricultural research and development has actually been falling because of budget pressures and internally or externally induced structural adjustment programmes.

The 'peace clause'

Article 13 of the Agreement on Agriculture sets out conditions under which its provisions supersede other WTO rights and obligations. This 'peace clause' is applicable for 9 years and set to expire at the end of 2003. The clause was designed to reduce the threat of trade disputes during the period of farm trade reform, especially in industrial countries. Its expiration will subject agricultural subsidies to the same disciplines as industrial subsidies. Any extension of the peace clause will require consensus, giving developing countries important political leverage in negotiations on agriculture.

At present, however, the green box support measures cannot be subject to countervailing duty action or other subsidy action nor the subject of complaints that they impair tariff concessions. Domestic and export subsidies that are not in breach of the reduction obligations cannot be legally challenged under the subsidies agreement. This means that countries are powerless to prevent the loss of export markets. While countervailing duties can be applied where such subsidies cause injury to domestic producers "due restraint" is expected to be shown in initiating countervailing duty investigations.

Subsidies: the overall picture

OECD members provide about $1 billion a day in agricultural subsidies—more than six times what they spend on official development assistance for developing countries (UNDP, 2002). Since 1997 these subsidies have increased 28 per cent; although EU and US spending under the Aggregate Measure of Support decreased, most of this spending was simply transferred into the 'green box'. As green-box spending surged, agricultural support in OECD countries increased—instead of dwindling in accordance with the intent of the Agreement on Agriculture. Indeed, the agreement appears to have led some industrial countries to start providing expensive subsidies, closing off cheaper, regulation-based controls that could benefit human development.

Half of OECD spending on agricultural support occurs in the EU, and 39 per cent in Japan. US support for agriculture rose to $28 billion in 2000, and the 2002 US Farm Bill (issued after the Doha conference) authorizes $180 billion in domestic farm support over the next 10 years. Some of the main reasons for and implications of the US legislation are analysed in box 5.5.

FOOD SECURITY, EMPLOYMENT AND LIVELIHOODS

The Agreement on Agriculture directly affects rural livelihoods, food security and farmer incomes. Thus all WTO members—particularly developing countries—need to have adequate policy space and flexibility to ensure food security and protect the employment and livelihoods of their populations.

Agriculture's non-market roles

Agriculture not only produces goods that are marketable and tradable, it also provides non-tradable public goods and services that are undervalued by the market. These public goods and services include environmental conservation, rural development, balanced regional development and, above all, food security.

Box 5.5 The 2002 US Farm Security and Rural Investment Act (Farm Bill)

The US led the calls for the Uruguay Round, and during it pushed for an Agreement on Agriculture. US negotiating positions on trade and agriculture have consistently echoed those of the Cairns Group, made up of the 18 industrial and developing countries most attached to liberalization of agricultural markets. Despite this and its international commitment to cut agricultural subsidies and tariffs, in May 2002 the US passed an extremely expensive piece of domestic legislation. The 2002 Farm Bill reinstates government payments intended to make up any shortfalls between market prices and government-set target prices—so-called counter-cyclical payments.

The Farm Bill governs not just agricultural production but also measures linked to agriculture and trade (export subsidies, credits and promotion), nutrition (including food entitlements for poor people), conservation, forestry, energy, research, rural development and credits for producers. The bill increases agricultural subsidies by almost 80 per cent, with $180 billion provisionally allocated over the next 10 years. Though such payments can be reduced if their value violates the Agreement on Agriculture, such amounts run counter to the spirit of the agreement and to the recent US proposal advocating liberalization of agriculture (see box 5.1).

Indeed, and especially against that background, the Farm Bill provoked enormous outrage in world trade circles. The contradictions between domestic politics and international trade policies could not be clearer. It is also ironic that the US has opened itself to criticism in this area at the same time that negotiators in Geneva are discussing ways of reducing the domestic support of WTO members—as a direct result of the US proposal seeking reductions in all 'trade-distorting' domestic support. With the new legislation the US can no longer pretend that it is trying to limit production (as in the past), because it has reinstated a target price through the use of counter-cyclical payments. This reintroduction of 'amber box' spending (agreed by all members as distorting production and trade and subject to scheduled reductions through the WTO) is what has upset the world community—that and the now-visible level of US spending on farm support, which is not new but has become harder to hide.

The Farm Bill is clearly not beneficial for developing country producers. It will stimulate production in the US that is not warranted by market signals. Unwanted production will flood world markets, not only directly in commercial sales and (often inappropriate) food aid, but also in the form of artificially cheap feed for livestock. Moreover, the bill is not good for most US farmers. It subsidizes agribusinesses, allowing them to buy very cheap, with the government then making up some of the difference with direct payments to farmers. (In 1998 the average US corn farmer received $30,000 in government subsidies and $8,000 in net income.) The loss on commercial sales is so large that most subsidies simply repay bank loans. Who benefits? The company buying corn for $1.80 a bushel that costs $2.70 a bushel to grow.

Rather than disciplining the market power of transnational agribusinesses, the US government is providing them with massive subsidies. In turn, US production of certain crops (such as wheat) is so high that the artificially low price in the US market becomes the world market price. Developing country farmers find themselves unable to compete with this artificial price and cannot compete in local markets with the rising imports that result. And producers in both industrial and developing countries are left without livelihoods, despite the value of their products.

The Farm Bill continues a long history of US government refusal to confront the lack of competition in its agricultural markets, which leaves US farmers with little choice in where to buy their inputs and where to market their produce. Over the past few years the US has experienced an unprecedented increase in market concentration in nearly all agricultural sectors—for example, three firms handle more than 80 per cent of US corn exports. Many US farmers opposed the Farm Bill, and some have proposed a Food From Family Farms Act to restore farmers' ability to earn their income from the market. Such an act would require regulating oligopolistic power in the market. Elements of this proposal were discussed during the Farm Bill hearings and are under consideration as separate legislation.

Source: Murphy, 2002; Biswajit Dhar, 2002, 'Subsidising US Farmers under AoA', *The Economic Times* (India), 9 August.

It is an almost universal belief that the right to food is inalienable since food is essential to life. There is also widespread agreement that food should be accessible to everyone, not just those with purchasing power. The 1996 World Food Summit concluded that 'food security exists when all people, at all times, have physical and economic access to sufficient, safe, and nutritious food to meet their dietary needs and food preferences for an active and healthy life' (FAO, 1996, article 1). Amartya Sen's entitlements approach provides a useful framework for exploring the impact of trade policy on food security at the household level (see Sen, 1999).[11] But the framework's focus on the household level misses important broader issues for food security, such as a country's foreign exchange constraints (Green and Priyadarshi, 2001). The two aspects—the household level and the broader issues—are equally important for food security and human development.

A fundamental tenet of the food security argument advanced by developing countries is that agriculture is a way of life and the means to sustainable livelihoods and employment—and so essential to human development for the vast majority of their populations. Even small changes in agricultural employment or prices can have major negative effects on food security and human development. Similarly, cheap or subsidized imports can jeopardize food security and rural livelihoods.

Developing countries' food security concerns differ from those of industrial countries because food accounts for a significant share of household spending among the absolute poor and middle-income groups who make up most of their populations. In Haiti, for example, rural households spend two-thirds of their income on food. For landless peasants—the poorest of the poor—this percentage climbs even higher (Oxfam International, 2002). By contrast, food accounts for a small and falling share of household spending in industrial countries.

There is widespread agreement that food security in developing countries is one of the most valid non-trade agricultural concerns. Although the Agreement on Agriculture recognizes the need to take this into account and countries are allowed to exempt public stockholdings for food security reasons, some argue that the agreement does not pay sufficient attention to ensuring food security or even food supply to world markets. (Export controls and restrictions, for example, work against this.) Critics also believe that food security is an important socio-political concern and national security issue that needs to be explicitly addressed in trade negotiations, especially for large developing agrarian economies.

From a human development perspective there can be little doubt that universal food security must be made a priority. Trade policy should not be the exclusive or even predominant focus of strategies aimed at achieving this objective: as Sen's framework indicates, trade policy is merely one means of ensuring or contributing to food security, and should not be viewed as an end in itself. Developing countries have traditionally had a range of domestic policy instruments to deal with food security, farmer livelihoods and other agricultural development objectives. But the design and implementation of certain parts of the Agreement on Agriculture— especially its disciplines on tariffs, domestic support and export subsidies—have constrained some of those policy choices. These have had different implications for different developing countries depending, for example, on whether they are food-importing or -exporting countries. The Agreement on Agriculture's impacts also differ for developing countries for whom food crops comprise a significant share of their tradables and for those who are not reliant on significant food imports but largely trade in commercial crops.

Developing countries' growing trade deficits in food

The emerging empirical evidence on subsidies has serious implications for food security, livelihoods and employment in developing countries. With rapidly grow-ing trade, developing countries have become much more dependent on food imports. In 1997 food trade totalled $460 billion—four times its value 20 years ear-lier. Developing countries' share of imports rose from 28 per cent in 1974 to 37 per cent in 1997, but their share of exports increased from 30 per cent to just 34 per cent. Thus the trade balance of developing countries in food commodities has turned negative, with a net deficit of $13 billion in 1997 (FAO, 1999a). Since the early 1970s the drop in food exports relative to imports has been especially sharp for the least developed countries (figure 5.1).

The Food and Agriculture Organization study of 16 developing countries cited earlier (FAO, 1999b) also finds a growing imbalance between exports and imports. In Egypt merchandise imports grew 50 per cent between 1995 and 1997 and the food bill increased 37 per cent—while exports rose only 17 per cent. Most of the other countries studied showed remarkably similar experiences with import surges, particularly of poultry and skim milk powder.

By contrast, few aggregate improvements in agricultural exports occurred dur-ing the agricultural reform period in these countries. Only Thailand increased food exports—although some case studies pointed to good prospects for non-tradi-tional exports, among them fruits and vegetables from Bangladesh, Fiji, Guyana, Jamaica and Pakistan. In all, however, the FAO study concluded that while trade liberalization led to an immediate and asymmetrical surge in food imports, the countries studied could not increase agricultural exports significantly because of protected markets and export subsidies in industrial countries. In some cases where countries were successful in raising the volume of exports, their value fell.

An even more serious trend, according to the same FAO report, is the rise in the trade deficit in cereals—from 17 million to 104 million tonnes over 30 years.

FIGURE 5.1

Food exports as a share of food imports in the least developed and other developing countries, 1971–99

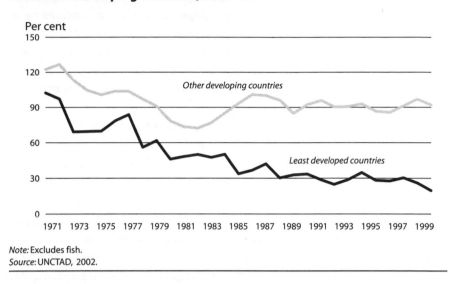

Note: Excludes fish.
Source: UNCTAD, 2002.

This development contradicts the flow of history: most countries, industrial and developing, have achieved food security through enhanced domestic production. Moreover, projections for the next 20 years indicate that almost all the increases in world food demand will take place in developing countries (FAO, 2000; Pinstrup-Andersen, Pandya-Lorch and Rosegrant, 1999). Historical experience shows that ensuring physical access to food in developing countries will be possible only if there is a minimal level of national self-reliance. Several factors can make it difficult to achieve such self-reliance, including limited foreign exchange for imports (and the high opportunity costs for other sectors, especially technology development, of spending scarce foreign exchange on food imports), an inability to increase exports quickly and poor physical infrastructure.

Limited national self-reliance for food has serious gender and other distributional dimensions. Thus the erosion of domestic food production resulting from trade liberalization has multiple repercussions for food security, social cohesion in rural communities and women's income, employment and status.

Food-insecure countries

Food-insecure countries must be differentiated from those that are not. The Marrakesh Agreement, the culmination of the Uruguay Round, recognized net food-importing developing countries as deserving special consideration. As indicated, even the most optimistic projections of welfare changes from agricultural liberalization acknowledge losers as well as winners. The losers include many developing countries—including some of the poorest least developed countries, because they are net food importers.

The losers were expected to suffer from rising food prices resulting from cuts in subsidies in food-exporting countries. The WTO Committee on Agriculture—and so the Agreement on Agriculture—identify net food-importing developing countries as a separate group from least developed countries (as classified by the UN) and low-income food-deficit countries. This decision committed WTO members to, among other things, provide sufficient food aid to meet developing countries' needs during the reform programme and to include technical assistance for agricultural productivity in aid programmes for the least developed countries and net food-importing developing countries.

Despite this agreement and the repeated requests of these countries, little has been done because the agreement does not legally compel industrial countries to provide food aid or technical assistance. According to Hesham Youssef (1999), a senior official in Egypt's Ministry of Foreign Affairs, food aid commitments to the least developed countries and net food-importing developing countries dropped after the Marrakesh Agreement. Between 1994 and 1997 food aid in cereals dropped by nearly two-thirds for net food-importing developing countries—and for Egypt by more than three-quarters. In addition, many donors (including Australia, Canada and Japan) reduced their technical and financial assistance during this period (though Norway increased it).

Over the past two decades the least developed countries and net food-importing developing countries have become less able to finance normal commercial imports of basic foods, reflecting weak growth in their export earnings and changes in their terms of trade (Shirotori, 2000). Since 1980 the least developed countries have accounted for a shrinking share of world exports of goods and services (figure 5.2). Moreover, in the late 1990s food imports accounted for a large share of merchandise imports in the least developed countries: more than 20 per cent in almost 20 countries, more than 30 per cent in more than 10 countries and 40 per cent or more in 4 countries (figure 5.3; see also figure 5.1).

Because a human development perspective places high priority on ensuring food security at all levels—country, household, individual—this trend must be reversed. Concerns about weak implementation of the Marrakesh Agreement's provisions for least developed and net food-importing developing countries were reflected in the Doha decision on implementation issues and concerns. The WTO Committee on Agriculture established an inter-agency panel to examine ways to improve access to multilateral financing for the least developed and net food-importing developing countries, to meet their short-term financing needs for commercial imports of basic foods (WTO Committee on Agriculture, 2001).[12] As part of its analysis the panel also considered the feasibility of establishing a revolving fund proposed by a group of net food-importing developing countries. The panel's final report recommended, among other things, improving access to existing IMF facilities and further examining the feasibility of establishing a borrowing facility for private food importers in least developed and net food-importing developing

FIGURE 5.2

*Shares of world exports of goods and services from the
least developed and other developing countries, 1980–99*

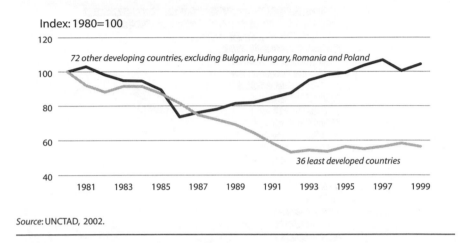

Index: 1980=100

72 other developing countries, excluding Bulgaria, Hungary, Romania and Poland

36 least developed countries

Source: UNCTAD, 2002.

countries (WTO, 2002). Discussions on the modality for such a facility continue in the sessions of the Committee on Agriculture.

At the country level a necessary question is whether the least developed and net food-importing developing country groupings capture all the countries that merit food security consideration in the context of the Agreement on Agriculture. Different views and criteria have been suggested. Diaz-Bonilla, Thomas and Robinson (2002), for example, categorize 167 countries using five measures of food security. They conclude that some of the categories used by the WTO appear inadequate to capture food security concerns. The authors classify as food insecure only 10 of the 18 developing countries identified by the WTO as net food-importing (11 if Egypt is included because of its high trade stress). But they identify many other food-insecure countries not included in this category.

By contrast, the UN list of least developed countries corresponds far more accurately to countries suffering from food insecurity. Diaz-Bonilla, Thomas and Robinson find that just three of the least developed countries are not food insecure. The authors also find a number of developing countries that are not among the groups of least developed or net food-importing countries—including El Salvador, Georgia, Mongolia and Nicaragua—but have food security profiles similar to others considered more vulnerable. The authors conclude that the category of net food-importing developing countries should use the least developed countries as its starting point, but include others classified as food insecure based on objective criteria. Whatever criteria are used, such a change would significantly increase the number of countries classified as food insecure.

Diaz-Bonilla, Thomas and Robinson also show that some industrial countries (Japan, Norway, EU countries) and high-income developing countries (Republic

FIGURE 5.3

Food imports as a share of all merchandise imports in the least developed countries, by country, 1997–99

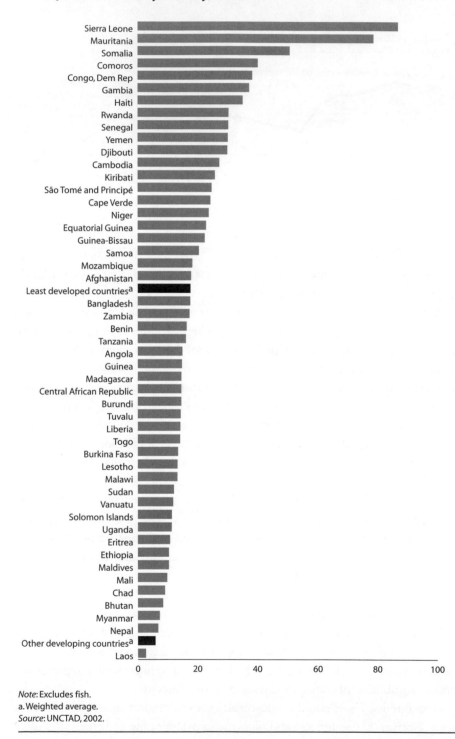

Note: Excludes fish.
a. Weighted average.
Source: UNCTAD, 2002.

of Korea) that have used multifunctionality to argue that food security is a national concern would not qualify as food insecure. In short, the study shows why WTO discussions on food security should be limited to food-insecure developing countries—while expanding the list of such countries.

Employment and livelihoods

Surging food imports have had severe employment effects in some developing countries. In Sri Lanka, for example, a significant increase in food imports since 1996 has caused a decline in domestic production of many food products—reducing rural employment. To sustain agricultural development and food security, the country must have greater flexibility in providing support to agricultural production in the short to medium term (FAO, 1999b).

Similar effects on farmer employment and livelihoods emerged in the Philippines after it signed the Agreement on Agriculture and in Mexico as a result of the North American Free Trade Agreement (NAFTA). Although NAFTA is not a WTO agreement, its agriculture agreement's effects on the employment and livelihoods of Mexican farmers are instructive (box. 5.6).

Implications of different types and scales of agricultural production

Dominant forms of agricultural production are fundamentally different in industrial and most developing countries. Differences stem not only from the technological inputs and production models used in subsistence and industrial agriculture, but also from the organization and basic objectives of these two production types.[13] The significant market failure and other institutional differences between developing and industrial countries increase the challenge for developing countries of shifting from traditional to non-traditional crop production. These differences also raise serious doubts about whether a trade regime based on market access can ensure farmer livelihoods and agricultural sustainability in developing countries—because the regime was designed on the assumption that industrial agriculture predominates in all countries. That is clearly not the case in most developing countries.

The agricultural economy of the Philippines, a middle-income developing country, illustrates some of these issues (Pascual and Gilpo, 2001). Although subsistence and industrial agriculture coexist, most of the country's farming involves small-scale production of traditional food and cash crops such as rice, coconuts, corn and other vegetables. These are typically cultivated on small plots averaging 1.5 hectares. Manual labour predominates; though some mechanization has occurred in rice production, there is very little in corn. As a result productivity is much lower than in industrial countries, where average rice yields are three times those in the Philippines—and corn yields are five times.

Moreover, in the Philippines the mechanized farming typical of industrial agriculture in industrial countries is found primarily on plantations dominated by

Box 5.6 Effects of agricultural trade agreements in the Philippines and Mexico

The Philippines and the Agreement on Agriculture

The Philippines experienced its first agricultural trade deficits since the 1970s in the six years following the 1994 Uruguay Round agreement. A net food exporter from the 1970s until the 1990s, the Philippines became a net importer by 2000, including from other Southeast Asian countries. In addition to significantly reducing domestic self-sufficiency in staples such as rice and corn, this change further depleted the country's foreign exchange reserves—already strained by debt. The shift has also hurt rural employment and livelihoods.

Agricultural export earnings were expected to increase by billions of pesos a year after 1994, generating 500,000 additional jobs a year. But instead, traditional exports such as coconuts, abaca and sugar have lost markets. Corn production suffered significant negative growth in 1994, 1995, 1998 and 2000 (from −2 to −12 per cent), partly because of cheaper subsidized imports. With incomes falling, some corn farmers in the southern Philippines have abandoned farming. Moreover, farms once devoted to staple crops have been converted into agribusiness plantations, industrial zones and real estate sites, displacing many rural people from their livelihoods and employment. By 1998 the agriculture sector had lost an estimated 710,000 jobs, and by 2000 another 2 million. Although the East Asian financial crisis and other factors played a significant role in this process, so did the Agreement on Agriculture.

Mexico and the North American Free Trade Agreement

Corn is more than Mexico's staple food: it plays a central role in the country's cultural heritage, with legend citing it as the source of humankind. But since signing the North American Free Trade Agreement (NAFTA) in 1994, Mexico has been flooded with corn grown by US farmers. Subsidized by billions of dollars from the US government, these farmers grow surplus crops for massive exports. Between 1993 and 2000 Mexican corn imports increased eighteen-fold. About a quarter of the corn consumed in Mexico now comes from the US, and that share is projected to increase. Cheap corn should mean cheaper food—yet the price of corn flour tortillas has not dropped. Prices stay high because a cartel of companies holds a monopoly on sales.

Small Mexican corn farmers—who account for 29 per cent of rural employment (1.7 million workers)—cannot compete with cheap corn imports from the US. In the absence of measures mitigating the negative distributional impacts of denying protection to small corn farmers, income and livelihood losses hurt women and poor farmers the most. Female corn farmers are typically engaged in subsistence production to feed their families or sell their produce in local markets. Poor farmers receive none of the huge subsidies that support their US competitors—and the small subsidies they once received from the Mexican government were slashed because of NAFTA.

Poverty has forced many poor farmers off the land, increasing migration to cities. The most vulnerable are the poorest peasants, who make up 40 per cent of Mexico's corn farmers and eat all the corn they grow. In theory the falling price of corn should not have affected them because they never sold their crops. Yet they have suffered because those slightly better off felt the squeeze and, as their incomes fell, could no longer afford to hire casual labour. Such jobs were crucial to the poorest farmers, and without this income they cannot survive on their land.

Beyond family tragedies is the shrinking of corn biodiversity—an important gene pool for the entire world. The poorest farmers were more likely to grow types of corn that can withstand infertile soils and other hostile environmental factors. Moreover, all these changes have come about at breakneck speed. NAFTA projected that the price of Mexican corn would fall in line with international prices over a 15-year period. It happened in just 30 months.

Source: Pascual and Gilpo, 2001; Oxfam International, 2002; Beneria and Mendoza, 1995.

foreign transnational corporations. Such plantations account for a small portion of the country's agricultural production and overall employment, and remit significant portions of their profits overseas. This situation—in a middle income country with relatively high education and health indicators—illustrates the difficulties of speaking of a 'level playing field' and 'free market competition' between subsistence and industrial agriculture. Subsistence agriculture like that in the Philippines is widely prevalent in developing countries, while transnational corporate industrial agriculture is largely a phenomenon of industrial countries.

Shifting from traditional to non-traditional agricultural exports requires intensifying inputs and upgrading technologies, and so involves dilemmas, choices and consequences (box 5.7). And even when circumstances are favourable—with generous development assistance and assured export markets—the results can be dismal.

Achieving human development goals will continue to be difficult as long as the Agreement on Agriculture is based on a market access paradigm that assumes all countries can engage equally in market-oriented agricultural production. The assumption that intensifying inputs and upgrading technologies can level the playing field between industrial and developing countries in the short to medium term also raises serious questions. Such policy measures would have serious distributional impacts and gender implications.

Food security and sustainable livelihoods are important gender concerns. Where women are mainly involved in traditional food production and men in non-traditional cash crop production, shifting from the former to the latter translates into benefits that favour men. Female household members typically lose their already limited control over cash crops and have to increase their household and cash crop work—increasing the gender bias in agricultural production (Campbell and Warner, 1997; Cagatay, 2001). Furthermore, even when women find work in commercial agriculture, they continue to be responsible for unpaid household labour.

Moreover, even where women's employment rises as a result of a shift to export-oriented production, they benefit only if they directly receive the higher prices of exported crops. Whether that happens depends on a host of factors often weighted against women: control over land and other productive resources, preferences for male labour as agricultural production becomes mechanized and access to credit, training and technology. To the extent that tax incentives for export promotion imply budget cuts for social services, women and children are affected most, both because of the direct effects of such cuts on health and other social

Box 5.7 Moving to non-traditional exports: The experience in Central America

In the 1980s Central America's debt crisis led to the promotion of non-traditional agricultural exports, with a focus on input-intensive methods. This policy, supported by the US Agency for International Development, encouraged exports from the region to markets worldwide, especially the US. Products promoted included melons, strawberries, broccoli, cauliflower, snow peas and squash shipped directly to US supermarkets.

Many small Central American farmers had little choice but to convert to the new crops. Trade policies had undercut the viability of traditional corn and bean cultivation, leaving them without the safety net of basic grain production for domestic markets and household consumption. Although the drive for new export crops led to impressive increases in production and exports in some countries, non-traditional agricultural exports often undermined the economic positions of small farmers. Among small farmers, common problems during this period included:

- Fluctuating prices and services. Early adopters of non-traditional crops were given extensive support: credit, full-time extension workers, certified disease-free seeds and purchase contracts with export companies. The first year of conversion was an outstanding success. Although seeds and contracts were not provided in the second year, more farmers planted the new crops based on the experiences of their peers the previous year. But many farmers suffered heavy disease losses because of the poor-quality seeds used, and about half defaulted on their credit. Moreover, US prices dropped in response to cheaper imports of these crops from other countries. In the third year all farmers defaulted on their credit in some areas. As a result the market began to show a bias against small producers. Larger producers were offered contracts more readily because packers and exporters thought they had better quality controls and because their smaller number made it easier and cheaper to contract with them.

- Limited access to capital and credit. Start-up costs were much higher for non-traditional than traditional crops. In one country a small farmer's costs for producing snow peas were nearly 15 times those for basic grains. Moreover, credit was difficult to obtain because of stringent criteria and high interest rates.

- Low bargaining power. Farm size was a major determinant of price: small farmers had less bargaining power and were more vulnerable to exploitation by intermediaries. Moreover, non-traditional crops offered the worst of all marketing worlds for small farmers. Such crops were perishable and not consumed locally—so if an export contract failed to materialize, the farmer could not get a good price locally.

- Limited knowledge and technology. Fairly high technological sophistication was required for non-traditional crops, such as in dealing with the risk of crop failure from pests and diseases. But large farmers had easier access to new technologies because they could afford to buy foreign technology and hire foreign experts. By contrast, small farmers depended on unreliable extension services. Moreover, foreign quality controls were difficult and expensive to comply with, and for small farmers often posed a major barrier to entering export markets.

- Dependence on costly inputs. New high-yielding seed varieties have been called 'high response' varieties because they respond to costly inputs. Farmers unable to afford such inputs suffered disproportionately, often losing their land. Their yields also declined in the absence of such inputs.

Source: Conroy, Murray and Rosset, 1996.

spending and because women often have to take on social roles previously supported by government spending.

Other human development problems arise even where women successfully engage in non-traditional exports—such as horticulture, which employs a large number of rural women. Technological and logistical developments and agricultural trade agreements have made flower exports easier and immensely profitable for transnational corporations. Kenya is the largest supplier of fresh-cut flowers to the UK, while half the flowers sold in the US comes from Colombia, where about 100,000 women work in greenhouses. But these positive employment effects have been counterbalanced by health and environmental costs unrelated to trade but still important from a human development perspective. Many flower plantations use harsh pesticides, lack safety equipment and flout national health and safety regulations, causing a range of illnesses among female workers—from nausea and headaches to asthma and miscarriages (White, 2001). The EU proposal for sustainability impact assessments could help in such situations.

Moreover, case studies suggest that trade liberalization in agricultural economies has significant distributional implications, both across social groups and in gender terms. It can disadvantage women or benefit them less than men even when traditional crop production increases (Cagatay, 2001). In Central America (see box 5.7) and many sub-Saharan African countries trade reform has tended to benefit medium-size and large producers at the expense of smaller ones. Because women—the backbone of agricultural production and food security—are primarily small farmers, this has had negative consequences for their economic welfare and for household food security. Growth in food imports can also result in cheaper goods, displacing local production and threatening the livelihoods of women whose income comes from selling traditional foods. Such developments have negative implications for the health and well-being of women and girls.

PROPOSALS FOR THE FUTURE

Agricultural activities are more liberalized in developing than in industrial countries—especially in many of the least developed countries and countries that have implemented structural adjustment programmes mandated by the IMF and World Bank. Thus developing countries believe that it is industrial countries' turn to liberalize in the new round of agricultural negotiations. Many developing countries also believe that the domestic support commitments under the Agreement on Agriculture were designed to reduce excess agricultural production in industrial countries. Developing counties want to increase their agricultural production (for example, by increasing productivity) and food security and work towards their broader development goals.

Two sets of proposals emerge from the discussion in this chapter. One involves the need for increased market access and reduced domestic support and export subsides in industrial countries, particularly Canada, the EU, Japan and the US. The other relates to the food security of developing countries and their need for greater flexibility in crafting policies for agricultural development. Though both sets of issues are crucial for achieving human development goals in developing countries, the discussion below emphasizes food security and agricultural development policies. This is because much has already been written on market access, domestic support and export subsidies, and in the international community there appears to be broad agreement on at least some of the proposals needed to address these issues—even if the political will to implement such policies is lacking in some industrial countries.

Still, the parameters of this long-standing debate are limited because most discussions on the way forward have focused on the roles of governments, farmers and, to a lesser extent, consumers. By contrast, there is a deafening silence on the role of transnational corporations and the concentration of market power. This silence means that both the academic models used to justify the overall benefits of the Agreement on Agriculture and the rhetoric of different negotiating positions (from both industrial and developing countries) are evading a crucial element of the political economy of agricultural trade. Until this issue is confronted—and it is hard to see how that will happen in the framework of current negotiations on agriculture—it will be difficult to achieve real progress on market access for developing countries in industrial countries or significant reductions in domestic support and export subsidies in the US and EU. Political will in industrial countries is a prerequisite for dealing with this asymmetry.

Market access, domestic support, export subsidies and export dumping

TARIFF PEAKS AND ESCALATION. There is a need to reduce tariff peaks and eliminate tariff escalation, particularly for agricultural exports and processed food exports of interest to developing countries. This issue is of crucial importance to many developing countries in the current round of agriculture negotiations. Some developing countries are proposing that industrial countries use the 'Swiss formula', which was used to reduce industrial tariffs during the Tokyo Round and can lead to disproportionately greater cuts on higher tariffs.[14] Other proposals, not necessarily mutually exclusive, include cutting tariffs on all products to a certain level (say, 25 per cent) over a five-year period. For products with especially high tariffs this will first entail lowering the tariff to a certain level (say, 50 per cent), then cutting all tariffs by a certain percentage (say, 50 per cent)—that is, harmonization followed by reduction. Binding deeper reductions on products of export interest to developing countries have been proposed for industrial countries, with maximum tariffs of 12 per cent. Special and differential treatment for developing countries includes lower tariff reductions, longer implementation periods and exemptions for the least developed countries. While there is no agreement on these proposals, a solution that conclusively deals with tariff peaks and escalation should be agreed at the 2003 WTO ministerial meeting in Cancun, Mexico.

DOMESTIC SUBSIDIES. Many developing countries have said that they will offer tariff cuts only after industrial countries have made clear their reductions in the Aggregate Measure of Support and export subsidies. If this approach is agreed, a developing country may be required to reduce its tariffs by a small amount or not at all for products that receive subsidies in industrial countries.

While some industrial countries' non-trade concerns are legitimate, there is a need to eliminate 'blue box' subsidies in particular. Given their nature, these subsidies should have been considered transitional. It would be desirable for them to be eliminated by January 2005, the mandated date for the conclusion of the Doha Round. For that to happen, agreement on this will need to be reached in Geneva and incorporated into the ministerial declaration that emerges from the 2003 WTO meeting in Cancun.

The Aggregate Measure of Support limits allowed under the 'amber box' should apply on a product-specific basis, not just in aggregate. Ideally subsidies allowed under this box should also be phased out, if possible by 2015—the same year targeted by the international community for the achievement of the Millennium Development Goals. In fact, such a commitment should be seen as a concrete target within goal 8 of those goals.

There is also a need to more clearly define, through tighter criteria, what can be allowed as part of the 'green box'. Ideally this should be the only box that industrial countries are allowed to use after 2015, with clear criteria on what it can include. Legitimate non-trade concerns of industrial countries should be dealt with through green box measures, which should be geared towards protecting small farmers. This is not the case for many of the measures currently allowed under the green box, including decoupling measures. In addition to protecting small farmers, some recent reform proposals for the EU Common Agricultural Policy—which seek to shift funds from direct payments to farmers to rural development and environmental programmes—could be accommodated within the green box.

EXPORT SUBSIDIES. All export subsidies should also be phased out by 2010. The Doha declaration aims at the eventual elimination of agricultural export subsidies, though no timeframe was agreed. While the EU will probably strongly oppose any timeframe, it is important to get agreement on a reasonable timeframe if the language of the Doha declaration is to have any meaning.

Products on which export subsidies cause the greatest disruption to developing countries' production and trade should be targeted for elimination within a shorter timeframe. Moreover, it is essential that article 10 of the Agreement on Agriculture be effectively implemented to establish disciplines over export credits, to prevent them from being used to circumvent obligations on export subsides. Food aid should be provided only in the form of grants.

EXPORT DUMPING. A related but broader issue, countries should commit to reducing and then eliminating export dumping of all agricultural products by 2010. While some argue that dumping can be dealt with through the use of countervailing duties by importing countries, this is not a realistic solution for small, powerless, poor countries. Export dumping issues can, however, be partly dealt with through the establishment of a proper safeguard measure for developing countries (see below).

The most effective way to eliminate export dumping, nevertheless, will be to secure appropriate legislation in the US, EU and other major grain exporters. Such legislation should ensure that export prices capture the full costs of production and transportation, including a reasonable profit. To help implement such legislation, and as a start, the OECD should publish the full costs of production estimates for all its member states and make these available to all importing countries. To the extent that these products benefit from green box subsidies, the prohibition of export dumping could be one of the conditions for extension of the peace clause.

Food security and sustainable agricultural development

All developing countries—but the least developed in particular—need more policy flexibility to ensure food security and protect the employment and livelihoods of their poor and vulnerable populations. Many proposals have been made on these issues by African countries, India and other WTO members. The most comprehensive, from a human development perspective, is the 'development box' (box 5.8).

There should be an agreement on the creation of a development box at the 2003 meeting in Cancun. To give developing countries the development policy flexibility they need to pursue human development goals, the development box should go beyond most proposals to date. Ideally it should be based on a positive rather than a negative list approach and apply only to developing countries (Kwa, 2002). Limiting to just a few the food security crops to be included on a negative list for exclusion from the Agreement on Agriculture would be ineffective from multiple perspectives. For example, while contributing considerably to food security, such an approach is unlikely to enhance agricultural biodiversity and sustainability or boost employment and livelihoods.

Even if a positive-list approach is unattainable, a development box with certain core features should be considered integral to any new agreement on agriculture in Cancun. Such a box should, among other elements, include a proper safeguard measure for developing countries as a WTO rule as well as enhanced tariff rate quotas based on experience to date—drawing on the recent Swiss proposal for such quotas and others that build on it.[15] Development box measures should also allow for the exemption of food security crops from tariff reductions, allow input and investment subsidies aimed at increasing and diversifying agricultural production and

Box 5.8 The development box

Many developing countries have argued that the agriculture sector presents a number of development concerns that reach well beyond food security and that the Agreement on Agriculture should recognize these through the creation of a 'development box'. Key rationales for this proposal include highlighting the inherent market failures in agriculture and emphasizing the need to protect certain widely agreed basic human rights. Both goals necessitate a public policy role in agriculture that should not be constrained except to prevent significant deliberate or inadvertent negative effects on other countries. The proposal is particularly relevant for countries that cannot afford to support their agricultural sectors with direct payments—that is, all developing countries.

Broadly speaking, proponents of the development box advocate provisions aimed at allowing them to adopt policies that ensure higher incomes, reduced vulnerability to price fluctuations and increased agricultural productivity, especially for food staples and poor farmers. Such provisions would give developing countries the flexibility to pursue a wide range of policies aimed at reducing poverty and achieving human development.

More specifically, the instruments within a development box could be targeted at crops, people, countries or all three. Most development box proposals recommend greater flexibility in market access disciplines for food security crops, food-insecure countries and low-income and resource-poor people. These proposals seek to protect and enhance production capacity for staple foods, provide and protect agricultural and rural livelihoods for poor people, protect small farmers and producers from highly subsidized export dumping and increase employment, food security and accessibility for the most vulnerable segments of the population.

The proposal applies only to developing countries, and within such countries focuses on low-income and resource-poor farmers and staple and food security crops—which provide the main source of livelihood for such farmers. If defined as cereal crops, which normally include a country's food staples, increased trade barriers are unlikely to have a major impact on trade between developing countries because cereals account for less than 10 per cent of developing countries' agricultural exports. Likewise, by maintaining such a focus, the proposal concentrates on supporting farmers who generally produce crops for domestic consumption, not export markets.

Source: Dominican Republic, Kenya, Pakistan and Sri Lanka, 2002; Green and Priyadarshi, 2001; Ruffer, Jones and Akroyd, 2002.

exports, and link the phase-out of protectionist barriers in developing countries to the phase-out of domestic support and export subsidies in industrial countries and food dumping by their producers as a result of such subsidies.

A revised Special Safeguard mechanism that is relatively simple, transparent and easy to administer will be of crucial importance and merits special attention. This safeguard should be invoked when import prices fall below an agreed trigger or import volumes rise above an agreed trigger (Ruffer, Jones and Akroyd, 2002). In conjunction with and as a supplement to this, developing countries should be able to raise bound tariffs for food security and other crops crucial to farmer livelihoods and agricultural sustainability if these were set too low (as India recently did with its previously zero bound tariff on rice). They should also be able to reduce tariffs on such crops much more slowly than current rules and timetables allow.

If a positive-list approach for product inclusion is agreed, clear criteria will be needed to ensure that developing countries do not abuse its intent. For example, all products that are significant agricultural exports of a country and that account for a significant share of the world export market (say, 3 per cent) should be included on a country's positive list and be subject to Agreement on Agriculture disciplines. Other clear, enforceable criteria will also need to be developed. These could include subjecting all exports with a positive Aggregate Measure of Support to Agreement on Agriculture disciplines by placing them on a country's positive list.

There are important areas of overlap between proponents of the development box and those from developing countries who emphasize food security as part of stronger, more operational special and differential treatment. But the development box proposal goes much further than seeking to address food security. It aims at giving developing countries the autonomy and flexibility they need to devise agricultural development policies that reduce poverty and promote human development. The development box proposal also targets poor and vulnerable people more clearly than do food security proposals.

Support for the concept of a development box appears mixed. Objections focus on the fact that it deals only with small farmers, not the landless rural poor who in many cases—as in Latin America—make up a significant portion of the population below the poverty line. The notion of an 'employment crop' to provide jobs for rural labourers has been suggested in response to this criticism, but the concept remains ill-defined. However, the Food and Agriculture Organization has done interesting work showing how a healthy farm economy is good for landless labourers. For example, as long as land holdings are not grossly inequitable, prosperous farms generate jobs both on the farm and for services such as construction (FAO, 2001b). This work merits further research.

Critics of the development box also argue that while it will benefit small producers, it will lead to higher prices for poor consumers in developing countries—especially countries with large urban poor populations. Advocates counter argue that revenues from higher tariffs on certain food imports can be used to compensate poor urban consumers in the short term. Furthermore, poor consumers rarely benefit from cheap imports because of market failures and structural impediments—which have led to the well-documented capture of a disproportionate share of lower-priced imports by transnational food conglomerates, traders and middlemen.

This political economy problem will need to be addressed by national governments if consumers are to benefit through lower prices. But as argued earlier, a long-term solution that guarantees low food prices for poor consumers in developing countries will not be found without significant increases in spending on research and development for the production of food staples in developing countries. Such spending—accompanied by technical assistance—needs to be made a priority by both developing and industrial countries.

The development box, especially if made operational through a positive-list approach, appears to have genuine potential for putting human development at the heart of the agriculture negotiating process. If accepted, it will mark a shift in the global trade regime towards a trade and human development regime—and create opportunities for replication in other trade negotiation areas. Thus the development box has value in itself and in symbolic terms, signalling that the trade regime can put human development and the needs of poor people at its core.

Specific instruments to operationalize the development box should emerge from the third phase of current agricultural negotiations, due to conclude in March 2003. These instruments should build on the proposals made in this chapter as well as those made in the Committee on Agriculture by the 'Friends of the Development Box' and in other studies (see Ruffer, Jones and Akroyd, ch. 6).

NOTES

1. Annex V:B provides an exception to the elimination of non-tariffs barriers for primary agricultural products that are dominant staples in the traditional diets of developing countries. Such countries are permitted to retain quantitative restrictions for 10 years subject to increasing minimum access opportunities, at which time any continuation must be negotiated. Only the Republic of Korea, the Philippines (both for rice) and Israel (for cheese and sheep meat) have invoked this provision.

2. Against this flexibility, Jordan's accession to the WTO after 1995 shows the difficulties that new members face in getting product-specific special treatment in Uruguay Round agreements. Jordan was one of the first developing countries to negotiate its accession to the WTO in the post–Uruguay Round period. It appears to have received 'WTO plus' terms in agriculture that have limited its flexibility, because it accepted relatively stringent conditions governing its agricultural trade policy—notably relatively low bound tariff rates. Subsequently, during negotiations in the Committee on Agriculture, Jordan proposed that modifications be made in the Agreement on Agriculture to permit developing countries to effectively address poverty alleviation, rural development, rural employment and desert reclamation. These include the possibility of a flexible tariff rate (on olive oil), measures to support sheep raising in desert areas and use of the Special Safeguard mechanism.

3. The Special Safeguard for agriculture differ from the General Safeguard Provisions covered under article XIX of GATT 1994 and the Agreement on Safeguards. The conditions to be met for agricultural products are less strict than those provided by the Agreement on Safeguards.

4. As cited in Anderson, Hoekman and Strutt (1999), Tangermann (1994) illustrates this by the example of a country with four items subject to tariffs: three sensitive ones with 100 per cent duty rates and one with a 4 per cent duty rate. It is possible to arrive at an unweighted average rate of 36.25 per cent, which would meet the unweighted 36 per cent tariff cut requirement, by eliminating the 4 per cent tariff and reducing the 100 per cent tariffs to 85 per cent—and so maintaining high levels of protection on sensitive products. This approach to implementing Agreement on Agriculture stipulations also results in high tariff dispersion rates.

5. Tariffs peaks in agriculture and food processing normally imply tariffs of 12 per cent or more. Tariff escalation occurs if a tariff increases as a good becomes more processed. For example, low duties on tomatoes, higher duties on tomato paste, and yet higher duties on tomato ketchup.

6. For example, limited capacity is a major reason African, Caribbean and Pacific countries have had very modest export success—despite their relatively free access to EU markets. African countries have especially limited capacity.

7. Bangladesh, Botswana, Brazil, Egypt, Fiji, Guyana, India, Jamaica, Kenya, Morocco, Pakistan, Peru, Senegal, Sri Lanka, Tanzania and Thailand.

8. 'Negative' Aggregate Measure of Support refers to a situation where the administered price of a product in a particular year is lower than its nominally fixed reference price. Some developing countries have suggested that such negative measures of support be deducted from the total Aggregate Measure of Support because they can be considered a tax on farmers—and because the total Aggregate Measure of Support should, by definition, be the sum of all subsidies and taxes.

9. The Aggregate Measure of Support is an index that measures the monetary value of government support to a sector. The Agreement on Agriculture's Aggregate Measure of Support includes direct payments to producers, input subsidies (such as for irrigation water), programmes that distort market prices to consumers (market price supports) and interest subsidies on commodity loan programmes.

10. Article VI of the General Agreement on Tariffs and Trade (1947) has two definitions of export dumping. The one more relevant to many agricultural exports is when there are no 'normal' prices and the export price in another market is less than the cost of producing the product in the country of origin plus a reasonable addition for selling cost and profit. This is referred to as the 'constructed' value of the product.

11. Sen identifies production, trade, labour and transfers (usually from government) as the four sources of food and potential food security. Each of these sources is affected by the Agreement on Agriculture to some degree. For example, spending on agricultural production is affected by the de minimis ceiling, while trade is affected by the tariff reduction stipulations and other aspects of the Agreement on Agriculture.

12. The panel consisted of experts from the Food and Agriculture Organization, International Monetary Fund, International Grain Council, United Nations Conference on Trade and Development and World Bank.

13. Industrial agriculture, in contrast to subsistence agriculture, is characterized by intensive use of high-cost or scarce inputs such as chemical fertilizers, pesticides, water and capital equipment, and generally relies on mechanization.

14. The Swiss formula is: $T1 = (cT0)/c + T0$, where $T0$ is the initial tariff, $T1$ the new tariff after the cut and c the reduction coefficient that determines the depth of the cut. The smaller the coefficient, the greater is the resulting tariff cut.

15. Switzerland recently proposed that a certain percentage of new tariff rate quotas be allocated to non-traditional exports from developing countries—an interesting option for developing countries with limited supply capacity (see www.blw.admin.ch/agrarbericht2/e/international/entwicklung.htm).

REFERENCES

Anderson, Kym, Bernard Hoekman and Anna Strutt. 1999. 'Agriculture and the WTO: Next Steps'. Paper prepared for the Second Annual Conference on Global Economic Analysis, 20–22 June, Helmaes, Denmark.

ABARE (Australian Bureau of Agricultural and Resource Economics). 2000. 'Developing Countries: Impact of Agricultural Trade Liberalization'. *ABARE Current Issues* 1 (July).

Beierle, Thomas C. 2002. 'From Uruguay Round to Doha: Agricultural Trade Negotiations at the World Trade Organisation'. Discussion Paper 02-13. Resources for the Future, Washington, DC.

Beneria, Lourdes, and Breny Mendoza. 1995. 'Structural Adjustment and Social Investment Funds: The Case of Honduras, Mexico and Nicaragua'. *European Journal of Development Research* 7 (1): 53–76.

Çağatay, Nilüfer. 2001. 'Trade, Gender and Poverty'. United Nations Development Programme, New York.

Campbell, D., and J. M. Warner. 1997. 'Formally Modeling a Gender Segregated Economy: A Response to William Darity Jr'. *World Development* 25 (12): 2155–58.

Conroy, Michael E., Douglas L. Murray and Peter M. Rosset. 1996. *A Cautionary Tale: Failed U.S. Development Policy in Central America.* Boulder, Colo.: Lynne Rienner.

Diaz-Bonilla, Eugenio, Marcelle Thomas and Sherman Robinson. 2002. 'Trade Liberalisation, WTO, and Food Security'. Discussion paper 82. International Food Policy Research Institute, Trade and Macroeconomics Division, Washington, DC.

Dominican Republic, Kenya, Pakistan and Sri Lanka. 2002. 'Non-Paper on the Development Box'. Paper presented at the special session of the World Trade Organization Committee on Agriculture, 4–8 February, Geneva.

Fan, Shenggen, Peter Hazell and Sukhadeo Thorat. 1999. 'Linkages between Government Spending, Growth, and Poverty in Rural India'. Research Report 110. International Food Policy Research Institute, Washington, DC.

FAO (Food and Agriculture Organization). 1996. 'Rome Declaration on World Food Security, World Food Summit'. Rome. [http://www.fao.org/wfs/index_en.htm].

———. 1999a. *Agriculture, Trade and Food Security: Issues and Options in the Forthcoming WTO Negotiations from the Perspective of Developing Countries.* Report of an FAO Symposium held in Geneva on 23–24 September 1999 at the United Nations. Rome.

———. 1999b. 'Synthesis of Country Case Studies'. Paper presented at the FAO Symposium on Agriculture, Trade and Food Security: Issues and Options in the Forthcoming WTO Negotiations from the Perspective of Developing Countries. Commodities and Trade Division, 23–24 September, Geneva.

———. 2000. *Agriculture Towards 2015.* Rome.

———. 2001a. 'Incorporating Food Security Concerns in a Revised Agreement on Agriculture'. Discussion Paper 2. FAO Roundtable on Food Security in the Context of WTO Negotiations on Agriculture. Geneva.

————. 2001b. 'Reducing Poverty, Buffering Economic Shocks: Agriculture and the Non-Tradable Economy'. Background paper prepared for the experts meeting on the Role of Agriculture Project, 19–21 March, Rome.

————. 2001c. 'Some Issues Relating to Food Security in the Context of the WTO Negotiations on Agriculture'. Discussion Paper 1. FAO Roundtable on Food Security in the Context of WTO Negotiations on Agriculture. Geneva.

GATT (General Agreement on Tariffs and Trade). 1994. 'Agreement on Agriculture'. [www.wto.org/english/tratop_e/agric_e/agric_e.htm].

Green, Duncan, and Shishir Priyadarshi. 2001. 'Proposal for a "Development Box" in the WTO Agreement on Agriculture'. Catholic Agency for Overseas Development and South Centre, Geneva.

Harrison, Glen, Thomas Rutherford and David Tarr. 1996. 'Quantifying the Uruguay Round'. In Will Martin and Alan Winters, eds., *The Uruguay Round and Developing Countries*. Cambridge: Cambridge University Press.

Heffernan, William, with Mary Hendrickson and Robert Gronski. 2002. 'Consolidation in Food and Agriculture System'. Report to the National Farmers Union. National Farmers Web site, 5 February. [www.nfu.org/documents/01_02_Concentration_report.pdf].

Josling, Tim. 1998. 'Agriculture Adjustments and the Uruguay Round Agreement on Agriculture: Some Issues Facing Countries in the LAC Region'. Stanford University, Institute for International Studies, Stanford, Calif.

Konandreas, Panos, and Jim Greenfield. 1996. 'Policy Options for Developing Countries to Support Food Security in the Post–Uruguay Round Period'. Food and Agriculture Organization, Rome.

Kwa, Aileen. 2001. 'Agriculture in Developing Countries: Which Way Forward? Small Farmers and the Need for Alternative, Development-Friendly Food Production Systems'. Focus on the Global South, Geneva.

————. 2002. 'Can the Development Box Adequately Address the Agricultural Crisis in Developing Countries?' Focus on the Global South, Geneva.

Lindland, Jostein. 1997. 'The Impact of the Uruguay Round on Tariff Escalation in Industrial Products'. Energy for Sustainable Communities Program 3. Food and Agriculture Organization, Rome.

Murphy, Sophia. 2002. 'Managing the Invisible Hand: Markets, Farmers and International Trade'. Institute for Agriculture and Trade Policy, Minneapolis, Minn.

OECD (Organisation for Economic Co-operation and Development). 2000. 'Agricultural Policy Reform: Development and Prospects'. Paris.

————. 2001a. 'Agricultural Policies in OECD Countries: Monitoring and Evaluation, Highlights'. Paris.

————. 2001b. *The Development Dimensions of Trade*. Paris.

Olson, Kent. 1999. 'Mixed News from 1998 Farm Records'. *Minnesota Agricultural Economist* 696 (spring).

Oxfam International. 2002. 'Rigged Rules and Double Standards'. Oxford, UK.

Page, Sheila, and Michael Davenport. 1994. 'World Trade Reform: Do Developing Countries Gain or Lose?' Special report. Overseas Development Institute, London.

Pascual, Fransisco, and Arze Gilpo. 2001. 'WTO and Philippine Agriculture: Seven Years of Unbridled Trade Liberalization and Misery for Small Farmers'. Integrated Rural Development Foundation, Quezon City, the Philippines.

Perroni, Carlo. 1998. 'The Uruguay Round and Its Impact on Developing Countries: An Overview of Model Results'. In Harmon Thomas and John Whalley, eds., *Uruguay Round Results and the Emerging Trade Agenda.* Geneva: United Nations Conference on Trade and Development.

Pinstrup-Andersen, Per, Rajul Pandya-Lorch and Mark W. Rosegrant. 1999. *World Food Prospects: Critical Issues for the 21st Century.* Washington, DC: International Food Policy Research Institute.

Ricupero, Rubens. 1999. 'Remarks'. Presented at the Food and Agriculture Organization Symposium on Agriculture, Trade and Food Security: Issues and Options in the Forthcoming WTO Negotiations from the Perspective of Developing Countries, 23–24 September, Geneva.

Ritchie, Mark, Suzanne Wisniewski and Sophia Murphy. 2000. 'Dumping as a Structural Feature of US Agriculture: Can WTO Rules Solve the Problem?' Institute for Agriculture and Trade Policy, Minneapolis, Minn.

Rodrik, Dani. 2001. 'The Global Governance of Trade As If Development Really Mattered'. United Nations Development Programme, New York.

Ruffer, Tim, with Stephen Jones and Stephen Akroyd. 2002. 'Development Box Proposals and Their Potential Effects on Developing Countries. Volume 1: Main Report'. Oxford Policy Management, Oxford.

Sen, Amartya. 1999. *Development as Freedom.* Oxford: Oxford University Press.

Shirotori, Miho. 2000. 'Notes on the Implementation of the Agreement on Agriculture'. In United Nations Conference on Trade and Development, *Positive Agenda and Future Trade Negotiations.* Geneva and New York: United Nations.

———. 2002. 'WTO Negotiations on Agriculture: The 13th Special Session on Agriculture—Market Access: Chairman's Oral Summary'. Report to the United Nations Conference on Trade and Development, Division on International Trade in Goods and Services and Commodities, and Commercial Diplomacy and Trade Negotiations Branch, 6 September, Geneva.

Stancanelli, Nestor. 1994. 'La agricultura en la Ronda Uruguay y el desarrollo de America Latina'. In *La Ronda Uruguay y el desarrollo de America Latina.* Santiago de Chile: CLEPI.

Supper, Erich. 2000. 'The Post–Uruguay Round Tariff Environment for Developing Country Exports: Tariff Peaks and Tariff Escalation.' In United Nations Conference on Trade and Development, *Positive Agenda and Future Trade Negotiations.* Geneva and New York: United Nations.

Tangermann, S., and T. E. Josling. 1994. 'The Significance of Tariffication in the Uruguay Round Agreement on Agriculture'. Paper presented to the North American Agricultural Policy Research Consortium Workshop on Canadian Agricultural Policy, February, Vancouver, Canada.

TWN (Third World Network). 2001. 'The Multilateral Trading System: A Development Perspective'. Background paper for Trade and Sustainable Human Development Project. United Nations Development Programme, New York.

Thomas, Harmon, and John Whalley. 1998. 'Uruguay Round Results and the Emerging Trade Agenda: Quantitative-based Analyses from the Development Perspective'. United Nations Conference on Trade and Development, Geneva.

UN (United Nations). 2002. *No Water, No Future*. New York.

UNCTAD (United Nations Conference on Trade and Development). 1995. 'Identification of New Trading Opportunities Arising from the Implementation of the Uruguay Round Agreements in Selected Sectors and Markets: Agriculture, Textiles and Clothing, and Other Industrial Products'. TD/B/WG.8/2 and TD/B/WG.8/2/Add.1. Geneva.

————. 1999a. 'Examining Trade in the Agricultural Sector, with a View to Expanding the Agricultural Exports of the Developing Countries and to Assisting them in Better Understanding the Issues at Stake in the Upcoming Agricultural Negotiations'. TD/B/COM.1/EM.8/2. Geneva and New York.

————. 1999b. 'General Features: Trade in Agriculture'. Commercial Diplomacy Programme, Geneva.

————. 1999c. *Trade and Development Report*. Geneva and New York.

————. 2000. *Positive Agenda and Future Trade Negotiations*. Geneva and New York.

————. 2002. 'The Least Developed Countries Report'. Geneva and New York.

UNCTAD (United Nations Conference on Trade and Development) and WTO (World Trade Organization). 1999. 'The Post–Uruguay Round Tariff Environment for Developing Country Exports: Tariff Peaks and Tariff Escalation'. TD/B/COM.1/14/Rev.1. Geneva.

UNDP (United Nations Development Programme). 2002. *Human Development Report 2002: Deepening Democracy in a Fragmented World*. New York: Oxford University Press.

UNIFEM (United Nations Development Fund for Women). 2000. *Progress of the World's Women*. New York.

White, Marceline. 2001. 'Women and Trade: Investing in Women—FTAA Investment Policies and Women'. Coalition for Women's Economic Development and Global Equality, Washington, DC.

WTO (World Trade Organization). 2001. 'WTO Agriculture Negotiations: The Issues, and Where We Are Now'. WTO Secretariat, Geneva.

————. 2002. 'Inter-Agency Panel on Short-Term Difficulties in Financing Normal Levels of Commercial Imports of Basic Imports of Basic Foodstuffs'. Report of the Committee on Agriculture's Inter-Agency Panel, Geneva.

WTO Committee on Agriculture. 2001. 'Report to the General Council on Implementation-Related Issues'. G/AG/11. Geneva.

Youssef, Hesham. 1999. 'Speech at FAO Symposium'. Cabinet of Egypt's Ministry of Foreign Affairs. 23–24 September, Geneva.

CHAPTER 6
COMMODITIES

The problems facing primary commodities (agricultural primary commodities and mineral commodities, but not fuel) are closely related to those afflicting agriculture, because about 80 per cent of commodity exports—for developing countries and for the world—are agricultural. Despite progress in diversifying exports and broadening national economic structures, most developing countries—86 of 144 for which data are available—still depend on commodities for more than half their export earnings. This number has remained virtually constant for the past ten years. Moreover, for many countries a large share of export income comes from only one commodity or just a few. For 55 countries, three commodities together account for more than half of export earnings.

A BRIEF HISTORY

In April 1942, during preparations for the Bretton Woods conference in New Hampshire, John Maynard Keynes ([1942] 1974) presented a memorandum to the Allies proposing an international institution for regulating world commodity markets as one of three major international institutions needed to regulate the world economy after World War II. His proposal outlined a series of commodity agreements and organizations for major commodities (tin, wool, wheat, maize, sugar, coffee, cotton and rubber), operating in an integrated manner under a general council for commodity organizations and relying primarily on buffer stocks.

Negotiations over international commodity arrangements were not new. Even before World War II such arrangements had been concluded for sugar, wheat, tea, natural rubber and tin, aimed at stabilizing prices or defending floor prices. But between 1945 and 1964 price-stabilizing international commodity arrangements were concluded for only three of these five commodities (wheat, sugar and tin) and for coffee. The commodity issue became one of the major concerns leading to the establishment of the United Nations Conference on Trade and Development (UNCTAD) in 1964.

Following the 1973 oil price increase by the Organization of Petroleum Exporting Countries (OPEC) and the 1974 call of the United Nations General

Assembly (1974, p. 6) for 'an integrated programme for . . . commodities of export interest to developing countries', negotiations under the auspices of UNCTAD led to the creation in June 1980 of the Common Fund for Commodities, a central financing mechanism. They also resulted in the conclusion of three new international commodity arrangements, for jute, natural rubber and tropical timber. Of these, only that for rubber included economic clauses for market intervention. The others, along with international study groups on nickel and copper, aimed at increasing market transparency through the publication of statistics and through research and development (R&D) and other development projects financed by the Common Fund for Commodities. After the collapse of the International Tin Agreement in 1985, successive renegotiations of the other international commodity arrangements resulted in a progressive abandonment of economic clauses aimed at price stabilization.

Since the 1970s there have been several major developments in global commodity markets:

- The structures of world commodity markets have altered significantly, both on the demand side (through mergers and acquisitions) and on the supply side (through the abolition of marketing boards). While concentration has often been helpful to market management and mergers and acquisitions can play a useful role, the changed market structures make reaching agreement on international commodity arrangements that would increase prices even more difficult than in the 1970s.

- Developing countries, particularly African and least developed countries and those in the African, Caribbean and Pacific (ACP) group, have suffered more from losses of market share in world commodity exports (excluding fuels) than from price declines for their commodities. Between 1970–72 and 1998–99 Africa's share in world commodity exports declined from 8.6 per cent to 2.6 per cent, that of ACP countries from 8.4 per cent to 2.4 per cent and that of the least developed countries from 4.7 per cent to 1.0 per cent. If these three groups of countries (which overlap to a large extent) had been able to maintain their 1970–72 market shares, their average annual export earnings in 1998–99 would have been far higher: US$41 billion higher for Africa, US$45 billion higher for the ACP countries and US$28 billion higher for the least developed countries. These losses are due in part to a loss in competitiveness and in part to the protectionism (through higher trade barriers and export subsidies) of industrial countries. Developing countries today account for only around 26–29 per cent of world commodity exports.

- Meanwhile, 14 of the 15 countries of the European Union (all except Denmark) have increased their market share in world commodity exports. So have China and some of the newly industrialized countries in Southeast Asia and Latin America, such as Indonesia, Thailand, and Mexico. For agricultural exports alone, the European Union's share rose from 28.1 per cent to 42.7 per cent between 1970 and 2000, that of China from 2.4 per cent to 4.3 per cent, that of Thailand from 0.9 per cent to 1.8 per cent and that of Mexico from 1.3 per cent to 1.9 per cent.[1]

- The share of developing countries in world exports of tropical products that are produced exclusively in these countries has fallen, as industrial countries import raw commodities and blend and pack them (or just pack and brand them without blending) for re-export at a much higher value. (For example, the share of developing countries in world coffee exports declined from 93 per cent to 75 per cent between 1970–72 and 1998–99.)

- Traditional commodity exports of developing countries have lost importance, overtaken by new, dynamic commodity sectors. Between 1970–72 and 1998–99 the value of world coffee exports increased by more than 4.4 times (from US$3.2 billion to US$14.2 billion) and that of tea by 4.3 (from US$0.7 billion to US$3.0 billion). Meanwhile, the value of world vegetable exports expanded by almost 14 times (from US$2.1 billion to US$29.2 billion), cut flowers by 22 (from US$0.2 billion to US$4.4 billion) and poultry by 41.5 (from US$0.2 billion to US$8.3 billion). Coffee, which used to be the foremost commodity export earner for developing countries, now ranks only fifth—behind fish, vegetable oils, fruits and wood.

- The prices of several major export commodities of developing countries have collapsed since the mid-1990s, leading to massive losses in foreign exchange earnings.

- Newly industrialized developing countries have become the most dynamic importers of commodities, underlining the importance of direct South-South trade in commodities.

THE SITUATION TODAY

Given the history of international commodity arrangements and other developments since the 1970s, trade in most commodities, unlike other agricultural and industrial products, continues to take place outside the framework of the General Agreement on Tariffs and Trade (GATT) and the World Trade Organization (WTO). Yet many if not most commodities are subject to tariff peaks and escalation, especially in industrial countries. In addition, numerous anti-dumping actions and the resurgence of voluntary export restraints are nullifying the potential benefits of liberalization in the minerals and metals sector.

The collapse in the prices of several major commodities of export interest to developing countries since the mid-1990s has fuelled calls for supply management schemes by producer associations of developing countries (along the lines of the OPEC model) aimed at raising the prices of developing country commodity exports from their dismally low levels. The fall in export prices and revenues has had dramatic consequences for human development, transmitted through lower employment, wages, incomes, livelihood security and social well-being (boxes 6.1 and 6.2). In developing countries typical export crops such as tea, coffee, cotton and sugar are often harvested by casual, unprotected and unregistered day labourers, many of whom in some countries are women.

Box 6.1 The case of coffee

In 2001 the composite indicator price for coffee was 44.62 cents a pound, a 30-year low and 68 per cent lower than the average of 138.04 cents in 1995. For developing country exporters, the drop in price represents an annual loss of export earnings estimated at US$7 billion. The real (inflation-adjusted) price of coffee beans has fallen to just 25 per cent of its level in 1960, so that the money farmers make from coffee can buy only a quarter of what it could 40 years ago (see figure).

The impact on export prices, revenues, employment and wages

The coffee sector in several Latin American and Caribbean countries has entered an unprecedented crisis, with repercussions for economic performance, balance of payments, employment and income. Hardest hit are Colombia, Costa Rica, El Salvador, Guatemala, Honduras and Nicaragua. In 2001 alone Central American countries lost US$713 million in coffee revenues (compared with their average export earnings of the late 1980s), equal to 1.2 per cent of the region's GDP for that year. In the same year about 170,000 jobs were lost in coffee farming, and US$140 million in wages. The unemployment and lower wages in the coffee sector affected some 1.6 million people in the poorest population groups.

In El Salvador coffee export earnings collapsed from US$311 million in 2000 to US$130 million in 2001 and to an estimated US$100 million in 2002. Direct jobs provided by coffee growers in the country are expected to decline from 150,000 in 1997 to 80,000 in 2002. In Guatemala the harvest labour force for the 2001/02 crop has been halved from 500,000 to 250,000. In Colombia, where coffee production accounts for 2 per cent of GDP and more than 500,000 families depend on coffee production for their livelihood, the downturn in the coffee industry in 2001 led to the loss of 257,000 jobs, of which 181,000 were in the coffee sector.

The same story is echoed in parts of sub-Saharan Africa. Ethiopia's export revenues from coffee fell 42 per cent, from US$257 million to US$149 million, between 1999–2000 and 2000–01. In Uganda, where roughly a quarter of the population depends on coffee in some way, coffee exports for the eight-month period before June 2002 remained at almost the same volume as in the year before while earnings dropped by almost 30 per cent. In the southern Indian state of Karnataka, which produces a large share of India's coffee, the number of plantation workers has fallen 20 per cent over the past two years.

Countries highly dependent on coffee export earnings are doubly disadvantaged. While the price of their exports tends to decline over time, the prices of their imports, often manufactured goods, do not fall or fall more slowly. Oxfam International reports that a coffee farmer in producer countries would have to sell more than twice as many coffee beans today as in 1980 to buy a Swiss army knife. A similar situation arises for debt and debt service, which are fixed in US dollars. For Uganda, for example, the falling value of coffee exports has negated the benefits of its debt relief under the heavily indebted poor countries (HIPC) initiative.

The impact on farmers' incomes and livelihoods

In stark contrast with the booming coffee industry in industrial consuming countries and the exceptional windfall profits of their coffee roasters and processors, coffee farmers in developing countries are going through their worst crisis ever. More than 125 million people depend on coffee for their livelihood, a large share of them in least developed countries. The recent collapse in coffee prices has hit rural economies worldwide, even in countries (such as Brazil and Vietnam) where production costs are low. In Brazil low returns led to reduced spending by farmers and rising unemployment. In Vietnam, one of the lowest-cost producers

Real price of coffee, 1960–2000

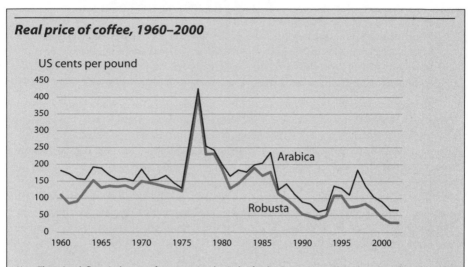

US cents per pound

Note: The price deflator is the manufactures unit value index for the G-5 countries (G-7 minus Canada and Italy) in constant 1990 US dollars.
Source: Oxfam International, 2002, based on World Bank data.

in the world, research in Dak Lak province suggests that the price farmers were receiving at the beginning of 2002 covered as little as 60 per cent of their production costs.

Indebted farmers who depend primarily on coffee for income, including for food purchases, have been forced to sell their farms to pay back their debts. Many have had to move to cities or join the illegal flow of emigrant workers to industrial countries. Others have had to switch to alternative crops—including proscribed drugs, as in Colombia, parts of Asia and much of Central America. In Bolivia, Colombia and Peru, where the conditions required for growing coffee are similar to those for growing coca—the raw material for cocaine—farmers are replacing coffee with coca. This brings its own set of problems—assaults, rape, prostitution and gang warfare.

The impact on families

The World Food Programme reported in March 2002 that the coffee crisis, combined with the effects of a drought, had left 30,000 Hondurans suffering from hunger, with hundreds of children so malnourished that they needed to be hospitalized. It also reported that farmers were selling their assets and cutting down on food. In Vietnam's Dak Lak province farmers dependent solely on coffee are now categorized as 'pre-starvation'. In January 2002 the European Union and the US Agency for International Development warned of increased poverty and food security problems among coffee farmers in Ethiopia.

Mohammed Ali Indris, a 36-year-old Ethiopian coffee farmer interviewed in March 2002, gave a graphic sense of how the price collapse had affected his family. The head of a household of 12, including the children of his deceased brother, he estimated that he will earn only US$60 from the combined sale of coffee and corn in 2002, down from around US$360 five years earlier.

'Five to seven years ago, I was producing seven sacks of red cherry [unprocessed coffee] and this was enough to buy clothes, medicines, services and to solve so many problems. But now even if I sell four times as much, it is impossible to cover all my expenses. I had to sell my oxen to repay the loan I previously took out to

(Box continues on next page.)

151

buy fertilizers and improved seed for corn, or face prison. . . . Earlier we could cover expenses, now we can't. . . . Three of the children can't go to school because I can't afford the uniform. We have stopped buying teff and edible oil. We are eating mainly corn. The children's skin is getting dry and they are showing signs of malnutrition'.

Hunger is particularly acute in households that have decided to devote a larger share of their land to coffee than to subsistence crops. Wherever coffee serves as a cash crop for subsistence farmers (such as in many African and some Asian countries), substantially less cash income is available for spending on food, medicine and education. Families that depend on money generated by coffee are withdrawing their children, particularly girls, from school. The price crisis also affects women directly since the male household head often goes to work elsewhere, for at least part of the year, leaving the women and children to work the land. The workload of women has also increased in families used to contracting casual labour to help with the coffee harvest. Women have to shoulder the extra workload now that such families can no longer afford casual labour.

Source: Megzari, 2002; Oxfam International, 2002; Fonseca, 2002; Osorio, 2002.

BOX 6.2 THE CASE OF COTTON

The global labour force directly involved in cotton production at the farm level probably exceeds 100 million, although at least twice that many people living in rural households benefit from cotton cultivation. In addition to direct farm employment, cotton production also provides employment in cotton ginning, transport and marketing. Many least developed countries depend heavily on cotton production and exports. But unlike coffee, which is produced exclusively in developing countries, cotton is also produced in industrial countries.

Much of the overproduction of cotton and the resulting collapse of its prices is due to production and export subsidies, mainly in industrial countries. (In 2001 the average US dollar price per pound of cotton was around 52 per cent lower than the 1995 average price.) The International Cotton Advisory Committee estimates that abolishing such subsidies would increase the world price by almost 75 per cent. This would provide more than US$1.2 billion in additional income a year to African cotton producers, most of whom live in least developed countries.

The decline in export earnings and government revenue in developing countries affects the investment in and availability of public goods, including health care, agricultural extension services and maintenance of feeder roads. And the gains in market share by industrial country cotton exporters, thanks to higher production and export subsidies, have led to significant losses in rural employment and income in some developing countries—particularly least developed countries—contributing to the spread of poverty.

While cotton farmers in industrial countries are shielded by subsidies from the negative effects of a price collapse and may even expand their market shares and revenues, cotton growers in developing countries have to bear direct effects through a loss of cash income and indirect effects through a loss of export earnings and government revenue. The decline in cash incomes has curtailed their access to basic foods, to medicines, to education for their children, to communications and to production inputs, further reducing their productive capacity and future incomes.

Source: Megzari, 2002; Fortucci, 2002.

Box 6.3 The case of shea butter

Shea butter is produced from shea nuts, which grow on a tree native to several African countries. Burkino Faso, with 1 million such trees, produces 25 per cent of the world's shea nuts. These are consumed locally and exported to Europe and Japan for the production of shea butter, used in chocolate, margarine, cosmetics and pharmaceuticals.

During colonial times shea butter intended for export to Europe was produced and handled much the same as other export commodities. Nuts were gathered and sold in the community, with low returns to the growers and those who prepared the nuts for export, most of whom were women. Shea processing facilities were set up by colonial enterprises in Bobo Dioulasso, where initial purification and packaging were done for easy transport to the world market.

At independence this chain was broken and replaced by unregulated intermediary services at the national level. Attempts to regulate the commodity and establish a national council for price stabilization in Burkina Faso failed, and access to financing to support the export of shea nuts and butter became difficult. But two markets grew steadily:

- The cosmetics industry, where the natural virtues of shea butter surpass those of alternatives in the production of hair lotions and healing and moisturizing creams. The shift from margarine making to beauty products has led to a demand for higher-quality shea butter.

- The chocolate industry, especially after the European Union adopted shea butter as a possible substitute for cocoa butter.

The growth in these markets has allowed women to increase their earnings by producing shea butter locally and thus adding value to the commodity.

The collapse of several major export commodities, including cocoa, opened new space for 'dynamic commodity sectors' such as shea butter and other vegetable oils. To take advantage of the new markets, however, shea producers needed to be able to negotiate a good price for their products. The gains from greater production of high-quality shea butter had to outweigh those from agriculture and subsistence farming, which women still considered their main source of livelihood.

Funding from several sources—the government of Luxembourg, the United Nations Fund for International Partnerships and the United Nations Development Fund for Women—supported the organization of women producers into a consortium enabling them to access larger markets and negotiate better prices. As members and later co-chairs of the national council of shea producers, the consortium was able to set a common basic price that was three times the price in 1998. They then negotiated directly with European companies, most notably with L'Occitane, the French cosmetics enterprise, which supplies Delta Airlines with shea butter–based products for use as in-flight cosmetics. In January 2000, under its first contract with the consortium, L'Occitane purchased some 60 tonnes of high-quality shea butter at twice the local market price.

Adding value to the raw commodity through local processing is a step towards greater competitiveness in the world market. But these gains remain modest in today's global trading environment, where the negotiating power of commodity producers is continually eroded and a broad array of cheaper substitutes are allowed.

Source: UNIFEM, 2000; Zaoude, 2002.

PROPOSALS FOR THE FUTURE

On the international backburner for too long, the commodity issue requires urgent attention in multilateral trade negotiations. The international community should give the issue serious consideration in post-Doha negotiations at the WTO. It should also give serious encouragement to developing country producer groups that wish to build South-South coalitions on specific commodities so as to increase their bargaining power in the international market. Small island developing states and a group of single commodity exporters have recently made specific proposals in the WTO in the context of the ongoing negotiations on agriculture. Three dimensions of commodity diversification should be promoted: horizontal (new dynamic products), vertical (adding value) and geographical (new market outlets). The production and export of shea butter by women in Burkina Faso illustrate what is possible when this is done (box 6.3).

Supply side

There is a need to address the supply constraints of developing countries and, in particular, to strengthen their capacity to process commodities, adding value before exporting them. Special consideration should be given to product differentiation, or 'decommoditization', of the export commodities of developing countries so as to allow them to capture the premiums on products with special qualities (such as gourmet coffees and high-quality teas).

Wherever feasible, the international community should encourage international schemes aimed at voluntary supply management with a view to achieving a better balance between supply and demand. Such schemes would avoid the waste of investment, depletion of non-renewable natural resources and excessive price volatility. These schemes should also assist high-cost commodity producers in overcoming exit barriers.

Market access

As proposed in chapter 5, the multilateral trading system needs to rationalize tariff structures and subsidies in agriculture and allow developing countries to support their own markets. There is an urgent need to reduce tariff peaks and eliminate tariff escalation, especially in industrial country markets.

Financing

The international and regional financial institutions and bilateral donors should take into account the escalating effects of financing projects aimed at increasing the production of a commodity in one developing country. Such projects can affect the commodity's price and the corresponding export earnings for other developing countries—and have even contributed to the collapse of prices. Gains achieved by commodity diversification in one country should not be more than offset by losses in all other producing and exporting countries.

The highest priority should be given to resource allocations that enhance the R&D abilities and competitiveness of developing countries and the capacity of their small farmers and producers to supply and market new commodities with dynamic market prospects and the potential for significant local value added, including organic products. To support this, all OECD countries should join the Common Fund for Commodities, and this institution should be given adequate resources to reach a critical mass in its operations.

Also warranting the highest priority is establishing effective compensatory financing schemes to help bridge shortfalls in export earnings. Market-based risk management instruments have proved ineffective over periods longer than a year or so, especially for least developed countries, whose needs are the most acute. Official development assistance can play an anticyclical role in this regard, at least in the short term.

Effective support should be provided to developing country farmers and other commodity producers to empower them to access appropriate multilateral commodity risk management mechanisms or new, alternative schemes combining traditional finite insurance (such as against natural catastrophes) with new risk management instruments. And because women, who make up the bulk of small farmers, have traditionally had restricted access to credit, these risk management schemes need to be tailored to women in particular.

NOTE

1. Computations by UNCTAD based on the Food and Agriculture Organization's FAOSTAT database. In the European Union, for example, France increased its market share of agricultural exports from 5.7 per cent to 8.1 per cent between 1970 and 2000, while Germany expanded its share from 2.6 per cent to 5.9 per cent, and the United Kingdom its share from 2.7 per cent to 4.1 per cent.

REFERENCES

FAO (Food and Agriculture Organization). 2002. FAOSTAT database. Rome. apps.fao.org/page/collections?subset=agriculture, accessed on 12 September 2002.

Fonseca, Luz Amparo. 2002. 'The Coffee Sector in Colombia'. United Nations Economic Commission for Latin America and the Caribbean, Santiago, Chile.

Fortucci, P. 2002. 'The Contribution of Cotton to Economy and Food Security in Developing Countries'. Paper prepared for the International Cotton Advisory Committee, Washington, DC.

Keynes, J. M. [1942] 1974. 'The International Control of Raw Materials'. *Journal of International Economics* 4: 299–315.

Megzari, Abdelaziz. 2002. 'The Commodity Issue: Preliminary Suggestions for the Contents of a Box on Commodities'. Background note for Trade and Sustainable Human Development Project. United Nations Development Programme, New York.

Osorio, Néstor. 2002. 'Aide-Memoire on the Global Coffee Crisis'. International Coffee Organization, London.

Oxfam International. 2002. 'Mugged: Poverty in a Coffee Cup'. Oxford.

United Nations General Assembly. 1974. *Resolution on the Establishment of a New International Economic Order*. Adopted at the Sixth Special Session of the United Nations General Assembly. Resolution 3202 (S-VI), A/9559. New York.

UNCTAD (United Nations Conference on Trade and Development). 1994. *Commodity Yearbook*. Geneva.

UNIFEM (United Nations Development Fund for Women). 2000. *Progress of the World's Women*. New York

Zaoude, Aster. 2002. 'The Case of Shea Butter in Burkina Faso'. Background note for Trade and Sustainable Human Development Project. United Nations Development Programme, New York.

CHAPTER 7
INDUSTRIAL TARIFFS

Developing countries attach great importance to levels of and changes in industrial tariffs because industrial products—defined as all non-agricultural products—account for more than 70 per cent of their exports (UNCTAD, 2002; WTO, 1994; Michalopoulos, 1999). Especially for industrial products with high value added, tariff levels and changes determine developing countries' effective access to industrial country markets as well as the extent to which their industrial strategies translate trade into benefits for human development.

Although the Generalized System of Preferences can increase developing countries' market access, the system does not cover some important products—mainly in sensitive sectors such as fish products and textiles and clothing. As a result developing countries face peaks and escalation in industrial countries' most-favoured-nation tariffs for such exports. Moreover, some developing countries are excluded from the system. In addition, the preferences are significantly underused because many exports do not qualify under the rules of origin and because of onerous documentation requirements.

African, Caribbean and Pacific (ACP) countries have been granted duty-free access to EU markets for non-sensitive products. In addition, most products from the least developed countries (many of which are ACP members) benefit from duty-free access to Quad markets—Canada, the EU, Japan, the US—and from preferences in some developing countries although some products of critical importance to them (such as textiles and clothing) do not qualify. Some developing countries have also obtained duty-free access to industrial country markets as part of free trade agreements, as with many Arab countries under Euromed agreements and Mexico under the North American Free Trade Agreement (NAFTA) and EU free trade agreement. But in general the increase in free trade agreements and customs unions among industrial countries has led to considerable tariff discrimination against developing country exports.

Even with the completion of the Uruguay Round of trade negotiations, industrial tariffs are higher in developing countries (for industrial country exports) than in industrial countries (for developing country exports). But this disparity is not entirely unwarranted, and analysis of industrial trade between the two groups of countries must take into account two important issues:

- *Market access.* Tariff peaks and tariff escalation occur in industrial country markets, especially for exports of significant interest to developing countries. Yet in many developing countries applied tariffs are much lower than most-favoured-nation rates.

- *Policy space.* Higher industrial tariffs in developing countries can often be justified as safeguards against deindustrialization and as providing the policy space needed to achieve human development objectives.

MARKET ACCESS SINCE THE URUGUAY ROUND

Market access depends largely on the tariffs imposed on a country's exports. Average tariffs are important, but tariff peaks and escalation can play an even more important role in determining the success and extent of industrial exports—both from and to developing and industrial countries.

Average tariffs

In industrial countries the average trade-weighted tariff on industrial imports fell to 15 per cent in the mid-1950s, 10 per cent in the late 1960s, 6 per cent in the late 1970s and about 4 per cent during the Uruguay Round. During the Uruguay Round developing countries also substantially reduced their industrial tariffs. India's average trade-weighted tariff on industrial products fell from 71 per cent to 32 per cent, Venezuela's from 50 per cent to 31 per cent, Mexico's from 46 per cent to 34 per cent, Brazil's from 41 per cent to 27 per cent and Chile's from 35 per cent to 25 per cent (Das 1998).

The average trade-weighted tariff on imports from industrial countries is about 11 per cent in developing countries, while the converse is approximately 5 per cent (OECD, 2001). Still, in OECD markets the trade-weighted, most-favoured-nation tariff for manufacturing exports from developing countries (3.4 per cent) is almost four times that for manufacturing exports from other OECD countries (Michalopoulos, 1999). Furthermore, during the Uruguay Round OECD countries cut their average tariff by nearly half for imports from other OECD countries—but by less than a third for imports from developing countries. This resulted in a 3 per cent average trade-weighted tariff on imports from other OECD members, compared with the 5 per cent (noted above) for developing countries (OECD, 2001).

Tariffs also vary among developing countries, especially for labour-intensive manufactured goods (though not in the form of full duty- and quota-free access). Average tariffs on manufactured goods fall as countries move from low- to middle- and higher income status (figure 7.1), and middle- and higher-income countries have lower levels of protection through tariffs and non-tariff measures. The leading developing country importers also have low tariffs (UNCTAD, 2002). Indeed, they all have tariffs lower than the low-income country average for products of relevance to them.

As economies grow and reach full employment, they become more willing to liberalize trade and lower tariffs. Yet many developing countries have been more

FIGURE 7.1

Simple tariffs on manufactured goods in three groups of developing countries

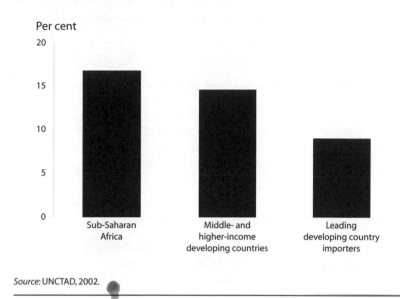

Source: UNCTAD, 2002.

active than OECD countries in cutting tariffs—and the speed and motivation for these cuts are a problem (box 7.1).

Indeed, many developing and transition economies are cutting tariffs much faster than is necessary or desirable from a human development perspective. Consider Mongolia. To conform to IMF loan conditions, it imposed a flat 5 per cent tariff in the second half of the 1990s—requiring abrupt, across the board cuts in its industrial tariffs. This change was not required under World Trade Organization (WTO) agreements and has impeded value addition and competitiveness in Mongolia's few areas of strategic advantage (such as cashmere production).

These trends, along with the evidence presented in box 7.1, should lead to a reconsideration of the view that trade restrictions among developing countries significantly contribute to fallacy of composition dilemmas and problems in increasing exports of traditional labour-intensive manufactures.

Tariff peaks and escalation

Despite the agreements reached during the Uruguay Round, industrial countries have maintained tariff peaks—defined as tariffs higher than 12 per cent—and tariff escalation on some industrial products of export interest to developing countries. Tariff peaks and escalation have undermined developing countries' efforts to export industrial products, produce and export processed raw materials and climb up the value-added chain for basic commodities.

Tariff peaks and escalation in industrial countries reflect the influence of domestic political forces opposed to import liberalization (VanGrasstek, 2001).

Box 7.1 Are industrial tariffs really higher in developing countries?
The case of labour-intensive manufacturing

Market access for labour-intensive exports is extremely important for developing countries because it mitigates the risk of 'fallacy of composition' (the view that what is good for one country is good for all countries) presented by these products. Yet most developing countries with the capacity and potential to expand labour-intensive exports have not gained much from Uruguay Round agreements and continue to face significant barriers especially in the markets of industrial countries.

Some analysts argue that developing country tariffs are too high and are responsible for many of the market access problems of developing countries, pointing out that 70 per cent of duties on developing country manufacturing exports are paid by other developing countries. But this argument becomes less convincing when trade patterns are examined more closely—particularly the variations among groups of developing countries.

Tariff and non-tariff measures are lower in middle- and higher-income developing countries than in low-income countries. For example, the 15–20 higher-income developing countries in Latin America and Asia have substantially liberalized trade. Relative to low-income countries, middle- and higher-income developing countries do not have a competitive edge in labour-intensive manufactures, and their import demand for such products is higher. Thus trade restrictions among developing countries do not play a central role in their market access and fallacy of composition problems.

Moreover, there is an imbalance between tariffs on labour-intensive manufactures in industrial and developing countries. First-tier newly industrialized economies apply lower tariffs to these products than do industrial countries. In addition, the tariffs imposed by many large developing country importers are similar to industrial country rates. And the 10 top developing country importers apply much lower tariffs to some labour-intensive manufactures (textiles and clothing, footwear, leather goods) from other developing countries than do high- and middle-income countries, including all the major industrial countries.

Looked at another way, industrial countries apply higher average most-favoured-nation tariffs to traditional labour-intensive manufactures—including textiles and clothing, footwear, and leather and travel goods—in which low-income developing countries have a stronger competitive position than they do to products of less interest to developing countries (such as computers and other office equipment and telecommunications, audio and video equipment). Thus the high industrial tariffs that industrial countries impose on critical industrial exports from developing countries are a crucial determinant of market access. This issue requires urgent discussion and resolution.

Source: UNCTAD, 2002, pp. 128–35.

The strength of this resistance is reflected in the classification of certain products as sensitive and subject to special internal procedures, as in the US Trade Act of 2002. Where such protection is not adequate, additional protection is often sought through anti-dumping duties and other forms of trade harassment.[1]

Tariff peaks. Quad countries (Canada, the EU, Japan, the US) maintain numerous tariff peaks on industrial products, especially food industry products, textiles and clothing, footwear, leather and travel goods, automotive products and consumer electronics and watches. Some of these peaks are as high as 900 per cent (Supper, 2000).[2]

On average, industrial countries—especially the Quad countries—grant high and generous tariff preferences to the least developed countries. Still, the preferences given by most Quad countries do not cover some products that would help the least developed countries develop their industrial sectors. These include textiles and clothing, footwear and leather products (Supper, 2000). Tariff peaks are particularly hurtful to the least developed countries because 11 per cent of their exports to the Quad countries are subject to the peaks, even though these constitute just 4 per cent of the Quad's total imports (Hoekman, Ng and Ollarreaga, 2001).

TARIFF ESCALATION. Tariff structures and levels form a barrier to market access in international trade. Tariff escalation raises the effective rate of protection on goods above the nominal tariff rate.[3] A study by the WTO concludes that bound tariffs since the Uruguay Round imply nominal tariff escalation in some sectors (cited in Supper, 2000).[4] Tariff escalation is particularly pronounced for products that offer developing countries the best chance of starting industrial exports—including food industry products, textiles and clothing, footwear, leather products, rubber products and wood industry products. For footwear, most-favoured-nation tariffs reach 260 per cent in Japan (for a pair of leather shoes valued at $25), and average 33–58 per cent for certain rubber, plastic and textile shoes in the US and 18 per cent for shoes in Canada (Supper, 2000, pp. 89–103).

Some of the products subject to tariff peaks or escalation (or both) are considered dynamic products of world trade. As a result developing countries' lack of market access constrains their human development possibilities by blocking their entry into dynamic industrial sectors—limiting their export earnings to traditional sectors. (box 7.2).

High tariffs in industrial countries also encourage developing country producers of labour-intensive manufactures to engage in wage competition—lower real wages, decreasing employment or both. Because women in developing countries are disproportionately employed in labour-intensive manufacturing, especially textiles and clothing, high tariffs seriously undermine their well-being.

HIGHER TARIFFS AND POLICY SPACE IN DEVELOPING COUNTRIES

From a human development viewpoint, higher industrial tariffs in developing countries are justified for two main reasons. The first is to avoid deindustrialization and build competitiveness: Binding industrial tariffs at low levels in developing countries—where industries do not have the capacity to withstand competition from cheaper imports—creates difficulties for their manufacturing sectors. The rapid reduction in industrial tariffs in sub-Saharan Africa since 1980 has resulted in deindustrialization in some countries (box 7.3). Many tariff cuts in developing

BOX 7.2 BANGLADESH'S LOST OPPORTUNITIES FOR HUMAN DEVELOPMENT DUE TO HIGH TARIFFS IN INDUSTRIAL COUNTRIES

Among the least developed countries, Bangladesh would be the biggest beneficiary of duty-free access to all products in the Quad countries (Canada, the EU, Japan, the US). The country's export revenues would increase 45 per cent, with exports of textiles and clothing to Canada and the US rising by more than $700 million in both cases.

The implied financial losses resulting from existing trade barriers also have important implications for poverty reduction efforts. More than 1 million women work in Bangladesh's textiles sector. The sector is the engine of growth in manufacturing, and because production is labour-intensive it generates a wide range of benefits. Increased exports to Canada and the US resulting from the withdrawal of tariff peaks and other restrictions would not only substantially increase employment, they would also help finance investment that the industry needs to prepare for more intense competition.

Source: South Bulletin, 2002.

countries are driven by crises (rather than full employment and rapid growth) or required as a condition of loans from international financial institutions.

An important issue for middle- and higher-income developing countries in building competitiveness is how to move from labour-intensive manufactures to high-skill, technology-intensive products. Doing so requires a solid development strategy, which could involve tariff protection in certain strategic industries. In addition, better access to industrial country markets increases export earnings for developing country industries and supports faster industrialization.

Such developments are especially crucial for the least developed countries. With full preferential duty- and quota-free access to Quad markets for tariff peak products, exports from the least developed countries to these markets are projected to increase 11 per cent (or $2.5 billion)—with a 30–60 per cent increase in exports of tariff peak products (Hoekman, Ng and Ollarreaga, 2001). This does not appear to be a zero-sum game: losses due to trade diversion would be less than 0.1 per cent.

The second justification for higher industrial tariffs in developing countries is to support human development expenditures. To generate much-needed tariff revenue, developing countries—especially low-income and least developed countries—must have a certain threshold of tariff protection. Like all developing countries (box 7.4), the least developed countries are in desperate need of savings, which currently average some 15 per cent of their GDP. To conduct social and industrial policies geared towards human development goals and to generate resources for industrial upgrading, governments of low-income (as well as upper-middle-income) countries need tariff revenues (Rao, 1999).

THE WAY FORWARD

The WTO's new work programme is an important step in recognizing tariff peaks and escalations, along with high tariffs, as targets to be reduced (WTO, 2001).

BOX 7.3 DO REDUCTIONS IN INDUSTRIAL TARIFFS RESULT IN DEINDUSTRIALIZATION?

- Senegal experienced large job losses after a two-stage trade liberalization programme that reduced the average effective rate of protection from 165 per cent in 1985 to 90 per cent in 1988. By the early 1990s employment cuts had eliminated one-third of manufacturing jobs (Weissman, 1990; ADB, 1995, p. 84).

- Côte d'Ivoire's chemical, textiles, footwear and automobile assembly industries collapsed after tariffs were cut 40 per cent in 1986 (Stein, 1992). Similar problems have plagued liberalization attempts in Nigeria. Capacity use fell to 20–30 per cent, and harsh effects on employment and real wages provoked partial policy reversals in 1990, 1992 and 1994.

- In Sierra Leone, Sudan, Tanzania, Uganda, Zaire, and Zambia liberalization in the 1980s generated a huge surge in consumer imports and sharp cutbacks in foreign exchange available for purchases of intermediate inputs and capital goods—with devastating effects on industrial output and employment. In Uganda capacity use in the industrial sector languished at 22 per cent, while consumer imports absorbed 40–60 per cent of foreign exchange (Loxley, 1989).

- Kenya's beverages, tobacco, textiles, sugar, leather, cement and glass sectors have struggled to survive competition from imports since a major trade liberalization program was introduced in 1993. During 1993–97 growth in output fell to 2.6 per cent and growth in manufacturing employment fell to 2.2 per cent (ADB, 1998; Kenya Ministry of Planning and National Development, 1998, p. 164).

- In Ghana manufacturing output and employment grew rapidly after liberalization in 1983, and generous aid from the World Bank greatly increased access to imported inputs. But when liberalization spread to consumer imports, stiffer competition caused manufacturing employment to plunge from 78,700 in 1987 to 28,000 in 1993 (ADB, 1995, p. 397).

- In Zimbabwe formal sector job growth stalled and unemployment doubled to 20 per cent after trade liberalization in 1990. Adjustment in the 1990s was also difficult for the manufacturing sectors in Cameroon, Malawi, Mozambique, Tanzania and Zambia. Import competition caused sharp contractions in output and employment, with many firms closing down (ADB, 1998, pp. 45, 51).

- In the early 1990s liberalization caused large losses in formal sector jobs and substantially increased underemployment in Brazil, Ecuador, Nicaragua and Peru. Evidence from other parts of Latin America is similarly discouraging, with indications that liberalization in the region has caused sharp—and possibly long-lasting—deteriorations in the distribution of income (Berry, 1998, p. 4).

Source: Buffie, 2001, pp. 190–91

Recognizing the importance of taking into account the needs and interests of developing and least developed countries, the programme aims at reducing tariffs, with a focus on products of export interest to these countries (Das, 2002). These reductions are expected to occur with less than full reciprocity in the reduction commitments requested of developing countries. These changes should go into effect as soon as possible and should include complete and binding duty- and quota-free access to industrial country markets for exports from the least developed countries.

Box 7.4 Trade taxes and development policy

Trade taxes (import tariffs and export taxes) are important policy instruments not only because they protect import-competing sectors but also because they provide revenue. Problems in mobilizing public revenue often force developing countries to rely heavily on trade taxes. Though their share of total tax revenue has declined over the past two decades because of trade liberalization, trade taxes remain an important source of revenue for developing countries—especially the least developed countries. Between the 1970s and 1998 trade taxes accounted for 36 percent of tax revenue in low-income countries, 29 per cent in lower-middle-income countries, 19 per cent in upper-middle-income countries and just 3 per cent in high-income countries.

Governments tend to deal with revenue losses resulting from reduced import taxes by cutting public spending, though not by the same amount. Most of these cuts affect social spending such as public investments in infrastructure, education and credit and interest rate subsidies. Increases in trade taxes are correlated with higher gross domestic investment, demonstrating a 'crowding in' effect on domestic capital formation. Thus trade taxes and spending policies can have a significant impact on human development and poverty reduction efforts as well as growth outcomes (through their impact on domestic investment).

Source: Rao, 1999; Khattry and Rao, 2002; Chu, 1990.

By themselves, however, these changes will have limited impact, because enormous pressures remain for developing countries to liberalize industrial tariffs as part of initiatives to form free trade areas with industrial countries. These initiatives include the Free Trade Area of the Americas, the EU-Mercosur (Southern Common Market) free trade area and the follow-up to the Cotonou Agreement, through which African, Caribbean and Pacific countries are to form free trade areas with the EU. Thus it is of considerable importance that provisions for special and differential treatment be introduced into GATT article 24.

As discussed, countries that have effectively integrated with the global economy did not liberalize trade and cut tariffs until after they achieved high, sustained growth. Thus developing countries should be allowed to maintain higher tariffs to provide the flexibility they need as part of their industrial and development efforts. Higher tariffs are necessary to avoid deindustrialization, establish competitiveness in vulnerable domestic sectors and generate resources for social and human development. The empirical record suggests that tariff liberalization will occur once higher levels of human development have been achieved and developing countries integrate with the global economy on their own terms.

The policy flexibility to maintain higher industrial tariffs is also necessary for another important reason. A major difference between industrial and developing countries is that industrial countries have the capacity to provide safety nets for people whose jobs or regions are affected by the increased imports that result from tariff reductions. For example, the first 150 pages of the 2002 US Trade Act set out provisions for assistance to workers and communities that stand to be affected by possible US concessions granted under the tariff negotiating authority provided in the act. Developing countries do not have such capacity. So, as a condition for further bound tariff liberalization, they should seek to establish financial windows that enable them to provide comparable safety nets.

NOTES

1. The recent imposition of high tariffs on US steel imports illustrates the political strength of the forces supporting protection in the sector.

2. In addition, 22 per cent of the tariffs at the six-digit level of the Harmonized System face a most-favoured-nation tariff of more than 15 per cent in at least one Quad country (Hoekman, Ng and Ollarreaga, 2001). Moreover, about 30 per cent of the tariff peaks in Quad countries exceed 30 per cent (Supper, 2000). Finally, 60 per cent of the tariff peaks apply to exports from developing countries to the major industrial countries (UNCTAD, 1999; UNCTAD, 2001).

3. Tariff escalation occurs when tariffs on processed goods exceed those on raw materials in a country's tariff schedule. Thus tariff escalation gives additional protection to domestic processing industries.

4. The study covers the Quad countries, Brazil, Hungary, India, Indonesia, Malaysia and Poland.

REFERENCES

ADB (African Development Bank). 1995. *African Development Report 1995*. New York: Oxford University Press.

———. 1998. *African Development Report 1998*. New York: Oxford University Press.

Berry, R. 1998. 'Introduction'. In A Berry, ed, *Poverty, Economic Reform and Income Distribution in Latin America*. Boulder, Colo.: Lynne Rienner.

Buffie, Edward. 2001. *Trade Policy in Developing Countries*. Cambridge: Cambridge University Press.

Campbell, Bonnie K., and John Loxley. 1989. 'The IMF, the World Bank and Reconstruction in Uganda'. In Bonnie K. Campbell and John Loxley, eds, *Structural Adjustment in Africa*. New York: St. Martin's Press.

Chu, Ke-young. 1990. 'Commodity Exports and Public Finances in Developing Countries'. In V Tanzi, ed, *Fiscal Policy in Open Developing Economies*. Washington, D.C.: International Monetary Fund.

Das, Bhagirath Lal. 1998. *An Introduction to the WTO Agreements*. Penang: Third World Network.

———. 2002. 'The New Work Programme of the WTO'. Third World Network, Penang.

Hoekman, Bernard, Francis Ng and Marcelo Ollarreaga. 2001. 'Eliminating Excessive Tariffs on Exports of Least Developed Countries'. Policy Research Working Paper 2604. World Bank, Washington, D.C.

Kenya Ministry of Planning and National Development, 1998. *Economic Survey 1998.* Nairobi, Kenya.

Khattry, Barsha, and J. Mohan Rao. 2002. 'Fiscal Faux Pas? An Analysis of the Revenue Implications of Trade Liberalization'. University of Massachusetts, Department of Economics, Amherst.

Michalopoulos, Constantine. 1999. 'Developing Country Goals and Strategies for the Millennium Round'. World Bank, Washington, DC.

OECD (Organisation for Economic Co-operation and Development). 2001. *The Development Dimensions of Trade.* Paris.

Prusa, Thomas J. and Susan Skeath. 2001. *The Economic and Strategic Motives for Anti-dumping Filings.* NBER Working Paper 8424. Cambridge, Mass.: National Bureau of Economic Research.

Rao, J. Mohan. 1998. 'Development in the Time of Globalization'. United Nations Development Programme, Social Development and Poverty Elimination Division, New York.

———. 1999. 'Globalization and the Fiscal Autonomy of the State'. Background paper for *Human Development Report 1999: Globalization with a Human Face.* United Nations Development Programme, New York.

South Bulletin. 2002. [www.southcentre.org/info/southbulletin/bulletin13/southbulletin13web-05.htm].

Stein, H. 1992. 'Deindustrialization, Adjustment and the World Bank and the IMF in Africa'. *World Development* 20 (6): 83-95.

Supper, Erich. 2000. 'The Post–Uruguay Round Tariff Environment for Developing Country Exports: Tariff Peaks and Tariff Escalation'. In *Positive Agenda and Future Trade Negotiations.* New York and Geneva: United Nations Conference on Trade and Development.

TWN (Third World Network). 2001. 'The Multilateral Trading System: A Development Perspective'. Background paper for the Trade and Sustainable Human Development Project. United Nations Development Programme, New York.

UNCTAD (United Nations Conference on Trade and Development). Various years. *Trade and Development Report.* Geneva.

VanGrasstek, Craig. 2001. 'The Political Economy of Residual Tariff Protection in the United States'. United Nations Conference on Trade and Development, Geneva.

Weissman, S., 1990. 'Structural Adjustment in Africa: Insights from the Experiences of Ghana and Senegal'. *World Development* 18: 1621–34.

WTO (World Trade Organization). 1994. 'General Agreement on Trade in Services'. Geneva. www.wto.org/english/docs_e/legal_e/final_e.htm

———. 2001. Doha 4th Ministerial—'Ministerial Declaration'. [www.wto.org/english/thewto_e/minist_e/min01_e/mindecl_e.htm].

CHAPTER 8
TEXTILES AND CLOTHING

As Adam Smith ([1776] 1998) pointed out, basic and proper clothing enables people to appear in public without shame and thus is an important means to human development. Clothing plays a crucial role in human development not only in the form of finished goods. The labour-intensive production of textiles and clothing generates significant employment—and productive employment provides people with the means for a decent standard of living and enhances their self-esteem and their participation in society. Moreover, in most economies, employment in textile and clothing production is biased towards women and thus has a gender dimension. But the processes often used in textile and clothing production may have serious adverse effects on human health and the environment. All these issues have implications for human development. So does the structure of international trade in textiles and clothing.

Textiles and clothing have received trade protection unprecedented in degree and duration. Indeed, even after the conclusion of the Uruguay Round agreements in 1994, which paved the way to trade liberalization around the world, strong inherent tendencies have remained to protect textiles and clothing. The issue of the liberalization of this trade has divided developing and industrial countries over the years. Even after the World Trade Organization (WTO) Ministerial Conference in Doha in 2001, the implementation issues that relate to the Uruguay Round agreement on textiles and clothing remain a key concern for developing countries.

THE ROAD TO AGREEMENT ON TEXTILES AND CLOTHING: A HISTORICAL REVIEW

The history of protectionism in textile and clothing trade is old and deeply rooted. Once an agreement on textile and clothing trade was reached, the tendency was to extend it again and again (box 8.1). For example, the Long-Term Arrangement, to commence 1 October 1962 and last for five years, was extended twice—first in 1967 and then in 1970—each time for three years. The story is the same for the Multifibre Arrangement (MFA).

Although box 8.1 identifies many of the milestones in agreements on textile and clothing trade, it does not cover some of the measures by individual countries

---

Box 8.1 Milestones in agreements on textiles and clothing trade

- December 1955: Japan unilaterally restrains exports of cotton fabrics and clothing to the US.

- January 1957: Japan and the US reach a five-year agreement limiting Japan's overall textile exports to the US.

- November 1958: The UK signs a voluntary restraint agreement on cotton textile and clothing imports from Hong Kong, China (SAR).

- September 1959: The UK signs similar restraint agreements with India and Pakistan.

- July 1961: Agreement is reached on the Short-Term Arrangement.

- February 1962: Agreement is reached on the Long-Term Arrangement (LTA), to last five years.

- April 1967: Agreement is reached to extend the LTA for three years.

- October 1970: Agreement is reached to extend the LTA for another three years.

- December 1973: Agreement is reached on the Multifibre Arrangement (MFA), to last four years.

- December 1977: The MFA is extended for four years.

- December 1981: The MFA is renewed for another five years.

- July 1991: The MFA is extended pending the outcome of the Uruguay Round negotiations.

- December 1993: The draft final act of the Uruguay Round provides for a ten-year phase-out of all MFA and other textile quotas under the Agreement on Textiles and Clothing.

Source: Aggarwal, 1985; Finger and Harrison, 1996.

---

or groups. For example, in 1971, the US negotiated voluntary export restraints on wool and human-made fibres with Asian suppliers, and in 1977 the European Economic Community negotiated bilateral arrangements with developing countries before agreeing to the extension of the MFA.

As many Asian countries began to develop their textile and clothing industries in the 1960s and particularly in the early 1970s, it became obvious to the governments of importing countries that a more comprehensive package of restraints needed to be designed. They considered this essential to effective regulation of the rapidly expanding spectrum of textile and clothing products emerging from developing countries and threatening the textile and clothing industries in industrial countries. While the MFA contained wording underlining the agreement's short duration—just long enough to permit structural adjustment in industrial countries—this short-term nature had by no means become apparent by the end of the 1980s. What had become apparent was that the entire set-up had become so complex that there seemed to be almost no reasonable solution but to phase out the

TABLE 8.1

Textile and clothing exports of 13 leading exporters, 1965–96

(per cent)

	Share in world exports				Growth rate		
					1965–	1973–	1983–
	1965	1973	1983	1996	73	83	96
Textiles and clothing	79	73	67	65	15	10	10
Textiles	79	73	67	72	13	8	9
Clothing	80	73	67	60	19	13	10

Note: The 13 exporters are Belgium-Luxembourg, China, France, Germany, Hong Kong, China (SAR), India, Italy, Japan, the Republic of Korea, Taiwan (province of China), Turkey, the UK and the US.
Source: WTO, 1997.

MFA during the Uruguay Round. Thus the Uruguay Round Agreement on Textiles and Clothing (ATC) was born.

Although no systematic study was done of the human development implications of all these events in textile and clothing trade, it is easy to point to some probable and possible effects. First, the measures taken by industrial countries to protect their textile and clothing sectors probably did not maximize global employment and income. Asian countries could have gained greater human development benefits if they had had free access to industrial country markets. Second, even in developing countries the protection of the textile and clothing sector might have limited the benefits in productivity, higher wages and employment to the workforce in that sector, which had few links with others. Third, protection of textiles and clothing might have led to distorted and inefficient resource allocation, limiting public resources for the basic social services critical for well-being, particularly for poor people.

GROWTH IN TEXTILE AND CLOTHING TRADE

How has the flow of world trade in textiles and clothing developed over the past 30 years? The performance of 13 leading exporters of these products provides a summary picture (table 8.1). On the whole the shares of the leading exporters have tended to slowly shrink over the years. But the picture is quite different for textiles than for clothing. In textiles the 13 leading exporters have nearly held their own shares since 1973, when the MFA was enacted. In clothing, however, these exporters have been continually losing market share to other countries, particularly developing countries.

Breaking down these trends between industrial and developing economies yields a more varied picture. In textiles, the industrial economies lost as much market share as the developing economies gained during 1973–96. In other words, a reallocation took place between the industrial and developing economies within the group of leading exporters, and other countries were unsuccessful in capturing market share. In clothing, major shifts took place between the industrial and developing economies within the group of leading exporters during the same period, but also between the leading exporters and other countries.

Indeed, analysis of the situation four years before the Uruguay Round agreements and three years afterward shows that since the ATC has been in effect, the exporters not in that top group in 1997 were the ones able to increase their world market share. This is particularly true for clothing exports, in which these exporters almost doubled their share—from 4 per cent to 7 per cent—in just the three years from 1994 to 1997.

Thus countries other than the leading exporters also had impressive growth in textiles and clothing. In many of these countries the rapid growth had significant effects in areas that may have direct implications for human development. Take the example of Bangladesh. During the past decade and a half the real growth in exports of ready-made garments (12 per cent) was more than twice the real growth in GDP in the same period. This rapid growth contributed to an increase in real per capita income and played an important part in reducing the incidence of poverty. It also contributed to a significant increase in female employment. In Bangladesh more than 90 per cent of the 1.8 million workers employed in the ready-made garment sector are women, mostly from rural areas (Bhattacharya and Rahman, 2000). As many studies have pointed out, this employment has not only contributed to women's income but has also had positive effects on their educational attainment, on their decisions about marriage and on the number of children they desire (see, for example, Bhattacharya and Rahman, 2000; Jahan, 2002; and Rose, 2002). More broadly, the employment has increased their economic independence and improved their position within the household, resulting in the empowerment and liberation of women in Bangladesh society.

At the same time these female workers have often been the victims of exploitation, oppression and mistreatment at their workplace. They are frequently underpaid, forced to put in long hours, given no lunch break and provided no proper toilet facilities. They are not allowed to unionize, and they are denied workers' rights. As has been widely reported, there have been instances in which factory work floors were put under lock and key and hundreds of female workers died when fire broke out. And there have been instances in which female workers were subjected to sexual exploitation and rape by their employers.

The intention here is not to weigh the negatives against the positives. Instead, it is to show that the textile and clothing sector provides an important opportunity for empowering women socially and economically in many developing countries—but the strategy must be to take advantage of the positives and eliminate the negatives. Moreover, the negatives female workers face in this sector should not be used as an excuse for slowing liberalization under the ATC nor as justification for protection. The textile and clothing sector has helped increase women's freedom in many societies, and the negatives they face should be put into context.

THE UNDERLYING DYNAMICS OF THE AGREEMENTS ON TEXTILE AND CLOTHING TRADE

Whether textiles and clothing have received much greater protection over the past four decades than other internationally traded goods is an important question, but it is not the key issue relating to the MFA. Instead, the key issue is that textiles and clothing were exempted from basic GATT disciplines because of a deal struck between importing and exporting countries. This deal was cut outside the GATT legal framework by selling exporting countries the right to continue to export given amounts of textiles and clothing to importing (that is, industrial) countries. The selling point was simple: the exporting countries could capture the rents from restricting supply.

There was a flip side, of course: the exporting countries had to accept the quantitative limits dictated to them. These limits were based largely on the past performance of those exporters. The use of past performance naturally led to discontent among those not initially members and spawned problems along the way. The deal was carried out under the pretence of being only temporary—that is, lasting just long enough to permit the necessary structural adjustment in industrial countries. Moreover, the purveyors of the deal retained the option to apply contingent protection measures (such as anti-dumping proceedings) if imports grew fast.

The differing effects of the Multifibre Arrangement on exporters

There is no denying that in many developing countries the textile and clothing trade under the MFA has yielded benefits with implications for human development. In Bangladesh, for example, the ready-made garment business grew from US$1 million in 1978 to US$4.5 billion in 2001, equivalent to 76 per cent of the country's exports. The apparel sector accounts for about a fourth of the economy's value added, a third of its manufacturing employment and a fifth of its annual investment. The sector employs about 1.8 million workers in its 2,800 factories and supports roughly US$2 billion of economic activity in such areas as banking, transport, insurance, packaging, real estate, utility services, consumer goods and hotels and tourism. About 80 per cent of garment accessories (such as belts, buttons and zippers), worth about US$0.5 billion, are now domestically produced. And the ready-made garment sector contributes about 85 cents of every dollar of incremental exports from Bangladesh (Bhattacharya and Rahman, 2000).

Yet the picture has been quite different in many other developing regions. In fact, in Africa the textile industry has had negative growth under the MFA. In 1974–94 the region's market share for eight textile products declined by an average of nearly 2.0 per cent a year, and its market share of cotton yarn by 0.1 per cent a year. So while the MFA has allowed the African textile industry some preferences, the industry has nevertheless shrunk (Sireh-Jallow, 2000). The MFA has thus undoubtedly had implications for human development.

The phase-out of the Multifibre Arrangement

The ATC, the agreed solution to the problems of the MFA, sets out a basic framework with some specific targets:

- The MFA is to be phased out in four tranches over ten years (1 January 1995, 1 January 1998, 1 January 2002 and 1 January 2005), encompassing 16 per cent, 17 per cent, 18 per cent and 49 per cent of all imports of specified textile and clothing products based on volumes in 1990.

- Imports of products not liberalized but under quota are allowed to grow by 16 per cent, 25 per cent and 27 per cent during the first three steps of the phase-out.

- Each of the four groups into which the spectrum of textile products has been broken (fabrics, clothing, made-up textile products and tops and yarns) must be included in each of the liberalization tranches during the ten years.

- The liberalization process for members is binding and final—that is, there is to be no extension of the quota phase-out beyond 2004.

For Africa the phase-out seems to have brought some benefits. For example, while its market share of the eight textile products declined by 0.7 per cent a year in 1994–96, this was significantly less than the 1.9 per cent annual decline between 1974 and 1994. And the market share of the African clothing industry grew by 0.1 per cent a year in 1994–96, a great improvement over the 2.5 per cent annual decline between 1974–94 (Sireh-Jallow, 2000).

But given the propensity of countries to protect their own interests, the ATC has defined a process for eventually integrating textiles and clothing under GATT principles that clearly allows too much leeway (box 8.2). The probable result will be less than optimal for human development in developing countries.

FACTORS AND EVENTS INFLUENCING THE PRESENT SITUATION IN TEXTILE AND CLOTHING TRADE

The present situation in textile and clothing trade is complex, reflecting the influence of several factors, events and trends.

Normal development trends

The effect of normal development trends can best be described as a growing up process in which countries switch to more physical- or human-capital-intensive areas of textile and clothing production as their incomes rise. The advance of economies such as the Republic of Korea and Taiwan (province of China) is particularly evident in their steadily growing share of the clothing export market as they became increasingly efficient in clothing production. In addition, in the early 1980s they shifted out of the labour-intensive production of clothing and concentrated on the capital-intensive production of textiles.

Box 8.2 Leeway in the Agreement on Textiles and Clothing

The Agreement on Textiles and Clothing (ATC) specifies and declares as binding the amount of ATC products (in essence, tariff lines of eight, ten or even more digits) to be brought under GATT principles. But it does not stipulate that textile and clothing products not under quota or other restraints will be more quickly brought under those disciplines. Thus the ATC products to be liberalized outnumber those specified in the Uruguay Round agreements and far outnumber those covered by actual restraints in the European Union, the US and other industrial economies. Moreover, nowhere does the ATC stipulate that the products covered by the Multifibre Arrangement (MFA) that are under quota but for which only the minimum quota is utilized (that is, cases of quota redundancy) should be integrated more quickly under GATT principles. And the volume treatment of ATC products ensures that the economic value of the products liberalized is only loosely correlated with the actual amount liberalized, because the prices of the products may be low.

In addition, the agreed upon increase in quota growth rates during liberalization means very little if the actual growth rates are small. Since the growth rates assigned to major suppliers are quite low, little can be expected from this stipulation. For example, for Hong Kong, China (SAR) 85 per cent of the products under quota have growth rates of 3 per cent or less, and for China the growth rates are less than 4 per cent. The growth rates for most Asian countries are less than 5 per cent.

Finally, the lack of agreement on the manner in which liberalized items are to be distributed across the four types of textile and clothing products to be liberalized, beyond the requirement that some amounts from each group must be included, left the door open to a perverse development: all sensitive products (largely clothing) have been shifted to the last liberalization tranche.

Source: Jahan, 2002.

Of course, some of this export growth must be attributed to the MFA, since countries maintained production activities, but with higher value added shares, to capture rent from the quotas they held. Thus it could be contended that the MFA hindered countries from following an efficient development plan: it kept productive resources flowing into the textile and clothing industries long after they should have been flowing into more efficient production activities such as consumer goods.

Shifting factor intensities of production

The difference in the capital intensities of production between the textile and clothing industries has been one factor driving trade flows in their products. But the MFA has also played a part. In the textile industry major advances in technology have helped maintain production in industrial countries. The greater capital intensity in the textile industry also helps explain why, given the possibility of efficiently carrying out different stages of production in different locations, it has become worthwhile for such countries as Germany, Italy and the US to produce the capital-intensive inputs and then have them made into clothes just east or south of their border.

But the pattern may change once non-tariff barriers are removed. It is quite likely that it was the MFA that kept major European producers from establishing large spinning and fabric manufacturing facilities in the countries with high productivity and low labour costs—that is, in Asia. After all, given the existence of quotas, the European companies could not be sure that such facilities would be able to produce at adequate capacity. But with quotas now being eliminated, these producers may invest in Asia—and indeed, there are indications that this is occurring.

Another issue relates to the production of machines. With ever-larger shares of the textile and clothing industries now being located in developing countries, textile machinery companies have begun to establish production facilities in these countries. These facilities not only assemble textile machines but also test them on-site. Even more important, the companies are creating machines better adapted to conditions in developing countries. But this shift will apply to only parts of the industry, since there are still reasons to maintain research and production facilities in industrial countries (such as the productive interface between the industry and technical universities).

Fallacy of composition

World trade in many manufactures, mainly labour-intensive products, has been accelerating, raising the risk that once export growth goes beyond some threshold, prices will drop sharply. This is the well-known problem of the fallacy of composition, or the adding up problem: on its own a small developing country can substantially expand its exports without flooding the market and significantly reducing the prices of the products, but this may not be true for the developing world as a whole or even for large countries such as China or India. Rapid growth in exports of labour-intensive products could potentially lead to a reduction in the terms of trade large enough so that the benefits of the increased volume of exports may be more than offset by losses due to lower prices—that is, to immiserizing growth.

The fallacy of composition may be quite relevant to trade in textiles and clothing, whose production is quite labour-intensive. Between 1980–98 textiles and clothing were among the most dynamic products in world trade, growing by an average of more than 13 per cent a year. They were surpassed only by electronic and electrical goods, with a growth rate of more than 16 per cent a year. Markets for clothing have been more competitive than those for most other manufactures. In 1997–98 the index of market concentration for clothing was about 400, compared with more than 800 for electronics. Moreover, developing countries have attempted simultaneous export drives in textiles and clothing. And there have been signs that the terms of trade have been weakening for developing countries in textiles and clothing.

But whether these trends will lead to the fallacy of composition in textile and clothing trade will depend on many other factors, including market access conditions for these products, the pace of diversification in developing countries' exports, the full implementation of the ATC and growth in China's market share. Developing countries face significant barriers to market access. Trade in textiles and clothing continues to be governed by quota regulations, and developing countries encounter high tariffs, tariff escalation and increased use of contingent forms of protection, notably anti-dumping actions and new barriers such as labour and environmental standards. Tariffs in most industrial countries increase with the level of processing for textiles and clothing, particularly compared with leather, foot wear and travel goods. Such products are often excluded from preferential tariff schemes such as the Generalized System of Preferences. And tariff peaks in industrial countries for non-agricultural products are concentrated in textiles and clothing. Taken together, clothing and footwear represent more than 60 per cent of developing country products affected by tariff peaks. Developing countries, by lowering tariffs on textile and clothing imports from other developing countries, could also reduce the risk of fallacy of composition in this sector.

The risk of fallacy of composition in textiles and clothing has serious implications for human development. With simultaneous export drives by developing countries, the prices of textiles and clothing may fall, leading to lower wages for the workers in this sector. Since most of these workers are unskilled, alternative employment opportunities are slim. The result will be greater job insecurity and lower income and purchasing power. The ripple effects will be felt in poorer health and education outcomes, lower standards of living and shaky safety nets. Since women make up most of the workforce in textiles and clothing, they will bear the brunt of all these adverse effects as well as a decline in their economic independence, participation and social empowerment.

The Multifibre Arrangement and its tariff and non-tariff barriers

It has been argued that of all the trade liberalization measures agreed to in the Uruguay Round, eliminating the MFA would yield the greatest global welfare gains. Based on a computable general equilibrium (CGE) model, it was estimated at the end of the Uruguay Round that liberalizing textile and clothing trade would account for almost 40 per cent of the total welfare gains expected from the trade liberalization measures (François, 1996). The model is subject to qualifications, and changes in the world economy since the model was estimated may alter some of its results (box 8.3). Yet it is broadly indicative of the significant global welfare losses stemming from protectionism in textiles and clothing.

Tariffs on textiles and clothing have long been high relative to those on other products. While the unweighted pre–Uruguay Round tariff in the European Union was 5.7 per cent for all manufactured products, for textiles it was 10.1 per cent and for clothing 12.3 per cent. The structure for US tariffs is assumed to be quite similar, though the tariff rates are higher on average. Post–Uruguay Round tariffs on textiles and clothing in industrial countries remain highest except for

BOX 8.3 WELFARE GAINS FROM LIBERALIZING TEXTILES AND CLOTHING TRADE: QUALIFICATIONS TO THE MODELS

Based on a computable general equilibrium (CGE) model, the global welfare gains from the liberalization of trade in textiles and clothing has been estimated to be 40 per cent of the gains from the liberalization of all trade. But this estimate and others based on similar models are subject to qualifications, as the models fail to take into account crucial aspects of the Multifibre Arrangement (MFA).

First, quota rents applied in the models as accruing to exporting economies reflect the world as it was in the 1980s, particularly the world as it was in Hong Kong, China (SAR). (Quota rents are the amounts paid by traders or producers that need quotas to holders of quotas in an exporting country for specific textile and clothing products destined for specific importing countries. The quota rents vary according to the level of demand and the monthly fluctuations in demand. To the extent that they remain in exporting countries, they represent the amount of income transferred to such countries from importing countries.) Times have changed, and quota rents in Hong Kong, China (SAR) and other exporting economies have been declining sharply and in many cases even approaching zero. Thus one of the main factors said to be reducing global welfare seems to be disappearing.

Second, economies such as Hong Kong, China (SAR), the Republic of Korea and Taiwan (province of China) have long since begun to produce offshore many of the textile and clothing products that they used to manufacture domestically. In doing so they are still taking advantage of quota rents. The CGE model calculations of welfare gains do not allow for capital flows from Hong Kong, China (SAR)—or other exporting economies—to a second economy and, perhaps more important, do not allow for the transfer back to Hong Kong, China (SAR) of rents accruing to this capital. Thus the models do not correctly take into account the distribution of the welfare gains among developing economies or regions—nor perhaps the size of those gains.

The straightforward CGE estimates of welfare gains from eliminating the MFA may well be wrongly specified and, to the extent that quota rents have not been correctly adjusted to current levels, overstated.

Source: Krishna and Tan, 1997.

those on agricultural products, ranging from three to five times the tariffs for all industrial goods. Moreover, the tariff reductions in this product category have been among the smallest (table 8.2). All this reflects the sensitivity of this sector to liberalization and the strong desire to continue to protect it. It also shows that industrial countries still need to reduce tariffs considerably to truly improve market access. Since the tariff rates have not changed much, there has probably been little effect on the trade in textiles and clothing of developing countries.

The quota system established under the MFA and now being eliminated by the ATC has also generated a structure of exporting countries that has little to do with comparative advantage and much to do with market shares based on the availability of quotas. And if this changing trend (gradual elimination of the quota system) points to likely developments under the system without quotas that is to be introduced on 1 January 2005, major lower-cost suppliers today will lose out to countries like China.

TABLE 8.2

***Post–Uruguay Round tariff rates and concessions
in selected countries and groups***
(per cent)

Product category	European Union		US		Developing countries		Industrial countries	
	Rate	Reduction	Rate	Reduction	Rate	Reduction	Rate	Reduction
Agriculture[a]	15.7	−5.9	10.8	−1.5	17.4	−43.0	26.9	−26.9
Textiles and clothing	8.7	−2.0	14.8	−2.0	21.2	−8.5	8.4	−2.6
Metals	1.0	−3.3	1.1	−3.8	10.8	−9.5	0.9	−3.4
Chemicals	3.8	−3.3	2.5	−4.9	12.4	−9.7	2.2	−3.7

a. Excludes fish. Data for agriculture include the tariff equivalents of non-tariff barriers.
Source: Finger and Harrison, 1996.

For developing countries, one of the most visible impacts of the MFA is the trend away from quota prices or rents. With the elimination of the quota system, these rents may disappear. And in some exporting economies the structure and location of quota rents may change. Consider the case of Hong Kong, China (SAR), the only economy for which consistent and reliable data on quota rents are available (box 8.4).

Regional trade agreements and changing locational demands

Regional integration schemes, together with the changes in locational demands resulting from just-in-time policies and ever-faster fashion cycles, have had a major effect on trade flows of textiles and clothing. For example, in Europe the completion of the single market, the expansion of the European Union and the attempts to integrate Central and Eastern European economies have all prompted textile and clothing industries to rethink corporate strategies. Given the importance of minimizing the economic distance between production and consumption locations in such a time-conscious industry as fashion, it is clearly easier to achieve just-in-time production, rapid reordering and a quick fashion response by working with neighbouring countries rather than Asian exporters. On the other side of the Atlantic, the North American Free Trade Agreement (NAFTA) has had a similar effect in shifting demand away from Asian suppliers of textiles and clothing.

BOX 8.4 QUOTA RENTS: THE CASE OF HONG KONG, CHINA (SAR)

Data on utilization rates and rents for quota in the European Union and the US show that Hong Kong, China (SAR) has been able to maintain quota rents only in knitted clothes, for which the value added content and the quality requirements are quite high. Its quota rents have dropped considerably in all other areas, even though quota utilization rates have remained quite high in many cases.

But this is only half the story. Producers from Hong Kong, China (SAR) have long since moved their production to offshore locations, where they are presumably capturing quota rents. Thus the welfare losses for consumers in importing countries may be just as large as before.

Source: Jahan, 2002.

In addition, in both Europe and the US, offshore processing legislation has enabled firms to circumvent MFA quotas and helped induce them to establish more than just arm's-length production platforms in neighbouring countries. The offshore processing trade also makes nearer locations cheaper. And because tariffs are applied only to the value added when domestically produced intermediate inputs are re-imported as a final or near-final product, it can lead to considerable cost savings relative to direct importation.

As a result of these forces, the flow of the European Union's trade in textiles and clothing has changed. Since 1993 Asian countries, particularly East Asian countries, have been losing out to Mediterranean countries—from Turkey to Morocco—in the markets of Germany, Italy, Sweden and the UK. And in the US market they have been losing out to Latin American countries, whose market share nearly doubled during 1990–97, accounting for almost all the decline in the share of imports from Asia.

Implications for human development

All these factors and events influencing the present situation in textile and clothing trade will have significant impacts with implications for human development. For example, regional trade agreements and changing locations of production and offshore processing trade will rob many developing countries of their potential for further growth and trade in textiles and clothing. Lost business will mean lost jobs and income, with women especially affected. Thus while textile and clothing trade will contribute to human development in some regions, it will do so only at the expense of others.

The changing factor intensities of production will lead to the concentration of capital-intensive—and higher value added—production of textiles and clothing in the industrial world. Meanwhile, many developing countries will continue to be engaged in less productive, low-skilled, lower value added activities, with little potential for boosting income, growth and other aspects of human development.

Tariff and non-tariff barriers in textile and clothing trade will continue to restrict developing countries' access to global markets, retarding their economic growth and thus their ability to generate employment and income. Moreover, lower export revenue may mean lower government revenue, limiting public provisioning of basic social services such as education and health care.

THE FUTURE OUTLOOK FOR TEXTILE AND CLOTHING TRADE

Only marginal progress has been made in phasing out MFA and other quotas on textiles and clothing. The world was successful in reaching an agreement on textile and clothing products in the form of the ATC. But in the Uruguay Round it has been just as unsuccessful in structuring the agreement in a way that will effectively bring textiles and clothing under the multilateral trade framework during the phase-out period. As the previous section shows, many factors have influenced the process over the years. And a look ahead suggests that many factors will continue to do so in the future as well.

The Agreement on Textiles and Clothing: Dilution and postponement

The ATC watered down the liberalization process by including a far wider range of textile and clothing products in the group to be liberalized than was ever included in the MFA to begin with. And it postponed any significant liberalization until the final tranche of 1 January 2005, when it is hoped that the most sensitive products will be subject to basic WTO disciplines.

This disingenuous result is best represented by simply noting that less sensitive products, such as tire cords, tampons and tents, were liberalized by Canada, the European Union and the US in the first liberalization tranche of 1 January 1995 (Baughman and others, 1997). But the European Union barely included the highly sensitive clothing sector, liberalizing only 1 per cent of the quota for clothing imports, rather than the targeted 17 per cent. The story for the US was much the same. For Hong Kong, China (SAR), which has Asia's second largest share of clothing among its exports (79 per cent), clothing accounted for some 6 per cent of the products liberalized in the first tranche, and only 4 per cent in the second tranche. With progress like this, how will things stand at the time of the last tranche in January 2005, when 49 per cent of products are supposed to be liberalized?

The potential dangers of contingent protectionism

Whether the shift in textile and clothing trade resulting from regional trade agreements or offshore processing trade can be considered a diversion away from efficient sources is an open question that requires in-depth analysis. It is most crucial to determine whether trade flows will remain essentially the same after all trade restrictions are removed.

It is true that the European Union and the US have generally wanted to exclude the most competitive textile and, especially, clothing products as long as possible. Since most of these happen to be produced in Asia, its countries have been most affected by slow growth in quotas and slow liberalization. Major importing countries and groups in the industrial world appear to be willing to continue with the status quo in textile and clothing trade, fostering the risk of an impasse in liberalization in 2005.

The ATC safeguard mechanism attempts to limit the leeway for instituting such protectionist measures. But there are ways of getting around the ATC safeguards, including, most seriously, anti-dumping measures and technical barriers to trade (box 8.5). The introduction of the ATC in 1995 was not followed by a surge in such contingent protectionist measures. But they do hold a potential for undermining the letter and spirit of the ATC in the future.

BOX 8.5 WAYS TO GET AROUND THE SAFEGUARDS OF THE AGREEMENT ON TEXTILES AND CLOTHING

One way to get around the safeguards of the Agreement on Textiles and Clothing (ATC) is to use anti-dumping measures. The other is to apply technical barriers to trade. In the days to come the process for initiating anti-dumping proceedings should be subject to revision. The biggest problem is that it is the industry claiming to be affected by dumping that is responsible for requesting an anti-dumping investigation. In the past such requests have sometimes been founded on incorrect—if not outright fabricated—information about who is dumping imports and how severe the effect of the dumping is.

The situation relating to technical barriers to trade is even more ambiguous. The Uruguay Round agreements do not question the right of countries to introduce technical standards that they feel are necessary. These standards merely have to be applied in a way that does not discriminate between foreign and domestic producers. Even the conditions under which the technical standards are applied are not subject to question. So far, however, there appears to be no proliferation of technical standards for textile and clothing products that are intended to serve as contingent protection.

Source: Jahan, 2002.

China's accession to the World Trade Organization

The accession of China to the WTO in 2001 has important implications for textile and clothing trade, particularly for many least developed countries. First, China is projected to be the biggest winner in the post-MFA era, taking over fully 10 per cent of the world garment trade in the next ten years (Spaninger, 1999a). Second, China is a major producer in almost every important export category for many least developed countries which specialize in low-value items. Third, China has shown excellent performance in the few categories that have been liberalized thus far. In the category including cotton dressing gowns, robes and the like, China's exports to the US market increased by 483 per cent between the first half of 2001 and the first half of 2002. In the same period such exports from Bangladesh, a least developed country, fell by 42.7 per cent. China also experienced a surge in overall garment exports to the US market in the first half of 2002, with its export volume increasing by more than 41 per cent and its export value by over 12 per cent compared with the first half of 2001. Meanwhile, Bangladesh saw its export volume to the US market fall by almost 10 per cent and its export value by over 14 per cent.

As countries like Bangladesh lose out to countries like China, many garment exporting countries in the developing world fear a bleak future, expecting extensive restructuring in the world garment trade in the post-MFA era. While the most competitive producers may prosper, many garment manufacturing units will close or downsize in low-income countries, with serious consequences for human development (box 8.6).

Box 8.6 Effects of phasing out the Multifibre Arrangement on human development in Bangladesh

Phasing out the Multifibre Arrangement (MFA) is likely to lead to the closure and downsizing of garment manufacturing units in Bangladesh—a potentially disastrous outcome for many of the estimated 1.8 million workers in the garment sector. Most of these workers are girls or young women who migrated from rural areas, often in response to a crisis—flooding or erosion, injury or illness of the primary income earner. Their families depend on their wages, and surveys show that 80 per cent of the families of garment workers would fall below the poverty line without that source of income.

Surveys have shown that without the wages of a garment worker, 80% of garment workers' families would fall below the poverty line. Female garment workers provide 46% of their total family income, while 23% of unmarried garment workers (both male and female) account for their families' primary source of income. Moreover, 70% of workers have migrated from rural to urban areas because of a push or crisis, such as displacement from flooding or erosion, or because the prime income earner has been injured or fallen sick. All in all, it is clear that workers' families can be expected to face enormous financial difficulties when a factory closes.

Closure of a large number of garment manufacturing units would leave few options for young female workers. The garment sector is the only source of large-scale formal employment for women. Other possibilities include tailoring, domestic work and office cleaning, but none of these jobs provides the comparatively high and consistent wages or relatively good working conditions found in the garment sector. Even worse, many female workers have little or no work experience outside garment production and thus few other skills. So the loss of garment jobs would translate into higher poverty and the loss of employment opportunities for women.

Moreover, the effects would be felt beyond the garment manufacturing sector. Many industries feed off garment exports—from textile and accessory production to transport, hotel, banking and shipping services. An estimated $2 billion in economic activity is derived from garment exports as a result of these linkages. The larger economy of the poor also relies heavily on garment workers' wages. Surrounding the garment factories are innumerable small shops and vendors selling food, cosmetics, clothing, medicines and the like. And with a sizeable share of garment workers' wages returning to villages as remittances, the village economy has received a big impetus from the garment industry. Thus a broad decline in that industry would harm far more poor people than most estimates suggest.

Source: Rose, 2002; Paul-Majumder and Begum, 2000.

An uncertain future

The major textile and clothing exporting countries, primarily in the developing world, increasingly distrust the major importing countries, primarily in the industrial world. And that trend is not good. At the 1996 WTO ministerial meeting in Singapore the developing countries' frustrations over the industrial world's intentions and actions with respect to textile and clothing trade led these countries to virtually threaten to allow this trade to collapse if significant changes were not made. The developing countries called for a structure of liberalization that would reduce the probability of an impasse in 2005 when the remaining 49 per cent of textile and clothing products have to be liberalized.

At the 2001 WTO Ministerial Conference in Doha liberalization of textiles and clothing was a key concern for developing countries in relation to the implementation of the Uruguay Round agreements. Annex II of the Doha Decision on Implementation-Related Issues and Concerns contains important provisions to encourage faster movement on liberalizing textile quotas and agreement by liberalizing countries to exercise restraint in applying anti-dumping measures for two years after textiles and clothing are fully liberalized. How these provisions will work in practice remains to be seen. But the present situation in textile and clothing trade suggests that the world may be sitting on a time bomb ready to explode on 31 December 2004.

The bigger picture—human development

All these issues need to be addressed in the context of human development. Implementing the ATC properly and in a timely way is not necessary just because the global community agreed to do so. It is also essential because liberalizing trade in textiles and clothing will bring economic and human development benefits to people in developing countries. Similarly, the issues of tariff and non-tariff barriers, anti-dumping, offshore processing and ATC safeguards should be tackled from that broader perspective. Taking the bigger picture into account, the policy implications are the following :

- It is important to ensure that quotas are eliminated and that the MFA is phased out by December 2004 and not replaced by escalating anti-dumping cases in textiles and clothing.

- Misuse of the ATC safeguard mechanism should not be allowed. Particular attention must be paid to technical barriers to trade, as they offer a way of getting around the safeguards.

- The phase-out of the MFA should reduce tariff protection in the large North American and European markets enough to allow access for competitive developing countries affected by regional trade arrangements.

- Supportive measures should be in place to assist the least developed countries and specific population groups in both developing and industrial countries, especially women, who may be worst affected by the MFA phase-out.

The immediate purpose of all these policy measures should be to expand developing countries' access to and opportunities in textile and clothing trade. But the ultimate aim should be to enhance the capabilities and choices of their people. In the final analysis the issues affecting textile and clothing trade should be viewed not merely as international trade issues but as broader human development issues.

REFERENCES

Aggarwal, Vinod K. 1985. *Liberal Protectionism: The International Politics of Organized Textile Trade.* Berkeley: University of California Press.

Baughman, L, Rolf Mirus, Morris Morkre and Dean Spaninger. 1997. 'Of Tyre Cords, Ties and Tents: Window-Dressing in the ATC?' *World Economy* 20 (4): 407–34.

Bhattacharya, Debapriya, and Mustafizur Rahman. 2000. 'Experience with Implementation of WTO-ATC and Implications for Bangladesh'. Centre for Policy Dialogue, Dhaka.

Finger, J Michael, and Ann Harrison. 1996. 'The MFA Paradox: More Protection and More Trade?' In Anne O. Krueger, ed, *The Political Economy of American Trade Policy*. Chicago: University of Chicago Press.

François, Joseph F. 1995. 'Assessing the Uruguay Round'. In Will Martin and L Alan Winters, eds, *The Uruguay Round and the Developing Economies*. World Bank Discussion Paper 307. Washington, DC.

———. 1996. 'A User's Guide to Uruguay Round Assessments'. WTO Staff Working Paper RD-96-003. World Trade Organization, Geneva.

Harhoff, Dietmar. 1991. 'R&D Incentives and Spillovers in a Two-Industry Model'. ZEW Discussion Paper 91-06. Zentrum für Europäische Wirtschaftsforschung GmBH, Mannheim, Germany.

Hertel, Thomas W., Will Martin, Koji Yanagishima and Bettina Dimaranan. 1995. 'Liberalizing Manufactures in a Changing World Economy'. In Will Martin and L Alan Winters, eds, *The Uruguay Round and the Developing Economies*. World Bank Discussion Paper 307. Washington, DC.

Jahan, Selim. 2002. 'Textile and Clothing Trade: Protectionism vs. Liberalization'. Background note for Trade and Sustainable Human Development Project. United Nations Development Programme, New York.

Krishna, Kala, and Ling Hio Tan. 1997. 'The Multifibre Arrangement in Practice: Challenging the Competitive Framework'. In David Robertson, ed, *East Asian Trade after the Uruguay Round*. Cambridge, Mass.: Harvard University Press.

Paul-Majumder, Pratima, and Anwara Begum. 2000. 'Gender Imbalances in the Export-Oriented Garment Industry in Bangladesh'. Policy Research Report on Gender and Development, Working Paper 12. World Bank, Development Research Group, Washington, DC.

Reinert, Kenneth J. 1999. 'Give Us Virtue, But Not Yet: Safeguard Actions under the Agreement on Textiles and Clothing'. *World Economy* 11 (2): 49–66.

Rose, Jonathan. 2002. 'The Garment Export Sector of Bangladesh: Threatened Industry and Endangered Workers'. Harvard University, John F Kennedy School of Government, Cambridge, Mass.

Sireh-Jallow, Abdoulie. 2000. 'Dynamic Competitiveness of Textile and Clothing Industry in Africa'. United Nations Economic Commission for Africa, Addis Ababa.

Smith, Adam. [1776] 1998. *The Wealth of Nations*. New York: Oxford University Press.

Spaninger, Dean. 1999a. 'Faking Liberalization and Finagling Protectionism: The ATC at Its Best'. Paper presented at the Economic Research Forum, Istituto Affari Internazionali and World Bank workshop on WTO 2000 Negotiations: Mediterranean Interests and Perspectives, Cairo, 14–15 July. Kiel Institute of World Economics, Kiel, Germany.

———. 1999b. 'Textiles beyond the MFA Phase-Out'. *World Economy* 22 (4): 455–76.

UNCTAD (United Nations Conference on Trade and Development). 2002. *Trade and Development Report 2002: Developing Countries in World Trade*. Geneva.

WTO (World Trade Organization). 1997. *Annual Report 1997*. Geneva.

Yang, Yongzheng, Will Martin and Koji Yanagishima. 1997. 'Evaluating the Benefits of Abolishing the MFA in the Uruguay Round Package'. In Thomas Hertel, ed, *Global Trade Analysis*. Cambridge, Mass.: Harvard University Press.

CHAPTER 9
ANTI-DUMPING

Under article VI of the General Agreement on Tariffs and Trade (GATT), a member country of the World Trade Organization (WTO) can unilaterally impose anti-dumping duties to protect its domestic industry from imports of 'dumped' goods and offset material injury caused by such imports. Anti-dumping practices, particularly anti-dumping duties, are thus targeted at firms, not governments (unlike countervailing duties), and are therefore not required to be imposed on a most-favoured-nation basis (unlike safeguard measures). These two characteristics make anti-dumping the politically least difficult measure to apply of the trade remedies available to WTO members.

Anti-dumping law originated in Canada at the beginning of the 20th century, out of a need to protect against predatory pricing. But it has since evolved to become the principal protectionist tool (box 9.1). During the first five years of the WTO agreements (1995–99) 1,229 anti-dumping cases were initiated, 66 per cent of them against developing countries (Third World Network, 2001). The rapid liberalization of trade regimes by developing countries has led them to pass anti-dumping legislation and to rely on it heavily, because it is the most effective way to counter increased import competition while still conforming with WTO disciplines.

Although developing countries have dramatically increased their use of anti-dumping measures, they nevertheless remain the main victims of such measures. Anti-dumping actions applied by countries with major markets can have a devastating impact on individual industries, affecting the entire economy and often 'nipping in the bud' emerging competitive industries—with serious consequences for human development. Developing countries have therefore pressed for tighter rules governing the use of anti-dumping measures and for improved provisions on special and differential treatment to take account of their vulnerability. They submitted a large number of proposals in the context of the implementation issues and concerns relating to the Uruguay Round agreements, which will be taken up in the negotiations mandated by the 2001 WTO Ministerial Conference in Doha.

BOX 9.1 THE ORIGINS, INITIAL USE AND EVOLUTION OF ANTI-DUMPING

Canada was the first to introduce anti-dumping legislation, in 1904, to protect its domestic steel industry from predatory pricing by US Steel. New Zealand followed in 1905, Australia in 1906 and the US in 1916, all citing predatory pricing by foreign exporters.

International anti-dumping agreements

The original General Agreement on Tariffs and Trade (GATT) of 1947 set out rules for the imposition of anti-dumping duties under article VI. By the 1960s, however, it became apparent that there was a need to introduce greater discipline in the use of these measures, and the Agreement on the Implementation of article VI (the first anti-dumping code) was negotiated in the closing phases of the Kennedy Round in 1966–67.

In the years between the Kennedy Round and the launching of the Tokyo Round in 1975, the use of anti-dumping measures—by Australia, Canada, the US and the European Community—increased significantly. This led to the negotiation of a second anti-dumping code during the Tokyo Round, which was accepted by a small number of mostly developed countries.

During the Uruguay Round a third anti-dumping agreement was negotiated. Although less than half the members of the World Trade Organization (WTO) have passed anti-dumping legislation, all accepted the agreement under the single undertaking.

Changing pattern of anti-dumping

Through the 1960s GATT members filed only about ten anti-dumping petitions a year. By the 1980s, however, more than 1,600 anti-dumping cases had been filed worldwide. Of these, 95 per cent were filed by the US, Canada, New Zealand, Australia and the European Community. Between 1990 and 1994 the US initiated an average of 53.4 anti-dumping cases a year, almost 25 per cent of the world total and more than any other country. Australia followed closely, initiating an average of 51.2 cases a year, while the European Union filed 34.6 and Mexico 24.6. A total of 16 countries initiated cases during this four-year period.

After the signing of the third anti-dumping agreement, in 1994, the pattern shifted: anti-dumping actions became fair play for developing countries too. These countries now account for half the cases filed. In 2000, for example, the US filed 47 cases, Argentina 45 and India 41. In 2001 India took the lead with 75 cases, followed by the US (74), the European Union (28) and Argentina (26). Since the anti-dumping rules provide a legal form of trade protection under the WTO, developing countries that had liberalized other trade restrictions and lowered tariffs were quick to adopt anti-dumping legislation. Just three years after signing the anti-dumping code, Mexico had filed more than 30 cases. Similarly, Argentina, which filed its first anti-dumping case in 1991, averaged almost 20 cases a year throughout the 1990s. Even so, many least developed countries, including a number of African countries, have complained of their inability to deal with what they perceive as massive inflows of dumped imports.

Source: Finger, 2002; Finger, Ng and Wangchuk, 2001; Grey, 1999; Prusa, 1999; US Congressional Budget Office, 2001.

THE FAULTY ECONOMIC LOGIC OF ANTI-DUMPING—INDUSTRY AND CONSUMERS BOTH SUFFER

Canadian and US domestic antitrust laws prohibit various forms of domestic price discrimination. It is often argued that the two countries' anti-dumping laws, which have influenced the development of anti-dumping legislation worldwide, arose as a means of responding to international price discrimination. But even if one assumes that the arguments for prohibiting domestic price discrimination are valid (though they are often contested), the case for prohibiting dumping is not analogous (Trebilcock and Howse, 1995).

Dumping has economic effects altogether different from those of domestic price discrimination and cannot be treated as an analogous issue. A seller dumps only if it charges its customers in the export market a lower price than it charges its customers in the home market. Therefore, unlike domestic price discriminators, which create both high-price and low-price markets in the country in which they are operating, dumpers can create only a low-price market in the country to which they are exporting (Trebilcock and Howse, 1995). In the case of dumping an importing country benefits from lower prices, which increase the consumer surplus—though at the expense of the producer's surplus.

According to economic theory, when the importing country imposes duties to raise the price to the level in the exporting country, it produces a net loss to its own economy, because the losses to consumers will almost always outweigh any gains to the producers that are thereby protected (Trebilcock and Howse, 1995). This is borne out by empirical evidence. For example, the US International Trade Commission, analysing eight anti-dumping measures by the US, estimated that every dollar of increased profit for producers cost the average consumer US$8.00. And it estimated that removing US anti-dumping and countervailing duty orders would have created a welfare gain of US$1.59 billion for the country in 1991 (Anderson, 1993). The logic behind anti-dumping duties, however, is that otherwise competitive producers should not be put out of business by unfair competition and that if the dumper is attempting to establish a dominant position in the market, dumping will permit it to raise prices later.

PROBLEMS WITH ANTI-DUMPING METHODOLOGY

Anti-dumping actions not only defy economic theory. They also rest on a methodology that suffers from serious problems in several areas: the miscalculations of price differences, the lack of transparency and apparent bias in proceedings and the high cost to defendants of countering the claim, along with the cost to exporting industries and importing consumers when the claim is approved. Vermulst (2000, p. 289) states in a recent United Nations Conference on Trade and Development (UNCTAD) study, '[the notion of unfairness can be said to form the current basis for anti-dumping legislation.'

One of the central problems of anti-dumping methodology relates to the many reasonable instances of a firm's selling its goods below cost—instances that would not be subject to claims under the domestic competition policies of most WTO members. For example, firms may price goods at less than cost to draw down inventories during a recession. Or they may price goods below cost when demand is not yet sufficient to increase economies of scale in production, but demand needs to be attracted. Similarly, a common practice in retail sales involves designating certain products as loss leaders, underpricing them to attract customers, who may then buy higher-priced items (US Congressional Budget Office, 2001).

In the case of domestic firms such non-predatory behaviour is largely legal and unrestricted. But anti-dumping legislation treats foreign firms differently. Differences in the business cycles of two trading countries, or situations in which an exporter lowers prices upon entering a new market to attract customers, become grounds for initiating an anti-dumping action, as do short-term exchange rate fluctuations. As Grey (1999, p. 2) puts it, 'in so far as the anti-dumping system penalizes import trade more severely than similar price discrimination in domestic commerce, [under competition law] the anti-dumping system is protectionist to that extent and by design.' An extensive OECD review of anti-dumping cases in Australia, Canada, the European Union and the US found that 90 percent of the instances of import sales considered to be unfair under anti-dumping rules would never have been questioned under national competition law—that is, if they had been domestic sales by a domestic enterprise. And far fewer than 10 per cent of the anti-dumping cases would have survived the much more rigorous standards of evidence that apply under competition law (OECD, Economics Department, 1996, p. 18).

Another complaint against anti-dumping legislation involves the ways in which anti-dumping is calculated and proved. The investigating authority is supposed to determine, on the basis of a fair comparison, whether an imported good is being sold at less than its normal price in the country of origin. Yet the comparison of the goods between two countries is often asymmetrical because, despite their similarity, they may differ in quality. This problem has especially affected China, which specializes in low-cost, low-quality goods. And China is more vulnerable because it is still subject to non-market economy criteria, which enable importing countries to calculate dumping margins (the amount by which the normal value of a good exceeds its export price or constructed export price) based on the prices in a proxy country. Moreover, as part of its accession to the WTO, China was obliged to accept a 15-year period under which it will potentially be exposed to such methodologies (see Law Press China, 2001).

In addition, when determining whether a good is being sold below cost, the investigating authority may overestimate costs by including extraneous costs. Or if it uses profit margin as a benchmark, it may impose unrealistically high profit margins (Vermulst, 2000). Lindsey (1999), reviewing 141 company-specific dumping determinations by the US Commerce Department between 1995–98, found that the methodology used (constructed cost) overstated profit rates. In no instance for which he found comparable data was the profit rate used less than twice the actual profit rate in the US industry.

EFFECTS OF ANTI-DUMPING ON DEVELOPING COUNTRY EXPORTERS

The initiation of an anti-dumping proceeding alone has a significant impact on the exporting industry targeted whether a claim is found to be valid or not. A government undertaking a dumping investigation can demand vast quantities of information with a short turnaround time. McGee and Yoon (1998) cite the case of an anti-dumping proceeding against the Japanese electronics firm Matsushita in which the US Department of Commerce demanded that 3,000 pages of financial information be translated into English. Although the department made the demand on a Friday afternoon, it imposed a deadline of the following Monday morning. Rather than comply with the request, Matsushita withdrew the product from the US market.

Such tactics can play havoc with resource-constrained developing countries. Empirical evidence shows that anti-dumping measures against developing countries can have an immediate effect on trade flows and prompt importers to seek alternative sources of supply. Even if duties are not finally imposed, the initiation of investigations itself creates a huge burden for developing countries, which feel that they have been 'harassed'. For example, in 1997, the year after the US issued an anti-dumping order against carbon steel, Argentine exports of carbon steel wire rod to that country declined by 96 per cent. Mexican exports of the same product fell by 94 per cent in the year preceding the duty imposition (UNCTAD, 2000, p. 7). In an econometric analysis of US anti-dumping cases Prusa (1999) found that imports fell on average by 15–20 per cent where investigations were dismissed.

Another example relates to the European Union, which, during 1994–97 repeatedly initiated investigations of grey cotton fabrics originating from China, Egypt, India, Indonesia, Pakistan and Turkey. According to the International Clothing and Textiles Bureau, the European Union's volume of imports of cotton fabrics from these six countries fell by 28 per cent between 1994 and 1997, while the countries' market share fell from 59 per cent to 41 per cent. The case was ultimately dropped, with no anti-dumping duties imposed (UNCTAD, 2000, p. 8).

Similarly, a recent study by the US Congressional Budget Office (2001, p. 18) argues that the effect of the WTO anti-dumping agreement goes beyond the statistics on how many cases are filed, since 'the mere existence of the anti-dumping policy and the knowledge that domestic industries are ready and willing to file cases if competition becomes too fierce can cause foreign firms to compete less aggressively in the US market to avoid having cases filed against them. The same may be true in other countries. And successful anti-dumping cases have caused the value of imports to fall on average by 30–50 per cent (Prusa, 1999). Such cases can have especially severe effects for developing countries.

Although developing countries far outnumber industrial countries, the two country groups initiated almost equal numbers of anti-dumping cases between 1995 and 1999 (figure 9.1). Most striking is the large number of cases against 27 transition economies in Eastern Europe and Asia, most of which (like China) are still exposed

FIGURE 9.1

Anti-dumping initiations, by country group, 1995–99

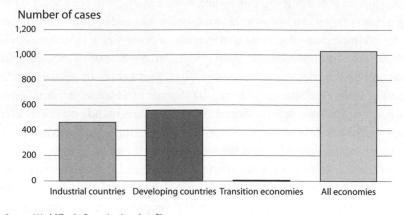

Source: World Trade Organization data files.

TABLE 9.1

Anti-dumping cases filed against transition economies, 1995–99

Filer group	Number of cases
Industrial countries	62
Developing countries	99
Transition economies	3
All economies	164

Source: World Trade Organization data files.

to non-market economy provisions in anti-dumping laws (table 9.1). Finger, Ng and Wangchuk (2001) argue that transition economies face the greatest intensity of cases. A recent case against Vietnam is illustrative (box 9.2). Interestingly, industrial country exporters are the least intensely targeted, while developing country exporters are almost three times as intensely targeted (Finger, Ng and Wangchuk, 2001, p. 6).

DEVELOPING COUNTRIES' GROWING USE OF ANTI-DUMPING

The use of anti-dumping correlates closely with the openness of an economy. As noted, developing countries undergoing liberalization during the 1990s came to view anti-dumping as a tool for helping to adjust to a liberalized trading regime (indeed, in keeping with this logic, the World Bank encouraged and assisted efforts in several developing countries to draw up anti-dumping legislation). In part because of this, developing countries have come to account for half of all anti-dumping cases initiated (figure 9.2). Moreover, it is feared that without a change in the anti-dumping legislation, it will be the main form of protectionism used in the textile industry from 2005.

BOX 9.2 ANTI-DUMPING ACTIONS AS TRADE HARASSMENT: THE CASE OF VIETNAMESE CATFISH

Developing aquaculture has become central to Vietnam's strategy for obtaining export earnings and providing alternative employment opportunities for poor farmers. A key fishery product has been catfish, which Vietnam began exporting to the US in 1996. By 2001 these imports had reached 9 million pounds, 1.7 per cent of US consumption of catfish.

Despite the limited market penetration, the Catfish Farmers of America launched a strong action against Vietnamese catfish imports, successfully lobbying the US Congress to pass a law specifying that only the species *Ictalurus punctatus*, of the family Ictaluridae, could be labelled *catfish*. Vietnamese catfish is of the family Pangasius. The organization also financed a campaign to convince consumers to buy only domestic catfish, describing Vietnamese catfish as raised in unhygienic conditions. This claim was found to be false by a US Department of Agriculture team that visited the fishery sites in the Mekong delta.

Even though Vietnam's catfish had to be labelled *basa* or *tra*, this did not prevent its catfish exports from growing. That led to the filing of an anti-dumping complaint against frozen fish fillets from Vietnam. Later, the US International Trade Commission determined that there was a reasonable indication that the US industry was threatened by material injury from the imports of 'certain frozen fillets' from Vietnam, sold in the US at less than fair value.

The case, which marks the first anti-dumping complaint against Vietnam, raises two interesting issues. The first relates to whether Vietnam will be treated as a non-market economy for the purposes of the investigation, which would require a special methodology using a proxy country as the basis for price comparisons (India has been proposed as the proxy). This not only would make a positive determination of dumping more likely, but also would have broader and more serious implications for Vietnam's terms of accession to the WTO, now being negotiated. The second issue relates to the definition of like product. While US law establishes that Vietnamese catfish are not catfish for the purposes of labelling, *basa* and *tra* are considered a like product for the purposes of the anti-dumping determination.

The Vietnamese exporters reportedly are paying a Washington, DC, law firm US$469 an hour to defend their case, while a catfish worker in the Mekong delta earns less than US$35 a month. This striking disparity demonstrates the need for more stringent multilateral rules and special and differential treatment in the form of meaningful thresholds for import shares to protect small developing country exporters and new market entrants from trade harassment.

Source: Nguyen Hong, 2002a, b; *Saigon Times Weekly*, 2002; Duc Dan, 2002; Luu Phan and Huynh Kim, 2002; Luu Phan, 2002; Tan Duc, 2002; *Vietnam News*, 2002a, b, c.

Developing countries face a conundrum: they must seek a balance between their need to export to industrial country markets and their need to protect domestic industries adapting to a free trade environment. For this reason they have chosen not to attack the anti-dumping system itself, but have instead sought to tighten the rules in such a way that their exporters will be less vulnerable to anti-dumping duties. They have made some progress in improving the application of existing provisions on special and differential treatment in their favour in the context of the dispute settlement process and have listed key anti-dumping issues for negotiation in their submissions on the implementation issues and concerns. These include such proposals as higher thresholds for import shares, higher dumping margins for

FIGURE 9.2

Anti-dumping initiations by industrial and developing countries, 1986–99

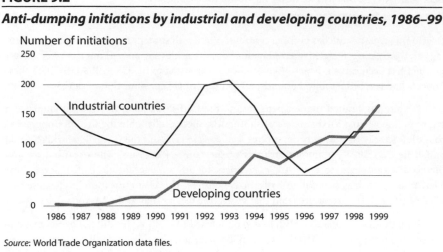

Source: World Trade Organization data files.

imports from developing countries and greater flexibility for least developed countries in applying anti-dumping measures.

Many developing countries, particularly those in Africa, have complained bitterly about what they perceive as massive dumping into their markets—which they have neither the expertise nor the administrative resources to counter and combat. While some countries, such as the US, have offered to assist them in strengthening their administration in this area, it is not clear that these efforts would be the best use of scarce resources in these developing countries, especially since they may never have the resources to send officials to conduct investigations in the exporting countries.

THE WAY FORWARD

The US remained intransigent against pressure for changes to anti-dumping rules until the WTO Ministerial Conference in Doha, where, as a result of intense pressure, it accepted the possibility of a review and clarification of anti-dumping disciplines with a view to tightening them. Still, the US Trade Act of 2002 creates impediments against any change in US anti-dumping law.

Anti-dumping as a protectionist tool tilts the balance of trade against developing countries, given the bias in industrial countries' legislation and the high costs of initiating and defending against anti-dumping cases. The anti-dumping agreement should be revised and consideration should be given to making other tools available, such as stronger domestic competition policy regimes. This would help reduce the incidence of cases stemming from short-term, natural fluctuations between the price levels of two trading countries as a result of different business cycles, exchange rate fluctuations or different levels of economies of scale in production. It is also vital that the agreement be revised to provide adequate thresholds for import shares in industrial countries, so that developing country industries entering the world market are not 'nipped in the bud' by anti-dumping actions in major importing countries.

Moreover, steps should be taken to eliminate bias in procedures by ensuring technical support to developing countries. This could be done by providing them sufficient time and resources to comply with the requests of an investigating authority. In addition, developing countries could be allowed higher *de minimis* dumping margins and import share thresholds in anti-dumping proceedings involving them (Vermulst, 2000). Revising the anti-dumping agreement to reduce unwarranted cases against developing countries could also help them gain greater benefits from their increased participation in world trade.

REFERENCES

Anderson, B. K. 1993. 'Anti-dumping Laws in the United States: Use and Welfare Consequences'. *Journal of World Trade* 27 (2): 99–117.

Duc Dan. 2002. 'An Ideal Breeding Environment'. *Saigon Times Weekly*, 10 August.

Finger, J. Michael. 2002. 'Issues and Options for US-Japan Trade Policies'. Robert M Stern, ed, *Studies in International Economics*. Ann Arbor: University of Michigan Press.

Finger, J. Michael, and Philip Schuler. 1999. 'Implementation of Uruguay Round Commitments: The Development Challenge'. World Bank, Development Research Group, Washington, DC.

Finger, J. Michael, Francis Ng and Sonam Wangchuk. 2001. 'Anti-dumping as a Safeguard Policy'. World Bank, Development Research Group, Washington, DC.

Grey, Rodney. 1999. 'The Relationship between Anti-Dumping Policy and Competition Policy'. UNCTAD Study Paper. United Nations Conference on Trade and Development, Geneva.

Kempton, Jeremy, Peter Holmes and Cliff Stevenson. 1999. 'Globalization of Anti-Dumping and the EU'. Sussex European Institute Working Paper 32. University of Sussex.

Law Press China. 2001. *Compilation of Legal Instruments on China's Accession to the WTO*. Beijing.

Lindsey, Brink. 1999. 'The US Anti-dumping Law: Rhetoric versus Reality'. Trade Policy Analysis 7. Cato Institute, Washington, DC.

Luu Phan. 2002. 'The Catfish War'. *Saigon Times Weekly*, 26 January.

Luu Phan and Huynh Kim. 2002. 'New Stature'. *Saigon Times Weekly*, 26 January.

Maskus, Keith, and John Wilson. 2000. 'Quantifying the Impact of Technical Barriers to Trade: A Review of Past Attempts and the New Policy Context'. Paper presented at the World Bank workshop Quantifying the Trade Effect of Standards and Technical Barriers: Is It Possible?, Washington, DC, 27 April.

McGee, Robert, and Yeomin Yoon. 1998. 'Anti-dumping and the People's Republic of China: Five Case Studies'. *Asian Economic Review* 41 (2): 208–17.

Ngoc Hai. 2002. 'Aid Group Slams US Catfish Charges'. *Viet Nam News*, 12–18 August.

Nguyen Hong. 2002a. 'Agifish Proves a Catch for Investors'. *Vietnam Investment Review,* 5–11 August.

———. 2002b. 'Catfish Spat Now "a Fight to the Finish"'. *Vietnam Investment Review,* 29 July–4 August.

OECD (Organisation for Economic Co-operation and Development), Economics Department. 1996. *Antitrust and Market Access: The Scope and Coverage of Competition Laws and Implications for Trade.* Paris.

Prusa, Thomas. 1999. *On the Spread and Impact of Anti-dumping.* NBER Working Paper 7404. National Bureau of Economic Research, Cambridge, Mass.

Saigon Times Weekly. 2002. 'The Competitive Edge of Basa Fish'. 27 July.

Tan Duc. 2002. 'Unexpected Famous'. *Saigon Times Weekly,* 5 January.

Third World Network. 2001. 'The Multilateral Trading System: A Development Perspective'. Background paper for Trade and Sustainable Human Development Project. United Nations Development Programme, New York.

Trebilcock, Michael J., and Robert Howse. 1995. *Regulation of International Trade.* London and New York: Routledge.

UNCTAD (United Nations Conference on Trade and Development). 1998. 'Globalization and the International Trading System: Issues Relating to Rules of Origin'. ITCD/TSB/2. Geneva.

———. 2000. *Positive Agenda and Future Trade Negotiations.* Geneva and New York: United Nations.

US Congressional Budget Office. 2001. *Anti-dumping Action in the United States and around the World: An Update.* Washington, DC.

Vermulst, Edwin. 2000. 'Anti-dumping and Countervailing Duties'. In United Nations Conference on Trade and Development, *Positive Agenda and Future Trade Negotiations.* Geneva and New York: United Nations.

Viet Nam News. 2002a. 'Seafood Exporters—Hurt by Catfish Row'. 17 August.

———. 2002b. 'US Catfish Industry Went Fishing for a Scapegoat and Hauled in Viet Nam'. 10 August.

———. 2002c. 'VASEP Seeks Fair Decision from US'. 10 August.

CHAPTER 10
SUBSIDIES

The Agreement on Subsidies and Countervailing Measures (ASCM) governs the use of subsidies and regulates the actions that countries can take to counter their trade impact. The ASCM builds on the Tokyo Round subsidy code (issued in 1979) but takes the important step of defining what a subsidy is, making it the first international agreement on acceptable levels of government support for production and trade.

Depending on its purpose, the ASCM defines a subsidy as prohibited, actionable or non-actionable. The ASCM does not apply to agricultural subsidies during the implementation period of the 'peace clause' of the Agreement on Agriculture— that is, until the end of 2003. Although the ASCM contains concrete measures providing developing countries with special and differential treatment, many of them believe that it has created an imbalance on measures that can be taken by industrial and developing countries. Developing countries also feel that the ASCM does not take into account their development needs. Thus they have made many proposals for improving it.

DEFINITION OF AND LIMITS ON SUBSIDIES

Like tariffs, subsidies support industrial promotion. But subsidies distort trade less than tariffs do because they affect only the production patterns of certain products, whereas tariffs affect both production and consumption. Multilateral trade negotiations, starting with the 1947 General Agreement on Tariffs and Trade (GATT), sought to discipline the use of subsidies. Initially weak provisions were tightened in 1955 with the addition of provisions on export subsidies. Then, in 1961, industrial countries accepted the prohibition of subsidies for industrial exports.

The Tokyo Round subsidy code imposed more stringent rules and, though optional, was accepted by many developing countries because acceptance was required for countries to benefit from the injury criterion in the US law on countervailing duties. During the 1980s subsidies persisted as an area of tension in international trade relations. By the launch of the Uruguay Round in 1986 it was evident that subsidies and the actions that could be taken against them needed to be more precisely defined (Sajjanhar, 2000).

The ASCM defines a subsidy as a government financial contribution that confers a benefit, whether directly or through an intermediate party. This definition includes such practices as government provision of goods and services, government forgoing of revenue that otherwise would have been collected and government provision of income or price support.

Specificity is a key concept in the agreement. To be actionable, a subsidy must be specific—targeted at an enterprise, industry or group of enterprises or industries. If a specific subsidy is determined to cause injury to domestic industries in an importing country, countervailing duties can be applied. If such subsidies displace exports in third country markets and cause serious prejudice to exporters, an accelerated dispute settlement mechanism is available. Prohibited subsidies include those contingent on export performance or on the use of domestic goods instead of imported goods. Prohibited subsidies are also subject to accelerated dispute settlement procedures. If the procedure confirms that the subsidy is prohibited, it must immediately be withdrawn, and there is no need to demonstrate injury or prejudice. (The restrictions on industrial subsidies in the ASCM are far more aggressive than those on agricultural subsidies in the Agreement on Agriculture; see chapter 5.)

The ASCM also defines certain subsidies that, although specific, are non-actionable—meaning that they cannot be challenged and that countervailing duties cannot be imposed. These include subsidies for industrial research and pre-competitive development activities, assistance to disadvantaged regions and certain types of assistance for adapting facilities to new environmental laws and regulations. These provisions, spelled out in article 8 of the agreement, were to apply for five years after its signing (through 1999 for WTO founding members), at which point a review was to occur to determine whether the category of non-actionable subsidies should be maintained. Because the review did not take place, these provisions have technically expired. But given the political importance of such subsidies in some industrial countries, there seems to be an unspoken agreement not to challenge them.

To apply countervailing duties, a country must follow ASCM provisions for establishing cases and investigation parameters. The agreement sets out the relevant economic factors to be included in assessing the state of the industry and requires that a causal link be established between the subsidized imports and the affected industry. If the subsidy is worth less than 1 per cent of the value of the imports, the investigation should be terminated. But cumulative assessment of injury is permitted, meaning that relatively small suppliers can be subjected to countervailing duties on the basis that they are contributing to the injury of the industry concerned. If countervailing duties are warranted, they can be imposed at a rate no greater than the amount of the subsidy benefit. Moreover, they must be removed within five years of their imposition unless a review determines that doing so would cause further injury.

Box 10.1 SUBSIDIES—A CRUCIAL TOOL FOR DEVELOPMENT

Large direct and indirect export subsidies were essential to the rapid growth of many of today's most successful developing economies at the early stages of their development. In East Asia's tiger economies—the Republic of Korea, Malaysia, Singapore, Taiwan (province of China)—subsidies played an important role in the export promotion policies used to develop new local industries. Korea's subsidies included export credits and long-term loans with negative real interest rates for firms able to meet export quotas (see chapter 1). Such policies enabled these economies to become world-class exporters of modern industrial products such as electronics, semiconductors and ships, moving well beyond the limits of their comparative advantages. Even countries that have tried to develop industries in line with their comparative advantage in international trade have used export subsidies. In the mid-1980s, for example, Chile instituted tax rebates to support exports of non-traditional goods—primarily processed natural resources—now considered a catalyst for the country's thriving wine, grapes and cellulose industries.

Source: Amsden, 1989; Helleiner, 1994; Silva, 1999; Wade, 1990.

ISSUES FOR DEVELOPING COUNTRIES AND HUMAN DEVELOPMENT

The ASCM provides special and differential treatment to developing countries through a series of time limits and through criteria related to income thresholds, trade values and subsidy levels. WTO members that are among the least developed countries or that have GNP per capita of less than $1,000 a year are not subject to the prohibition on export subsidies. As a result of the decision on Implementation-Related Issues and Concerns issued at the WTO's 2001 ministerial conference in Doha, Qatar, a developing country will receive this treatment until its per capita GNP exceeds this level for three consecutive years. In addition, countries that lose this treatment as a result of achieving higher GNP per capita are covered again if their GNP per capita falls back below this level. Other developing countries were given eight years (until the end of 2002) to meet the new obligations.

Developing countries also benefit from different thresholds in the application of countervailing duties. Imports from developing countries enjoy higher thresholds in terms of subsidies per unit and the volume of imports benefiting from a subsidy.

Still, developing countries perceive that significant imbalances remain in the ASCM's treatment of industrial and developing countries. Given the importance of subsidies in early stages of industrial development (box 10.1), these imbalances will likely accentuate human development problems in developing countries, causing further divergence in countries' development levels. Moreover, many developing countries have not been permitted to use even the flexibility mechanisms they enjoy under the ASCM, because international financial institutions' loan conditions require the reduction and elimination of the generally applicable, non-specific subsidies that are non-actionable under the agreement. Such conditions ignore the rights enjoyed by developing countries under the WTO agreement, requiring these countries to make, in effect, additional trade concessions that go

---

Box 10.2 SMALL ECONOMIES, EXPORT SUBSIDIES AND COUNTERVAILING ACTIONS

To operate efficiently and not rely unduly on domestic markets, world-scale plants in small developing countries must export a large portion of their production—typically 45–85 per cent. Also quite typically, the bulk of such exports may go to just one of the country's larger trading partners. When such exports are subsidized, they are liable to inspire countervailing duties in larger trading countries. Because such action is usually applied to a large portion of the plant's output, it can be extremely damaging.

By contrast, a similar plant receiving similar subsidies in a larger trading country generally exports a small portion of its production, meaning that its profits will not be seriously affected by countervailing duties applied on its exports to a small country. Thus countervailing duties may encourage investors to locate production in larger trading countries that often resort to countervailing duty action.

Source: UNCTAD, 1994.

---

far beyond their WTO obligations and commitments. This set-up illustrates the lack of coherence in global economic policy making.

While the Tokyo Round subsidy code allowed developing countries to maintain export subsidies when necessary for development, the ASCM extends the prohibition of export subsidies to most developing countries—limiting, above all, their policy flexibility. The problems facing developing countries in the application of the export subsidy provisions relate to their need to use export subsidies for development purposes and to the failure of the provisions to take into account certain characteristics of developing countries, undermining their international competitiveness.

Export subsidies have been important instruments in the development of many industrial and developing countries (Helleiner, 1994; see box 10.1). Prohibiting industrial export subsidies also inherently discriminates against smaller countries, where domestic production can be viable only if a large portion is exported. Many of these countries are not low-income and so do not qualify for the exemption from the ASCM that applies to the least developed countries and others with GNP per capita below $1,000 a year (box 10.2).

Encouraged by a coalition of transnational corporations, many developing countries perceived that the end-2002 expiration of the transition period under which they were permitted to apply export subsidies would undermine the operations of their free trade zones. Thus these countries successfully sought an extension in the context of the Doha decision on implementation-related issues and concerns. Some developing countries opposed this extension, however, arguing that it was granting permission for poor people in developing countries to subsidize rich investors and consumers in industrial countries.

In East and Southeast Asia, for example, up to 80 per cent of the workforce in export processing zones is female (UNIFEM, 2000). While the evidence on gender wage inequality and gender wage gaps are mixed, there is clearer evidence that labour market deregulation weakens workers' rights in general and women's in particular. Working conditions in export processing zones are good examples, as many are exempt from local labour laws. (Sen, 1999).

Furthermore, contrary to the Tokyo Round code—which prohibited only export subsidies—the ASCM prohibits both export subsidies and subsidies contingent on the use of domestic over imported goods (Sajjanhar, 2000). In practice this means that countries cannot use subsidies to support import substitution policies.

Non-actionable subsidies, as defined in article 8 of the ASCM, are also significantly biased against developing countries. The subsidies used primarily by industrial countries—for research and development and to support disadvantaged regions—are non-actionable. Yet subsidies to promote the development of national industries—the tool used most often by developing countries to diversify and upgrade their export industries—are either prohibited or actionable. The concept of non-actionable subsidies should be further developed, however, because it could give developing countries the flexibility needed to pursue human development policies.

In several areas the rules do not take into account the inherent characteristics of developing countries. An example is the high cost of capital in these countries, which was a major element in Canada's successful challenge to Brazil's support to its aircraft industry. Another is the difficulty that many developing countries have in administering an effective value added tax system. This means that many taxes on inputs cannot be rebated when the products are exported, resulting in an effective tax on exports.

Because economic policies tend to be biased towards male breadwinners, women are often left with more work (the triple burden; see chapter 1) and less pay. Given women's importance in agriculture and food security (see chapter 5), this has led to biases in agricultural policies and affected consumption patterns. Thus trade-related allocations for export subsidies and export credits, as well as other subsidies and allocations in national budgets, should bear in mind gender and other biases. Likewise, interest rate subsidies (in the context of monetary policies) should be formulated to recognize, reduce and eventually eliminate such biases. Viet Nam has tried to address this problem by maintaining a subsidy programme, notified in the context of its WTO accession negotiations, that enables firms to obtain a reduction in corporate income tax for expenses incurred promoting the health and upgrading the skills of female employees.

The more favourable treatment of agricultural (as opposed to industrial) subsidies is seen as creating another major imbalance between industrial and developing countries. Current rules permit industrial countries to retain massive export subsidies on agricultural products but effectively prohibit those used by developing countries. Moreover, the subsidies from industrial countries dwarf those from developing countries. Under the Agreement on Agriculture the US can provide $363 million in export subsidies for wheat and wheat flour, and the EU can provide

> **Box 10.3 Fishing for subsidies**
>
> Although the fisheries sector shares many characteristics with agriculture—particularly as a major provider of employment and export earnings in developing countries—it is not covered by the Agreement on Agriculture. Yet the ASCM fails to address the massive subsidies provided to the fishing industries of certain major industrial countries. This subsidization has led to excess fishing capacity around the world. This, in turn, has led the fleets of subsidizing countries to overfish in the high seas and motivated their governments to negotiate imbalanced agreements for access to the territorial waters of developing countries. The result has been a depletion of fish stocks, reduced incomes for poor fishers in developing countries and threats to their food security. Fishery subsidies have been recognized as a priority item under the WTO rules and trade and environment mandates in the Doha declaration.
>
> *Source:* UNEP, 2000; ICTSD, 1999; Deere, 2000.

$1.4 billion (Cairns Group, 2000). By comparison, in 1996 Chile's entire non-traditional export subsidy program cost $126 million (Macario, 1998)—and most other developing countries have much less capacity to provide subsidies. Another problem arises from fisheries subsidies in some industrial countries (box 10.3).

THE WAY FORWARD

The Doha work programme gives developing countries the opportunity to advance their proposals for changes to the ASCM (Das, 2002). These proposals—included in the 'Compilation of Outstanding Implementation Issues Raised by Members'—can be addressed in negotiations on WTO rules, with the objective of achieving greater policy space for human development.

Given the successful use of subsidies by the East Asian 'tiger' economies, the revised agreement should provide other developing countries with the option of using this policy instrument for industrial development. Subsidies should be examined from the perspective of domestic policy space. A new category of non-actionable subsidies essential to the development of developing countries would be an important step forward, providing these countries with more flexibility to implement export subsidies.

REFERENCES

Amsden, Alice. 1989. *Asia's Next Giant: South Korea and Late Industrialization.* Oxford: Oxford University Press.

———. 2001. *The Rise of 'The Rest': Challenges to the West from Late-Industrializing Economies.* New York: Oxford University Press.

Das, Bhagirath Lal. 2002. 'The New Work Programme of the WTO'. Third World Network, Penang, Malaysia.

Deere, Carolyn. 2000. *Net Gains: Linking Fisheries Management, International Trade and Sustainable Development.* Washington DC: Island Press.

Helleiner, Gerald K. 1994. 'Introduction'. In Gerald K. Helleiner, ed. *Trade Policy and Industrialization in Turbulent Times: New Perspectives.* Routledge: New York.

ICTSD (International Centre for Trade and Sustainable Development). 1999. *Fish for Thought.* Geneva.

Macario, Carla. 1998. 'Why and How Do Manufacturing Firms Export Evidence from Successful Exporting Firms in Chile, Colombia and Mexico'. Ph.D. diss. University of Missouri, Columbia.

Porter, Gareth. 2000. 'Fisheries, Subsidies, Overfishing, and Trade: Towards a Structured Discussion'. Environment and Trade Monograph Series. United Nations Environment Programme. Nairobi, Kenya.

Sanjjanhar, Ashok. 2000. 'Subsidies'. In *Positive Agenda and Future Trade Negotiations.* Geneva and New York: United Nations Conference on Trade and Development.

Sen, Gita. 1999. 'Engendering Poverty Alleviation: Challenges and Opportunities'. *Development and Change* 30: 685–92.

Silva Torrealba, Francisca. 1999. 'La inversión en el sector agroindustrial Chileno'. Serie Reformas Económicas 46. CEPAL, Santiago, Chile.

UNCTAD (United Nations Conference on Trade and Development). 1994. *Assessment of the Outcome of the Uruguay Round.* Geneva.

UNIFEM (United Nations Development Fund for Women). 2000. *Progress of World's Women.* New York.

Wade, Robert. 1990. *Governing the Market: Economic Theory and the Role of Government in East Asian Industrialization.* Princeton: Princeton University Press.

CHAPTER 11
TRADE-RELATED ASPECTS OF INTELLECTUAL PROPERTY RIGHTS

'If nature has made any one thing less susceptible than all others of exclusive property, it is the action of the thinking power called an idea…. that ideas should freely spread from one to another over the globe, for the moral and mutual instruction of man, and improvement of his condition seems to have been peculiarly and benevolently designed by nature'.

—*Thomas Jefferson, 1813*

The contentious introduction of the Trade-Related Aspects of Intellectual Property Rights (TRIPS) Agreement into the framework of the multilateral trade regime has probably aroused more controversy than any outcome of the Uruguay Round. This stems from the far-reaching implications of TRIPS for human development in the spheres of technology, public health, education, and conservation, stewardship and ownership of traditional knowledge and biological resources.

THE TRIPS AGREEMENT

The TRIPS Agreement aimed at establishing minimum standards of intellectual property rights (IPR; see annex 11.1 and box 11.1). The agreement has three broad components. The first sets out the content and overall direction of the goals and objectives. Member nations agree to provide minimum standards of protection for all intellectual property applied to all technologies in products and processes. Intellectual property includes copyrights, trademarks, geographical indications, industrial designs, integrated circuits, patents and trade secrets. The aim is to balance innovation and dissemination of technology to the mutual advantage of producers and users so as to promote social and economic welfare (Parts I and II, articles 1–40).

The second component defines the broad civil and administrative procedures for enforcement of IPR (Part III, articles 41–64; Parts IV and V), with details on state obligations, provisional measures and remedial measures under the dispute settlement mechanism. The third component focuses on the needs of technology consumers. In return for the rights provided in the first section, it recognizes the

Box 11.1 TRIPS: A HISTORICAL PERSPECTIVE

The first attempt at a multilateral agreement on intellectual property rights (IPR) protection began with the Paris Convention of 1883, where 14 countries agreed on broad principles on equality of treatment, right of priority, independence of patents, general principles on compulsory licensing and revocation of patents and rules of unfair competition. By 1998, 155 countries were signatories to the Paris Convention. It played an important role in the spread of national patent legislation, though the patterns of legislation differed depending on country circumstances and requirements.

In the late 1960s and 1970s, a group of developing countries, led by the Andean Group, began a reassessment of intellectual property, its implications for development and the need to revise the Paris Convention to make it more compatible with developing country interests. As part of this revisionist movement, many developing countries that already had patent legislation tried to make it more balanced and flexible. This trend towards weakening IPR protection in developing countries and the increasing importance of new knowledge-based technologies were major considerations for the US in pushing for IPRs to be on the multilateral trade agenda. The US and the EC introduced IPR protection in the General Agreement on Tariffs and Trade (GATT) negotiations during the Tokyo round of 1978 in a draft proposal in connection with anti-counterfeiting measures. As no agreement was reached, the US circulated a new draft in 1982 and raised it in a GATT experts meeting in 1985.

Meanwhile, the US Trade and Tariff Act of 1984 linked intellectual property protection to the application of the generalized system of preferences. In 1988, the Omnibus Trade and Competitiveness Act extended this further by authorizing the US trade representative to list countries that had been given deadlines to improve their IPR protection; threatening them with sanctions if compliance did not follow. Developing countries, meanwhile, were only willing to discuss the clarification of existing GATT rules such as articles IX and XX(d) on measures to restrict trade in counterfeit goods. They treated any discussion of substantive IPR norms as beyond the competence of GATT and within the exclusive jurisdiction of the World Intellectual Property Organization (WIPO). After two years of analysis, at the senior officers' meeting in Geneva, the GATT mandate was clarified with explicit reference to standard setting, dispute settlement and transitional arrangements.

The first draft proposal was submitted by the European Economic Community, followed by proposals from the US, Switzerland and Japan and was based on the assumption that inadequate, discretionary or excessive protection of intellectual property could distort and impede trade and should as such be dealt with within the GATT framework as part of a single undertaking. Fourteen developing countries responded with detailed proposals on trade in counterfeit and pirated goods and the principles for the use of intellectual property rights. These proposals also included detailed discussions of scope of patents, compulsory licensing, control of anti-competitive practices and the like. This allowed the chairman of the negotiating group to consolidate various texts and prepare a comprehensive proposal for discussion at the ministerial meeting in 1990 that led to the successful conclusion of the negotiations on TRIPS in December 1993. In its final form, TRIPS built on earlier agreements at the Paris, Berne, Rome and Washington conventions but was the first that explicitly linked IPRs to trade sanctions.

Source: UNCTAD, 1994; Roffe, 2000.

need for transitional arrangements, technology transfers and technical cooperation for the least developed countries (Parts VI and VII, articles 65–73).

The provisions in the agreement that protect intellectual property are specific,
binding and actionable. These include the scope of IPRs (all products and processes
in all technologies), the length of patent protection (20 years), the scope of exceptions allowed (limited to very specific cases) and the legal compliance required
from domestic patent laws in member countries. Non-compliance can be challenged under the World Trade Organization's (WTO) dispute settlement mechanism. By contrast, provisions with the potential to benefit technology consumers
(mainly developing countries), such as technology transfer and technical cooperation, while also binding in theory, are vaguely worded, making them difficult to
enforce. Non-compliance with these provisions is hard to prove and, on a practical level, subject to no penalty. Attempts to develop a code of conduct for technology transfer have also failed (Roffe, 2000).

The Doha Declaration, as discussed later, is an important step towards making the TRIPS Agreement more development friendly. It has clarified the need to
interpret TRIPS from a public health perspective and, in accordance with articles
7–8 (social and economic objectives), is a useful guideline for interpreting not just
TRIPS, but also other agreements.

TRIPS has important human development implications for public health,
technology and knowledge and biological resources. Developing countries are
likely to be worse off under TRIPS if it is viewed from a human development perspective, and alternate models of IP protection should be designed. The bargaining framework of the WTO is inherently inappropriate for an asymmetric
agreement such as TRIPS, and intellectual property protection issues should be
delinked from trade sanctions.

In the interim, countries should use the flexibilities available in the TRIPS
Agreement to interpret and implement it in a manner that furthers human development goals. This requires using compulsory licensing provisions in a systematic
and efficient way, setting the correct precedents in disputes, adopting alternative
sui generis systems that balance rights and obligations where mandated and using
the review mechanism of the agreement to provide additional assistance to developing countries.

TRIPS IN THE CONTEXT OF DEVELOPMENT

The economic rationale for protection of intellectual property stems from market
failure. Like other public goods, knowledge is non-rival (so quantity does not shrink
with consumption), is non-excludable (and is therefore easy to reproduce) and its
original costs of production are high. In the absence of intervention, therefore, it is
likely to be underproduced. Intervention can take various forms. The government
can produce or finance the production of knowledge, it can subsidize the private

---

BOX 11.2 EMPIRICAL EVIDENCE ON INTELLECTUAL PROPERTY RIGHTS

Patents. Ginarte and Park (1997) find that patent laws have became stronger in the 1990s. Maskus and Penubarti (1995) find a U-shaped relationship between patents and per capita income, indicating that at low levels of income, patents fall as income rises and, beyond a threshold level, patents rise with per capita incomes. The World Bank puts this threshold at US$7,750 in 1985 prices. Maskus (2000) also infers that effective patent rights are likely to remain limited unless income levels in developing countries rise well above current levels.

Trade. Maskus and Penubarti (1997) also postulate that stronger patents have ambiguous effects on trade; they can increase imports (due to the lower deterrence costs and the increased effective demand due to the exit of local imitators) or can decrease imports if the host country firms hold the patents.

Ability to engage in imitation. Smith (1999) finds that as patent laws become stronger, countries with strong imitative capabilities see the greatest increase in manufacturing imports, while countries with weak imitative abilities see deterioration in their terms of trade.

Technology diffusion. Models that try to measure the impact of IPRs on technology diffusion have given mixed results. Helpman (1993) and Glass and Saggi (1995) find that once a strong patent regime is adopted, the rate of innovation slows, which leads to a slowdown of the global rate of innovation as well.

Foreign direct investment. Lee and Mansfield (1996) find that weak IPRs have a significant negative impact on the location of US foreign direct investment and on R&D facilities. Maskus (1998b) estimates the joint impacts of the activities of transnational corporations and finds that foreign direct investment measured by the asset stock reacts positively to patent strength. Question marks remain, however, on robustness. Braga and Wilmore (1991) and Gould and Maskus (2000) show that IPRs are by themselves insufficient to promote foreign direct investment.

Quality of technology transfer. Davies (1977) and Contractor (1980) show that weak IPRs reduce the quality of technology transferred. However in conjunction with an overall hospitable framework of regulation (taxes, investment rules), the IPR regime influences a firm's perception of its returns on knowledge-based assets. Further, the likelihood that the most advanced technologies will be transferred rises with the strength of the IPRs. Also, rapidly growing developing countries are likely to strengthen their IPRs as they move up the technology ladder.

Access to specific technologies. Sharing of data, scientific research, information, genetic materials and research tools affects knowlege building and scientific enterprise, particularly in developing countries.

Source: Maskus, 2000a (chapter 4 and others). All sources cited here are listed in Maskus.

---

costs of producing knowledge or it can grant temporary ownership rights to knowledge producers. Normally, some combination of these interventions is used to increase the pool of knowledge. Granting temporary rights requires a legal IPR system that provides and regulates these rights. The TRIPS Agreement is an attempt to reinforce this system at the international level.

Appropriate intervention strategies depend on perceived benefits and costs. The potential benefits from an intellectual property regime are increased innovation and technology transfer. An intellectual property regime also creates temporary monopolies and restricts access to technology for imitators. The empirical evidence on the role of IPRs is inconclusive precisely because it is difficult to isolate the impact of IPRs from that of other factors that affect innovation, promote investment in research and create markets for intellectual property (see box 11.2).

TRIPS in an unequal world

TRIPS and its expected impact on rewarding knowledge creation need to be seen against the backdrop of the world as it exists today. In 1998, the high-income countries of the Organisation for Economic Co-operation and Development (OECD) accounted for 86 per cent of total patent applications filed and 85 per cent of scientific and technical journal articles published worldwide, earning over 97 per cent of worldwide royalties and license fees (UNDP, 2001; World Bank, 2002). In contrast, the least developed countries earned 0.05 per cent of worldwide royalties and license fees in the same year. In this context, TRIPS works against latecomers or imitators by increasing the price of technology and restricting their options for technological catch-up. Further, it affects future economic development, which is likely to increasingly rely on the power of ideas and information, threatening to leave behind countries that lack research capacity.

Empirical research has also shown that weak IPRs have been used by countries with low levels of technological capacity until they reached a level of development at which their industries could benefit from intellectual property protection (see box 11.2). The history of intellectual property protection in developed countries confirms this trend. As Chang (2000) points out, most developed countries allowed the patenting of imported inventions by their nationals. The Netherlands abolished its 1817 patent law in 1869, treating patents as other monopolistic practices, and reintroduced it in 1910 under pressure from its neighbors. Other examples are Britain before 1852 and Austria and France. Even though the nature of technology has changed, this historical evidence is telling about the relevance of a standardized intellectual property regime for countries at hugely varying levels of income and technological capability.

Further, the World Bank (2001) estimates that (of a sample of 26 developed countries) TRIPS will lead to rent transfers to 9 of them of US$41 billion (in 2000 dollars).[1] These transfers are a natural outcome of the unequal distribution of technology and technological capacity and raise the overall cost of the TRIPS Agreement for countries with already scarce resources.

Today, the main beneficiaries of intellectual property protection are largely transnational corporations, which can use intellectual property laws to own and control research and development, while the world's poorest people face higher prices and restrictions on access to new technologies and products. Intellectual property protection on educational material, essential drugs and medical equipment is likely to hurt poor consumers. Yet, the true impact of TRIPS is variable. Producers in countries with fledgling technological capabilities can benefit from TRIPS.[2] At the same time, intellectual property protection on sunrise technologies and R&D-intensive industries is likely to stymie developing country efforts to acquire, imitate and learn from them.

Within the developing world variation is also high. As pointed out by the 2002 Commission on Intellectual Property Rights (CIPR) report, in 1994 China, India and Latin America contributed to nearly 9 per cent of research expenditure world-wide, while sub-Saharan Africa contributed to only 0.5 per cent and all other developing countries contributed only 4 per cent. Also, as the report argues, apart from differences in technological capabilities, developing countries are also vastly different in their socio-economic conditions. It is difficult, therefore, to justify the imposition of an across-the-board, one size fits all approach to intellectual property protection. Ultimately, the impact of TRIPS must be measured by whether it allows poor countries to close the technology (and therefore income) gap or helps widen it or by whether it helps poor people and national development.

TRIPS and the multilateral trade regime

The asymmetric relations of developed and developing countries in the context of TRIPS do not fit with the mutual bargaining framework of the WTO. The WTO agreements are negotiated agreements, and concessions are traded to make all members better off. In the case of TRIPS, low-income countries are predominantly technology consumers and have little to bargain with. The expected gains from TRIPS are unlikely without a range of complementary policies such as investment in tertiary education and research capabilities, reward mechanisms in research sectors and an appropriate investor climate—all of which depend on different government policies.

The negative implications of TRIPS meanwhile are clear and immediate in the form of restricted access and higher prices for protected goods. Enforcement of TRIPS through the dispute settlement mechanism allows for retaliation against non-compliance through trade sanctions. For countries already hurt by TRIPS, this means fewer exports and less income for producers. Despite developed country arguments to the contrary, TRIPS itself is trade restricting since it creates monopoly rights and prevents the entry of cheaper, generic versions of products.[3] It is therefore at odds with the aims of the WTO of furthering economic development through increased trade. TRIPS does not necessarily assist in either and is both inappropriate and potentially harmful as part of the WTO framework.

IMPLICATIONS FOR DEVELOPING COUNTRIES: LINKS WITH HUMAN DEVELOPMENT

The TRIPS Agreement has not been fully implemented in most developing countries, since they have an extended transitional period of up to 2005. The least developed countries have, in general, until 2006 to implement TRIPS and until 2016 to implement the patent provisions of TRIPS dealing with pharmaceutical products. However, most developing countries have national intellectual property systems of various types, and the potential implications of TRIPS are clear.[4] This section examines the links of TRIPS with human development in greater detail with a focus on public health, technology and knowledge creation, and food security, biological resources and traditional knowledge. It highlights the implications of TRIPS, the flexibilities it offers and the challenges it raises for meeting human development goals.

Public health

The research-based pharmaceutical industry, characterized by high initial investment in R&D and ease of imitation of final products, is a prime candidate to benefit from TRIPS. articles 27–34 of the TRIPS Agreement deal with patents (for provisions, see annex 11.1) and are particularly relevant for public health and human development.[5]

TRIPS affects access to drugs and medical equipment in the following ways:

- *Increasing prices.* The most common private finance mechanism for health care in the majority of developing countries is out-of-pocket payment, since governments cannot provide large scale subsidized health care. Out-of-pocket payments in developing countries exceed 90 per cent of total payments, much higher than the 20 per cent in developed countries (WHO, 2000). Other important determinants include the presence of trained medical personnel, well-functioning healthcare infrastructure, comprehensive reach and adequate medical supplies—all of which require resources. However, all these determinants (including access to drugs) need to be addressed simultaneously. Notwithstanding this, drug prices are a critical determinant of access to health care. Patented drugs are substantially more expensive than generic versions. According to the Federal Trade Commission in the US, generic drugs cost 25 per cent less than their patented counterparts and, after two years, the price differential is 60 per cent. Several studies for developing countries have estimated the impact of patents on drug prices (Fink, 2000; Watal, 2000; Lanjouw, 1997; and Subramanian, 1995). Their estimated increases range from 12 per cent to 68 per cent once TRIPS is implemented.[6] In the case of anti-retroviral drugs for HIV/AIDS, patented drugs that cost US$10,000–$12,000 per patient per year are available for US$200–$350 in their generic form (see box 11.3).

- *Producing generic versions.* Some developing countries have the technical capacity to produce generic versions of drugs. Others have the capacity to produce formulations but not active ingredients. Still others rely almost completely on imports. For those with production capacity, TRIPS restricts reverse engineering and increases the waiting time for generic versions of patented drugs to the length of protection (20 years). For countries that rely on imports of patented drugs, the implications are as yet unclear. As the next section shows, articles 30 and 31 can be interpreted to permit generic production, but implementation problems remain.

- *Fuelling Research.* Patents have clearly fuelled the pharmaceutical industry in the developed world, creating incentives for further research. The Pharmaceutical Research and Manufacturers of America estimated research costs at US$30.3 billion for 2001 compared to US$8.4 billion in

BOX 11.3 BRAZIL'S EXPERIENCE WITH IMPLEMENTING TRIPS

Brazil's experience with patent protection in the pharmaceutical sector is instructive. Before implementing TRIPS, Brazil did not afford protection to products nor pharmaceutical processes. This policy needed to be altered as a result of the Uruguay Round. Brazil, at the same time, has created one of the most ambitious anti-retroviral drug programs among developing countries through imaginative legislative and administrative procedures. By 2000, Brazil had more than 536,000 cases of HIV infection. Since 1996, the Brazilian Ministry of Health has implemented a policy of universal access to anti-retroviral drug therapy and by December 2000 had treated some 95,000 patients. This represents US$300 million in expenditure to buy the 12 drugs that make up the anti-HIV cocktail. Simultaneously, the government encouraged a strong generics industry that supplied 40 per cent of all anti-retroviral drugs used nationwide.

This combination of free access to drugs with an extensive health infrastructure was supported by national legislation. The Brazilian intellectual property law of 1996 (article 68[1]) requires the patent holder to manufacture the product in Brazil. If this does not happen, the government can issue a compulsory license to another producer, unless the patent holder can show that local production is not feasible. Both these provisions are well within TRIPS parameters. However, the US challenged the provisions of article 68(1). Brazil insisted that the law was central to the country's public health policy and its threat of compulsory licensing has been instrumental in its negotiations with pharmaceutical companies to reduce prices on imported anti-retroviral drugs. On June 25, 2001, the US government withdrew its WTO Panel against Brazil and, in turn, Brazil agreed to hold talks with the US before applying article 68. More recently, Brazil threatened to use the provision when its negotiations with Roche over lowering prices of nelfinavir (marketed as Viracept by Roche) broke down. Eventually, Roche agreed to lower the price by another 40 per cent; article 68 was not invoked.

The Brazilian AIDS program has shown significant results. There has also been a 60-80 per cent reduction in AIDS-related opportunistic infections, a four-fold reduction in hospitalization rates and an overall savings to the government of more than US$490 million during 1996-2000 in procurement costs alone. And finally, between 1996-2000, average locally produced drug prices fell by 72.5 per cent, while imported drug prices fell by only 9.6 per cent.

Source: UNDP, 2002.

1990 and US$1.97 billion in 1980. In the developing world, some countries are also beginning to develop research-based pharmaceutical industries. But private research is driven by the promise of patent rents. The Global Health Forum (2001) estimates that of the US$70 billion spent globally on health research, less than 10 per cent is spent on diseases that comprise 90 per cent of the world's health burden — despite the fact that most of the poorest countries of Africa have offered patent protection since at least 1984 and, in some cases, since 1977.[7] In the last 25 years, scientists have developed only two new drugs for tuberculosis, while research outlays for malaria are only US$100 million.[8] Clearly, patent systems like TRIPS do not ensure pioneering research into the diseases of the poor.

THE DOHA DECLARATION. The Doha Declaration on TRIPS and Public Health reaffirms the right of developing countries to interpret the TRIPS Agreement through a public health perspective. Specifically, the declaration states that 'the

TRIPS Agreement does not and should not prevent members from taking measures to protect public health.' It explicitly recognizes the flexibility within TRIPS to grant compulsory licenses and the right of countries to determine the grounds on which these are granted. Paragraph 6 of the Doha Declaration also recognizes the problems for countries with 'insufficient or no manufacturing capacity in the pharmaceutical sector' and instructs the Council to find a solution regarding compulsory licensing for them 'expeditiously' (by the end of 2002).

The Doha Declaration is an important milestone in the TRIPS debate. It paves the way for a more public health-friendly interpretation of TRIPS by explicitly recognizing that intellectual property rights are subservient to public health concerns.[9] It is a political, rather than a legal statement and should be used as a reference point for more public health-friendly interpretations of TRIPS if disputes arise.

OPPORTUNITIES AND CHALLENGES FOR PUBLIC HEALTH UNDER **TRIPS.** TRIPS is a broad framework and contains several flexible provisions that developing countries need to use. At the same time, several challenges remain in ensuring that TRIPS articles are interpreted and implemented in a public health-oriented manner. Some of these are illustrated below.

- *Articles 7 and 8, and the Doha Declaration.* The objectives and principles in these articles and in the Doha Declaration affirm that IPRs should be 'conducive to social and economic welfare' and members may adopt measures that are needed to 'protect public health and nutrition....provided [that they] are consistent with the provisions of the Agreement'.

  Articles 7 and 8 are guiding principles and should be used for a pro-public interest interpretation of TRIPS. The Doha Declaration extends the transitional period available to least developed countries until 2016.

- *Article 6 and parallel imports.* TRIPS does not explicitly address the issue of international exhaustion of property rights, leaving individual member countries to decide whether to recognize that the right of patent is exhausted at sale, and consequently, if parallel imports are legal.

  TRIPS allows countries to use parallel imports to source patented products legally from anywhere in the world. Countries like Argentina, Japan, Australia and the US have adopted the international exhaustion principle. At the same time, South Africa's attempt to use the principle for parallel imports led to a lawsuit from 39 pharmaceutical companies (later withdrawn) and pressure from the US, illustrating implementation problems under TRIPS.

- *Article 30 and exceptions to rights.* TRIPS allows for exceptions to rights under article 30. Members can provide 'limited exceptions' to patent rights for legitimate interests of third parties, as long as they do not unreasonably prejudice the interests of the patent holder, are limited and do not conflict with the normal exploitation of the patent.

  Article 30 can be interpreted so that members may authorize the production, sale and export of public health-related products without the consent of the patent-holder as a limited exception, especially in the case of countries that do not have the capacity for generic production. For this to happen, the TRIPS Council needs to adopt a liberal interpretation of article 30. In the only dispute on article 30, (Canada-Generic Pharmaceuticals), the panel followed a much more restrictive interpretation of 'limited exception'. While article 30 has the potential to resolve the access to drugs problem, it has not been interpreted in a development friendly manner as yet and is open to legal challenge.

- *Article 31 and compulsory licenses.* Article 31 allows for authorization for use without the consent of the patent-holder. Compulsory licenses can be provided based on individual merit; such licenses should be issued only after efforts have been made to secure voluntary licenses on reasonable terms and have failed (exceptions are allowed in the case of a national emergency). They are predominantly for use in the domestic market, are non-exclusive and temporary. Specifically, TRIPS allows for compulsory licensing in cases of emergency, anti-competitive practices, public non-commercial use and dependent patents (Correa 1999).

Article 31 allows production of generic versions of patented products. Countries like Canada and the US have used compulsory licenses extensively for pharmaceutical companies, biotechnology and chemicals. But the Brazilian case (see box 11.3) highlights the difficulties faced by developing countries in implementing article 31. The Doha Declaration categorically states that countries have the right to grant compulsory licenses and the freedom to determine the grounds on which they are granted. Yet, several outstanding issues remain.

For adequate access, the definition of countries with 'insufficient manufacturing capacity' needs to include countries that lack capacity to produce active ingredients as well as formulations. It should also include countries that may have the capacity to produce generics, but have markets that are too small to justify production.

Import of generic drugs by these countries under article 31 requires clarification on compulsory license requirements by the importing country as well as by the country in which the drugs are produced. Article 30 is a simpler, administratively easier and more direct mechanism for achieving the same and can be a solution to the access problem, if clarified by the TRIPS Council.

Technology and knowledge creation

The raison d'etre of the TRIPS Agreement is the commercial exploitation of ideas. Notwithstanding its serious implications for public health, its most profound implications lie in the areas of research and development and diffusion of technology. Developing countries are net technology importers; consequently, the first impact of an international patent regime that they experience is a rise in the cost of purchasing technology.

TECHNOLOGY AND HUMAN DEVELOPMENT. Technology is critical for enhancing productivity and spurring economic growth. Investments in research and development correlate positively with high levels of income. High-income countries invested 2.4 per cent of their GDP in 1998 compared with 0.9 per cent for low-income countries. Innovation is central to a strong technological base, which in turn allows countries to build high value-added products and remain 'ahead of the curve'. Lall (2001) has developed an index of 'domestic capabilities' by combining two separate indices: an industrial performance index and a technology effort index.[10] He has classified countries based on their capabilities. Not surprisingly, the world's poorest countries fall into the bottom quintile. The causality operates both ways: lack of resources inhibits the ability to invest in research, and the low investment in research contributes to continuing poverty.

TECHNOLOGY AND *TRIPS.* The complex relationship between technology and intellectual property is mediated by industry characteristics, the rate of technological change, local economic circumstances and the distribution of market power.

- *Restricting absorption of technology.* From an economic viewpoint, innovation can be encouraged through either subsidies or patents, though the use of patents has increased significantly during the last decade.[11] Viotti (2001) points out that technical change for 'latecomer' developing countries comes through diffusion and incremental innovation, which begin with absorption and imitation in active learning systems that eventually evolve into innovation systems. TRIPS increases the costs of purchasing, and thereby of absorbing, patented technology. Patents also restrict access to the original technologies, opening incremental innovation to litigation based on claims of infringement.

- *Inhibiting innovation?* For industries in which innovation is cumulative and complementary, patents can reduce overall innovation and social welfare (Bessen and Maskin, 2000; Garfinkel and others, 1991; Stallman, 2002).[12] The software, computers and semi-conductor industries of the US are such examples. Strong protection began only in the 1980s.[13] A number of small firms had built on the common pool of ideas in the public domain to produce new ideas and products. Stronger patent rights parceled out that common pool under patents and cross-licensing agreements and forced new entrants to 'reinvent the wheel'. In many cases, inventing around software patents was difficult, raising the cost and time of innovation. Consequently, stronger patents have correlated with a period of stagnancy in R&D among firms that patented the most. TRIPS extends these stronger patents to fledgling software and semiconductor industries in developing countries, making it more difficult for them to catch-up.

- *Making acquisition of technology more difficult.* Developing countries acquire technology in four broad ways: through embedded technology in capital goods imports, through direct foreign investment, through purchase or foreign technology licensing, or through technology transfer through assistance. Empirical evidence shows that the relative importance of intra-firm technology flows has increased since the mid-1980s as a way of transferring technology (Kumar, 1997). This was spurred by the emergence of new technologies in information, electronics and biotechnology. Companies see these technologies as key to long-run competitiveness and are keen to preserve their monopoly. TRIPS consolidates knowledge ownership and reduces opportunities for learning and imitating for new entrants.[14]

- *Impeding the spread of knowledge.* TRIPS raises the cost of copyright-protected educational material. In the software industry, only a small segment of developing country populations can afford copyright-protected software, and non-compliance can be penalized through retaliatory measures. TRIPS can also reduce the quality of software that comes into a country. In the case of hardware, a few large firms own significant blocks of patents and under TRIPS can control the terms on which technology is distributed. Finally, developed country firms also control the information industry. Technology has made it possible both to permit inexpensive copying and access to information and to control and, to some extent, restrict this access (encryption, licensing, online subscription). In 1998, for example, the US Congress passed the Digital Millennium Copyright Act on anti-circumvention measures, which are far more restrictive and, if internationalized, will render TRIPS flexibility on fair use irrelevant and widen the technology gap (Correa, 1999).

Developing countries also lack the legal infrastructure to deal with abuse of monopoly power as effectively as developed countries (CIPR, 2002). This makes it more important for developing countries to design an IPR regime that is the right mix of incentives and access to meet their needs.

Finally, patent enforcement incurs significant costs. Domestically, apart from the initial costs of establishing the institutional structures, training personnel and building mechanisms for filing and examining and enforcing patents, enforcement also varies greatly by industry characteristics. In high-innovation industries, the cost of patent searches to check the existence of 'prior art' can be prohibitive. Internationally, TRIPS brings with it the threat of litigation with high costs. For developing countries, this raises the question of opportunity costs and priorities—whether developing countries should invest in patent litigation and search infra-structure or use the resources to address more important development objectives. The cost of setting up the institutional structure for TRIPS (estimated between US$250,000 and US$1.2 million[15]) could instead be used towards more urgent development expenditures such as achieving the Millennium Development Goals.

OPPORTUNITIES AND CHALLENGES FOR TECHNOLOGY UNDER TRIPS. At the same time, TRIPS offers opportunities and challenges for technology acquisition and use. Among them:

- *Articles 66 and 67.* Developed countries are expected to provide incentives to their enterprises to encourage technology transfer to least developed countries to help them create a 'sound and viable technological base'. They are also expected to provide, on request, technical and financial cooperation on legal and institutional issues for countries to help them become TRIPS compliant.

Articles 66 and 67 have not been implemented even as symbolic measures. Technology transfer has not occurred in any recorded, coherent or consistent manner. Technical Assistance has been narrowly limited to TRIPS compliance, without reference to implications for human development.

- *Copyrights and the software industry.* TRIPS reflects the current international ambiguity of the 'expression' dilemma. It treats software programs as 'expressions' protected by copyright. To the extent that these programs merely codify ideas or laws of nature, they cannot be patented, though on proof of industrial application, many are routinely patented in the US. TRIPS is not explicit on software codes as being 'industrial applications' or merely 'codification of laws of nature'. Some argue that national laws can therefore legitimately provide for reverse engineering and deny protection to user interfaces, but the current debate on this is unresolved.[16]

Strict enforcement of copyright laws under TRIPS can reduce access to computer programs unless balanced with fair-use provisions for educational and research purposes.

- *Bolar Provisions.* This provision allows for the use of an invention without the patentee's authorization so that approval for the generic version can be obtained before the patent expires. This permits marketing of a generic version as soon as the patent expires. Since generic competition lowers prices, the Bolar exception increases the affordability of off-patent products. Since the commercialization of the product does not take place while it is on patent, this early working provision is compatible with article 30.

While TRIPS does not explicitly refer to this exception, the WTO in the dispute between Canada and the EU ruled that an early working exception is consistent with TRIPS even in the absence of an extended period of protection for the patent. So developing countries can use the Bolar Provision to speed up the production of generics. However, the right to manufacture and stockpile before the expiration of the patent was not deemed consistent.[17]

- *Experimental use.* TRIPS does not explicitly prevent countries from providing exceptions to patents for experimentation.

Several countries have built experimentation provisions for scientific or academic purposes into their national legislation. These include Argentina, Brazil, Mexico, the Andean Group and the U.S.

- *Applicability of patents, scope of claims and patentability requirements.* As a framework, TRIPS sets international standards and parameters for what constitutes a patent regime but leaves their detailed articulation to the national level. For example, TRIPS requires nations to award patents on the basis of 'novelty' but leaves them to define 'novelty'. If drafted carefully and flexibly, national patent laws could disallow patents for certain chemical categories and still leave them TRIPS-compliant.[18]

Many developing and least developed countries lack the capacity to design legislation appropriate to their development interests and to defend their domestic legal policies in the face of international pressure. The freedom to set appropriate standards in novelty, prior art and the like is important to build into legislation and needs to be actively used by developing countries.

Food security, biological resources and traditional knowledge

Article 27.3(b) of the TRIPS Agreement allows members to exclude plants and animals and biological processes for the production of plants and animals, other than microorganisms and non-biological or microbiological processes, from patentability. It also requires member nations to extend intellectual property protection to plant varieties through either patents or a *sui generis* system or any combination thereof (see annex 11.1).

The TRIPS Agreement does not explicitly prevent or promote the formulation of additional measures that provide for farmers' rights, or the sharing of benefits in genetic resources or traditional knowledge with countries or communities, as long as these measures do not violate the minimum standards laid down under the Agreement. Most of these measures lie outside the scope of TRIPS though some TRIPS provisions can be used (see annex 11.2) in some cases.

ARTICLE 27.3(B) AND HUMAN DEVELOPMENT: FARMERS' RIGHTS AND FOOD SECURITY. The issue of protection for plant varieties is central to the world's food supply. Plant breeding can generate higher yields and lead to seed varieties with stronger resistance to drought, pests and disease.

Many plant varieties come from seeds that farmers in developing countries have selected and sown for many years; these practices form the basis of food security and livelihoods for communities throughout the developing world. Where subsistence-based production is dominant, it is critical to maintain farmers' freedom to save, exchange and replant their own seed.

However, as the biotechnology industry has expanded, it has sought to demand protection for genetically modified seed varieties in order to guarantee returns for high R&D investment costs. Similarly, as developing countries build their industrial seed production capabilities, their views on the utility and shape of a patent and plant variety protection system will also change. 'In areas with good access to urban markets, even small-scale farmers may see a shift to modern hybrids as an attractive option because of their high yield potential. In this case, private sector companies are the main seed suppliers' (FAO, 2001, p. 37) and private breeding companies may wish to seek greater protection.

But with large numbers of farmers engaged in subsistence farming for at least part of the time, a *sui generis* system that protects the rights of farmers to exchange and replant protected seeds is critical to ensuring food supply and livelihoods. This was also acknowledged internationally, at the UN Food and Agriculture Organization Conference-approved International Treaty on Plant Genetic Resources on Food and Agriculture 2001, which established a multilateral system of access to plant genetic resources for food and agriculture, as well as of fair and equitable sharing of the benefits obtained from their use. It also included provisions on farmers' rights.

Several international efforts to create such systems have already occurred. The Union for the Protection of Plant Varieties (UPOV) models of 1978 and 1991 are two such examples. The 1978 model allowed farmers to save seeds for their own use and breeders to freely develop new seeds.[19] The 1991 convention restricts these exceptions; farmers' privilege is optional but the breeders' exception is preserved. It also implements a *sui generis* system of plant variety protection through which the commercial interests of plant breeders are protected.[20]

The implications of plant variety protection are uncertain and vary according to circumstances (Rangnekar, 2001). A preliminary study in the US showed that it led to increased seed prices for farmers, a falling role for public investment in plant breeding and reduced information flow from the private to the public sector. It also did little to stimulate plant breeding (Butler and Marion, 1996). Further, genetic modifications increase gene uniformity, and this can affect biodiversity in the long run. Developing countries need to encourage incentives for new seed development without restricting the rights of farmers to save and replant seeds through an appropriate *sui generis* system.[21]

However, TRIPS is essentially an inappropriate model for property rights that do not follow the conventional Western model (based on individual rights), and TRIPS mandates countries to deal with the requirements of these community rights through the creation of appropriate *sui generis* systems.

The gender dimension of the impact of IPRs on biodiversity is often overlooked. TRIPS affects women's reproductive health, agriculture, food security and traditional knowledge in health care and medicines. Women are affected in many direct and indirect ways by IP since they are the primary users and protectors of biodiversity. They produce 50 per cent of all food in the world and are also responsible for collecting food, fodder, fuel and water. In the poorest rural households in developing countries, traditional diets often consist of a finely balanced mix of cultivated crops and plants and fruits found in the wild. Women, more than men, tend to use the forest as a source of a wide variety of insects, plants and plant products to supplement the basic diet, especially during food shortages.

Common property resources have been used as grazing lands for animals, communal sources of water and forest resources for food and income. The protection of agricultural biodiversity and common property resources is therefore crucial to the livelihood and food security of poor people in rural areas, particularly women and girls, who are responsible for family welfare but tend to fare worse than the male members in food intake and nutrition. Privatisation of biological resources directly affects women, who lack resources to purchase them and are left relying on shrinking and increasingly degraded common property resources.

TRADITIONAL KNOWLEDGE AND BENEFIT SHARING. The 1992 Convention on Biodiversity promotes the need to 'respect, preserve and maintain' traditional knowledge for 'the conservation and sustainable use of biological diversity' and encourages the 'equitable sharing of benefits arising from the utilization of such knowledge' (article 8(j)). Many developing countries have lobbied for an expansion of IP concepts to enable more effective 'protection'[22] of traditional knowledge. In recent years, there has also been increasing attention to the importance of greater recognition of the value and contribution of traditional knowledge to public health and community development.

Traditional knowledge and indigenous knowledge are not the same. Traditional knowledge can refer to knowledge that is in some way nationally held (such as ayurvedic medicine and Chinese herbal medicine), while indigenous knowledge is often associated with groups that are or have historically been marginalized or are trying to pursue a traditional lifestyle. Both traditional and indigenous knowledge have been used for generations by local communities and have contributed to the development of crop varieties, food security and medicines, as well as the emergence and continuation of artistic work in the form of music, handicrafts and artisanship.[23] Traditional knowledge tends to be passed down over generations and held collectively (at the community or national level). It provides legitimacy, as a first step towards benefit sharing of the knowledge and the resources that these communities possess. Further, it is important for the economic development of indigenous communities, since recognition of traditional knowledge protects them against misappropriation or loss, and compensation can also help in broadening its use (Correa, 2001). But, as Correa also points out, protection could also reduce access to and sharing of this knowledge. Many indigenous communities express concern about traditional knowledge being in the 'commons' because that exposes it to private interests that could steal from this commons and use the knowledge as a tool for their future exploitation. Governments need to design protection systems that balance out these costs and gains for their communities' futures.

Unlike other intellectual property, protection for traditional knowledge is not a prerequisite for encouraging future innovation. It is aimed at preserving ownership and sharing the benefits from the commercial exploitation of this knowledge rather than rewarding its creators. From a human development perspective, it is important to prevent corporate misappropriation of knowledge that is already in the public domain. It is also important to codify this knowledge and place it in the public domain with the cooperation of the communities to which it belongs and to clarify rules for benefit-sharing following the same principles that apply to all other sectors—that of balancing the rights of owners and consumers. Indigenous peoples have their own ways of managing and sharing their knowledge, and this will require an acceptance of different models of property rights (collective, customary, community-based rights as opposed to individual rights).

SUI GENERIS SYSTEMS. Several models of *sui generis* legislation have been proposed and enacted by various countries (see box 11.4). They demonstrate the heterogeneity of developing country intellectual property requirements for best preserving the interests of their populations. Specifically, these systems depart from (but do not conflict with) TRIPS in one of the following manners: they explicitly recognize

> **BOX 11.4 ILLUSTRATIVE SUI GENERIS SYSTEMS**
>
> 'Community rights are natural, inalienable, pre-existing or primary rights. The rights of local communities over their biodiversity leads to the formalization of their existing communal control over biodiversity. This system of rights, which enhances the conservation and sustainable use of biological diversity and promotes the use and further development of knowledge and technologies is absolutely essential for the identity of local communities and for the continuation of their irreplaceable role in the conservation and sustainable use of this biodiversity'.
>
> *—African Model Legislation for the Protection of the Rights of Local Communities, Farmers and Breeders and for the Regulation of Access to Biological Resources, African Union*
>
> 'The collective intellectual property of indigenous knowledge, technology and innovations is guaranteed and protected. Any work on genetic resources and the knowledge associated therewith shall be for the collective good. The registration of patents in those resources and ancestral knowledge is prohibited'.
>
> *—Article 124, Constitution of the Bolivarian Republic of Venezuela, 1999*
>
> 'The State expressly recognizes and protects, under the common denomination of *sui generis* community intellectual rights, the knowledge, practices and innovations of indigenous peoples and local communities related to the use of components of biodiversity and associated knowledge. This right exists and is legally recognized by the mere existence of the cultural practice or knowledge related to genetic resources and biochemicals; it does not require prior declaration, explicit recognition nor official registration; therefore it can include practices which in the future acquire such status. This recognition implies that no form of intellectual or industrial property rights protection regulated in this chapter, in special laws and in international law shall affect such historic practices'.
>
> *—Article 82, Biodiversity Law, The Republic of Costa Rica 1998.*

collective or community rights; they establish different criteria for different product forms and services (separate systems for traditional knowledge, plant varieties, artistic creations) and they define rights in terms of remuneration and benefit sharing. TRIPS provides the flexibility for countries to adopt appropriate *sui generis* systems depending on their specific needs.

TRIPS 'PLUS'

Apart from TRIPS, there are several other regional and bilateral IP agreements that have troubling implications for human development. Many of these agreements are more stringent than the TRIPS Agreement and considerably diminish the room for maneuver for developing countries. Countries that have signed onto these agreements cannot take advantage of the flexibilities in TRIPS discussed above either.

Stricter IP provisions that set the wrong precedents
These agreements go beyond TRIPS in terms of IPR protection. The revised Bangui Agreement of 1999, for example, recognizes regional exhaustion of IPRs and therefore restricts parallel importing to countries that are part of the agreement (see box

---

BOX 11.5 THE REVISED BANGUI AGREEMENT, 1999

The Organisation Africaine de la Propriété Intellectuelle (African Intellectual Property Organization) has regulated intellectual property in 15 countries of Francophone Africa since the Bangui Agreement in 1977. In 1999, the Bangui Agreement was revised to bring it in line with the TRIPS Agreement. This was important because four of the member nations (Cameroon, Côte d'Iviore, Gabon and Senegal) expected to be TRIPS compliant by January 1, 2000. The Bangui Agreement is equivalent to the national patent law in each of these 15 member countries, and in its revised version goes well beyond the TRIPS Agreement.

The Bangui Agreement recognizes the regional principle of exhaustion of rights, limiting parallel imports to member countries only. Further, compulsory licenses can no longer be granted if the product can be imported; in other words, the lack of locally available patented products is no longer valid reason for compulsory licenses. Licenses to meet special needs can also be granted only for local use and not for imports, leaving unresolved the problem of countries with no production capacity. The revised Bangui Agreement has not yet been ratified by all its members and is therefore not yet in effect. However, its binding conditions make it harder for these countries to source cheaper generics through imports and to promote generic production domestically, leaving few options for access to cheaper drugs.

11.5). The Bilateral Free Trade Agreement between the US and Jordan limits the scope of compulsory licensing to remedies against anti-competitive practices, for non-commercial, governmental use, or in the case of an emergency when the licensee is either a government agency or a government designee, and for failure to meet working requirements (where imports are included in the definition of 'working'). By signing these treaties, developing countries are restricting their policy options without adequate evidence on the impact of these higher standards on human development outcomes.

Other such bilateral agreements that go beyond TRIPS include US agreements with Cambodia, Ecuador and Singapore; EU agreements with Morocco, Palestine and South Africa; and the Swiss-Vietnam treaty (GRAIN, 2001). These agreements are setting a dangerous precedent. By committing to higher standards of protection than mandated under TRIPS, these countries become unable to take advantage of the flexibilities offered under TRIPS. Any attempts to make TRIPS more human development friendly, therefore, will be meaningless for these countries unless they can ensure that their commitment to TRIPS overrides their bilateral and regional commitments.

Harmonization of intellectual property laws

Some agreements seek to harmonize intellectual property laws; the EU-Tunisia agreement requires Tunisia to join the Budapest Treaty by 2002 and binds it to UPOV 1991 as the model *sui generis* system for protection of plant varieties.[24] The EU-Bangladesh Treaty obliges Bangladesh to make 'best effort' to join UPOV 1991 by 2006. The US-Vietnam treaty has similar conditions on UPOV and extends protection to encrypted program-carrying satellite signals apart from the IPRs covered under TRIPS.

SETTING THE AGENDA

TRIPS is clearly the most controversial of WTO agreements because of its scope and nature. Despite its exceptions and flexibilities, it has the potential to restrict access to medicines, technology and knowledge, with disturbing implications for indigenous knowledge and food security. An alternative to TRIPS, either within or outside the ambit of the WTO, ought to be debated at the highest level. In the interim, TRIPS can be made more development friendly through key changes to the design of the agreement and in its interpretation and implementation.

Alternative models of intellectual property rights

The relevance of TRIPS is highly questionable for large parts of the developing world. Its asymmetric nature makes it unsuitable to be included in a trade bargaining and negotiation context. While benefits can arise from protecting intellectual property, certain preconditions need to be in place before the gains can be expected. The underlying issue is deeper: countries at low levels of human and technological capability cannot benefit significantly from TRIPS. The experience of developed countries has also shown that strong patents follow industrial development rather than lead it. In Pareto optimal welfare terms, the preceding analysis shows that developing countries are not likely to be even *at least as well off* under TRIPS as they would be outside it. From a development perspective, therefore, TRIPS should be revisited as a required agreement in the multilateral trading regime.

While there has been substantial thinking on alternative models for intellectual property in the last few decades, clearly much more research is required to generate models relevant to the development context of different countries.[25] A related question is how the intellectual property discussions, even if they are to remain a part of the WTO, can be delinked from trade sanctions. This is particularly important because WIPO, which should be the appropriate organization for this function, has an extremely narrow and technical mandate that restricts it to 'promoting protection'. It needs to do much more to help countries design development friendly regimes. Member nations need to begin dialogues to replace TRIPS—and equivalent top-down schemes of substantive IPR harmonization—with alternate intellectual property paradigms that are unrelated to trade sanctions and may include, but are not restricted to:

- An intellectual property ladder, where more stringent laws apply to countries at higher levels of income and technology use, and countries progress from one level of protection to another with improvements in their Human Development Index/Millennium Development Goal indicators.

- A TRIPS-minus model that significantly reduces the length of protection and scope of coverage and increases national decision-making authority on standards and coverage of protection while maintaining a minimalist agenda at the international level.

- An IPR regime with specific opt-out clauses for certain kinds of property rights and specific industries.
- Separate IP regimes for collective and individual rights.

To strengthen the case for replacing TRIPS, there is an urgent need to undertake extensive research and monitoring programmes to measure the potential welfare implications of TRIPS (and alternative intellectual property regimes) on different sectors and segments (consumers, small farmers, large entrepreneurs) of the population.[26]

Admittedly, replacing or fundamentally altering TRIPS will not be easy or sudden, given the differences in national positions on this issue. However, it is critical to begin serious thinking about it at an inter-governmental level.

In a parallel vein and in the interim, governments will need to use TRIPS as best as they can to further their social and economic development objectives. This requires modification in the way the agreement is interpreted and implemented.

Interpretation and implementation of TRIPS

There is little indication, apart from the Doha Declaration, that TRIPS has really been interpreted in the true spirit of balance between rights holders and users. From a legal perspective, the generalist language employed in TRIPS has worked both ways for developing countries; it has allowed for flexible interpretation, but also left the text open to dispute. The latitude in the text requires tremendous specialized legal capacity, which most developing countries lack. Moreover, the experience of Brazil (see box 11.3) has shown that efforts to use this flexibility provoke strong opposition from the developed world.

Finally, the enforcement mechanism—the cross-retaliation mechanism of the dispute settlement process—takes little account of differences in capacity to retaliate. This is costly and harmful for developing countries. Exceptions are limited and specific, and the burden of proof falls on the alleged violator. In practice, this considerably reduces the power of the exceptions.

TRIPS has not been implemented fully in most developing countries, and its future will depend on the decisions taken by the dispute settlement body, which will determine to what extent the agreement is implemented in line with the social and economic development objectives of member nations. On a priority basis, member nations need to:

- Facilitate implementation of exceptions to rights. Compulsory licensing procedures need to be simplified, made easier to invoke and made broader in scope. *Human Development Report 2001* (UNDP 2001) specifies five features of a suitable legal structure (administrative approach, strong government use provisions, production for export, reliable rules on compensation and dispute demand disclosure), which should be used as parameters to determine the ease of implementation of articles 30 and 31. There is also talk of countries invoking broader exceptions, for example, with respect to research tools, life forms, particular technologies of interest to poverty reduction in developing countries and indigenous knowledge.

- Set the correct precedents in disputed cases. Much of the impact of TRIPS will depend on how the dispute settlement body interprets the agreement with reference to its social and economic objectives, the first test being the use of the Doha Declaration. Although the text is clearly ambiguous, the manner in which decisions will be taken will indicate the actual latitude that the agreement allows. The multilateral trade regime has a responsibility to ensure that interpretation is in line with human development concerns so that further disputes, retaliation and litigation are minimized.

- Create alternative protection regimes as allowed under TRIPS. *Sui generis* regimes to protect plant varieties and integrated circuits need to be designed as appropriate, and there should not be multilateral pressure to promote a particular system (such as UPOV 1991) in countries in which it is not appropriate.

- Under the mandated review mechanism, extend the transition periods for compliance for all developing countries, not just the least developed countries. In addition, strengthen articles 67 and 66.2 to establish time-bound, concrete and measurable parameters for technical assistance and technology transfers in accordance with the development needs of different countries.

Additional policy interventions

Finally, no multilateral intellectual property regime in itself can guarantee that human development objectives will be met. Active government policy intervention is needed in:

- Designing national legislation that addresses human development needs in terms of access to health care and the resources and opportunities for technological progress.

- Ensuring that products are priced to market and, irrespective of their patent status, are affordable to consumers. Part of this strategy should aim at encouraging growth of the generic drug industry and promoting a competitive market structure.

- Investing in research and development, which is critical to developing technological competence. Results of publicly funded R&D, in developed and developing countries, including patents, could then be voluntarily licensed to producers in developing countries.

Any multilateral agreement should reflect a balance of interests among countries and their constituents. An agreement will not be sustainable if the interests of one or more constituents are under- or overrepresented. TRIPS as well as any equivalent system of top-down harmonization needs to better balance the interests of its largest constituency: the poorest sections of the world population. Until the TRIPS Agreement allows their concerns to be adequately addressed—or, at the very least, not actively harmed—it will run counter to its own stated objectives.

ANNEX 11.1

Main provisions of the TRIPS Agreement

Aspect of agreement	Main provisions
Type of protection	
Copyright and related rights (performers, recordings, broadcasting organization rights)	Protection to expression (as in the Berne Convention)
	Computer programmes (source or object code) treated as literary works
	Term of protection: minimum term of 50 years from publication or creation (if publication was not made within 50 years from creation) for works not belonging to natural persons
Trademarks	Inclusion of trademarks for goods and services
	Term of protection: seven-year periods, renewable indefinitely
	Compulsory licensing not allowed
Geographical indications	Protection of geographical indicators that identify a good as originating from a certain place where a given quality, reputation or other characteristic of the good is essentially attributable to its geographical origin
	Special protection for wines and spirits
Industrial design	Term of protection: 10 years
Patents	All fields of technology, for products and processes for 20 years
	Patentability of plants and animals excludable (other than microorganisms); however, members are required to protect plant varieties through patents or a *sui generis* system
	Exceptions to exclusive rights: Article 30, limited exceptions allowed
	Article 31, compulsory licensing allowed under specific conditions
	Burden of proof reversed to the infringer of a process patent rather than the right-holder
Integrated circuits	Protection to layout designs for a minimum of 10 years
	No trade in protected layout designs; an integrated circuit containing a protected design or a product containing an integrated circuit that contains a protected design
	Exceptions in cases where the traders are unaware, and had no reasonable way of knowing, that the article contained a protected layout design, in which case, they are required to pay the right holder 'reasonable royalty'
Undisclosed information	Protection of commercial trade secrets
	Provision for protection of data for new chemical formulations needed for pharmaceutical or agricultural products against unfair commercial use, unless disclosure is necessary for public interest
Anti-competitive practices	Freedom to restrict rights in case of anti-competitive practices due to abuse of intellectual property rights, and due consultations with other member nations

Enforcement	Fair, transparent procedures
	Review by judicial authority, no obligation to establish separate judicial system dedicated to IPR resolution
	Provisional measures and measures at the border need to be made available
	Provision for criminal procedures and penalties (imprisonment or monetary fines) in the case of trademark and copyright violations
	Dispute settlement moratorium until 2000 for non-violation cases
Transitional arrangements	Transition periods for developing countries (2000) and least developed countries (2005) subject to extension
	Members that do not recognize patent rights in pharmaceutical and agricultural products as of date of entry need to provide mechanisms for filing patent applications and provide exclusive marketing rights for five years or provide patent protection, whatever is earlier
Review and amendment	Biennial review mechanism established
	Amendments based on consensus subject to WTO general rules for amendments to an agreement

Source: Agreement on Trade-Related Aspects of Intellectual Property Rights, Annex 1C, WTO Agreement.

ANNEX 11.2

TRIPS and traditional knowledge

Options under TRIPS	Interpretation and implementation issues for developing countries
Patents—novelty and inventive requirements	
Latin American countries have argued that processes to use this knowledge and resources may still be protected if their application fulfills the novelty requirement.	Traditional knowledge is not, according to TRIPS language, 'new, does not involve an inventive step and is not necessarily capable of industrial application'. Novelty and inventive requirements are hard to fulfill, since this knowledge has often been in use for generations and is community-based, which means that no effort has been made to keep it confidential.
Copyrights and trademarks	
Artistic expressions of traditional knowledge-holders in the form of literary works, theatrical or pictorial works, textiles, pottery, sculptures, tapestries, carpet designs and the like can be copyright-protected. Further, all goods and services that belong to native communities, different guilds and the like can be identified through trademark protection, which will differentiate and brand them for commercial purposes.	Copyrights and trademarks are also inappropriate because of the collective ownership of this knowledge. National legislation needs to clarify the communal nature of traditional knowledge and specify that it be deemed eligible for copyright protection. This has been done by Bolivia, China, and Morocco.

Geographical indications

Identifying certain products or services as belonging to the particular region from which the product or service derives its characteristics is a powerful way of protecting native industry. Geographical indications currently used primarily for wines and spirits could be extended by developing countries to protect traditional products.

Geographical indications currently cover only wines and spirits. Many developing countries are keen to extend coverage to products that are of special importance to them. Geographic indications do not protect knowledge or technology; they only prevent the misleading use of certain indications by other parties.

Protection of undisclosed information

Traditional secrets of native and indigenous communities that have potential technical or economic value can be protected under Article 39 of the TRIPS Agreement as protection against unfair competition. Control over such information can allow for its regulation in terms of formulating contractual agreements, licensing it and earning remuneration from it.

Most important, TRIPS leaves details of guidelines, classification, and benefit sharing to the countries, which has generated controversial patent grants. Examples include the Ayahuasca plant from Brazil, turmeric from India, and quinoa from the Andean region. Some of these patents were revoked on appeal (turmeric, for example), but these examples illustrate the inability of the TRIPS Agreement to deal with the consequences of Article 27.3b.

NOTES

1. The nine countries are the US, Germany, Japan, Switzerland, UK, Australia, Netherlands, France and Ireland. It should also be noted that some of these transfers come from developed countries. However, given that developing countries are net technology consumers, the bulk of the transfers can be assumed to come from them (World Bank, 2001, p. 133, table 5.1).

2. These include Brazil, China, India, Republic of Korea, Mexico and South Africa (UNDP, 2001).

3. Developed countries have argued that in the wake of increased trade in knowledge-intensive goods, IPR protection is necessary across markets. However, this argument is flawed on several grounds. One, the choice to sell or not depends primarily on the purchasing power of the local populations, not the kind of IPR regime in place as seen in the case of emerging markets like China. Two, increased trade does not imply IPR protection for *all* products in *all* countries and depends on the relative weights different societies place on the rights of sellers versus consumers. Poor countries simply cannot afford the monopoly pricing consequences of TRIPS. Further, since trade occurs in the context of these widely different socioeconomic conditions, the harmonization of laws will not by itself create effective demand for patented products. It is possible, however, that the absence of property rights in other markets can reduce the incentive for full disclosure by patent holders in developed markets because of fears of imitation, and this may affect innovation in the long run. However, this can be balanced through other more appropriate policy interventions in disclosure regulation, research incentives and related areas.

4. Several least developed countries have strict IPR laws through regional or bilateral agreements and are de facto TRIPS compliant already.

5. According to WHO estimates for 1998, infectious diseases accounted for 13.3 million of a worldwide total of almost 54 million deaths. For low- and middle-income countries, one third of the deaths were due to treatable conditions of communicable diseases, shortfalls in maternity care or nutritional deficiencies. These include HIV/AIDS, malaria, tuberculosis, diseases that increase infant mortality (such as diarrhea, diphtheria, tetanus and measles) and the varied causes of maternal mortality. Among these, HIV/AIDS has probably become the most dangerous disease faced by the world today. Since its emergence nearly 20 years ago, over 60 million people have been infected; it is now the leading cause of death in Sub-Saharan Africa and the fourth largest killer worldwide (UNAIDS and WHO, 2001).

6. This was based on increases in the patentable segments of drug markets for select countries. These specific studies were conducted for Argentina and India using detailed price data (WTO, 2001).

7. The Organisation Africaine de la Propriété Intellectuelle (African Intellectual Property Organization) members, comprising 15 countries of Francophone West Africa, have offered a system of pharmaceutical product and process patents since the *Bangui Agreement* of 1977, and the African Regional Industrial Property Organization members, comprising 14 Anglophone countries, have offered pharmaceutical patent protection since at least 1984 (www.ohadalegis.com/anglais/intell per cent20property.htm# membership and www.aripo.wipo.net/protocol.html).

8. This is equivalent to US$2.2 per disability-adjusted life year (DALY), 1/20 of the global average (WHO, 2002, p. 79). DALY measures the number of life years lost due to premature mortality and the number of life-year equivalents lost due to chronic disability.

9. The Doha Declaration was also significant because for the first time, developing countries, led by the African group, and others such as Brazil and India decisively negotiated for a development friendly outcome.

10. The technology effort index is based on two variables: the R&D financed by productive enterprises and the number of patents taken out internationally (in the US) and then standardized and averaged to give a technological intensity index. The industrial performance index is based on manufacturing value added per capita, exports per capita, medium- and high-technology products as proportions of exports and manufacturing value added (Lall, 2001).

11. From an economic point of view, subsidies are a first-best option, since they directly reward innovators; at the same time, they require that the cost of innovation be estimated ex ante and are therefore difficult to implement. By contrast, patents are a second-best solution, since they distort prices and create monopolies. But they are easier to implement because the cost of innovation has already been incurred.

12. Cumulative as in 'each successive innovation builds on the previous one', and complementary as in 'each potential innovator takes a somewhat different research path and enhances the overall probability of reaching a particular goal' (Bessen and Maskin 2000).

13. For more details, see Bessen and Maskin (2000).

14. In some cases, capacity constraints are the impediment. The *sui generis* regime on integrated circuit designs under TRIPS does not prevent reverse engineering. However, few developing countries possess the requisite knowledge or resources to do so.

15. The UN Conference on Trade and Development (UNCTAD, 1996a) estimates these costs for upgrading, training and administration for selected countries.

16. This is primarily because of differing interpretations by US and European courts. Recent rulings in Europe, however, are moving closer to the US position of higher protection, which may imply more stringent implications of TRIPS under case law.

17. WT/DS114/R, 17 March 2000, EU vs. Canada, where the EU challenged a Canadian law that allows for a similar exception to not only allow tests, but also produce and stockpile for release immediately after the patent expires.

18. Detailed illustrations of these forms and conditions can be found in Correa (2000) for the pharmaceutical industry.

19. Members of the 1978 Convention are Australia, Austria, Argentina, Bolivia, Brazil., Chile, China, Colombia, Czech Republic, Ecuador, Finland, Hungary, Japan, Kenya, Mexico, Norway, Panama, Paraguay, Poland, Portugal, Slovakia, Trinidad and Tobago and Ukraine.

20. Members of the 1991 Convention are Belgium, Bulgaria, Canada, Denmark, France, Germany, Ireland, Israel, Moldova, Netherlands, New Zealand, Russia, South Africa, Spain, Sweden, Switzerland, UK and US.

21. The 1978 UPOV version offered one such model, though it is by no means the only model that combines these goals.

22. The term *protection* is the subject of much confusion and contention. On the one side are groups that seek protection of traditional knowledge through IP to enable its commercial exploitation. Some see it as a way to use IP tools to protect traditional knowledge and biological resources from misappropriation and misuse. Some see the possibility that IP protection could be used as a tool for enhancing recognition of the value of traditional knowledge. And some see IP protection as a way to secure certain knowledge as privately held assets that can be commercialized for economic development. There is strong debate about the extent to which IP can advance any of these objectives and the role of IP among a range of other possible policy instruments for advancing these goals. On the other side are those who argue against protection through IP and for the protection of traditional knowledge through investments in communities and their livelihoods. Some groups want to contain the scope of IP, preventing its application to traditional knowledge in any way, to guard against the danger that foreign corporations could appropriate local knowledge through IP tools. And some argue against the commodification of knowledge that comes with the assignment of ownership rights. There are also concerns that governments will appropriate traditional knowledge for national benefit or for elites to benefit.

23. WIPO defines traditional knowledge as 'tradition-based literary, artistic or scientific work; performances, inventions, scientific discoveries, designs, marks, names and symbols, undisclosed information and all other tradition-based innovations and creations resulting from intellectual activity in the industrial, scientific, literary or artistic fields' (WIPO, 2001, p. 25).

24. The Budapest Treaty obliges countries to recognize the physical deposit of a sample of a microorganism as disclosure of an invention for the purpose of patent

protection. For this, the treaty—which has 49 member states, 47 of them from developed countries—relies on a network of recognized international depository authorities which operate special rules on access to the biological samples, especially to avert potential patent infringement. There are 31 depository authorities in 19 countries, all but 2 of them being developed countries (GRAIN, 2001).

25. UNCTAD did significant research in this area in the 1970s (UNCTAD, 1996b).

26. As is being carried out as part of the WHO Essential Drugs Monitor program.

REFERENCES

Abbott, Frederick. 2002. 'Compulsory Licensing for Public Health Needs: The TRIPS Agenda at the WTO after the Doha Declaration on Public Health'. Occasional Paper 9. Friends World Committee for Consultation, Quaker United Nations Office, Geneva.

Attaran, Amir, and Lee Gillespie-White. 2001. 'Do Patents for Antiretroviral Drugs Constrain Access to AIDS Treatment in Africa?' Special Communication. *Journal of the American Medical Association* 286 (15): 1886–92.

Barton, John. 2001. 'Differentiated Pricing of Patented Products'. CMH Working Paper Series WG4:2. World Health Organization, Commission on Macroeconomics and Health, Geneva.

Bessen, James, and Eric Maskin. 2000. 'Sequential Innovation, Patents, and Imitation'. Working Paper. Massachusetts Institute of Technology, Department of Economics. Cambridge, Mass.

Boullet, Pascal, and Gilles-Bernard Forte. 2000. 'Drug Patents in French-Speaking Africa'. Joint Mission Report, Médecins sans Frontières–World Health Organization–UNAIDS, Geneva.

BRIDGES Trade News Digest. 2001. 'TRIPS and Public Health vs. TRIPS and Pandemics?' September. International Centre for Trade and Sustainable Development, Geneva.

Butler, B. J., and B. W. Marion. 1996. *The Impacts of Patent Protection in the U.S. Seed Industry and Public Plant Breeding.* Madison: University of Wisconsin.

Chang, Ha-Joon. 2000. 'Intellectual Property Rights and Economic Development-Historical Lessons and Emerging Issues'. Background paper for *Human Development Report 2001.* United Nations Development Programme, New York.

CIPR (Commission on Intellectual Property Rights). 2002. 'Integrating Intellectual Property and Development Policy'. London.

Clarke, George. 2001. 'How the Quality of Institutions Affects Technological Deepening in Developing Countries'. Policy Research Working Paper 2603. World Bank, Development Research Group, Washington, D.C.

Cohen, Joel. 2000. 'Harnessing Biotechnology for the Poor: Challenges Ahead Regarding Biosafety and Capacity Building'. Background paper for *Human Development Report 2001.* United Nations Development Programme, New York.

Convention on Biological Diversity. 1992. [www.biodiv.org/convention/articles.asp].

Correa, Carlos. 1999. *Intellectual Property Rights and the Use of Compulsory Licenses: Options for Developing Countries.* Trade Related Agenda, Development and Equity (TRADE) Working Paper 5. Geneva: South Center.

———. 2000. *Integrating Public Health Concerns into Patent Legislation in Developing Countries.* Geneva: South Center.

———. 2001a. 'Public Health and Patent Legislation in Developing Countries'. *Tulane Journal of Technology and Intellectual Property* 3(1).

———. 2001b. 'Traditional Knowledge and Intellectual Property?' Quaker United Nations Office Discussion Paper. QUNO, Geneva.

———. 2001c. 'The TRIPS Agreement: How Much Room to Maneuver?' Background paper for *Human Development Report 2001.* United Nations Development Programme, New York.

———. 2002. 'Review of the TRIPS Agreement: Fostering the Transfer of Technology to Developing Countries'. Third World Network, Geneva. [www.twnside.org.sg/title/foster.htm].

CUTS (Consumer Unity and Trust Society). 2001. 'Negotiating the TRIPS Agreements: India's Experience and Some Domestic Policy Issues'. Research Report 0111. Center for International Trade, Economics, and Environment, Jaipur.

Drahos, Peter. 2002. 'Developing Countries and International Intellectual Property Standard-Setting'. Study prepared for the UK Commission on Intellectual Property Rights. CIPR, London.

Dutfield, Graham. 2002a. 'The Doha Declaration on TRIPS and Public Health: Does it Change Anything?' *Trade Negotiations Insights* 1 (1): 1–2. International Centre for Trade and Sustainable Development, the European Centre for Development Policy Management, and the Overseas Development Institute, Geneva.

———. 2002b. 'Literature Survey on Intellectual Property Rights and Sustainable Human Development'. Intellectual Property Rights and Sustainable Development Series. UNCTAD/ICTSD Capacity Building Project on Intellectual Property Rights and Sustainable Development. UN Conference on Trade and Development/International Centre for Trade and Sustainable Development, Geneva.

Escudero, Sergio. 2001. *International Protection of Geographical Indications and Developing Countries.* Trade Related Agenda, Development and Equity (TRADE) Working Paper 10. Geneva: South Center.

FAO (Food and Agriculture Organization). 2001. *The State of Food Insecurity in the World: Food Insecurity—When People Live with Hunger and Fear Starvation.* Vienna.

Fink, Carsten. 1999. 'Entering the Jungle of Intellectual Property Rights Exhaustion and Parallel Imports'. Paper presented at conferences on 'Competitive Strategies for Intellectual Property Protection' organized by the Fraser Insitute, Santiago Chile and Buenos Aires, Argentina.

———. 2000. 'How Stronger Patent Protection in India Might Affect the Behaviour of Transnational Pharmaceutical Industries'. Policy Research Working Paper 2352. World Bank, Development Research Group, Washington D.C.

Fink, Carsten, and Carlos A. Primo Braga. 1999. 'How Stronger Protection of Intellectual Property Rights Affects International Trade Flows'. Policy Research Working Paper 2051. World Bank, Washington, D.C.

Fink, Carsten, Carlos A. Primo Braga, and Claudia Paz Sepulveda. 1998. 'Intellectual Property Rights and Economic Development'. TechNet Working Paper. World Bank, Washington D.C.

Gallini, Nancy, and Suzanne Scotchmer. 2002. 'Intellectual Property: When Is It the Best Incentive System?' In Adam Jaffe, Joshua Lerner and Scott Stern, eds, *Innovation Policy and the Economy*, vol. 2 Cambridge, Mass.: MIT Press.

Garfinkel, Simson L. 1994. 'Patently Absurd'. *Wired.* July: 104–06.

GRAIN (Genetic Resources Action International). 1998. *Intellectual Property Rights and Biodiversity: The Economic Myths—Global Trade and Biodiversity in Conflict.* Issue 3, October.

———. 1999. 'Beyond UPOV: Examples of Developing Countries Preparing Non-UPOV *Sui Generis* Plant Variety Protection Schemes for Compliance with TRIPS'. [http://www.grain.org/publications/nonupov-en-p.htm].

———. 2000. 'For a Full Review of TRIPS 27.3(b): An Update on Where Developing Countries Stand with the Push to Patent Life at WTO'. [www.grain.org/publications/tripsfeb00-en-p.htm].

———. 2001. 'TRIPS-Plus through the Back Door: How Bilateral Treaties Impose Much Stricter Rules for IPRs on Life than the WTO'. In Cooperation with South Asia Network on Food, Ecology, and Culture (SANFEC), Rome.

Juma, Calestous. 1999. *Intellectual Property Rights and Globalization: Implications for Developing Countries.* Center for International Development Science, Technology and Innovation Discussion Paper 4. Harvard University, Cambridge, Mass.

Kumar, Nagesh. 1995. 'International Linkages, Technology and Exports of Developing Countries: Trends and Policy Implications'. INTECH Discussion Paper 9507. United Nations University, Institute for New Technologies, Maastricht.

———. 1997. 'Technology Generation and Technology Transfers in the World Economy: Recent Trends and Implications for Developing Countries'. INTECH Discussion Paper 9702. United Nations University, Institute for New Technologies, Maastricht.

Lall, Sanjaya. 2001. 'Indicators of the Relative Importance of IPRs in Developing Countries'. UNCTAD/ICTSD Capacity Building Project on Intellectual Property Rights and Sustainable Development. UN Conference on Trade and Development/International Centre for Trade and Sustainable Development, Geneva.

Lichtenberg, Frank. 2001. 'Are the Benefits of Newer Drugs Worth Their Cost? Evidence from the 1996 MEPS'. *Health Affairs* 20 (5): 241–51.

Love, James. 2001a. 'Compulsory Licensing Models for State Practice in Developing Countries, Access to Medicine and Compliance with the WTO TRIPS Accord'. Background Paper for *Human Development Report 2001.* United Nations Development Programme, New York.

———. 2001b. 'Implementing TRIPS Safeguards with Particular Attention to Administrative Models for Compulsory Licensing of Patents'. Paper presented at the WHO meeting in Harare, Zimbabwe, Consumer Project on Technology, Washington D.C.

Mangeni, Francis. 2000, *Technical Issues on Protecting Plant Varieties by Effective Sui generis Systems.* Trade Related Agenda, Development and Equity (TRADE) Occasional Paper 2. Geneva: South Center.

Maskus, Keith. 1998a. 'The International Regulation of Intellectual Property'. *Weltwirtschaftliches Archiv* 123 (2): 186–208.

———. 1998b. 'The Role of Intellectual Property Rights in Encouraging Foreign Direct Investment and Technology Transfer'. *Duke Journal of Comparative and International Law* 9 (1): 109–62.

———. 2000a. *Intellectual Property Rights in the Global Economy*. Washington D.C.: Institute for International Economics.

———. 2000b. 'Regulatory Standards in the WTO: Comparing Intellectual Property Rights with Competition Policy, Environmental Protection and Core Labor Standards'. Working Paper 00-1. Institute for International Economics, Washington, D.C.

McCalman, Phillip. 2001. 'Reaping What You Sow: An Empirical Analysis of International Patent Harmonization'. *Journal of International Economics* 55:161–286.

Nayyar, Deepak. 1999. 'Intellectual Property, the New Millennium and the Least Developed Countries: Some Reflections in the Wider Context of Development'. In *The New Millennium, Intellectual Property and the Least Developed Countries: A Compendium of the Proceedings of the First High Level Interregional Roundtable on Intellectual Property for the LDCs*. Geneva: World Intellectual Property Rights Organization.

Oxfam GB. 2001. 'Drug Companies vs. Brazil: The Threat to Public Health'. Policy Briefing Note, Cut the Cost Campaign. London.

Oxfam International. 2001. 'Formula for Fairness: Patient Rights before Patent Rights'. Oxfam Company Briefing Paper 2. London.

Panagariya, Arvind. 1999. 'TRIPS and the WTO: An Uneasy Marriage'. University of Maryland, Center for International Economics, College Park.

Patel, S., P. Roffe, and A. Yusuf. 2000. *International Technology Transfer: The Origins and Aftermath of the United Nations Negotiations on a Draft Code of Conduct*. Dordrecht: Kluwer Law International.

Rangnekar, Dwijen. 2001. 'Access to Genetic Reources, Gene-Based Inventions and Agriculture'. Study Paper 3a. UK Commission on Intellectual Property Rights, London.

Rasiah, Rajah. 2002. 'TRIPS and Capability Building in Developing Economies'. INTECH Discussion Paper 2002-1. United Nations University, Institute for New Technologies, Maastricht.

Roffe, P. 2000. 'The Political Economy of Intellectual Property Rights—A Historical Perspective'. In J Foudez, M Footer and J Norton, eds. *Governance, Development and Globalization*. University of Warwick.

Saggi, Kamal. 2000. 'Trade, Foreign Direct Investment and International Technology Transfer: A Survey'. Policy Research Working Paper 2349. World Bank, Development Research Group, Trade, Washington D.C.

Scotchmer, Suzanne. 1999. 'Cumulative Innovation in Theory and Practice'. University of California, Goldman School of Public Policy and Department of Economics, Berkeley.

Shiva, Vandana, Afsar H. Jafri, Gitanjali Bedi, and Radha Holla-Bhar. 1997. 'The Enclosure and Recovery of the Commons'. Research Foundation for Science, Technology and Ecology, New Delhi.

Stallman, Richard. 2002. 'Software Patents—Obstacles to Software Development'. Paper presented at the University of Cambridge Computer Laboratory, sponsored by the Foundation for Information Policy Research. [www.cl.cam.ac.uk/~mgk25/stallman-patents.html].

Stilwell, Matthew, and Elizabeth Tuerk. 2000. *Non-Violation Complaints and the TRIPS Agreement: Some Considerations for WTO Members.* Trade Related Agenda, Development and Equity (TRADE) Occasional Paper 1. Geneva: South Center.

Stilwell, Matthew, Elizabeth Tuerk, and Catherine Monagle. 2000. *Review of TRIPS Agreement under Article 71.1.* Trade Related Agenda, Development and Equity (TRADE) Occasional Paper 3. Geneva: South Center.

Subramanian, Arvind, and Jayashree Watal. 2000. 'Can TRIPS Serve as an Enforcement Device for Developing Countries in the WTO?' *Journal of International Economic Law* 3 (3): 403–16.

Tansey, Geoff. 1999. 'Trade, Intellectual Property, Food and Biodiversity: Key Issues and Options for the 1999 Review of Article 27.3(b) of the TRIPS Agreement'. Discussion Paper. Quaker Peace and Service and Quaker United Nations Office, London.

Tripathi, Ruchi. 2000. 'Implications of TRIPS on Livelihoods of Poor Farmers in Developing Countries'. Paper presented at a conference in Berne, Switzerland, 13 October 2000. Action Aid.

UNAIDS and WHO (World Health Organization). 2001. *AIDS Epidemic Update December 2001.* Geneva.

UNCTAD (United Nations Conference on Trade and Development). 1994. 'Assessment of the Outcome of the Uruguay Round'. Geneva.

———. 1996a. 'Strengthening the Participation of Developing Countries in World Trade and the Multilateral Trading System'. TD/375/Rev.1. Geneva.

———. 1996b. 'The TRIPS Agreement and Developing Countries'. UNCTAD/ITE/1. Geneva.

———. 1999. 'Trade, Sustainable Development and Gender'. Paper prepared in support of the themes discussed at the pre-UNCTAD X Expert Workshop on Trade, Sustainable Development and Gender, 10 January, Geneva.

———. 2002a. 'Capacity Building and Technical Cooperation for Developing Countries, especially LDCs, and Economies in Transition in Support of Their Participation in the WTO Doha Work Programme'. Draft proposal. UNCTAD/RMS/TCS/1. Geneva.

———. 2002b. *Trade and Development Report 2002. Developing Countries in World Trade.* Geneva.

UNDP (United Nations Development Programme). 2001. *Human Development Report 2001: Making New Technologies Work for Developing Countries.* New York: Oxford University Press.

———. 2002. 'TRIPS and Brazil'. Background note for Trade and Sustainable Human Development Project. United Nations Development Programme, New York.

Viotti, Eduardo. 2001. 'National Learning Systems: A New Approach on Technical Change in Late Industrializing Economies and Evidences from the Cases of Brazil and South Korea'. Center for International Development Science, Technology and Innovation Discussion Paper. Harvard University, Cambridge, Mass.

WHO (World Health Organization) and UNAIDS. 1998. 'Guidance Modules on Antiretroviral Treatments'. WHO/ASD/98.1, UNAIDS/98.7. Geneva.

————. 1999. *Globalization and Access to Drugs: Perspectives on the WTO/TRIPS Agreement*. Health Economics and Drugs. DAP Series 7. Geneva.

————. 2000. *World Health Report*. Geneva.

————. 2001a. *Globalization, Patents and Drugs: An Annotated Bibliography*. Health Economics and Drugs. EDM Series 10. Geneva.

————. 2001b. *Globalization, TRIPS and Access to Pharmaceuticals*. WHO Policy Perspectives on Medicines 3. Geneva.

————. 2001c. *Network for Monitoring the Impact of Globalization and TRIPS on Access to Medicines*. Health Economics and Drugs. EDM Series 11. Geneva.

————. 2002. *Commission on Macroeconomics and Health*. Geneva.

World Intellectual Property Rights Organization (WIPO). 1999. *The New Millenium, Intellectual Property and the Least Developed Countries*. Geneva.

World Bank. 2001. *Global Economic Prospects and the Developing Countries 2002*. Washington, D.C.

WTO (World Trade Organization). 1994. *Agreement on Trade-Related Aspects of Intellectual Property Rights*. Agreement Establishing the WTO, Annex IC. [www.wto.org/english/docs_e/legal_e/final_e.htm].

Zinnbauer, Dieter. 2000. 'The Dynamics of the Digital Divide: Why Being Late Does Matter'. Background paper for *Human Development Report 2001*. United Nations Development Programme, New York.

CHAPTER 12

TRADE-RELATED INVESTMENT MEASURES AND INVESTMENT

Governments use two measures to attract and regulate foreign direct investment: performance requirements (such as local content, local manufacturing, export performance and technology transfer requirements) and investment incentives (such as loans and tax rebates). Performance requirements are intended to ensure that foreign investment contributes to the host country's development and is consistent with its policy goals.

Investment incentives involve a wide range of fiscal and monetary policy tools. When these incentives are related to trade in goods, they are called Trade-Related Investment Measures (TRIMs). Some TRIMs entail performance requirements. Such measures have been extremely important for many developing and some industrial countries, often serving as part of broad strategies aimed at achieving economic growth, industrialization and technology transfer. TRIMs have also been used to guard against and counter anticompetitive and trade-restrictive business practices—particularly those of transnational corporations.

This chapter begins by analysing the TRIMs agreement—its history, its relationship to development and its possible future. The chapter then discusses investment more broadly, because the two issues are closely related. The discussion focuses on foreign direct investment, arguing that it—not portfolio flows—should be the focus of any discussion on investment in the World Trade Organization (WTO). The chapter then traces how the nature of such investment has changed and analyses how it can contribute to human development. The chapter also highlights what a multilateral investment agreement might cover under the WTO, and concludes by identifying some of the prerequisites and flexibilities needed for a multilateral investment agreement.

THE TRIMS AGREEMENT

The TRIMs agreement aims at eliminating the trade-distorting effects of investment measures taken by WTO members. It does not introduce any new obligations, but merely prohibits TRIMs considered inconsistent with the provisions of the 1994 General Agreement on Tariffs and Trade (GATT) for both agricultural and industrial goods. Measures deemed inconsistent with the agreement were to be identified (by the countries where they were in effect) within 90 days of 1 January 1995, the day the WTO came into existence.

Industrial country members were expected to eliminate these measures within two years, while developing countries were given five years and the least developed countries seven years. The agreement provides flexibility on these deadlines if a country is experiencing implementation difficulties for development, finance or trade reasons. For example, some developing countries were recently granted an extension through 2003.

The agreement does not define TRIMs or provide objective criteria for identifying them, leaving it to members to decide which of their TRIMs are illegal. This approach allows considerable room for interpretation and dispute, though TRIMs that do not violate the national treatment obligations of GATT article III or the prohibition on quantitative restrictions of article IX are clearly permitted. The agreement calls for increased transparency in administering TRIMs, allowing countries to challenge measures they consider non-transparent.

Guidance on TRIMs was provided only through an illustrative list that identifies measures inconsistent with national treatment and local content requirements and with the prohibition on quantitative restrictions that link imports to export performance through trade or foreign exchange restrictions or through export restrictions based on domestic sales. Thus the TRIMs agreement does not prohibit export performance requirements. But subsidies linked to such requirements are covered under the Agreement on Subsidies and Countervailing Measures (ASCM) and subject to its disciplines.

Although investment measures that do not violate GATT articles III and IX are permitted, countries that have recently joined the WTO have been obliged to eliminate additional performance requirements as part of the terms of their accession—notably requirements related to export performance and technology transfer. Similar 'WTO plus' demands are being made on countries in the process of accession to the WTO, including least developed countries (see UNCTAD, 2002).

WHERE WE ARE NOW

The 2001 WTO Ministerial Conference in Doha, Qatar, remained deadlocked on investment and the three other 'Singapore issues' (competition policy, trade facilitation, transparency in government procurement). Most industrial countries, especially EU members, wanted to start negotiating an agreement on these four issues after the Doha conference, while many developing countries wanted to continue studying them (box 12.1). The Doha declaration agreed to continue studying the issues until the 2003 conference in Cancun, Mexico. Although it is not inevitable that negotiations on these issues will begin after the Mexico conference, pressure for such an outcome has intensified since Doha.

BOX 12.1 THE HISTORY OF INTERNATIONAL AGREEMENTS ON INVESTMENT

Attempts to reach international agreements on investment have a long history. In the late 18th and the 19th centuries the European powers and the US set standards for the protection of foreign investment that were superior to national treatment. Furthermore, host countries were not permitted to interfere with or expropriate foreign assets.

Latin American countries were the first to challenge the favourable treatment of foreign investors. The 1868 Calvo Doctrine established the same rights for foreigners and nationals and prohibited countries from intervening to enforce the claims of their citizens in other countries. Between World War I and II the League of Nations was stalemated on this issue, and since World War II industrial countries have been unsuccessful in their efforts to establish an international regime for the protection of international investment.

The 1947–48 United Nations Conference on Trade and Employment considered investment in its discussions on the expansion of international trade. Investment measures formed part of a wider discussion of restrictive business practices, and the Havana charter for an International Trade Organization (ITO) contained provisions on such measures. But the negotiations leading to the charter and eventually to the GATT showed that governments were not prepared to subject their investment policies to international rules and disciplines.

Following the failure to establish the ITO, industrial countries implemented policies bilaterally through investment promotion and protection treaties and agreements. Such treaties were intended to ensure that investors' property would not be expropriated without prompt, adequate and effective compensation, non-discriminatory treatment, transfer of funds and dispute settlement procedures. In addition, in the late 1950s an evaluation of restrictive business practices was carried out by a GATT group of experts, focusing on activities of international cartels and trusts that could hamper the expansion of world trade and interfere with GATT objectives.

Later the issue of international investment surfaced at the United Nations, where developing countries sought international approval for their sovereign aspirations and tried to alter the international investment standards that had prevailed in the colonial period. One outcome was the UN General Assembly's Charter of Economic Rights and Duties of States, passed in 1974. Article 2 of the charter provided for the rights of every state to regulate and exercise authority over foreign investment in conformity with its national objectives and stated that no state would be compelled to grant preferential treatment to foreign investment. The draft Code of Conduct for Transnational Corporations, issued by the United Nations Center on Transnational Corporations, addressed a range of additional issues—almost all of which remain unresolved because most industrial countries opposed a legally binding status for the code. In addition, the Set of Multilaterally Agreed Equitable Principles and Rules for the Control of Restrictive Practices, negotiated under the United Nations Conference on Trade and Development, covered investment and competition policy issues—and suffered the same fate.

After the conclusion of the GATT's Tokyo Round in 1979, renewed attempts were made to bring under its purview a limited number of performance requirements imposed on foreign investors by host countries, particularly local content and export performance requirements (TRIMs). Though many developing countries continued to maintain that foreign direct investment was beyond the GATT's purview, the US and some other industrial countries argued that such performance requirements affect trade and should be addressed by the trade regime.

A 1982 dispute over administration of the Foreign Investment Review Act, brought by the US against Canada, significantly boosted its efforts to bring investment under the purview

(Box continues on next page.)

of multilateral trade disciplines. While many delegations were sceptical about bringing such a dispute to the GATT, its council finally decided to allow a panel to investigate the US claim. Among other things, the panel ruled that Canada's practice of requiring foreign direct investors to purchase Canadian goods was inconsistent with GATT article III:4, though not with article XI:1. The US-Canada dispute set the stage for a more effective challenge of TRIMs at the multilateral level. The ruling also appears to have led to an amendment in US trade legislation to address investment issues more directly.

Investment was a major issue in the Uruguay Round, featuring in and affecting discussions and agreements on trade in services (GATS), TRIMs, Trade-Related Aspects of Intellectual Property Rights (TRIPS), government procurement and subsidies. The 1988 Omnibus Trade and Competitiveness Act, which provided the US with negotiating authority for the Uruguay Round, had explicit language on investment. TRIMs were viewed by the US as preventing its transnational corporations from designing coherent global strategies, and their removal became a main negotiating issue for the US and some other industrial countries during the Uruguay Round.

During the negotiations attempts were made to go beyond TRIMs to develop a regime for investment in general, including the right of establishment and national treatment. Industrial countries also argued for the elimination of all TRIMs, rather than just minimizing and avoiding their adverse affects on trade. Most developing countries differed from the US, Japan and other industrial countries on two main counts: whether multilateral disciplines should be limited by existing GATT articles or expanded to develop an investment regime; and whether some or all actionable TRIMs should be prohibited or dealt with case by case, based on a clear demonstration of their direct and significant restrictive and adverse effects on trade. The US and Japan favoured an all-encompassing investment regime, with TRIMs as one part of it. Developing countries called for strict adherence to the GATT mandate and for limiting negotiations to investment measures with direct and significant adverse effects on trade. While developing countries managed to limit the scope of the TRIMs agreement during the Uruguay Round, article 9 called for a review of the agreement's operation within five years of its entry into force—with a view to determining whether it should be complemented with provisions on investment and competition policy.

In addition, the General Agreement on Trade in Services (GATS), which takes a 'positive list' approach, covers investment liberalization since it includes commercial presence as one of the modes of service supply (mode 3). In fact, it is believed that the term 'trade in services' was coined as a way of bringing investment within the scope of Uruguay Round agreements in a more forceful way than the TRIMs agreement would allow due to opposition from developing countries. Most developing countries opposed bringing trade in services under the purview of multilateral disciplines and agreed only on the condition that it be kept separate from negotiations on trade in goods. Thus while TRIMs were discussed during negotiations on goods, the GATS was discussed in separate negotiations on services. Nevertheless, the US and transnational private sector actors devoted substantial efforts to ensuring that 'trade in services' was defined to include investment and that it would become acceptable terminology. Thus it is no surprise that the maximum market access commitments under the GATS have been achieved under mode 3, especially in financial services and telecommunications.

Regional agreements such as the North American Free Trade Agreement (NAFTA) go further than the TRIMs agreement and the GATS, providing national and non-discriminatory treatment to foreign investment. NAFTA also prohibits a number of performance requirements. For this reason services are clearly differentiated from investment in NAFTA. In addition, by January 1997 there were 1,330 bilateral investment treaties in 162 countries—up from fewer than 400 treaties in the early 1990s.

Major differences remain on the issue of bringing investment under multilateral trade disciplines. Not satisfied with the TRIMs agreement, industrial countries maintained intense pressure for the inclusion of four new issues (investment, competition policy, trade facilitation, government procurement) at the first WTO ministerial conference, held in Singapore in 1996. Investment was probably the most important to them. Despite most developing countries' resistance to the inclusion of these issues, members agreed that all four (subsequently dubbed the 'Singapore issues') should be studied further in working groups, with a view to recommending whether negotiations should take place on them at a future ministerial conference. The scope of the government procurement discussion was limited to transparency, not market access.

At the same time, the Organisation for Economic Co-operation and Development (OECD) began trying to reach a Multilateral Agreement on Investment among its members—only to fail, indicating how difficult it is to agree on investment issues even among countries at similar levels of human development.

Source: UNCTAD, 1994; Gibbs and Mashayekhi, 1998; UNDP, 2002; Ganesan, 1998.

Many developing countries contend that, based on the implementation experience so far, the TRIMs agreement has not taken into account their development requirements. They are particularly concerned about the agreement's negative effects on employment and value added, because it prohibits late-industrializing countries from pursuing domestic content polices. Such policies were crucial to the successful development strategies of today's industrial countries and East Asia's newly industrialized countries.

Developing countries have put forward a number of reasons for maintaining TRIMs. Among these are ensuring the fullest, most efficient contribution of investment to their economic development. For example, TRIMs may allow small firms to expand to full competitive scale and can be used to channel foreign direct investment to bring infant industries to maturity. In doing so, such enterprises are likely to increase domestic employment and valued added. TRIMs can also mitigate the problems of disadvantaged regions and enhance investment's contribution to building and upgrading domestic technological capacity, increasing the value-added share of exports. In this context the TRIMs agreement is viewed by many developing countries as a major impediment to upgrading technology and increasing value added.

Developing country governments have also argued that TRIMs counter the trade-restrictive and -distorting strategies of transnational corporations. For example, local content requirements can be used to increase employment, protect the viability of local firms and avoid overpricing by transnational corporations. Local content requirements can also be a necessary response to vertically integrated transnational corporations that dominate the market.

For example, the electronics industry derives little local content from developing countries despite having significant operations in them. This is because many of the corporations that dominate the industry prefer to source components and parts from parent companies or foreign affiliates—even if parts of comparable quality are available domestically in developing countries. As a result most of the value added from the industry goes to transnational corporations.[1]

Implementation of the TRIMs agreement has posed a number of challenges for developing countries. These include the difficulty of identifying TRIMs covered by the agreement and ensuring their timely notification to the WTO, the inadequacy of the transition period for phasing out prohibited TRIMs and disputes arising from the lack of clarity between the GATT, the TRIMs agreement and the Agreement on Subsidies and Countervailing Measures. Of greatest concern, however, are dispute settlement rulings involving prohibitions on local content requirements—rulings that many developing countries view as running counter to their interests.

Although a number of countries have de-emphasized the use of local content in recent years, such requirements continue to be used in both developing and industrial countries—particularly in the automotive sector, where they are most widespread in developing countries.[2] Accordingly, since the TRIMs agreement came into force, this sector has seen the largest number of disputes lodged by industrial against developing countries. Between 1995 and February 2002, 11 complaints in the automotive sector (involving not just local content requirements but also subsidies, incentives and foreign exchange balancing) were brought by Japan, the European Communities and the US against four developing countries with large potential automotive markets: Brazil, India, Indonesia, and the Philippines. Rulings have been made on six of these complaints—four against Indonesia and two against India. Japan's complaint against Indonesia (and similar subsequent complaints against Indonesia by the EU and US) illustrates a number of development concerns (box 12.2).

THE WAY FORWARD

A positive response to some of the implementation concerns of developing countries was the July 2001 decision of the WTO Council for Trade in Goods to extend until the end of 2001 the transition period for the TRIMs notified under article 5:1. Another two-year extension was made available upon request and upon the fulfilment of certain conditions, such as the presentation of a phase-out plan for TRIMs.

Though useful in the short run, these extensions do not deal with the fundamental problem of the TRIMs agreement: it does not give developing countries the policy space they need to use certain development policy instruments—such as local content and other performance requirements—that could enhance their value added, employment and trade competitiveness.

The TRIMs agreement may not be in the best interests of developing countries and human development. Thus it should be reassessed, with a view to rolling back its prohibition on the use of instruments that enhanced the development prospects of today's industrial and newly industrialized countries. In addition, TRIMs and GATS (General Agreement on Trade in Services) provisions on

---

BOX 12.2 COMPLAINTS ABOUT INDONESIA'S CAR PROGRAMME

In 1997 Japan asked a WTO panel to investigate its complaint that Indonesia was in violation of a number of articles of the TRIMs agreement. (The EU and US reserved third-party rights in the case.) Indonesia had not given notification of the disputed measures because it believed that its national car programme, which included local content requirements, did not violate the TRIMs agreement. It felt that the measures it was taking were more appropriately discussed under the Agreement on Subsidies and Countervailing Measures (ASCM).

The panel, however, judged the local content requirements as violating article 2 of the TRIMs agreement. Further, the panel concluded that the tariff and luxury sales tax exemptions Indonesia provided as incentives through its car programme were specific subsidies that had caused serious prejudice to the interests of the complainants. This interpretation of article 5 of the ASCM indicated that TRIMs could be adjudicated under the ASCM as well.

This case brings together most of the TRIMs-related implementation concerns identified by developing countries. Most important, like many other developing countries, Indonesia felt that it was being denied legitimate development measures for the promotion of its automotive industry. Regardless of the particular merits of Indonesia's national car programme, the automotive industry has long been viewed as central to the development of many large, populous developing countries with large internal markets. The rapid development of the automotive industry in such countries has significant multiplier effects and backward linkages, with positive implications for domestic value added, technological capacity and employment.

Despite other significant problems with Indonesia's car programme, including its demise due to domestic political pressures and the conditions imposed by international financial institutions during the East Asian crisis of the late 1990s, the programme appears to have had implications for both the TRIMs agreement and future negotiations on investment in the WTO. Although Indonesia did not appeal the panel's report because the financial crisis made it impossible for the programme to continue, the issues raised in the complaint have led many developing countries to regard the TRIMs agreement as hostile to their development interests and designed to maintain the industrialization and technology gap between industrial and developing countries.

Source: Tang, 2002.

---

performance requirements should be made consistent: the GATS allows them while the TRIMs agreement prohibits many.

If a rollback is not possible, it will be necessary to rethink the parameters of the TRIMs agreement through the application of special and differential treatment exemptions for local content requirements, especially in the automotive and electronics industries of developing countries. These industries should be prioritised because they are dynamic, with significant potential for contributing to human development outcomes. As some have argued, there may also be value in rethinking the TRIMs agreement to focus it on trade-related investment measures with direct and negative implications for trade, as opposed to the current outright prohibition of certain measures. In addition, any discussions on bringing other investment measures under multilateral disciplines should be approached with caution, keeping in mind the experience with TRIMs so far.

INVESTMENT

OECD discussions on the Multilateral Agreement on Investment (see box 12.1) were all-encompassing, reaching beyond traditional notions of foreign direct investment to cover nearly every type of tangible and intangible asset (OECD, 1997). Thus in addition to foreign direct investment the proposed agreement included both intellectual property and portfolio investment.

The motivations for the failed OECD discussions and the investment discussions in the WTO appear to have a lot in common, even if the types of investment covered by the WTO Working Group on the Relationship Between Trade and Investment are likely to be more limited. The common motives seem to be the strategic interests of transnational corporations to ensure uniform global rules that will reduce both their transactions costs and the uncertainty surrounding their investment decisions while simultaneously giving them secure property rights. Since the vast majority of transnational corporations are based in OECD countries, it is not surprising that reaching a multilateral agreement on investment with such an emphasis is a high priority for OECD governments.

But from a developing country perspective these motivations imply an inherent asymmetry in the discussions, because so far the discussions have focused on the rights of foreign investors in host countries—not their obligations. From a human development perspective, key issues include whether foreign direct investment is supportive of human development and whether a multilateral agreement on investment in the WTO will give developing countries the policy flexibility and autonomy they need to pursue their human development goals. Given that the TRIMs agreement has been in effect for more than seven years, it will be important to take its experience into account while making such an assessment.

While the 2001 Doha declaration does not explicitly define what is meant by investment for WTO discussion purposes, the relevant paragraph reads: 'recognizing the case for a multilateral framework to secure transparent, stable and predictable conditions for long-term cross-border investment, particularly foreign direct investment, that will contribute to the expansion of trade'. This suggests that any proposed agreement in the WTO can be expected to focus on long-term foreign direct investment, not short-term portfolio capital flows.

This interpretation is consistent with the frequent reminders of developing countries since the 1996 Singapore ministerial conference that the working group in this area was established with the understanding that its work would be limited to foreign direct investment (cited in Correa 1999). Given the Doha emphasis and Singapore understanding, it can be reasonably expected that the Working Group on the Relationship Between Trade and Investment will, at least initially, focus exclusively on foreign direct investment.

The changing nature of foreign direct investment

There is growing recognition that in the context of financial globalization, some of the long-standing characteristics of foreign direct investment (such as its stability and long-term nature) that have differentiated it from portfolio investment may be eroding, making their distinction increasingly blurred. This has complicated the debate about the nature of foreign direct investment and its potential and real benefits for human development. Almost a decade ago a World Bank study illustrated the changing nature of foreign direct investment in the context of financial liberalization (Claessens, Dooley and Warner, 1993). It argued that 'bricks and mortar' investments can easily be converted into liquid assets and remitted out of a country. The study stated that:

> 'Because direct investors hold factories and other assets that are impossible to move, it is sometimes assumed that a direct investment inflow is more stable than other forms of capital flows. This need not be the case. While a direct investor usually has some immovable assets, there is no reason in principle why these cannot be fully offset by domestic liabilities. Clearly a direct investor can borrow in order to export capital, and thereby generate rapid capital outflows'. (cited in Singh, 2001)

In such situations there is no documentation that distinguishes foreign direct investment from other financial capital. Retained profits, repatriated out of the host country, now account for a significant portion of foreign assets—as much as 50 per cent in the case of US-based foreign investors.

Clearly, foreign direct investment in this form cannot be compared with domestic capital accumulation. As a result, Singh (2001) argues that in the context of financial globalization, a first-order issue is understanding what foreign direct investment comprises. He indicates that the past decade probably saw the largest volume of cross-border mergers and acquisitions in world history. While most took place between industrial countries, mergers and acquisitions also greatly expanded in developing countries in the second half of the 1990s. Excluding China, the share of mergers and acquisitions in the combined foreign direct investment of developing countries rose from an average of 22 per cent during 1988–91 to 72 per cent during1992–97 (UNCTAD, 1999b). Moreover, most of this was in form of acquisitions, not mergers.

This trend accelerated during and after the 1997 East Asian financial crisis. Singh argues that the implications of this trend are troubling for developing countries because, unlike 'greenfield' investment (which represents a net addition to the capital stock of developing countries), foreign direct investment in the form of an acquisition may not represent any addition in terms of capital stock, employment or even output. But as others note, such investment could lead to positive effects in terms of subsequent investment, technology transfer and short-term balance of payments effects. While there is no conclusive evidence on the human development impacts of this form of foreign direct investment, on balance it appears less likely to create value added in developing countries, at least in the short run, compared with traditional greenfield investment in productive assets that add to the host country's capital stock.

Finally, it is important to bear in mind that, contrary to a widespread view, not all foreign direct investment is in the form of equity. Much is in the form of high-interest-bearing loans and of an intrafirm nature. Sometimes these loans are even government guaranteed.

Foreign direct investment and development

Despite features that can make foreign direct investment expensive, and important changes in its evolving nature, most developing countries welcome it because they believe that it can contribute to their development objectives. This is because the potential development role of certain types of foreign direct investment is almost universally acknowledged. Still, important disagreements remain about whether all foreign direct investment is development friendly and about the nature of the pre-requisites and conditions—including the role of government policy—in ensuring that it plays a positive development role.

Proponents of foreign direct investment and its inclusion in the multilateral trade regime argue that, on balance, it has a positive impact on human development, especially through its technology transfer and domestic productivity spillover effects (WTO, 1996). Over the past two decades such optimism about the economic growth, technology transfer and productivity consequences of foreign direct investment have led most developing countries to unilaterally lower barriers to foreign investment, including portfolio capital. Country after country has adopted regimes friendly to foreign direct investment and transnational corporations, with at least 103 countries offering special tax concessions to foreign corporations that have established production or administrative facilities within their borders since 1998 (Avi-Yonah, 1999, cited in Hanson, 2001). This, despite widespread evidence and agreement that such incentives, offered largely for reasons of competition between developing countries, play a relatively small role in the location decisions of all but footloose foreign investors (such as those attracted to export processing zones). Indeed, since most foreign investors are interested in domestic market opportunities in developing countries, there is evidence that such incentives merely lower the collective potential gains of developing countries from foreign direct investment.

Is all foreign direct investment good for human development?

While there is little disagreement that foreign direct investment can play an important role in enhancing human development, a more important question is whether all foreign direct investment is good for human development. Many proponents argue for a multilateral investment agreement in the WTO because they believe it will provide security and predictability to foreign investors, enhancing foreign direct investment—which is assumed to be good for developing countries.

There have been numerous studies on the impact of greenfield foreign direct investment in different countries, sectors and settings. The results have been mixed, with no conclusive evidence in any one direction. Such investment has been used for different purposes. For example, Latin American countries have often relied on foreign direct investment to finance balance of payments deficits, while Asian countries have used it more for technology transfer. Foreign direct investment can be expensive and unsustainable if used for balance of payments purposes. It is also much harder to differentiate from financial capital if it is used in this manner.

In a number of cases foreign direct investment has not realized its human development potential. Firm-level evidence from a large sample of manufacturing plants in developing countries fails to indicate the existence of productivity spillovers related to foreign direct investment. Indeed, the presence of transnational corporations appears to depress the productivity of domestic plants in some countries—with negative consequences for employment and other human development variables (Hanson, 2001).

Lost opportunities for technology transfer through foreign direct investment are also well documented. In fact, successful, sustainable technology transfer through foreign direct investment has been more the exception than the rule. Moreover, foreign direct investment may be an expensive way of achieving technology transfer. This is because, given the many risks associated with foreign direct investment, investors need to ensure high rates of return—exceeding the interest rates that typically apply on foreign loans for imports of capital goods.

Moreover, foreign direct investment can have negative development effects through its balance of payments impact, especially in the context of financial liberalization. As Kregel (1996) argues, 'FDI [foreign direct investment] may have both a short and a longer-term structural influence on the composition of a country's external payment flows. While financial innovation allows FDI to have an impact in the short run which is increasingly similar in terms of volatility to portfolio flows, the more important aspect is the way it may mask the true position of a country's balance of payments and the sustainability of any combination of policies....Accumulated foreign claims in the form of accumulated FDI stocks may create a potentially disruptive force that can offset any domestic or external policy goals.'

So, whatever the potential merits of foreign direct investment for human development—and there are many—it is by no means always a positive influence on the variables that are most important for advancing human development in developing countries: employment, productivity and technology transfer. A comprehensive review of experiences with foreign direct investment perhaps summed up the evidence best when it concluded that 'in terms of the impact of FDI on different parameters of development…FDI promises more than it delivers' (Kumar, 1996, p. 40).

Some kinds of foreign investment are preferable to others. Because not all types of foreign direct investment are equally desirable, less may be better than more unless all of it is of the desirable kind. Moreover, foreign direct investment in certain sectors may be preferable to others. In other words, developing countries need to both attract foreign direct investment selectively and govern it effectively if it is to play a positive role in human development.

What really matters?

While development-friendly foreign direct investment should be welcomed, the empirical evidence suggests no clear correlation between the volume of foreign direct investment and development success. Some of the most successful countries have not relied heavily on foreign direct investment. For example, Japan and the Republic of Korea relied only marginally on foreign direct investment for their success (South Center, 1997; see also UNCTAD, 1997). While such flows were higher for Korea than for Japan (as a share of gross fixed capital formation), they were among the lowest for all developing countries—including those in sub-Saharan Africa. Moreover, foreign direct investment flows to Japan were minimal not just for the decade of comparison (1984–93) but for the entire period after World War II. Data for Korea for 1970–94 show a similar pattern (South Center, 1997).

Appropriate government intervention matters—and can make the crucial difference. Though its foreign direct investment was low, Korea made strategic and effective use of the investment it did receive. This was in no small measure due to the government, which imposed important restrictions on foreign direct investment, stipulating both local ownership and performance requirements.

The more recent experiences of China, the developing world's largest recipient of foreign direct investment for much of the past decade, reinforce this earlier pattern (UNCTAD, 2002a). China also confirms that regulatory constraints do not significantly or negatively affect the amount of foreign direct investment that a country is able to attract. Malaysia, another successful recipient of foreign direct investment despite significant controls and regulations, appears to be further proof of this (UNCTAD, 1999a). By contrast, many of the countries with the least regulation and most foreign investment–friendly regimes (many in Africa) appear to have been the least successful in attracting foreign direct investment and other capital flows.

Southeast Asian countries also appear to indicate that foreign direct investment has been most successful when governments have integrated it with their national development plans, rather than allowing it unfettered market access. Certain government policies and instruments (such as local content and other performance requirements, and certain controls on investment) have often made the crucial difference to a foreign investment's prospects of being development-friendly.

Moreover, the most useful foreign direct investment has been that driven less by market access needs and more by the 'flying geese' pattern—where foreign direct investment moved from Japan to East and Southeast Asia, ensuring a dynamic division of labour and enhancing productivity and technology in all participating developing countries.[3] So, from a human development perspective it appears that the volume of foreign direct investment is far less important than how it is directed by both source and host countries and how it is integrated with a developing country's national development plans and requirements.

A multilateral regime is not essential to attract foreign direct investment

The legal security provided by a multilateral investment agreement under the WTO may improve perceptions of the investment climate in a developing country (see below). But the most important factors in attracting sustainable, development-friendly foreign direct investment do not include the nature of the legal regime—whether bilateral or multilateral. This is not surprising: ample literature indicates that the more important factors are primarily domestic in nature. These factors include political and economic stability, market size, labour productivity, the quality of health, education and physical infrastructure and the quality of institutions, including their transparency.

If the presence of a multilateral investment agreement is not a major factor in attracting development-friendly foreign direct investment, the case for such an agreement will rest primarily on whether it is able to increase government autonomy in policy-making—particularly in directing foreign direct investment towards human development goals. Such an agreement will also need to be more attractive for developing countries than relying on existing bilateral investment treaties and making commitments through mode 3 of the GATS, which addresses the commercial presence of foreign investors but allows a 'positive list' approach. Many developing countries are reluctant to give up the flexibility provided by bilateral investment treaties, which allow them to tailor different agreements to different objectives without fear of disputes and retaliatory sanctions (Ganesan, 1998).

A multilateral investment agreement under the WTO

The key issue is whether a multilateral agreement on investment under the WTO would limit the policy space of developing countries in a way that precludes the successful policies and investment strategies pursued by countries such as Malaysia, where foreign direct investment played a significant role in the economy and contributed to human development.

What would a multilateral investment agreement most likely cover that is not already covered by the TRIMs agreement and mode 3 of the GATS? The 2001 Doha declaration instructed the Working Group on the Relationship between Trade and Investment to focus on 'scope and definition; transparency; non-discrimination; modalities for pre-establishment based on a GATS-type, positive list approach; development provisions; exceptions and balance of payments safeguards; consultation and the settlement of disputes between Members.'

Although there are no firm proposals at this stage, industrial countries pushing for such an agreement are likely to ask for commitments from developing countries that cover at least the following: the right of establishment for foreign investors, most-favoured-nation treatment, national treatment, investment incentives and protection, abolition of performance requirements still allowed under the TRIMs agreement and binding dispute settlement (Singh, 2001).

Even more important, the WTO investment agenda appears mainly concerned with market access through wide-ranging pre-establishment commitments (such as ensuring that most sectors are open to foreign investment on a non-discriminatory basis; Winters, 2002). As such, a multilateral investment agreement under the WTO is likely to differ considerably from bilateral investment treaties, which have been popular with developing countries because they provide national treatment to foreign investors in the post-establishment phase only, and do not place any restrictions on host countries in identifying and following home grown foreign direct investment policies (Ganesan, 1998).

A multilateral investment agreement would limit policy space

Some critics have questioned whether the notion of a multilateral framework on investment is compatible with the need to preserve flexibility in development policies and strategies. By its nature a multilateral framework aspires to a one-size-fits-all approach—which, while recognizing some differences between countries, allows few lasting exceptions. Such a framework appears unlikely to provide the policy autonomy and flexibility that developing countries need for another important reason: investment discussions in the WTO focus on the pre-establishment phase—which sectors are open to investment and to whom (Winters, 2002).

A focus on the pre-establishment phase will not increase foreign direct investment because the factors most essential to attracting and sustaining foreign direct investment are domestic in nature and come into play only in the post-establishment phase. Moreover, a preoccupation with the pre-establishment phase will reduce—and possibly eliminate—a government's ability to allow only foreign direct investment that promotes its development interests and has a positive impact on human development.

More specifically, a multilateral investment agreement focused on the pre-establishment phase will mean that countries will no longer be able to restrict the types of assets that may be acquired by foreigners, specify the structure of ownership and lay down requirements for the future operations of foreign investors (such as employment of local workers, use of local raw materials and export requirements). All these policies were crucial elements in the pre-WTO policy arsenals of the East and Southeast Asian countries that have been most successful in enhancing human development since World War II.

Moreover, in negotiations on any multilateral investment agreement, industrial countries will seek to reduce the choice of development instruments available to developing countries—such as performance requirements currently allowed under the TRIMs agreement (see the US Trade Act of 2002, title XXI, section 2102). A multilateral investment agreement, even one based on a GATS-style positive list approach as intended by the Doha declaration, will nevertheless be binding. Acceptance of the national treatment principle, for example, would limit the ability of host governments to restrict or exclude investment in certain sectors and require that local ownership clauses and other currently permitted performance requirements be specified in country schedules. This would also limit the ability of governments to control and direct domestic investment for development purposes, including by reducing the flexibility provided by bilateral investment treaties. Moreover, transgressions of the agreement will invite disputes and retaliatory sanctions.

Relationship with the General Agreement on Trade in Services

There is also concern that a multilateral investment agreement could 'swallow' the GATS by incorporating mode 3 commitments into an agreement that would provide much less flexibility for developing countries. The North American Free Trade Agreement (NAFTA), for example, contains general obligations on investment that do not distinguish between investments in goods and services.

In some cases developing countries have not been able to maintain their GATS limitations. For example, in Thailand investment liberalization measures imposed by the International Monetary Fund (IMF) after the 1997–98 financial crisis opened up the distribution services sector despite GATS commitments. This has resulted in an influx of large foreign retailers, hurting the many small domestic retail businesses that employ many Thais (*South-North Development Monitor*, 'Thailand: Local Retailers up in Arms over Foreign Retail Chains', 16 August 2002).

Mechanism for investor-state disputes

Another aspect of multilateral negotiations on investment of great concern from a human development perspective is the possible inclusion of an investor-state dispute mechanism—particularly if the NAFTA investor-state clause or the failed OECD Multilateral Agreement on Investment is used as a model. NAFTA, the trade agreement with the most extensive investor rights, shows why there is and should be cause for concern (box 12.3).

The draft agreement that failed in the OECD reflected the aspirations of many industrial countries, and contained both state-to-state and investor-to-state dispute settlement mechanisms. State-to-state arbitration was to follow a process similar to that of the WTO Dispute Settlement Understanding in its early stages. The International Centre for the Settlement of Investment Disputes was to be called in to establish rules if an amicable solution could not be reached. But the draft agreement also allowed for an investor-to-state arbitration system. While it remains unclear what dispute resolution mechanism would be chosen if there were to be a multilateral investment agreement under the WTO, the NAFTA illustrations make

BOX 12.3 TWO EXAMPLES OF NAFTA'S CHAPTER 11 ON INVESTOR-STATE RELATIONSHIPS

Metalclad Corporation

Investors have used the investor-state provision of NAFTA to aggressively challenge a wide range of laws and regulations. For example, an arbitration tribunal found violations of NAFTA investment rules stemming from a Mexican municipality's decision to deny a permit to Metalclad Corporation for a hazardous waste facility in 1997. The state governor of San Luis Potosi ordered that the facility be closed after a geological audit showed that the facility would contaminate the state's water supply. The governor then declared the site part of a 600,000-acre ecological zone. Metalclad claimed that this amounted to expropriation and sought $90 million in compensation.

The decision was based on a selective reading of NAFTA objectives, with a focus on the promotion of investment. This ignores the counterbalancing sections in the preamble to the NAFTA identifying environmental protection and sustainable development as equal underlying principles. The tribunal ruled that environmental factors were legally a federal issue and could not be used as a basis for denying a municipal permit. Thus a critical underpinning of this decision is challenging Mexican law on municipalities' authority when it comes to environmental issues—despite the fact that local authorities are closest to the problem caused by big facilities such as waste transfer stations.

In terms of levels of government and domestic law, the decision also creates uncertainty about the application and scope of minimum provisions for international standards—as well as about the tribunal's interference with domestic law. Moreover, the legitimacy of a test for closure based only on the significance of its impact on the investor, with no consideration of the purpose of the measure taken by the government, raises a broader question: should considerations of damage to investor interests be enough to decide on cases affecting human health and the environment?

Methanex

Methanex is a Canadian company that manufactures a key ingredient of methyl tertiary butyl ether (MTBE), an additive that makes gasoline burn cleaner. The US Environmental Protection Agency has classified MTBE as a potential carcinogen. California state officials cite studies showing that MTBE causes cancer on laboratory animals and symptoms such as headaches and nausea in humans. Most gasoline components stick to the soil. MTBE, however, is highly solvent, leaking even from reinforced tanks and moving at a great pace into water wells. Because of this additive the water in Santa Monica, California, is undrinkable—and the cleanup costs to the city are estimated to be about $300 million. Moreover, the cleanup could take 30 years.

In 1999 California ordered a phase-out of MTBE that would end in a complete ban by the end of 2002. Several other US states have followed suit. Methanex, on the other hand, claims that the problem is leaking gasoline tanks, not MTBE. Another Methanex claim is that the California governor ordered the ban because he received campaign contributions from a US manufacturer of ethanol. This argument led to another grounded in NAFTA chapter 11, article 1106, which prohibits host governments from 'showing a preference for domestic goods and services'. Methanex also claims that 'any violation of an international principle for the protection of trade or investment is also a violation of the NAFTA article 1105 requirement that state measures be fair, equitable and in accordance with international law'. The company's complaint seeks to expand the scope of NAFTA chapter 11 to allow the investor-state process to litigate any trade law issue.

> This time involving a basic human need, drinkable water, the investor-biased provisions of NAFTA make it difficult for governments to regulate businesses that threaten human health and the environment. Methanex wants US taxpayers to compensate it for $970 million in profits lost due to the ban. The broad definition of expropriation allows such bans to be viewed as indirect expropriation and so may entitle the investor to compensation. The Methanex case will be decided under terms of international treaties by a panel of arbitrators chosen by the US State Department and Methanex. As in other cases, these investor-state disputes will be settled behind closed doors.
>
> These two cases show that NAFTA chapter 11 forces governments to spend significant resources defending their regulatory and judicial processes from investor challenges. As a result the three NAFTA countries are likely to have to pay investors considerable sums just to defend their public interest regulations.
>
> *Source:* IISD and WWF, 2001; Hemispheric Social Alliance, 2001.

it clear that this is a matter of considerable importance—with significant human development and opportunity cost implications for developing countries.

Reconciling the most-favoured-nation principle

Another concern that will need to be addressed is reconciliation of the most-favoured-nation principle, which is basic to all multilateral trade agreements, with the special treatment conferred under bilateral investment treaties and regional agreements to ethnic overseas investors in countries such as China and India. This issue is important because evidence suggests, for example, that in a number of cases ethnic overseas investment is more development-friendly. There is also the question of whether application of the most-favoured-nation principle will imply that the terms in regional agreements (such as the NAFTA chapter 11 investor-state arbitration procedure) will be incorporated in a multilateral investment agreement.

Will the smallest and most vulnerable countries benefit from a multilateral investment agreement?

Advocates of a multilateral investment agreement make some important arguments. One is that the smallest, most vulnerable countries are always better off in multilateral than in bilateral agreements because of the unequal power relationships between countries. This is a valid argument, but only if the multilateral agreement can be guaranteed to be more flexible and to increase development policy autonomy. As the previous analysis shows, this is unlikely: an investment agreement under the current world trade regime will likely considerably limit developing countries' policy autonomy.

Moreover, it cannot be assumed that a multilateral investment agreement will negate the need for bilateral investment treaties. Both types of agreements coexist in trade and other areas; one is not a substitute for the other. A new multilateral investment agreement, in addition to adding another layer that may reduce their policy autonomy, will likely also drain the limited human resources of developing countries especially the least developed, smallest and most vulnerable among them.

Once in, especially as part of the single undertaking, it would also be harder for such countries to withdraw from a multilateral agreement. Such action would be met by threats of dispute claims and retaliatory sanctions or by demands for further unilateral concessions.

Lower transactions costs are not inevitable...

Another argument for a multilateral agreement is that it should lower transactions costs, especially for the poorest and most vulnerable developing countries, as a result of one agreement replacing the multitude of bilateral ones. While this may be true for multilateralism over bilateralism more generally, it is doubtful that a multilateral investment agreement will replace bilateral investment treaties, at least in the short-term—especially if bilateral agreements offer more favourable terms and more flexibility. Rather than reducing transactions costs, a multilateral agreement may actually increase them for developing countries, especially the poorest and most vulnerable.

Equally important, a multilateral agreement is unlikely to reduce transactions costs for foreign investors. As Hoekman and Saggi (1999, p. 16) argue, 'it seems that the major proportion of the transactions costs associated with foreign direct investment is likely to arise from differences in language, culture, politics and the general business climate of a host country. Familiarizing oneself with the investment laws of a country seems trivial in contrast to these more daunting challenges that exist regardless of whether the country is a signatory to a multilateral or bilateral investment agreement'.

...and higher opportunity costs may not be justified

Finally, it is questionable whether policy-makers in developing countries could justify the opportunity costs of diverting scarce human and other resources to negotiating and administering new issues such as investment. This is because of the questionable development value of such an agreement and their arguably more pressing domestic and poverty reduction priorities.

Indeed, experts have argued that taking high-quality human and other resources away from such domestic priorities is unlikely to be their best possible economic use (Rodrik, 2001; Winters, 2002). Even if confined to the trade area, developing country priorities and those of poverty reduction lie much more in the traditional 'border' areas (agriculture and textiles)—where they should logically invest their limited resources if they wish to maximize their gains.

Notes

1. UNCTAD (2002a) discusses the role of Japanese foreign direct investment in the international networks of the electronics industry and their policies towards local parts and suppliers. The analysis also highlights how little of the value added from these networks remains in developing countries.

2. Local content requirements also occur in the tobacco, audiovisual, pharmaceutical, computer equipment and food processing industries.

3. A number of commentators, including various Trade and Development Reports from the United Nations Conference on Trade and Development, have elaborated on the important differences between US and Japanese foreign direct investment and transnational corporations in this respect. The US has generally been motivated more by market access reasons, while Japan was motivated—especially in Southeast Asia—by the need for a dynamic division of labour.

REFERENCES

Amsden, Alice H. 2000. 'Industrialization under WTO Law—High-Level Round Table on Trade and Development: Directions for the Twenty-first Century'. Paper presented at the 10th United Nations Conference on Trade and Development, 12 February, Bangkok.

———. 2001. *The Rise of the 'Rest': Challenges to the West from Late-Industrializing Economies.* New York: Oxford University Press.

Chang, Ha-Joon. 2002. *Kicking Away the Ladder: Development Strategy in Historical Perspective.* London: Anthem Press.

Claessens, Stijn, Michael Dooley and Andrew Warner. 1993. 'Portfolio Capital Flows: Hot or Cold?' In *Portfolio Investment in Developing Countries.* World Bank Discussion Paper 228. Washington, DC.

Correa, Carlos. 1999. 'Preparing for the Third Ministerial Conference of the World Trade Organization (WTO): Issues for the Member States of the Islamic Development Bank in the Built-In Review of the Agreement on Trade-Related Investment Measures (TRIMs) of the WTO'. Study for the Islamic Development Bank. University of Buenos Aires, Argentina.

Deere, Carolyn. 2000. *Net Gains: Linking Fisheries Managaement, International Trade and Sustainable Development.* Washington DC: Island Press.

Ganesan, Arumugamangalam V. 1998. 'Strategic Options Available to Developing Countries with Regard to a Multilateral Agreement on Investment'. Discussion Paper 134. United Nations Conference on Trade and Development, Geneva.

Gibbs, Murray, and Mina Mashayekhi. 1998. 'Uruguay Round Negotiations and Investment: Lessons for the Future'. United Nations Conference on Trade and Development, Geneva.

Hanson, Gordon H. 2001. 'Should Countries Promote Foreign Direct Investment?' G-24 Discussion Paper 9. United Nations Conference on Trade and Development, Geneva, and Harvard University, Center for International Development, Cambridge, Mass.

Hemispheric Social Alliance, 2001. 'NAFTA Investor Rights Plus: An Analysis of the Draft Investment Chapter of the FTAA'. [www.art-us.org/index.html].

Hoekman, Bernard, and Kamal Saggi. 1999. 'Multilateral Disciplines for Investment-Related Policies?' Paper presented at the Institutional Affari Internazionali Conference on Global Regionalism, 8–9 February, Rome.

IISD (International Institute for Sustainable Development) and WWF (World Wildlife Fund). 2001. 'Private Rights, Public Problems: A Guide to NAFTA's Controversial Chapter on Investor Rights'. Winnipeg, Manitoba, Canada. [iisd.org/trade/ilsdworkshop/resources.htm].

Kregel, Jan A. 1996. 'Some Risks and Implications of Financial Globalisation for National Policy Autonomy'. United Nations Conference on Trade and Development, Geneva.

Kumar, Nagesh. 1996. 'Foreign Direct Investments and Technology Transfers in Development: A Perspective on Recent Literature'. Discussion Paper 9606. United Nations University and Institute for New Technologies, Maastricht.

Malhotra, Kamal. 2002. 'Doha: Is It Really a Development Round?' Trade, Environment and Development Policy Paper. Carnegie Endowment for International Peace, Washington, DC.

OECD (Organisation for Economic Co-operation and Development). 1997. 'Main Features of the MAI'. Paper presented at the OECD symposium on the Multilateral Agreement on Investment, 3–4 April, Seoul.

Rodrik, Dani. 2001. 'The Global Governance of Trade As If Development Really Mattered'. Background paper for Trade and Sustainable Human Development Project. United Nations Development Programme, New York.

Singh, Ajit. 2001. 'Foreign Direct Investment and International Agreements: A South Perspective'. T.R.A.D.E. Occasional Paper. South Centre, Geneva.

South Centre. 1997. 'Foreign Direct Investment, Development and the New Global Economic Order. A Policy Brief for the South'. Geneva.

Tang, Xiaobing. 2002. 'Experience of Implementation of the WTO Agreement on Trade-Related Investment Measures: Difficulties and Challenges Faced by Developing Countries'. United Nations Conference on Trade and Development, Geneva.

UNCTAD (United Nations Conference on Trade and Development). 1994. 'Assessment of the Outcome of the Uruguay Round'. Geneva.

———. 1997. *Trade and Development Report*. Geneva.

———. 1999a. *Trade and Development Report*. Geneva.

———. 1999b. *World Investment Report*. Geneva.

———. 2002a. *Trade and Development Report*. Geneva.

———. 2002b. 'WTO Accessions and Development Policy'. Geneva.

UNDP (United Nations Development Programme). 2002. 'A Brief History of Multilateral Discussions on Investment'. Background note for Trade and Sustainable Human Development Project, New York.

Winters, L. Alan. 2002. 'Doha and the World Poverty Targets'. Paper presented at the Annual World Bank Conference on Development Economics, 29 April, Washington, DC.

WTO (World Trade Organization). 1996. *WTO Annual Report: Trade and Foreign Direct Investment*. vol. 1. Geneva.

WTO (World Trade Organization) and UNCTAD (United Nations Conference on Trade and Development). 2002. 'Trade-Related Investment Measures and Other Performance Requirements'. Council for Trade in Goods, Geneva.

CHAPTER 13
GENERAL AGREEMENT ON TRADE IN SERVICES

The provision of services has become one of the most important determinants of global GDP and trade. Thus it has critical implications for human development. Efficient and equitable infrastructure and social services are crucial to countries' competitiveness and people's well-being. Excluding public services, services account for more than 60 per cent of GDP in industrial countries and 50 per cent in developing countries (Corner House, 2001).

Services are also the fastest growing component of international trade, jumping from US$0.4 trillion in 1985 to US$1.4 trillion in 1999—equal to almost one-quarter of global trade in goods and about three-fifths of foreign direct investment flows (Mashayekhi, 2002). In 1997 industrial countries accounted for about two-thirds of trade in services (exports and imports).

From a development perspective the General Agreement on Trade in Services (GATS) is one of the most important agreements in the World Trade Organization (WTO). The agreement regulates the cross-border flow of trade and investment in services and provides important opportunities for developing countries. But it is not without problems. The human development impact of the agreement will depend on its implications for WTO members' ability to formulate development policies (policy space) and on whether the potential of several of its articles is realized.

FEATURES AND STRUCTURE OF THE AGREEMENT

The GATS provides a legal framework for trade in services, defined to cover a range of areas including transport, investment, education, communications, financial services, energy and water services and movement of persons. The agreement also calls for the negotiated, progressive liberalization of regulations that impede trade and investment in services. Negotiations within this framework could have major implications for human development.

The inclusion of trade in services in the Uruguay Round was largely due to initiatives by transnational financial and telecommunications corporations to include investment in the General Agreement on Tariffs and Trade (GATT). While this provoked resistance from developing countries (box 13.1), the eventual compromise

BOX 13.1 THE GENERAL AGREEMENT ON TRADE IN SERVICES:
HISTORY AND WHERE WE ARE NOW

History

Trade in services was first covered by international trade agreements during the Uruguay Round, but the history of such discussions dates to the late 1970s. At that time the US aimed to expand GATT rules to facilitate the expansion of the global operations of transnational corporations within a predictable and universal contractual framework. The concept of trade in services was invented for this purpose. With a few exceptions, developing countries did not support the idea of bringing trade in services into trade negotiations, because they thought that doing so was a veiled attempt to introduce investment into the negotiations.

Their concerns were heightened by the US negotiation mandate through the 1984 Trade and Tariff Act, which lumped services and investment together under 'trade'. Developing countries accepted the inclusion of trade in services in the Punta del Este declaration of 1986 only on the condition that negotiations on trade in services would occur separate from those on trade in goods, with a clear development orientation. The first meetings on services concentrated on defining 'trade in services'. Industrial countries argued that the presence of a supplier in the foreign market, through some form of investment, was necessary for most services.

At the Montreal midterm ministerial meeting in 1988 it was agreed that the definition of trade in services should include movement of factors of production where such movement was essential to suppliers. This was perceived as a victory for developing countries because it was initiated by a group of them, including Argentina, Colombia, Cuba, Egypt, India, Mexico, Pakistan and Peru. Developing countries had been trying to establish symmetry between capital and labour, and this was a step in that direction. But this definition did not cover permanent establishment or immigration—only activities characterized by specificity of purpose, discreteness of transactions and limited duration.

Between the Montreal and Brussels ministerial meetings (in 1990) much work was done to refine the definitions both of trade in services and of 'barriers' to such trade. The definition was drawn up to cover 'the supply of service by a service supplier of one Member, through commercial presence in the territory of any other Member'. Measures restricting market access and covering all modes of supply were listed in article XVI of the GATS. It was decided, at the insistence of developing countries, that national treatment should be a subject for negotiation of specific sectoral and subsectoral commitments.

The structure of the GATS reflects proposals by developing countries. There had been considerable discussion about whether the commitments should be in the form of a 'negative list' (meaning that schedules would be comprised of measures that each country wished to maintain that were exceptions to a common set of rules) or a 'positive list' (where the schedules would set out the actual access and national treatment commitments that each member was willing to accept for each service sector included). The negative list was seen as infeasible for a number of reasons—the most important being that there was no agreement on a common objective or target. It was also felt that a negative list would be unmanageably long, inevitably including mistakes and oversights, in addition to automatically including new services emanating from technological advances. However, for each sector included on the positive list, all barriers to market access and deviations from national treatment would be bound.

Where we are now

At the end of the Uruguay Round it was agreed to continue negotiations on three sectors and one mode of supply (movement of natural persons) under the GATS. Agreements have since been reached on basic telecommunications and financial services, resulting in substantial liberalization commitments—especially in the form of access to investment (see box 12.1 for a brief history of investment discussions). Maritime transport, which was not completed in the first round of negotiations, was included in the 2000 negotiations. Commitments on the movement of natural persons are limited in scope (see below). Thus these sectoral negotiations did not provide reciprocal benefits for developing countries.

At the end of the Uruguay Round the GATS also left open for future negotiations articles on emergency safeguard mechanisms, government procurement and subsidies. Negotiations on these issues were not completed in the first round and so have become part of the new round. Negotiations in the new round involve two phases: a rule-making phase during which rules for services on subsidies, safeguards and government procurement are negotiated, and a request and offer (market access) phase during which members negotiate further market access. During this new bargaining phase countries are expected to negotiate on a bilateral basis with specific sectoral requests and offers. The market access phase was formally launched in April 2002 and started with the June 2002 special session of the Council for Trade in Services. Member countries are expected to table their initial offers by March 2003.

Source: Gibbs and Mashayekhi, 1998, 1999; CIEL, 2002; Woodroffe, 2002; WTO, 2002; UNCTAD, 1994.

was a four-mode classification system. The 'modes of supply' or categories of service delivery regulated by the agreement are:

- Cross-border supply (mode 1), covering services supplied 'from the territory of one Member into the territory of any other member'—such as services provided by international postal or telephone companies.

- Consumption abroad (mode 2), covering services provided 'in the territory of one Member to the service customer of any other Member'—such as services provided to tourists.

- Foreign commercial presence (mode 3), covering services supplied 'by a service supplier of one Member, through commercial presence of any other Member'—such as the establishment of branches of banks in host countries or the acquisition of foreign companies.

- Presence of natural persons (mode 4), covering services supplied 'by a service supplier of one Member, through the presence of natural persons of a Member in the territory of any other Member'—such as services provided by foreign technicians or workers temporarily employed in host countries.

The GATS provides a framework for countries to select sectors and subsectors that they will subject to principles of market access (article XVI) and national treatment (article XVII), and to lay down conditions for such access and treatment.

The design of the GATS stands out among WTO agreements in several ways. For example, it includes both general disciplines that apply to all service imports and specific commitments to be listed in country schedules, with application only to certain sectoral measures that a government explicitly agrees to cover. The general commitments, to be accepted by all parties, include most-favoured-nation treatment, trans-

---

BOX 13.2 OVERALL COVERAGE OF THE GENERAL AGREEMENT ON TRADE IN SERVICES

Application to government measures. According to its article I:1, the GATS applies to measures taken by member governments at any level and in any form, including laws, regulations, administrative decisions— even unwritten practices affecting trade in services. The agreement also applies to non-government bodies exercising powers delegated by any level of government (article I:3.a.ii).

Application to means of supplying a service internationally. The four modes of the GATS system regulate all possible means of international service provision, including government action. Through this feature the agreement covers not just traditional cross-border trade in services but also all possible means and sources of service provision.

Exceptions. None except for services supplied in the exercise of government authority (as well as certain services in the air transport sector). Article I:1.3.c of the GATS stipulates that services supplied in the exercise of government authority must not be provided on a commercial basis and must not be supplied in competition with one or more other suppliers. This exclusion is often pointed to as evidence of the agreement's flexibility. But the scope of this exclusion may be quite narrow, because many 'public services' involve competitive and commercial (such as fees) aspects.

Source: WTO, 1994, 2001; OECD, 2001; Sinclair and Grieshaber-Otto, 2002; CIEL, 2002.

---

parency rules and increasing participation of developing countries (box 13.2).[1] Specific sectoral commitments involve market access and national treatment.

OPPORTUNITIES PROVIDED BY THE AGREEMENT

The GATS could help enhance human development in developing countries. Its 'positive list' approach offers flexibility, and several of its articles are potentially beneficial.

Sector-specific commitments and bottom-up features

Subject to specific negotiations, commitments are made on market access and national treatment for specific sectors and supply modes. The article on market access stipulates that unless a sector or mode is listed in a country schedule, there should be no limits on the number of service suppliers, the value of transactions and assets, the number of service operations and quantity of output, the number of natural persons employed and the participation of foreign capital. Except as stipulated under the most-favoured-nation principle and its exemptions of the national treatment principle under the GATS, foreign service providers should receive the same (best) treatment as domestic providers.

The positive-list approach leaves member country governments potentially free to choose which sectors and supply modes to include in their liberalization obligations (box 13.3). Each member also determines the services included in their schedules, prescribing terms, limits and conditions for specific commitments on market access and national treatment (Das, 1998a).

> **BOX 13.3 AN EXAMPLE OF A GOVERNMENT SCHEDULE ON A MODE OF SERVICE: CHILE AND MODE 3**
>
> The schedule of commitment of Chile stipulates the following criteria for the granting of commercial presence:
>
> - The effect of commercial presence on economic activity, including the effect on employment; on the use of parts, components and services produced domestically; and on exports of services.
>
> - The effect of commercial presence on productivity, industrial efficiency, technological development and production innovation.
>
> - The effect of commercial presence on competition in the sector concerned and other sectors; on consumer protection; on the smooth functioning, integrity, and stability of the market; and on national interest.
>
> - The contribution of commercial presence to integration in the world markets.
>
> Measures scheduled as limitations are:
>
> - Minimum requirements for training and employment—such as requirements for a specific number of directors to be nationals, effective control of the enterprise by the domestic shareholders, training of local employees and employment of domestic subcontractors.
>
> - Local content requirement—for example, a certain percentage of screen time in private film screening must be devoted to domestic films or advertisements (80 per cent local content).
>
> - Surcharges and different tax rates—for example, a duty-free system with exemption from import duties applicable only to domestic producers.
>
> - Access to technology—for example, a foreign service supplier should use appropriate and advanced technology, equipment and managerial experience and be obligated to transfer its technology and pass on its experience to the domestic personnel (the build-transfer-operate concept).
>
> - Information relating to operations—for example, a foreign service provider must furnish prompt and accurate reports on operations, including technological, accounting, economic and administrative data.

When a member makes a specific commitment, it can determine (or limit) the number of persons who will reside in the country as service providers, as well as the maximum number and type of establishments needed and permitted in the country. Similarly, the agreement gives members the flexibility to levy conditions, qualifications and standards for market access and national treatment in specific sectors (table 13.1). If a government has not specified a sector in its schedule of commitments, it is under no obligation to provide market access and national treatment in that sector.

Moreover, the GATS allows governments to add further limitations to, and to withdraw from, commitments they had made previously as long as they compensate

TABLE 13.1

An example of a government schedule for engineering services

Limits on market access	Limits on national treatment	Additional commitments
Supply mode 1: unbound	Supply mode 1: unbound	
Supply mode 2: unbound	Supply mode 2: unbound	
Supply mode 3: only through incorporation, with a foreign equity ceiling of 51 per cent	Supply mode 3: none	
	Supply mode 4: unbound	
Supply mode 4: unbound except as indicated in the horizontal section cutting across all sectors		

Note: 'Unbound' means that the government is not liberalizing a supply mode. 'None' means that there are no limits on a supply mode—the government pledges full liberalization and market access. These are extreme cases; qualifications and conditions exist between the two (see box 13.3).
Source: Das, 1998a, p 110.

member governments whose service suppliers may be adversely affected. The GATS contains two types of general exceptions—relating to legitimate public policy concerns and essential security interests—that also reflect its potential flexibility. In addition, article X on safeguard measures, often highlighted by supporters of the GATS, would allow governments to act in an emergency to protect or safeguard domestic service suppliers against services that threaten to cause 'serious injury'. (Negotiations on emergency safeguards, which are opposed by some industrial countries, were to have been concluded by 1 January 1998 but are still under way.)

Increasing participation of developing countries and respect for national policy objectives and development levels

Article IV of the GATS stipulates that the increasing participation of developing countries will be facilitated through specific negotiated commitments.[2] The article regulates three areas:

- The strengthening of developing countries' domestic services capacity, efficiency and competitiveness through, among other things, access to technology on a commercial basis.

- The improvement of developing countries' access to distribution channels and information networks.

- The liberalization of market access in sectors and modes of supply of export interest to developing countries.

Through the inclusion of article IV, the GATS recognizes the basic 'asymmetry' between industrial and developing countries in the situation of services, and especially that between least developed countries and the other member countries. The article obliges industrial countries to support developing countries in strengthening their domestic service sectors by providing effective market access for their exports. Developing countries remain potentially free to pursue further market access by undertaking liberalization and seeking reciprocal concessions on access in sectors of export interest to them.

The article also tasks industrial country members with establishing contact points to help developing country service suppliers gain access to information on the commercial and technical aspects of the supply of services; on the registration, recognition and obtaining of professional qualifications; and on the availability of services technology. This provision strengthens the transparency obligation, which stipulates that governments should publish or make publicly available all the relevant laws and regulations related to market access and discriminatory restrictions for all service sectors (Mashayekhi, 2000a).

Article XIX, on the negotiation of specific commitments, operationalizes article IV through its part IV (on progressive liberalization). Article XIX:2 provides that liberalization should take place with due respect for national policy objectives and the level of development of parties, both overall and in individual sectors. Developing countries will be allowed appropriate flexibility to open fewer sectors, liberalize fewer types of transactions, progressively extend market access in line with their development situation and, when providing access to their markets for foreign service suppliers, attach conditions aimed at achieving the objectives referred to in article IV.

This flexibility is beneficial for maintaining the policy space of developing countries. The article enables developing country members to take measures to strengthen their services capacity—such as measures relating to technology transfer, conditions on network access for foreign service suppliers, employment requirements and other national policy measures, including subsidizing their service sectors (UNCTAD, 1994). The main challenge is to translate these provisions into meaningful commitments by industrial countries and their service suppliers.

PROBLEMS CREATED BY THE AGREEMENT: ACTUAL FLEXIBILITY

The GATS is not without problems from the perspective of developing countries, especially in terms of policy development. These problems arise primarily from its practical application and the ability of developing countries to derive full benefit from the actual flexibility of the agreement and the operationalization of beneficial articles. This section discusses problems relating to the actual flexibility of the agreement. The next discusses issues relating to the operationalization of beneficial articles.

Policy space for developing country governments requires that they have the flexibility to manoeuvre, including the ability to reverse policy decisions if necessary. The GATS potentially offers that flexibility. But this potential is difficult to realize in practice because of the time and high costs that it involves. Several issues raise concerns about whether developing countries can benefit from this potential flexibility.

Power bargaining

Mashayekhi (2000b) argues that the actual bargaining process and imbalances in negotiating leverage between developing and industrial countries do not allow developing countries to take advantage of the flexibilities and provisions (like those in articles IV and XIX) that the GATS provides. Thus the voluntary offer process does not work properly. The request-offer modality, though preferable to other modalities on the table, imposes implicit—and even explicit—pressure to offer commitments (box 13.4). Because of this intense pressure, governments that lack the power and capacity to resist may be pushed to make rushed decisions on which sectors to liberalize and what kinds of limitations to place on specific commitments.

This pressure takes several different forms. First, an inherent pressure emanates from the nature of the agreement, even in its written form. The principle of progressive liberalization implies that a country needs to increase its liberalization commitments progressively. In the ongoing round of service negotiations, which started in March 2000, industrial countries intend to push for greater liberalization, including by developing countries. For example, the US proposal of 13 July 2000 for the 'Framework for Negotiation' states its challenge as the 'significant removal of . . . restrictions [on trade in services] across all services sectors, addressing measures currently subject to GATS disciplines and potentially measures not currently subject to GATS disciplines, and covering all ways of delivering services' (Office of the US Trade Representative, 2000, quoted in TWN, 2001, p 68). The US followed through with detailed requests to more than 120 countries in July 2002.

Second, there has been intense pressure on developing countries during the negotiation process to liberalize key service sectors. The initial specific commitments agreed to by developing countries during the Uruguay Round were made under this kind of pressure. One example often cited is the US refusal at the end of the Uruguay Round to conclude a financial services agreement. This led to two years of intense negotiations on financial sector liberalization, throughout which Southeast Asian countries such as Malaysia came under intense pressure to open their financial sectors to US and European Union (EU) service providers (TWN, 2001; Sinclair and Grieshaber-Otto, 2002; Raghavan, 1997b). Another example of this pressure in the request process is a recent EU negotiating stance: unless developing countries liberalize their banking and insurance markets, the European Union will not enlarge market access for developing countries' agricultural, textile and clothing products.

Developing countries acceding to the WTO have found themselves in a weak position to resist such pressures. Most countries that have recently acceded, including China but also small countries such as Jordan and Oman, have schedules of concessions much longer and much more intrusive than those accepted by the original

---

Box 13.4 THE REQUEST-OFFER APPROACH AND THE FORMULA APPROACH

New approaches are being proposed in the ongoing round of service negotiations that would accelerate liberalization, which is already advancing too fast for developing countries. Formula approaches multilateralize request-offer processes across members, sectors and modes of supply. The purpose is to identify subsectors and commitments on market access and national treatment by mode and measure that would be assumed by all members or a critical mass. The US has proposed a formula approach in electronic commerce, while Australia, Chile and New Zealand have proposed removing all residency and nationality requirements.

Many argue that the proposed approaches—such as the cluster, formula, horizontal modalities or even negative list approach—may change the nature of the GATS. Contrary to the request-offer approach, the formula approach, which may result in a switch (at least implicitly) to a negative list approach, does not allow for gradual liberalization. Most developing countries have opposed the formula approach and also oppose making their schedules uniform.

Some additional proposals have been developed for application across all members, without regard to their level of development. Two such proposals are the reference paper on basic telecommunications and the annex to the understanding on financial services. In the annex, for example, most developing countries decided to follow the GATS approach rather than the formula and negative list approach. But the formula approach could be useful in cases where substantial commitments have been made—in mode 3, for example, for tourism, telecommunications, financial services and professional and business services. It could also be useful for developing countries to adopt a formula approach in mode 4 on the basis of a proposal by Pakistan centred on removing the economic needs test based on occupation, simplifying visa and work permit regimes and overcoming barriers posed by qualification standards and licensing requirements.

Source: Mashayekhi, 2000b; UNCTAD, 2002.

---

developing country members of the WTO. In this context it should be recalled that all countries were required to negotiate a schedule of commitments on services as a condition for WTO membership. In the current negotiations, however, they need not make further commitments unless these are judged to be in their development interest or are made in return for effective applications of articles IV and XIX or meaningful reciprocal concessions in other sectors.

Third, there is significant external pressure on developing countries, especially indebted countries, to liberalize their services sector and develop privatization schemes to generate resources. The International Monetary Fund (IMF) and the World Bank have asked developing country governments, as part of the conditions for loans or debt relief, to privatize state enterprises and impose user fees on services essential to poor people (through cost recovery programmes), such as education, health care, water and sanitation. While this policy has recently been reversed for user fees in education, the power imbalance between developing and industrial countries remains critical in determining whether the GATS can deliver its flexibility in practice.

Problems in actual reversibility

Governments need to retain some important domestic regulations that are potentially inconsistent with the GATS and may wish to add others as development needs
arise or change. Despite the potential flexibility provided through horizontal limitations (provisions applying to foreign suppliers of all services that have been
scheduled) and specific limitations in country schedules, it is difficult if not impossible for developing country governments to take advantage of this flexibility in
practice. Horizontal limitations are determined when initial schedules are prepared, and it is difficult for a developing country to add a new one (for a more
detailed discussion of this difficulty, see Woodroffe, 2002 and Sinclair and
Grieshaber-Otto, 2002, p 30 ff). Limitations to specific commitments are complex
and can be more problematic for developing countries. Like horizontal limitations,
these limitations must be determined while making the initial commitments, and
while a member country may add new limitations after its initial commitments,
this is arguably difficult.[3]

Most developing countries, especially the least developed ones, lack crucial
data and information to assess which sectors and subsectors to limit in their schedules and what kinds of regulations to keep or impose at the time of the initial commitment. This makes the decision-making about what kinds of limitations to
include in their schedules very difficult. In practice, the lack of information works
against the flexibility of the GATS in three areas.[4]

First, enormous knowledge and foresight are required to determine which
areas to liberalize and what kinds of limitations to include in country schedules,
and there are major shortcomings in the data on world trade in services. Even rough
data for assessing the value of concessions exchanged in service negotiations are
not readily available to member countries. The current data on trade in services are
based on the IMF's balance of payments statistics. The data set is highly aggregated
and does not reflect the four-mode classification in the GATS (TWN, 2001). The
UN and the United Nations Conference on Trade and Development (UNCTAD)
tried to address the data issue during the Uruguay Round, but these attempts have
not been sustained.

Second, the agreement lacks clarity. The GATS does not give a sufficiently clear
definition of services nor of the sectors in which they fall (Woodroffe, 2002).
Moreover, certain GATS provisions, such as the government authority exclusion,
are undefined and untested. This implies that not scheduling commitments in a
specific sector—or scheduling limitations in that sector—does not necessarily provide protection, depending on how the commitments are interpreted and by
whom.[5]

Third, the GATS applies to all levels of government. In developing countries
such as India local governments provide essential services and yet are often unaware
of the commitments the federal government makes in international forums, even
though they are bound by those commitments. Moreover, in the specific case of

India the federal government is concerned that the GATS could undermine the provision of essential services at the local level and that it will be unable to influence or contest this process. At the same time, in many cases (though perhaps less so in India) there may be a lack of communication between trade negotiators and ministries or subnational governments about existing programmes and regulations that may be inconsistent with the GATS. This structural problem may mean that reversals of commitments will be needed, but this possibility is not sufficiently recognized in the GATS.

Problems of general exceptions

Implementing general exceptions under GATS article XIV is difficult for developing countries. To successfully invoke article XIV, governments must demonstrate that any challenged measure is 'necessary' to meet certain legitimate public policy concerns, such as the protection of human health. This is difficult and costly for developing country governments, which constantly need to maintain important public interest measures and regulations and put new ones into place.

HUMAN DEVELOPMENT IMPLICATIONS OF THE AGREEMENT AT THE SECTORAL LEVEL: OPERATIONALIZING BENEFICIAL ARTICLES

Among the main impacts of the GATS is its effect on policy space for human development. The agreement puts pressure on governments to deregulate their domestic markets, privatize public entities and open their markets to the rest of the world.

The GATS has two related mechanisms that operationalize its influence on policy space for human development. First, GATS rules such as market access and national treatment have a human development impact through their effect on governments' ability to formulate domestic development policy, especially public and industrial policy. Second, GATS directly affects key sectors related to components of human development. Among these sectors, those of most interest to developing countries are public services, financial services, the movement of natural persons (mode 4) and some sectors of export interest, such as construction services.

Human development implications of the principle of market access

Market access measures have implications for member governments' ability to pursue a development strategy, especially given the imbalances in commitments between developing and industrial countries (see below). Development policy may require that governments protect some service sectors, but under the principle of market access a government that wishes to do so may be challenged. Development policy may require, for example, that a government limit the number of service suppliers in such sectors as banking or telecommunications. Or a government may wish to direct some of the savings in the economy towards industrial and agricultural producers and provide tax breaks to domestic firms, as was done in successful East

Asian and Latin American economies—thereby limiting the amount of savings controlled by foreign-based banks. Such measures will require that the government have the flexibility to at least regulate the number of service suppliers and the value of transactions or assets.

The national treatment principle and the priorities of development

A vital part of the investment strategy in successful developing economies (such as those in East Asia) has been the creation of an enabling environment for promising domestic companies in key sectors. To achieve this, governments have needed to ensure, for example, that the banking sector favours domestic firms in allocating credit. Similarly, an important part of an industrial strategy is requiring foreign investors to use local suppliers, hire local staff and transfer technical know-how. The GATS permits such performance requirements in the services sector. The challenge for developing country governments is to ensure that the commitments they make allow the necessary policy space and reflect an overall development strategy, especially a human development strategy.

Such commitments should recognize the differences between domestic and foreign firms in their interaction with the labour force and the environment and their response to volatility. Foreign firms are likely to be much less inclined to maintain cooperative relations with the labour force, and they may be less willing to protect and preserve the environment. And they have an inherent tendency to 'cut and run' if the social and political environment does not favour their interests. This makes it necessary for governments to implement policies favouring domestic establishments, which are more stable and 'there for the long haul'.

Imbalances in commitments and market access

Operationalizing the development-oriented articles of the GATS (articles IV and XIX:2) must also involve action at the sectoral level. An analysis of the GATS from a human development perspective must include a sufficient sectoral and modal analysis of its human development impact. Accordingly, the negotiations on services will have to deal with the tension and even contradictions between the interests of industrial countries that see the GATS primarily as an opportunity for increasing market shares in developing countries and those of developing countries that see market access as one means to their development (UNCTAD, 2002, p 2).

Developing country governments have made substantial commitments and accepted a larger share of full market access bindings under the cross-border and commercial presence supply modes than industrial countries. This implies the precommitment of future policies without any implementation experience. By contrast, industrial countries have made very few liberalization commitments, especially in mode 4. A similar imbalance is apparent in sectors of export interest to developing countries. Delivered mainly through mode 4, these sectors include those in which developing countries have niche opportunities, such as health, transport, tourism, construction, education, audiovisual services, energy-related services and professional and business services (Mashayekhi, 2000b).[6]

The important lack of market access provided to developing countries under mode 4 is analysed in detail below. Beyond this, several critical market access barriers to service exports from developing countries have been identified:[7]

- Subsidies, including horizontal subsidies and investment incentives, provided in industrial countries in sectors of export interest to developing countries. The effect of subsidies is especially critical in such sectors as construction, where developing country service providers now have an obvious financial disadvantage. But it is also important in some high-technology services of particular interest to a few developing countries.

- Technical standards and licensing, especially for the provision of professional business services. The non-recognition in industrial countries of many developing country qualifications and standards also serves as a significant market access barrier.

- Lack of access to information and distribution networks such as those in telecommunications and air transport services (through 'alliances').

Supply constraints in developing countries also constitute an effective market access barrier to their exports of goods and services.

Increasing developing country participation in services trade requires eliminating these imbalances in market access and supply constraints, a need that calls for action by industrial countries. Mashayekhi (2000b, p 183) suggests that

> *'Positive measures could be taken by developed countries to implement article IV, for example, through encouraging investment in services sectors in developing countries, transfer of technology and access to distribution channels and information networks by providing incentives such as fiscal advantages for enterprises which undertake investment and facilitate access to technology and distribution channels and information networks in developing countries'.*

In turn, this would require that developing countries identify sectors of interest because of their export potential or role in national human development. These sectors should constitute the basis for further negotiations. In the current phase of placing requests and offers, for example, developing countries need to invoke the flexibility granted under article XIX to initiate a substantive discussion on the current imbalances stemming in part from their limited supply capacity (Das, 2002).

The GATS, public services and social policy

The GATS has important potential policy implications for the provision of public services. Part of the reason is that half of all foreign direct investment in developing countries goes to the provision of services—and much of this to public services (Oxfam, 2002). Since the negotiations on basic social services have not yet been completed, many developing countries have not committed themselves in such areas as health and education, services that governments have traditionally provided or heavily subsidized. Accordingly, developing countries face pressures relating to the deregulation of markets for public services and the commercialization of these services. There are three main sources of concern.

First, as indicated, GATS rules do not apply to services provided in the exercise of government authority (see box 13.2). But the criterion of government authority does not necessarily prevent the agreement from intruding into the basic services critical to the poor. Sinclair and Grieshaber-Otto (2002), among others, argue that since the agreement does not clearly define the key terms 'commercial' and 'in competition with', the WTO panels and the appellate body will rely on their own interpretations. Developing such interpretations may be problematic, however, because it is difficult to find any developing country government that is the sole supplier of any public service. Health and education services are supplied by a constantly changing mix of public and private enterprises. This means that a government entity providing a service will potentially be 'in competition with' private enterprises, opening the way to challenge and retaliation within the WTO dispute settlement system (Sinclair and Grieshaber-Otto, 2002).

Moreover, the GATS restricts the activities of monopolies and exclusive service suppliers, public or private. Many developing country governments continue to rely on public monopolies to provide basic services such as education, health care, rail transport, postal services, health insurance, water distribution and power generation and transmission. Monopolies must be scheduled as limitations or dismantled in sectors covered by a country's specific commitments (article XVI). The GATS also exposes public monopolies to charges that they are competing unfairly in listed sectors outside the scope of their monopoly (article VIII).[8] In addition, the compensation requirement—in cases where a new monopoly is established or an existing one expanded—could be very costly for member countries, especially for developing ones. If the government of a country that has committed its health insurance sector decides to expand its compulsory health insurance coverage to prescription drugs or home care, it could be challenged under the GATS.

Second, the GATS does not force governments to privatize, but it facilitates the commercialization of basic public services, especially when combined with the other pressures for privatization that developing countries face—whether because of resource constraints or because of conditions in structural adjustment programmes. Privatization of basic social services is already quite problematic in developing countries. Many have been unable to privatize social services with a corresponding increase in competition—that is, without the involvement of mostly foreign private monopolies. In Latin America, for example, the privatization of utilities resulted in public monopolies being replaced by private ones (Oxfam, 2002). Leaving social services in the hands of private monopolies may have important adverse consequences, especially for equity in access to basic services, because of the user fees involved. This will further marginalize segments of the population, including the poor and women.

Rapid privatization and commercialization of health services without regard to equity and accessibility, combined with the pressures to reduce public spending in health, can be especially harmful to human development. Cost recovery pro-grammes introducing user fees and price increases for health services led to a decline of up to 50 per cent in the use of medical services in countries such as Ghana, Kenya and Nigeria. This has contributed to higher child mortality, greater incidence of tuberculosis and sexually transmitted diseases and an increase in maternal deaths. In Nigeria maternal deaths rose by 56 per cent (Corner House, 2001).

Privatization of water supply is another area of concern in developing coun-tries, because it can restrict poor people's access to water services. In some cases the commercialization of water supply has produced mixed results at best. In Bolivia, where one-third of the population has no access to clean water, privatization improved access to piped water but also increased water prices (Oxfam, 2002). Because the price elasticity of demand for water is higher among poor people than among the non-poor, price increases will widen the gap in water consumption in Bolivia. In the capital of Mauritius, the privatization of water services has meant that poor families have to spend up to 20 per cent of their income on water (World Bank, 2000).

One way to increase access to water is through cross-subsidization, by increas-ing taxes in rich regions and using the funds to finance lower water prices in poor regions. But unless a government had foreseen the use of cross-subsidies and included pertinent qualifications in its schedule, it would be unable to prevent for-eign companies that supply water in rich areas from benefiting from its GATS com-mitments, since any measures the government may wish to take would be inconsistent with 'national treatment'.

Most developing country governments cannot afford to leave basic social ser-vices completely to private—including foreign—competition. The provision of these services affects vital concerns such as equity, human rights, social justice and state responsibility—in short, many components of human development (Oxfam, 2002). Thus opening basic services to foreign competition and subjecting them to GATS rules, which may induce further deregulation through channels such as power bargaining, may be problematic, especially where regulatory capacity is weak (Oxfam, 2002).

Third and related to this, new proposals on domestic regulation (article VI:4) are being negotiated through the Working Party on Domestic Regulation. These negotiations are aimed at, among other things, ensuring the quality of public ser-vices. If accepted, these proposals may force governments to further deregulate public services and weaken other public interest regulations. And they may reduce even existing policy flexibility by intruding into aspects of government policy involving non-discriminatory government regulation of services.

Proposals on expanding the domestic regulation clause would not eliminate governments' right to regulate the quality of services, but they would restrict the means available to do so. If challenged, regulations on the quality of services would come under the scrutiny of a dispute panel, compelling governments to undertake a difficult and costly exercise to prove that the regulations are necessary. Governments would need to demonstrate through a 'necessity test' that the regulations are not unnecessary trade restrictions—and are necessary to ensure the quality of service.

The necessity test could limit governments' ability and flexibility to undertake policy and regulatory reform in important service sectors. A narrowly defined notion of necessity could also lead to the harmonization of domestic policies based on those of industrial countries, reinforcing a 'one size fits all' approach to public policy in this vital area (Mashayekhi, 2000b). Moreover, if adopted, the necessity test may facilitate the questioning by trade bureaucrats, under the multilateral rules of trade, of regulations adopted and implemented by a democratically elected governing body, undermining the role of domestic courts and legislators (Woodroffe, 2002).

The GATS mode 3 (commercial presence) is the main vehicle through which trade in health care occurs.[9] When all the parts of the agreement as well as new proposals are combined with pressures on economic policy (including the GATS obligations), commercial presence may easily mean that a country's health care system will be left to foreign private multinationals. Foreign investment in health care is dominated by giant multinationals based in the US and Europe (Hilary, 2001). While foreign investment may be needed to fill many gaps in the health sectors of developing countries, it is risky to leave a country's health care system to always-fluid foreign direct investment: the departure of such investment could lead to the system's collapse, especially where regulatory capacity is weak.[10]

Liberalization and deregulation of financial services

Effective, broad-based financial services are a crucial element of development policy. But as the East Asian financial crisis and others before and after it have shown, rapid liberalization of financial services such as banking and insurance is likely to cause instability in already fragile economies. Commitments for liberalization under the GATS may be inconsistent with developing countries' capacity to regulate their financial sectors, providing a recipe for financial crisis (Oxfam, 2002). But most government regulatory interventions in specific financial subsectors will likely be inconsistent with the GATS.

National treatment and most-favoured-nation principles are likely to work to the benefit of foreign financial firms, which have greater financial strength, more sophisticated information technologies and greater economies of scale than developing countries' domestic financial firms, as well as the ability to move between and within countries. Under the GATS provisions, which pressure countries to deregulate their financial markets, a country with commitments in this sector may be unable to protect its own banking industry through tax breaks, credit and interest rate subsidies and the like. This would undermine the creation of capacity in financial institutions for longer-term credit support to firms generating new technologies or employment, as well as the development of new financial instruments for small and medium-size enterprises.

Rapid and progressive liberalization in financial services could be detrimental to small and medium-size enterprises in both the financial sector (through direct effects) and the industrial sector, especially in infant industries. Women, and thus human development, could be especially affected where women own and operate small and medium-size enterprises, particularly in the informal sector (box 13.5). GATS commitments could limit member governments' ability to direct preferential credit to and cross-subsidize small and medium-size enterprises in keeping with their industrial and human development policies.

Moreover, liberalization and deregulation of financial markets, especially in developing countries with weak regulatory capacity, can lead to instability, resulting in adverse human development outcomes. A large share of global capital flows

---

BOX 13.5 WOMEN AND FINANCIAL LIBERALIZATION

There is insufficient evidence to conclude that financial liberalization cannot benefit women. But based on the little research that has been undertaken, it is clear that the claims that liberalizing financial markets will broaden access to these markets and expand opportunities for saving and credit have not been proved for women.

Disproportionately excluded from the formal sector, women in developing countries often must turn to informal sector providers of financial services. The informal financial sector, unregulated and unsupervised, is dominated by providers that typically offer loans at very high interest rates. Still, it does provide access to credit for consumers and small enterprises largely excluded from the formal banking sector. Informal financial services are offered by a wide range of individuals and enterprises—from friends and family to pawnbrokers, specialized moneylenders, sector-specific lenders and rotating savings and credit associations. Women are more likely than men to be excluded from the formal sector, since they tend to conduct smaller transactions, hold fewer assets for collateral and, in some instances, may be unable to obtain bank loans without their husband's approval.

A detailed literature review by BRIDGE (a network striving for gender equity as an outcome of development) examines the direct and indirect effects of financial liberalization in developing countries and looks at the gender impact at the macro, meso and micro levels. The study concludes that institutional barriers between formal and informal financial sectors persist even after markets are liberalized. A case study of four Sub-Saharan African countries comes to the same conclusion. Moreover, the BRIDGE review provides little evidence that financial liberalization has benefited women. The one exception: women receiving remittances from family members working overseas may benefit from greater access to deregulated foreign exchange markets.

Source: Gammage and Jumelle, 2002, p 70; Baden, 1996; Aryeetey and Nissanke, 1998.

originate in industrial countries and take the form of highly liquid capital seeking arbitrage profits—and are thus an extremely unreliable source of development finance (UNCTAD, 1999). Liberalization of financial services in developing countries may quicken the flow of this footloose capital. This occurred in the recent East Asian financial crisis, which, in many respects, resulted in a serious setback to human development.

UNCTAD's *Trade and Development Report 2001* (2001b) outlines key standards for financial markets necessary for maintaining national and international financial stability. These standards relate to macroeconomic policy and data transparency, institutional and market infrastructure and financial regulation and supervision. While the GATS may encourage data and policy transparency, it may make it difficult to regulate other areas in financial systems. Financial liberalization, for example, is likely to make it more difficult to strengthen standards for corporate governance and banking supervision, crucial for promoting domestic financial stability.

Movement of natural persons

Mode 4 of the GATS covers not labour migration, but temporary cross-border movement of skilled and unskilled labour. There are strong theoretical and empirical justifications for the temporary movement of labour in the services sector (box 13.6). Nevertheless, there are significant barriers to this, resulting in an imbalance between the international movement of capital and that of labour.

The lack of commercially meaningful commitments by industrial countries on the movement of natural persons is the basic source of the imbalance in services trade (Mashayekhi, 2000b). In the Uruguay Round, commitments scheduled under mode 4 were limited largely to two categories: intra-company transferees regarded as 'essential personnel', such as managers and technical staff linked with a commercial presence in the host country; and business visitors—short-term visitors who are generally not gainfully employed in the host country (WTO, 2001). Since these categories consist mostly of higher-level senior professionals linked to mode 3, the commitments benefit industrial countries more than their developing country counterparts (Butkeviciene, 2000; Mashayekhi, 2000b).

The barriers to market access under mode 4 are broadly related to the nature of the commitments; strict visa, nationality, residency and licensing requirements; lack of recognition of qualifications and the existence of wage comparisons; and economic needs tests. There are also price-based restrictions, such as visa fees, exit and entry taxes, airport taxes and licensing fees (CUTS, 1999; Mashayekhi, 2000b). Other important barriers to market access include lack of transparency in measures relating to the movement of natural persons and lack of clarity relating to the existence, implementation and application of policy guidelines relating to work permits (Butkeviciene, 2000).

While industrial countries are pushing to deepen the commitments under mode 3—such as in financial services and health and other basic services—a major

Box 13.6 International movement of labour: Theory and empirics

International movement of labour occurs for a complex set of reasons. The major structural explanation at the macro level is disparities in income levels and employment opportunities between countries. On the supply side, unemployment and poverty are the main explanations. Alongside these 'push factors' are 'pull factors' on the demand side, both static and dynamic, such as cross-country differences in wage levels and employment opportunities at any point in time as well as the differences in the income stream and the quality of life over a period of time. Because of the segmentation of the labour market, push factors dominate in some parts of the market and pull factors in others. For example, 'brain drain' is explained mostly by pull factors, while unskilled labour migration is better explained by push factors.

Demand-side factors determining the movement of natural persons between poor and rich countries include labour shortages in the rich countries. There are different ways to compensate for labour shortages. Capital or trade flows can be substituted for labour, or labour can be imported from abroad. For the services sector capital and trade flows are unlikely to work because 'services are not quite as tradable as goods and even international trade in services often requires physical proximity between the producer and the consumer for the service to be delivered, because these are services which cannot be stored and transported across national boundaries in the same way as goods' (Nayyar, 2000, p 9).

There is justification for international migration of labour from many perspectives. According to traditional trade theory, the free movement of labour, like that of capital, between two countries results in efficiency gains for both. International labour migration also helps to optimize resource allocation and maximize economic welfare for the world as a whole, just as free movement of capital is supposed to do. International movement of labour can also be logically justified on the basis of rights and equality: it is perfectly reasonable to argue that any provision for capital or commercial presence of corporate entities should be matched by provisions for labour or temporary migration of workers across borders, 'just as the right-of-establishment for corporate entities (capital) has an analogue in the right-of-residence for persons (labour)' (Nayyar, 2000, p 25).

There are also empirical grounds for freer international movement of labour. Using computable general equilibrium (CGE) modelling, Walmsley and Winters (2002) estimate the effects of increasing temporary workers' permits in industrial countries by 3 per cent of their current skilled and unskilled workforces—permitting about 8 million skilled and 8.4 million unskilled workers to enter. (The problems in CGE modelling, especially those relating to degree of aggregation, should be noted here.) The potential economic benefits are huge: while some estimates project that complete liberalization of trade in goods would lead to global gains of US$66 billion a year, complete liberalization of the movement of natural persons is expected to yield gains of more than US$150 billion a year. Moreover, the global gains from mobility of unskilled labour would exceed those from mobility of skilled labour, since lost inputs for developing country production resulting from transfers of unskilled labour are likely to be less in value added terms than those resulting from transfers of skilled labour.

Winters (2002) argues that many of the extremely poor still would not benefit from the new opportunities to work abroad. But they might benefit, at least in the beginning, from simple trickle-down and increased tax revenues from those who do benefit. And in the long run higher returns to the skills needed for mobility may encourage people to seek greater education—and governments to provide it (Winters, 2002).

Despite all the potential benefits, international migration of labour, as measured by new immigrants per 1,000 world inhabitants, declined between 1970 and 1990. This trend contrasts

(Box continues on next page.)

with that in trade and capital flows. World exports increased from 12.1 per cent of global GDP in 1985 to around 20 per cent in the late 1990s. Total flows of foreign direct investment rose from US$55.7 billion in 1985 to US$395.4 billion in 1997 and US$637 billion in 1998. The turnover in foreign exchange markets expanded from US$15 billion in the 1970s to US$1.5 trillion in 1998. And international bank lending jumped from US$265 billion in 1975 to US$4.2 trillion in 1994 (UNDP, 1999).

It is important to understand the reasons behind this asymmetry between capital and labour, as '[t]his asymmetry, particularly that between the free movement of capital and the unfree movement of labour across national boundaries, lies at the heart of inequality in [the] rules of the game for globalization in the late twentieth century' (Nayyar, 2000, pp 15–16). This imbalance exists and grows for a variety of reasons related to ideology, interests and institutions. It is difficult to separate these three, as they are all part of the political economy of globalization. But the major determining factor of the imbalance appears to be institutional aspects involving industrial country commitments on the movement of natural persons under the GATS, reinforced by the other two factors.

shortcoming of the GATS from a human development perspective remains the lack of operationalization of its provisions on the movement of labour. These provisions could cover a wide range of service exports of interest to developing countries, including construction services (see box 13.8 in next section).

There is no similar restriction on the movement of capital in the GATS—indeed, the GATS encourages the free movement of capital through financial services liberalization. Shukla (2000) and many others argue that this has created a heavy bias in favour of the movement of capital, technology-intensive services and industrial countries. Today, transnational corporations based in foreign countries account for about 33 per cent of global services, while the transfer of labour accounts for only 1 per cent (McCulloghy, Winters and Cirera, 2001; Oxfam, 2002).

There is also a great imbalance in the application of the GATS between skilled workers and semi- and unskilled workers. Rather than facilitating the movement of unskilled labour between countries with a surplus of such labour (developing countries) and those with a deficit (industrial countries)—which could create a 'win-win' situation—the commitments on the movement of natural persons focus on professionals, who are favoured by and may also come from industrial countries. This imbalance also exacerbates the 'brain drain' problem in developing countries. In Jamaica, for example, 50 per cent of nursing positions remain vacant because Jamaican nurses are working in North America. Cuban and Indian doctors are among the favourites in industrial countries (Corner House, 2001).

This imbalance raises human development concerns in developing countries. In the health sector, for example, developing countries with an insufficient stock of professionals import them from those with routine surpluses, such as the Philippines. This might seem to be a good market solution, but it has allowed governments to put off addressing problems in their domestic career structures and to depress standards in the health profession (ICN, 1999). More important, many of the countries that export doctors and other professionals have shortages themselves.

Weighed against the losses, such benefits as remittances and the skills that professionals bring with them when they return—if they return—may not be sufficient compensation.

But while there is an apparent imbalance—generating other kinds of imbalances—in the agreement, the issue is not clear-cut. Major developing countries are keen to have access to industrial country labour markets for their independent professionals, and industrial countries are eager to have these professionals (Winters, 2002). In fact, the governments of some developing countries—such as India, which received the most workers' remittances in 1998—promote migration biased towards skilled labour out of a belief that qualified professionals constitute part of their competitive advantage in the world market (Butkeviciene, 2000; Corner House, 2001).

Greater and more secure access to industrial country markets for skilled people from developing countries could be beneficial in the medium and long term. But Winters (2002) argues that a key to reducing poverty and international and domestic inequalities is effectively extending mode 4 to less-skilled and, ultimately, unskilled workers.

Indeed, developing countries are interested in market access (not linked to investment) for persons in all categories (Butkeviciene, 2002). For most sectors covered by the GATS, the movement of natural persons would offer developing countries a great potential advantage for promoting their trade in services.

Among the barriers to market access noted above, the economic needs test seems to be the most controversial for and detrimental to service exports through the movement of natural persons from developing countries. There are several proposals for remedying the situation. Among these is a proposal by Pakistan for economic needs test exemption lists, by profession or sector or both (proposal to the preparations for the third ministerial, cited in Mashayekhi, 2000b).[11]

India has also developed proposals (box 13.7). It recommends that governments:

- Provide free and accessible information about the movement of personnel.
- Provide equal treatment of all foreign nationals.
- Standardize or harmonize qualifications and experience with the help of agreements.
- Remove all restrictions on temporary movement of professionals, salary and wage comparisons with residents and local competency or certification requirements, such as medical boards (CUTS, 1999).

THE WAY FORWARD

Based on the discussion in this chapter, it can be argued that the most immediate action needed is to operationalize the development-friendly aspects of the GATS.

BOX 13.7 SOME OF INDIA'S PROPOSALS ON REMOVING LIMITATIONS ON THE MOVEMENT OF NATURAL PERSONS

Economic needs tests
- Multilateral norms need to be established to reduce the scope for discriminatory practices in the use of economic needs tests.

- Clear criteria need to be laid down for
  - Applying such tests.
  - Establishing norms for administrative and procedural formalities.
  - Specifying how the results of such tests would restrict entry by foreign service providers.
- Fewer occupational categories should be made subject to such tests, and consensus should be reached on those categories.

- Specified occupational categories of professionals should be exempted from economic needs tests.

Administrative procedures relating to visas and work permits
Multilateral guidelines and norms are needed to tackle administrative procedures relating to visas and work permits, as these can negate even the limited market access available.

- Member countries should work towards a more transparent and objective implementation of visa and work permit regimes.

- Temporary service providers should be separated from permanent labour flows, so that normal immigration procedures would not hinder the commitments on temporary movement of labour. This could be achieved by introducing a special GATS visa for personnel categories covered by horizontal and sectoral commitments undertaken by a member in mode 4 under the GATS or through a special subset of administrative rules and procedures within the immigration policy framework.

- In both these cases the conditions for entry and stay should be less stringent than those for permanent immigration.

- The above would be possible if the recommendations on specificity, finer classification and wider coverage of personnel categories and transparency are reflected in the sectoral and horizontal commitments, achieving minimum discretion and greater certainty.

- The main features would include:
  - Strict time frames within which visas must be granted (two to four weeks at most).
  - Flexibility in granting visas on shorter notice for selected categories of service providers.
  - Transparent and streamlined application processes.
  - Mechanisms for finding out the status of applications, the causes of rejection and the requirements to be met.
  - Easier renewal and transfer procedures.
  - GATS visas for selected companies for use by employees temporarily posted abroad.
  - Adequate built-in safeguard mechanisms to prevent temporary labour from entering the permanent labour market.

Source: WTO, 2000b.

This will require that developing countries themselves press for negotiating modalities, in the exchange of offers and requests, that ensure that articles IV and XIX are effectively implemented at the sectoral level. In addition, the agreement should be strengthened by specifying the actions required to achieve or make the three goals of article IV legally enforceable.

The policy space needed to promote human development should not be traded for market access advantages in, for example, goods sectors. The provisions that impede developing countries from realizing the flexibility in the agreement should be modified. And the requirements for the reversal of commitments and additions to limitations in country schedules should be eased.

As recognized by the Doha work programme, special provisions in GATS articles IV and XIX:2 enable developing countries to participate in the international services trade in a much more efficient and equitable way. Consistent with the spirit of these articles, the international community and developing countries need to find ways to make liberalization more development friendly. This could best be done at the sectoral level. Assistance should be provided to developing countries in selecting sectors and subsectors to liberalize, in determining limitations and in making requests for access to industrial country markets in areas most important for developing countries as well as in areas significant for human development (boxes 13.8, 13.9 and 13.10).

The GATS architecture should be kept intact—though improved through the adoption of such methods as the conditional offer approach—but the agreement must be simplified and its coverage reduced. The agreement should also be improved through clearer language and limits in its scope.

BOX 13.8 CONSTRUCTION: A SERVICE SECTOR OF INTEREST TO DEVELOPING COUNTRIES

The world construction market is estimated at US$3.2 trillion. Over the past two decades projects in developing countries, primarily in infrastructure, have accounted for up to 70 per cent of the construction business opportunities in international markets, as measured by the size of contracts.

Construction as a share of GDP varies across countries, ranging from 2–3 per cent to more than 7 percent. But because of its labour-intensive nature, construction remains a relatively large employer, accounting for an average 10 per cent of total employment. In developing countries the sector has great potential to reduce rural poverty and provide opportunities for women. Moreover, many developing countries, especially those in Asia, have great capacity to export construction services—but barriers to the movement of natural persons limit their market access. Visa and residency requirements and economic needs tests, even for projects of short duration, often appear to penalize nationals of developing countries.

One way to enhance developing countries' access to construction markets would be to include local companies in designing and implementing international construction projects. This has proved to be the most effective way for developing countries to obtain access to technology.

Source: Butkeviciene, Benavides and Tortora, 2002.

BOX 13.9 SERVICES AND HUMAN DEVELOPMENT: THE ENERGY SECTOR

Energy is probably the biggest business in the world economy, with a turnover of US$1.7–2 trillion a year. The World Energy Council estimates that between 1990 and 2020 global investment in energy will total some US$30 trillion at 1992 prices.

Energy is key to achieving the social, economic and environmental aims of sustainable human development—and energy services are crucial in providing efficient access to energy in support of development. Developing countries thus face the challenge of achieving more reliable and efficient access to energy through greater availability of energy services. To ensure that the link between market access and development is clearly established, access to developing country energy markets could be made conditional on the transfer of technology and managerial know-how, the acceptance by foreign suppliers of public service obligations and the setting up of alliances between foreign and domestic firms, including small and medium-size enterprises.

Negotiations on energy issues are ongoing, with the aim of achieving the broadest possible market access and national treatment commitments. Canada, Chile, the European Union, Japan, Norway, the US and Venezuela have all submitted proposals. Except for the Venezuelan proposal and to some extent the Norwegian one, all proposals call for a total liberalization of energy services. The Norwegian and Venezuelan proposals emphasize the need to promote trade for all and to secure a share of the trade in energy services for developing countries.

From the perspective of developing countries, two related issues appear to be quite important in the ongoing GATS deliberations: 'classification' and 'additional provisions'. If classification permits sufficient precision in defining specific energy services, as is argued in the Venezuelan proposal, it will help facilitate an approach under which developing countries can undertake more informed commitments in specific areas, liberalizing their markets not in 'one go' but in line with their national development strategies. This possibility is very important in view of the US preference for 'technological neutrality'.

Developing countries should try to relate their liberalization commitments to articles IV and XIX:2, especially provisions such as transfer of technology and access to distribution channels and information networks, with a view to increasing the competitiveness of their firms in the supply of energy services. Similarly, attaching a set of public service obligations to an annex or reference paper applicable to the energy sector could ensure that developing countries obtain benefits that they may be unable to effectively negotiate with stronger trading partners or investors in a bilateral context.

Three objectives can be pursued with this strategy: levelling the playing field, establishing a clear link between energy and human development and avoiding creating 'race to the bottom' competition among developing countries, in which countries lower their requirements in an effort to attract investment.

Source: Butkeviciene, Benavides and Tortora, 2002.

The multilateral trading system for services could also be improved in several more specific areas:

- Concrete measures and their time frames should be established for improving commitments on the movement of natural persons, especially unskilled workers, with a view to reducing the asymmetry between these

> **BOX 13.10 SERVICES AND HUMAN DEVELOPMENT: THE ENVIRONMENT SECTOR**
>
> The global environment market reached an estimated US$522 billion in 2000. While industrial countries—mainly the US and countries in Western Europe—accounted for 85 per cent of this market, demand for energy in these countries has collectively grown by only 2–3 per cent annually in recent years. By contrast, strong growth in energy demand is forecast in transition economies and subsequently in developing countries as domestic policy and development assistance programmes combine to create a market out of the tremendous need for environmental equipment and services.
>
> To reinforce both equity and efficiency, a strong, effective regulatory and incentive framework is needed for private actors providing environmental services. In some cases, such as water, developing countries should be cautious in liberalizing their markets and privatizing public entities. The environmental services sector presents equity problems in ensuring universal access to clean water. It also raises the important question of how to secure the participation of domestic firms in delivering services. Developing countries may wish to set conditions under which all private companies are to operate, possibly setting maximum prices for consumers, determining the percentage of profit that should be reinvested in infrastructure and establishing public service obligations. To help build capacity in developing countries, market access requirements might include training of personnel, a minimum local content requirement and transfer of technology and managerial know-how.
>
> *Source:* Butkeviciene, Benavides and Tortora, 2002.

commitments and those made on the mobility of capital. Explicit and implicit barriers, such as immigration and visa requirements and economic needs tests in industrial countries, need to be effectively addressed and resolved.

- Developing countries may seek to introduce the conditional offer approach to operationalize the provisions under articles IV and XIX:2.[12] This approach would recognize the differences in capacity and development levels between different countries. However, developing countries would also need to identify what is needed to improve their participation in selected service sectors and suggest including and negotiating additional disciplines to facilitate this.

- In the interests of human development it is vital that governments have greater flexibility in exempting basic public services—such as health, water, education and social protection—from the progressive liberalization principle. Mechanisms need to be in place to ensure that the exemption of government authority is understood not in terms of means of delivery but in terms of function (Hilary, 2001). This requires strengthening the GATS government authority exclusion. International cooperation is needed to prevent the unnecessary privatization of basic social services or the recourse by developing country—especially least developed country—governments to schemes such as cost recovery programmes to remedy resource constraints in financing basic social services. The 20/20 initiative constitutes a good framework for such cooperation. This initiative, proposed by the UN in the early 1990s, encourages developing countries to allocate about 20 per cent of their national budgets, and developed countries about 20 per cent of official development assistance, to basic social services.

- The rules of the global trading regime should not constrain developing country governments from strengthening their existing domestic regulation and policies and introducing new ones if necessary. Requirements such as the necessity test and 'the least trade restrictiveness' criteria should not be made binding constraints.

- An urgent need is to address the lack of information, and thus lack of foresight, that limits the ability of developing countries to choose service sectors and subsectors to liberalize in line with their human development needs. Solving this problem is also important in order to create an effective and beneficial temporary safeguard provision, as countries will need appropriate data to show that the injury to domestic service sectors is in fact caused by increased imports and access granted to foreign suppliers. The solution will require an agreement on data collection and collation at the national and international levels in all four modes of supply. At the same time, developing countries will need to undertake national data estimations, for example, by using options theory (Raghavan, 2000).

- A full assessment of the human development impact of liberalizing services trade in developing countries needs to be carried out, based on complete and improved data and information. The provision in article XIX:3 requires the WTO Council for Trade in Services to assess the consequences of liberalizing services trade overall and at the sectoral level. This assessment should be carried out more completely. Moreover, it should include not only the direct impact of liberalization and deregulation across service sectors, but also the indirect and longer-term impact on components of human development, including the impact on marginalized groups such as poor women. Finally, in keeping with the Doha mandate on technical assistance and capacity building, a rapidly accessible funding mechanism should be put into place for developing countries willing to conduct an assessment, or to request an assessment, on trade in services (CIEL, 2002).

NOTES

1. Another important general obligation relates to monopolies and business practices (Mashayekhi, 2000a).

2. This section draws on UNCTAD (1994, 2001a), Mashayekhi (2000a) and WTO (2002).

3. Adding limitations to specific commitments is a long, complex process that can begin only three years after the commitment was made. Moreover, the other members must be notified at least three months before the change. If a negotiated settlement is reached, the government must compensate others by replacing the withdrawn commitments with substitutes that satisfy all WTO members. If a negotiated settlement is not reached, the withdrawing government faces retaliation (article XXI also permits cross-retaliation) not limited to service sectors (Sinclair and Grieshaber-Otto, 2002). Furthermore, according to the principle of progressive liberalization, even existing limitations can be challenged in the future, so effectively there is reverse flexibility.

4. This discussion draws largely on Woodroffe (2002) and TWN (2001).

5. For example, Canada has not committed its health services, but has committed its data processing without limitations. That raises the question of whether the management of health records falls under health services or data processing services (Sinclair, 2000; Sinclair and Grieshaber-Otto, 2002).

6. According to Mashayekhi (2000b, p 174), these sectors have been identified in UNCTAD's sectoral analysis and the outcomes of the sessions of the Commission on Trade in Goods and Services.

7. This discussion draws heavily on Mashayekhi (2000b).

8. Sinclair and Grieshaber-Otto (2002, pp 46–47) cite the example of education: 'Where a government makes specific commitments covering private education, this could trigger complaints that post-secondary institutions are abusing their monopoly position. For example, if a university offers a non-credit course that competes with courses offered by private training institutes, it could be exposed to charges that it is leveraging its monopoly position by using facilities and faculty supported by its monopoly status outside the scope of this monopoly.' Similarly, since China's entry into the WTO, China Post, the national postal administration, has faced charges from international courier companies that it is abusing its monopoly position by regulating the prices private couriers must charge when delivering parcels under 500 grams. The country is facing a difficult decision in the dispute, as the postal monopoly has come to rely on revenue from the fast-growing express market to subsidize its national postal network. This cross-subsidy has allowed China Post to withstand government cutbacks and fulfill its mandate, providing postal services throughout the entire country (McGregor, 2002).

9. When the provider is a powerful multinational, mode 3 is only part of the service provision; different companies can provide different aspects of health services through different modes. In the Indian state of Maharashtra, for example, the World Bank supports a private hospital through medical equipment and personnel (modes 3 and 4). The project is co-funded by a pharmaceutical giant, Wockhard, which is linking up with a giant US health insurance provider (mode 1) (Corner House, 2001).

10. There is also a need to address the issue of developing country access to industrial country markets for health services. According to UNCTAD (2002), portability of insurance is a precondition for increasing the participation of developing countries in international trade in health services. Also necessary for effective liberalization of market access is recognition of the qualifications of medical and other health professionals and measures to facilitate the temporary movement of persons in selected categories and occupations. Necessary too is recognition of measures aimed at protecting the health of the population in developing countries as a social obligation of their governments.

11. The economic needs test can be used for public policy purposes only with certain clear guidelines, which do not currently exist under the GATS (Butkeviciene, 2000).

12. According to the conditional offer approach, developing countries would be willing to undertake liberalization commitments in line with article XIX:2 if industrial countries would undertake to implement certain provisions and additional commitments for implementing article IV on the increasing participation of developing countries.

REFERENCES

Ahmad, Mushtaq. 2000. 'Pakistan and the GATS: An Assessment of Policies and Future Prospects'. Paper presented at the World Bank workshop WTO 2000 South Asia, New Delhi, 13 February.

Aryeetey, E., and M. Nissanke. 1998. *Financial Integration and Development: Financial Gaps under Liberalization in Four African Countries.* London: Routledge.

Baden, Sally. 1996. 'Gender Issues in Agricultural Market Liberalisation'. Report 41. Prepared for Directorate General for Development of the European Commission. BRIDGE, London. [www.ids.ac.uk/bridge/Reports/re41c.pdf].

Baden, Sally, and K. Milward. 1995. 'Gender and Poverty'. BRIDGE Briefings on Development and Gender, Report 30. University of Sussex, Institute of Development Studies, Brighton, UK.

Butkeviciene, J. 2000. 'Movement of Natural Persons under GATS'. In United Nations Conference on Trade and Development, *Positive Agenda and Future Trade Negotiations.* Geneva and New York: United Nations.

———. 2002. 'Market Access in Services'. Paper presented at the Workshop on Market Access, United Nations Conference on Trade and Development, New York, 8–9 January.

Butkeviciene, J., D. Benavides and M. Tortora. 2002. 'UNCTAD Services Performance in Developing Countries: Elements of the Assessment'. Paper presented at the World Trade Organization Symposium on Assessment of Trade in Services, Geneva, 14–15 March. United Nations Conference on Trade and Development, Geneva.

Chanda, Rupa. 1999. *Movement of Natural Persons and Trade in Services: Liberalizing Temporary Movement of Labour under the GATS.* New Delhi: Indian Council for Research on International Economic Relations.

CIEL (Centre for International Environmental Law). 2002. 'Services Assessment and the Market Access Phase of the WTO Services Negotiations'. Geneva.

Corner House. 2001. 'Trading Health Care Away? GATS, Public Services and Privatisation'. London.

CUTS (Consumer Unity and Trust Society). 1999. 'Professional Services under the GATS: Implication for the Accountancy Sector in India'. No 10/1999. CUTS Centre for International Trade, Economics and Environment, New Delhi.

Das, Bhagirath Lal. 1998a. 'An Introduction to the WTO Agreements'. Third World Network, Penang, Malaysia.

———. 1998b. 'Restoring Balance to Services in WTO'. SUNS–South-North Development Monitor, no 4336. SUNS, Geneva. [www.sunsonline.org/trade/process/followup/1998/12020298.htm].

———. 2002. 'The New Work Programme of the WTO'. Third World Network, Penang, Malaysia.

Dhanarajan, S. 2001. 'The General Agreement on Trade in Services'. Oxfam, Oxford.

Gammage, Sarah, and Y. Clement Jumelle. 2002. 'Framework for Gender Assessments of Trade and Investment Agreements'. Women's EDGE, Global Trade Program, Washington, DC.

Gibbs, Murray, and Mina Mashayekhi. 1998. 'The Uruguay Round Negotiations on Investment: Lessons for the Future'. [www.unctad.org/en/docs/investgm.pdf].

———. 1999. 'Lessons from the Uruguay Round Negotiations on Investment'. *Journal of World Trade* 33 (6).

Gupta, I., B. Goldar and A. Mitra. 1998. 'The Case of India'. In S Zarilli and C Kinnon, eds, *International Trade in Health Services: A Development Perspective*. Geneva: United Nations Conference on Trade and Development and World Health Organization.

Hilary, John. 2001. 'The Wrong Model: GATS, Trade Liberalisation and Children's Right to Health'. Save the Children UK, London.

ICN (International Council of Nurses). 1999. 'Nurse Retention, Transfer and Migration: Position Statement'. Geneva.

Malhotra, Kamal. 1999. 'Economic Renovation, User Fees and the Provision of Basic Services to Vulnerable Families: Lessons for Vietnam'. Paper prepared for Save the Children Alliance, Hanoi; and United Nations Children's Fund, Hanoi.

Mashayekhi, Mina. 2000a. 'GATS 2000 Negotiation Options for Developing Countries'. Working paper 9. South Centre, Geneva.

———. 2000b. 'GATS 2000: Progressive Liberalization'. In United Nations Conference on Trade and Development, *Positive Agenda and Future Trade Negotiations*. Geneva and New York: United Nations.

———. 2002. 'Market Access in Services'. Paper presented at the Workshop on Market Access, United Nations Conference on Trade and Development, New York, 8–9 January.

McCulloghy, N., A. Winters and X. Cirera. 2001. 'Trade Liberalisation and Poverty: A Handbook'. Centre for Economic Policy Research, London.

McGregor, Richard. 2002. 'China's Postal Service "Restricting" Competitors'. [www.cecc.gov/pages/hearings/060602/clarke.php3].

McGuire, Greg. 2002. 'How Important Are Restrictions on Trade in Services?' Paper presented at the Workshop on Market Access, United Nations Conference on Trade and Development, New York, 8–9 January.

Michalopoulos, C. 1999. 'Developing Country Goals and Strategies for the Millennium Round'. World Bank, Washington D.C.

Mwanza, A. 1999. 'Effects of Economic Reform on Children and Youth in Zimbabwe since 1991'. Save the Children, Harare.

Nayyar, D. 2000. 'Cross Border Movement of People'. Working paper 194. United Nations University, World Institute for Development Economics Research, Helsinki.

Njinkeu, Dominique, and Thierry Noyelle. 2000. 'Overview of African Implementation Experiences and Proposals for Development-Focused GATS Negotiations'. African Economic Research Consortium, Nairobi, Kenya.

OECD (Organisation for Economic Co-operation and Development). 2001. 'Open Services Markets Matter'. TD/TC/WP (2001)24/PART1/REV1. Working Party of the Trade Committee, Paris.

Office of the US Trade Representative. 2000. 'U.S. Proposal in the WTO Framework for Negotiations in Services'. Submitted to the World Trade Organization. Washington, DC.

Oxfam. 2002. *Rigged Rules and Double Standards: Trade Globalisation and the Fight against Poverty*. Oxford.

Raghavan. Chakravarti 1997a. 'Close Encounters at the WTO'. *Third World Economics* 175: 16–31.

———. 1997b. 'A New Trade Order in a World of Disorder'. In J. M. Griesgraber and B. G. Gunter, eds, *World Trade: Toward Fair and Free Trade in the Twenty-First Century*. Vol 5 of Rethinking Bretton Woods Series. London and Chicago: Pluto.

———. 2000. 'A Comment on the New Round of Services Negotiations'. Paper presented at Third World Network Seminar on Current Developments in the WTO: Perspective of Developing Countries, Geneva, 14–15 September.

Shukla, S. P. 2000. 'From GATT to WTO and Beyond'. United Nations University, World Institute for Development Economics Research, Helsinki.

Sinclair, S. 2000. 'GATS: How the World Trade Organisation's New "Services" Negotiations Threaten Democracy'. Canadian Centre for Policy Alternatives, Ottawa.

Sinclair, Scott, and Jim Grieshaber-Otto. 2002. 'Facing the Facts: A Critical Guide to WTO and OECD Claims about the GATS'. Canadian Centre for Policy Alternatives, Ottawa.

Sitthi-amorn, C., R. Somronthong and W. S. Janjaroen. 2001. 'Some Health Implications of Globalization in Thailand'. *Bulletin of the World Health Organization* 79 (9): 889–90.

Swan, M., and A. Zwi. 1997. *Private Practitioners and Public Health: Close the Gap or Increase the Distance?* London: London School of Hygiene and Tropical Medicine.

TWN (Third World Network). 2000. 'A Comment on the New Round of Services Negotiations'. Paper presented at Third World Network Seminar on Current Developments in the WTO: Perspective of Developing Countries, Geneva, 14–15 September.

———. 2001. 'The Multilateral Trading System: A Development Perspective'. Background paper for Trade and Sustainable Human Development Project. United Nations Development Programme, New York.

UNCTAD (United Nations Conference on Trade and Development). 1994. 'Assessment of the Outcome of the Uruguay Round.' Commercial Diplomacy Programme, Geneva.

———. 1999. *Trade and Development Report 1999*. Geneva.

———. 2001a. 'Tools for Multilateral Trade Negotiations on Trade in Services'. Commercial Diplomacy Programme, Geneva.

———. 2001b. *Trade and Development Report 2001*. Geneva.

———. 2002. 'Note on the New Approach to Services Negotiations by Developing Countries'. Geneva.

UNDP (United Nations Development Programme). 1999. *Human Development Report 1999*. New York: Oxford University Press.

———. 2002. 'Work Programme on Trade in Services: Energy'. [www.vnn.vn/design/undp/index.html].

Walmsley, T., and A. Winters. 2002. 'Relaxing the Restrictions on the Temporary Movement of Natural Persons: A Simulation Analysis'. University of Sussex, School of Social Sciences, Brighton, UK.

Whitehead, M., G. Dahlgreen and T. Evans. 2001. 'Equity and Health Sector Reforms: Can Low-Income Countries Escape the Medical Poverty Trap?' *The Lancet* 358: 833–36.

Winters, A. 2002. 'Doha and the World Poverty Targets'. Paper presented at the World Bank Annual Conference on Development Economics, 29–30 April, Washington, DC.

Woodroffe, Jessica. 2002. 'GATS: A Disservice to the Poor—The High Costs and Limited Benefits of the General Agreement on Trade in Services for Developing Countries'. World Development Movement, London.

World Bank. 2000. *World Development Report 2000/2001: Attacking Poverty*. New York: Oxford University Press.

WTO (World Trade Organization). 1994. 'General Agreement on Trade in Services'. Annex IB, Establishing the WTO. Geneva. [www.wto.org/cnglish/docs_e/legal_e/final_e.htm].

———. 2000a. 'Agricultural Trade Performance by Developing Countries, 1990–1998'. WTO Secretariat, Geneva. G/AG/NG/S/6.

———. 2000b. 'Communication from India: Proposed Liberalization of Movement of Professionals under General Agreement on Trade in Services (GATS)'. Council for Trade in Goods, Geneva. S/CSS/W/12/Corr.1.

———. 2000c. 'The Effects of the Reduction Commitments on World Trade in Agriculture'. WTO Secretariat, Geneva. G/AG/NG/S/11.

———. 2001. 'GATS: Fact and Fiction'. Trade in Services Secretariat, Geneva.

———. 2002. 'Services Negotiations'. [www.wto.org/english/tratop_e/serv_e/serv_e.htm].

Zarilli, Simonetta. 2002. 'International Trade in Energy Services and the Developing Countries'. United Nations Conference on Trade and Development, New York.

CHAPTER 14
COMPETITION POLICY

Competition policy refers to a set of laws and regulations aimed at maintaining a fair degree of competition by eliminating restrictive business practices by private enterprise. According to Graham (2000, p. 205), competition policy includes 'both anti-monopolies (antitrust) and regulation of state aid (i.e. subsidies and subsidy-like measures)'. Restrictive (or anticompetitive or unfair) business practices are those that limit entry into a market by other enterprises or regulate supply in a way deemed harmful to other (existing or potential) producers or to consumers. Such practices include collusion, predatory pricing behaviour, capacity expansion that deters market entry and mergers and acquisitions that reduce competition.

Competition policy thus aims at limiting monopoly so as to encourage competition and its beneficial welfare effects. While competition policy may help particular firms or consumers, in principle it aims not at helping specific competitors but at establishing conditions of competition. A key characteristic of competitive market conditions is that 'sellers and potential sellers be as free as possible to enter and leave the market as they see fit—or, in other words, that markets be contestable' (Graham, 2000, p. 207).

There are two main analytical questions relating to competition policy. First, are domestic competition policies needed, and if so, what should their nature be? And second, is an international competition policy needed, and if yes, should it be established in the World Trade Organization (WTO)?

As a brief history of competition policy in the international context shows, efforts to produce an international agreement on such policy have long been under way (box 14.1).

EXPERIENCE WITH DOMESTIC COMPETITION POLICY AND LESSONS FOR DEVELOPING COUNTRIES

Until recently most developing countries have operated without a formal competition policy, because no such policy was needed. Most developing country governments exercised considerable control over economic activity. If a government

BOX 14.1 COMPETITION POLICY IN THE INTERNATIONAL CONTEXT: A BRIEF HISTORY

In the context of trade, competition policy cannot be viewed separate from investment, since the two issues are closely linked. Efforts have been made to reach international agreement on competition policy before. Attempts to reach agreement on the United Nations General Assembly's 1980 'Set of Multilaterally Agreed Equitable Principles and Rules for the Control of Restrictive Practices' failed because most industrial countries disagreed with developing countries' desire to make rules legally binding. The United Nations Center on Transnational Corporations' code of conduct for transnational corporations, which can be viewed as relating to both investment and competition policy issues, met with a similar fate two decades ago.

Ironically, it is now industrial countries that seek a binding multilateral agreement, though of a very different kind and in a very different forum—the World Trade Organization (WTO). And it is now developing countries that oppose this. Industrial country groups such as the European Union now support a WTO agreement on trade and competition policy largely for reasons of market access much like those motivating their desire for a multilateral agreement on investment in the WTO. While the General Agreement on Trade in Services (GATS) has provided some expansion of market access in public utilities, telecommunications and financial services, a WTO-based competition code would clearly extend industrial countries' market access possibilities further. According to Graham (2000, p. 218),

> U.S. telecommunications services providers are certainly in favour of the ending of government policies that grant monopoly rights in the provision of telecommunications services to local providers. Such rights have long been insurmountable barriers to market access. Although many nations are now in the process of ending or substantially modifying state-sanctioned telecommunications monopolies, these markets nevertheless will remain highly regulated and probably not very contestable. Further market opening measures by the WTO in this domain are welcomed by providers that stand to gain market access.

Japan, while vigorously in favour of a competition policy agreement in the WTO, apparently has a different motivation. It would like to see such an agreement effectively address the panoply of anti-dumping practices (Graham, 2000). According to Graham (2000), this risk to the anti-dumping regime is precisely the reason that the US Department of Commerce is not actively pushing a competition policy agreement in the WTO.

Some WTO agreements already contain elements of competition policy. Anti-dumping actions aim specifically at predatory and below-cost pricing behaviour deemed unfair to domestic producers. Many services in developing countries are provided through state-owned monopolies, and article VIII of the GATS requires signatories to 'ensure that the supplier does not abuse its monopoly position to act in a manner which is inconsistent with the national treatment obligations and specific commitments made by the member in respect of the service' (Vautier, Lloyd and Tsai, 1999, p. 19). Thus the WTO has dealt with competition issues as they relate to specific aspects of trade.

If a binding competition policy were agreed on in the WTO, investment regulation under the Agreement on Trade-Related Investment Measures might need revision. Similarly, conflict might arise with the Agreement on Trade-Related Aspects of Intellectual Property Rights, which allows anticompetitive practices: intellectual property protection restricts contestability based on the grounds that such restrictions promote greater innovation over the long term.

Recognizing the relevance of anticompetitive practices to the direction and volume of international trade flows, the December 1996 WTO Ministerial Conference in Singapore identified competition policy as one of the four 'Singapore issues'. It also established a working group on 'the interaction between trade and competition policy' whose major tasks included *'ensur[ing] that the development agenda is taken fully into account'* (WTO, 1999, annex 1; emphasis added). The working group was encouraged to seek cooperation with other organizations, such as the United Nations Conference on Trade and Development (UNCTAD). Just as for investment, the 2001 Doha ministerial declaration did not formally launch negotiations but makes it possible to negotiate an agreement after the fifth ministerial conference in Mexico in 2003 if there is explicit consensus to do so.

According to the Doha ministerial declaration (article 23, p. 9), 'negotiations will take place after the Fifth Session of the Ministerial Conference on the basis of a decision to be taken, by explicit consensus, at that session on modalities of negotiations' [that is, how the negotiations are to be conducted].

Source: Milberg, 2002; UNDP, 2002.

perceived uncompetitive behaviour, it often intervened directly (such as with the prices of medicines). Indeed, until 1990 only 16 developing countries had a formal competition policy.

But with deregulation, privatization and liberalization over the past two decades, this situation has changed in most developing countries. With encouragement and help from the WTO and international financial institutions, 50 more countries completed their competition law in the 1990s and another 27 are doing so (Singh, 2002). About a third of WTO members still lack such legislation.

The experiences of industrial countries with domestic competition policies provide useful lessons for developing countries as they formulate their own domestic policies. The first and perhaps most important lesson is that a variety of domestic competition regimes coexist across the industrial world. The US, European Union and Japan, for example, have each used different competition policies and have modified them as needed. This approach has required flexibility and domestic policy space.

The US has focused on antitrust actions. Its vigilance in enforcing antitrust policies has fluctuated over time. It recently moved away from automatically prosecuting practices that threaten competition, regardless of the context or consequences, towards a competition policy that considers anticompetitive practices case by case, taking both context and consequences into account (see Baker, 1999).

The European Union's competition policy is aimed at promoting the harmonization of its members' national competition policies. Its competition law has been described as focusing largely on static efficiency and being less specific about issues relating to social policy and state subsidies (see Audretsch, Baumol and Burke, 2001).

Competition policy in Japan has evolved since the 1940s. The period most relevant for developing countries is 1950–73, when Japan was much more like a newly industrializing country than it is today. This period of rapid economic growth and competition policy was coordinated closely with industrial policy. Implemented by the Ministry of Trade and Industry (MITI), industrial policy dominated competition policy, which was enforced by the Fair Trade Commission. MITI sought high rates of profit and reinvestment for industry, an objective requiring such 'anticompetitive' actions as sponsoring cartels, coordinating investment by rival firms and intervening in firm exit and entry. All these, according to Singh (2002, p. 24), 'contributed to the high concentration ratios observed in the Japanese economy.'

Cartels were not viewed as necessarily bad. MITI managed the situation by playing oligopoly firms off against one another, rewarding those with good performance in exports or technological innovation with subsidies and protection from imports. The ministry's promotion of both cooperation and competition among cartels and oligopoly firms may have sacrificed static efficiency for the sake of maximizing long-term productivity growth—'dynamic efficiency'. The case of Japan may bear some similarities to that of Germany, where the government encouraged rather than opposed cartels in many instances.

A recent World Bank (2002) survey of competition laws in 50 countries that have introduced them also reported important inter-country differences in the definition of dominance, the treatment of cartels and the enforcement of the laws. The variation in competition policies across industrial countries and other countries included in the recent World Bank survey indicates that here, as in trade policy more generally, one size does not fit all. Developing countries should take care to adopt competition policies that fit their circumstances. Countries must retain the flexibility and policy space to regulate competition in a way that supports their long-term development strategy. The design of their competition policy should take into account their level of development, their institutions of labour relations and innovation and their place in the world economy. And given the rapid changes in technology and the heightened mobility of capital today, developing countries must also focus on these dynamic factors in developing their competition policies.

Japan's experience since World War II, with its emphasis on dynamic forces and on combining cooperation and competition, appears to provide the most useful lessons for developing countries. This is supported by the experiences of other East Asian countries, of China more recently and even of industrial districts in Italy (Singh, 2002). But in the context of today, perhaps the more important lesson from industrial country experience is that developing countries should be able to have competition policy regimes that differ from one another. And they should design their domestic competition laws and regulations to be flexible and dynamic enough to respond to and even pre-empt the changing circumstances of a rapidly globalizing world. Indeed, Audretsch, Baumol and Burke (2001) suggest that industrial countries should move to a more dynamic policy as well.

A second lesson for developing countries is that industrial countries have not applied domestic competition policies across the board but instead have been highly selective across sectors and even firms. According to US competition policy experts Graham and Richardson (1997, p. 34),

> 'Competition policy is usually tailored to sectoral public interest regulation—especially in transportation, telecommunications, and utilities—and often tailored to industrial policies that favor agriculture or high-technology sectors over others. . . . Competition policy has never been applied indiscriminately to financial markets. . . . Occasionally, competition policy even differentiates among competing firms, with state-owned or state-chartered firms treated with more leniency'.

This implies that an 'across the board' domestic competition policy regime is likely to be inappropriate. Countries will need to retain the flexibility to choose the sectors to which they wish to apply it.

A third lesson for developing countries is that most industrial countries developed competition policy quite recently—certainly only after they had attained levels of economic development far beyond those of most developing countries today (see Chang, 2002, chs 2 and 3). US policy began taking shape during the late 19th century, while Europe and Japan have effectively enforced competition regulations only during the past 50 years. In some cases (France, the UK) statutes existed largely on paper.

Thus competition policy arrived late in the industrial countries relative to their level of economic development. And it has both varied considerably across countries and been applied selectively across sectors and interest groups within countries. This should not be surprising, since most industrial countries pursued economic development strategies allowing considerable protectionist and anti-competitive behaviour, aimed at promoting the development of domestic industrial capacity and attaining dynamic efficiency through technological advance. Developing countries need to learn the right lessons from the experience of countries that have already achieved industrialization.

THE NEED FOR DOMESTIC COMPETITION POLICY IN TODAY'S WORLD

Both domestic and international economic developments in the past two decades suggest that it is important for developing countries to establish formal competition policies. Domestically, the enormous structural changes caused by deregulation and privatization are the main reason for this need. Without appropriate national competition policies, privatization is much more likely to reduce social welfare and undermine human development (Singh, 2002). Internationally, the boom in cross-border mergers poses a potentially significant threat to competition in developing countries. Mergers can increase the market power of transnational corporations' affiliates operating in developing countries and create 'increased barriers to entry and contestability' (Singh and Dhumale, 1999, p. 7).[1] Such mergers can be particularly harmful to the interests of the late industrializing countries, whose firms are still building the capacity to compete in international markets.

Moreover, along with the potential benefits of inward foreign direct investment come potential risks.[2] One such risk is that socially beneficial domestic competition will be reduced. Inward foreign direct investment can spur competition among domestic firms and move them to an internationally competitive level of productivity. But in the absence of an appropriate and effective domestic competition policy, foreign firms can crowd out domestic investment, stifle domestic competition, reduce domestic productivity growth, raise domestic prices and diminish prospects for industrialization.

Domestic competition laws and their enforcement should be designed to restrain anticompetitive behaviour by large domestic private corporations, limit or pre-empt abuses of monopoly power by large transnational corporations and support human development objectives. This is where the experience of Japan and other East Asian countries is likely to be most useful.

But even the most effective competition policy will be unable to constrain the global anticompetitive behaviour of large transnational corporations. That will require the cooperation of industrial countries, where most such corporations are based. And it will require an appropriate framework for international cooperation on competition issues, similar to the failed proposals put forth by developing countries two decades ago. The need remains as urgent as ever.

AN INTERNATIONAL AGREEMENT ON COMPETITION POLICY IN THE WORLD TRADE ORGANIZATION

Expanded activity by transnational corporations in developing countries might lead these countries to support the adoption of an international competition policy. Many already do so, prompted by concern about the static inefficiency that may result from the anticompetitive practices of such corporations. Although domestic policy could regulate this anticompetitive threat, an international policy would presumably give countries some influence over purely foreign mergers and acquisitions. But should such international cooperation be in the WTO?

Arguments in favour of this include restraining anticompetitive behaviour and cartelization by large industrial country corporations, disciplining the Agreement on Trade-Related Aspects of Intellectual Property Rights and blunting the potency of anti-dumping laws by bringing them into the normal framework of predation under competition law (Singh, 2002). Joseph Stiglitz argues that the predation test is much stricter than the anti-dumping measures that countries have been using under the WTO (Singh, 2002).

Economists disagree about the possible benefits that might accrue to developing countries from a WTO-based competition policy. Perroni and Whalley (1998) estimate a significant positive effect, equivalent to as much as 6 per cent of developing countries' national income. They argue that gains could result from several factors: fewer predatory anti-dumping actions against developing countries, less price gouging on imported inputs and increased domestic competition.

Hoekman and Holmes (1999), however, are sceptical about the ability of a WTO-based agreement to reduce anticompetitive merger activity in developing countries.[3] They believe there is a risk that negotiations will lead to an agreement serving mainly the industrial countries that want market access, particularly where large private or state enterprises control an industry. According to Hoekman and Holmes (1999, p. 16), a WTO-based agreement is unlikely to be helpful because

> 'the agenda is likely to be dominated by market access issues more than international antitrust.... [T]he WTO process is driven by export interests (market access), not national welfare considerations, and there is no assurance that the rules that will be proposed or agreed will be welfare enhancing'.

These concerns have been mirrored in the discussions of the WTO Working Group on Trade and Competition Policy. Among the issues debated are whether a uniform international competition policy is needed and, if such a policy should emerge, whether the WTO is the appropriate organization to enforce it.

Most important for the issues raised in this book, the working group's annual reports reveal much concern among developing country members that a WTO-based agreement would limit their ability to pursue policies promoting sustainable development, particularly industrial policies and infant industry protection under certain circumstances. The importance of this concern cannot be overstated; such policies have played an essential part in every case of successful industrialization leading to human development over the past 300 years.[4]

A key lesson from the historical and current experience of industrial countries is that any international cooperation framework in this area must allow participating countries the flexibility to design different competition policies and to adapt their policies over time. A uniform competition policy in the WTO seems unlikely to be able to do this.

Equally important, if such a framework is established in the WTO, governments will have to give large transnational corporations 'national treatment'—that is, the same treatment they accord domestic enterprises—both before such firms have decided which sector to enter and after the firms are established. This could easily lead to results harmful to both local development and global efficiency. For example, it should be permissible for a developing country to allow domestic corporations to merge or establish a minimum critical mass of R&D activity, to enable them to compete more effectively with large transnational corporations, while at the same time denying such merger opportunities to foreign transnational corporations. But this would violate the WTO's national treatment principle (Singh,

2002). It could also bring cross-retaliation against the developing country in another area as part of the WTO's dispute settlement procedure.

THE WAY FORWARD

The discussion of the benefits and costs of international cooperation on competition in the WTO highlights a difficult dilemma for developing countries: even the most appropriate and effective domestic competition policy will be unable to contend with the real or potential anticompetitive behaviour of large transnational corporations. This problem suggests a need for an international agreement on competition policy regardless of whether there is one on investment. Yet for the reasons discussed, a competition policy agreement under the current multilateral trade regime is unlikely to provide developing countries with the policy space or the outcomes they need from an internationally agreed competition policy. Moreover, violations of the national treatment or other principles of the WTO will open them to cross-retaliation, causing new problems. This situation calls for at least two sets of actions.

First, developing countries should continue to build their own domestic competition policies, both to regulate domestic monopoly and to control the possible anticompetitive behaviour of transnational corporations. Countries that do not have a domestic competition policy should begin to develop one. Such policies should be designed to thwart anticompetitive practices detrimental to long-term development, whether those unfair practices come from foreign or domestic enterprises. And they should encourage the development of services, technology, genuine infant industries, efficient public utilities and managerial and marketing capacity and allow flexibility in the choice of sectors for application.

Second, developing countries should coordinate competition policy as much as possible with other countries. Member countries of the European Union have done this, and those of Mercosur and the Asia-Pacific Economic Cooperation (APEC) have also begun sharing information and even harmonizing policy. The APEC agreement is based on four core principles: non-discrimination, comprehensiveness, transparency and accountability—a good starting point for any coordinated agreement (see Vautier and others, 1999, for an overview).

There is an important reason why such cooperation should be independent of and outside the existing multilateral trade rules: international competition policy involves a broader range of issues than those related to international trade. Among these are regulatory and social objectives very different from the WTO's efforts to promote free trade through market access.

NOTES

1. Hoekman and Holmes (1999) argue that international mergers that create anticompetitive markets are one important reason for developing countries to pursue an international competition policy in the WTO. Another relates to cases in which

anticompetitive export cartels are not restrained because it is not in the interest of the cartel's home country to do so.

2. For a discussion of the benefits and costs of a development strategy led by foreign direct investment, see Milberg (1999).

3. This point is also made in the 2001 report of the WTO Working Group on Trade and Competition Policy (WTO, 2001b, para 58).

4. Evidence on the first wave of industrialization can be found in Chang (2002). The experience of the late industrializers is described in Amsden (2001).

REFERENCES

Amsden, Alice. 1989. *Asia's Next Giant.* New York: Oxford University Press.

———. 2001. *The Rise of the Rest: Challenges to the West from Late-Industrializing Economies.* New York: Oxford University Press.

Audretsch, D. B., W. J. Baumol and A. E. Burke. 2001. 'Competition Policy in Dynamic Markets'. *International Journal of Industrial Organization* 19 (5): 613–34.

Baker, Donald I., and J. William Rowley, eds. 1998. *International Mergers: The Antitrust Process.* 2d ed. London: Sweet & Maxwell.

Baker, J. 1999. 'Developments in Antitrust Economics'. *Journal of Economic Perspectives* 13 (1): 181–94.

Best, M. 1991. *The New Competition.* Cambridge: Cambridge University Press.

Chang, H. 2002. *Kicking Away the Ladder: Development Strategy in Historical Perspective.* London: Anthem.

Fagerberg, J. 1995. 'User-Producer Interaction, Learning and Comparative Advantage'. Special issue on technology and innovation. *Cambridge Journal of Economics* 19 (February): 243–56.

———. 1996. 'Technology and Competitiveness'. *Oxford Review of Economic Policy* 12 (3): 39–51.

Graham, E. 2000. 'Trade, Competition, and the WTO Agenda'. In J Schott, ed, *The WTO after Seattle.* Washington, DC: Institute for International Economics.

Graham, E., and D. Richardson. 1997. 'Issue Overview'. In E. Graham and D. Richardson, eds, *Global Competition Policy.* Washington, DC: Institute for International Economics.

Hoekman, Bernard, and Peter Holmes. 1999. 'Competition Policy, Developing Countries and the WTO'. Policy Research Working Paper 2211. World Bank, Washington, DC.

Julius, D. 1990. *Global Companies and Public Policy.* New York: Council on Foreign Relations for the Royal Institute of International Affairs.

Linder, S. 1961. *An Essay on Trade and Transformation.* Uppsala, Sweden: Almqvist & Wiksell.

Lloyd, Peter John. 1999. *International Trade Opening and the Formation of the Global Economy.* Translated by David Colander and Mark Blaug. Cheltenham, UK: Edward Elgar.

Lloyd, Peter John, and K. Vautier. 1999. *Promoting Competition in Global Markets: A Multi- National Approach.* Cheltenham, UK: Edward Elgar.

Milberg, William. 1999. 'Foreign Direct Investment and Development: Balancing Costs and Benefits'. In United Nations Conference on Trade and Development, *International Monetary and Financial Issues for the 1990s.* Vol 11. New York.

_____. 2002 'Trade and Competition Policy'. Background note for United Nations Development Programme Trade and Sustainable Human Development Project, New York

OECD (Organisation for Economic Co-operation and Development). 1998. *Open Markets Matter: The Benefits of Trade and Investment Liberalization.* Paris.

Perroni, C., and J. Whalley. 1998. 'Competition Policy and the Developing Countries'. In H Thomas and J Whalley, eds, *Uruguay Round Results and the Emerging Trade Agenda: Quantitative-Based Analyses from the Development Perspective.* New York: United Nations.

Porter, M. 1990. *The Competitive Advantage of Nations.* New York: Free Press.

Singh, A. 2002. 'Competition and Competition Policy in Emerging Markets: International and Development Dimensions'. Revised version of a paper prepared for a G-24 Technical Group meeting, Beirut, March 2002. University of Cambridge, Faculty of Economics and Politics.

Singh, A., and R. Dhumale. 1999. 'Competition Policy, Development and Developing Countries'. Working Paper 7. South Centre, Geneva.

UNCTAD (United Nations Conference on Trade and Development). 2000. *World Investment Report.* Geneva.

UNDP (United Nations Development Programme). 2002. 'Trade, Competition, Policy, and Development'. Background note for United Nations Development Programme Trade and Sustainable Human Development Project, New York.

Vautier, Kerrin, Peter John Lloyd and Ing-Wen Tsai. 1999. 'Competition Policy, Developing Countries, and the WTO'. World Bank, Washington, DC. [www1.worldbank.org/wbiep/trade/manila/compet_DC_WTO.pdf].

World Bank. 2002. *World Development Report 2002: Building Institutions for Markets.* New York: Oxford University Press.

WTO (World Trade Organization). 1999. 'Report of the Working Group on Trade and Competition Policy to the General Council'. Geneva.

————. 2000. 'Report of the Working Group on Trade and Competition Policy'. Geneva.

————. 2001a. 'Doha Ministerial Declaration'. [www.wto.org/english/thewto_e/minist_e/min01_e/mindecl_e.htm].

————. 2001b. 'Report of the Working Group on Trade and Competition Policy'. Geneva.

CHAPTER 15
TRANSPARENCY IN GOVERNMENT PROCUREMENT

All economic activities undertaken by national, provincial or municipal governments— whether providing physical infrastructure, purchasing and maintaining defence equipment or providing public goods such as education and health care— require procuring intermediate goods and services. The procurement of goods and services by different tiers of government accounts for 10–20 per cent of GDP, a significant share of national public finance. Globally, non-defence-related procurement amounts to an estimated US$1.5 trillion (Hoekman, 1998). Among developing countries, procurement is estimated to account for 9–13 per cent of GDP (Choi, 1999). How procurement is undertaken is therefore crucial for the implementation of development policy.

GOVERNMENT PROCUREMENT UNDER THE MULTILATERAL TRADE REGIME

Government procurement is exempted from the basic rules of national treatment in article III of the General Agreement on Tariffs and Trade (GATT). The idea of negotiating a multilateral agreement to establish transparency in government procurement was broached during preparations for the first ministerial meeting of the World Trade Organization (WTO), soon after its creation. But there is a widespread perception that negotiations on transparency in government procurement will inevitably extend to market access issues. Indeed, several countries have expressed a hope that this will occur as a natural second step following the discussions of transparency. As former US Trade Representative Charlene Barshefsky said,

> '*The study on procurement [by the WTO working group established as a result of the first WTO ministerial meeting in Singapore in 1996] is intended to be the first step toward an agreement on transparency practices in government procurement. . . . [T]his initiative will, as we continue to push it, help create an environment where businesses can expect a fair share in competing for contracts with foreign governments*' (quoted in Khor, 1996, p. 4).

Box 15.1 **GOVERNMENT PROCUREMENT AND THE WORLD TRADE REGIME:**
A BRIEF HISTORY

A code providing a mechanism for bringing purchases by government agencies under fundamental disciplines of national treatment and transparency was negotiated during the Tokyo Round, and modifications to this code were negotiated during the Uruguay Round. Unlike most Tokyo Round codes, the Government Procurement Agreement (GPA) remained plurilateral (meaning that countries were not obligated to become signatories). The GPA was not incorporated into the 'single undertaking' despite the ministerial decision setting out procedures for accession to the agreement in Marrakesh, and it was based on a 'positive list' approach. Today the GPA has 27 signatories, but despite its positive list approach, none of them is a developing country.

After the 1996 WTO ministerial meeting in Singapore, WTO member countries identified transparency in government procurement as one of the four areas that required further study before a decision could be made on whether they should be taken up in multilateral trade negotiations. A working group was formed to undertake 'analytical and exploratory' tasks. The group was not to negotiate new rules or commitments, and it was to look only at transparency in procurement (not national treatment).

How transparency was to be defined remained ambiguous, however. The GPA uses a broad definition of transparency, covering technical specifications (article VI), tendering procedures (article VII), qualification of suppliers (article VIII), invitation to tender (article IX), selection procedures (article X), time limits (article XI), documentation requirements (article XV) and publication of awards and of reasons why tenders have failed (article XVIII). All these come into operation only above a certain threshold of procurement value.

Many industrial economies, such as Canada, Japan, the US and the European Union, were keen to begin negotiations on a new agreement on government procurement despite the continuing resistance from developing countries. These tensions surfaced at the 2001 WTO ministerial meeting in Doha. Paragraph 26 of the Doha ministerial declaration was thus drafted to clarify the agenda on procurement, making it clear that:

- Negotiations will begin after the fifth ministerial meeting in 2003 only if there is explicit consensus at that session on modalities of negotiation.

- The negotiations will be limited to transparency and will not include market access issues.

- A multilateral agreement on transparency in government procurement would lead to a requirement for technical assistance and capacity building in poorer countries.

Source: WTO, 2001; Srivastava, 1999.

Similarly, the European Commission, in a paper presented during the Geneva preparations process for the first WTO ministerial meeting in Singapore in 1996, stated that it 'fully supports Ministers taking decisions ... which lead to define ways and means ... to reduce or eliminate trade distortive effects of domestic government procurement measures of all WTO members' (quoted in Khor, 1996, p. 7).

But any extension of the government procurement negotiations into market access issues would be troublesome from a development perspective. The current negotiation agenda is limited to transparency, but there is a widespread perception that this will be a first step towards 'multilateralizing' the Government Procurement Agreement (GPA)—that is, making accession to the agreement obligatory rather than voluntary (box 15.1). While transparency requires only that governments disclose information, purchasing norms and contractual terms, proponents of an agreement aim to use it to make the domestic procurement business more accessible to foreign firms. A natural corollary of the transparency principle would be a move to the principle of national treatment of suppliers regardless of ownership, affiliation and origin of products or services. For these reasons an analysis of government procurement cannot be restricted to the advantages and disadvantages of transparency alone. The implications of these negotiations, as well as those of future potential discussions on market access, need to be evaluated from a human development perspective.

THE DEVELOPMENT DILEMMA

Transparency brings several important benefits for development and democracy. First, it can enhance welfare. Fair and clear procedures of procurement increase its efficiency, freeing scarce development resources for other public programs. Srivastava (1999) estimates the potential savings on purchases in India at up to US$7.8 billion a year. Second, transparency and openness in procurement procedures can check overt corruption and reduce opportunities for covert rent seeking and nepotism, again saving public resources and enhancing the quality of resource allocation. Third, in principle the GPA allows countries to secure export opportunities offered by government procurement of other signatory members.[1] Finally, transparency is among the cornerstones of good governance; it increases accountability and introduces checks and balances in the day-to-day activities of governments.

But how transparency is defined is important. It will bring these benefits as long as its scope is restricted to the availability of information on rules and procedures rather than extended to the harmonization or overhauling of procurement practices. But if transparency is defined very broadly, it could encroach on domestic policy space and lead to higher administrative and logistical costs.

The possible extension of a government procurement agreement into market access issues has more ambiguous implications for development.

Policy space in the context of small and medium-size enterprises
By increasing the number of policy constraints on governments, accession to a new procurement agreement could restrict their policy choices in developing and supporting small and medium-size enterprises, making it more difficult to optimize the implementation of development policy.

The strongest argument that countries have put forward against the national treatment principle is the need to protect their small-scale industries from competition. The reasons for protecting these industries often transcend economic logic to embrace equity, social cohesion, employment and political considerations. Small-scale cottage industries and indigenous and women's organizations are often protected from competition because they are seen as facing an uneven playing field and thus expected to need early support and nurturing to grow and thrive.

Government departments are often required to offer price as well as purchase preferences to these industries, giving them an assured market. The expectation is that these protected industries will generate employment and spur local innovation. In India, for example, procurement rules stipulating that certain products must be purchased exclusively from the small-scale sector, even if the prices charged are up to 15 per cent higher than those offered by the closest competition, are clearly intended to promote artisans and small-scale firms (Srivastava, 1999). Small firms are also often exempted from paying tender fees and benefit from other concessions.

Thus the government procurement market can offer small businesses a secure base to launch their products. And during economic downturns, governments opting for fiscal stimulus packages can use procurement from small and medium-size enterprises to generate employment and stimulate economic recovery.

Implementation costs

Implementing the GPA, or its future variant, will involve significant costs associated with changing from one procurement regime to another. There will also be substantial costs involved in harmonizing government procurement regimes in federal government systems, especially if the rules cover not only central but also state and municipal governments and state-owned procurement entities. Choi (1999) argues that the immediate economic costs of accession to a government procurement agreement might be smaller domestic supply, higher unemployment and a greater bureaucratic burden resulting from the need to comply with detailed transparency and procurement guidelines and reporting requirements. Given competing development priorities and limited resources, these measures could have substantial opportunity costs for developing countries.

A DIRECTION FOR THE FUTURE

Transparency in government procurement procedures is likely to enhance efficiency, clarity and the ease of supply of goods and services for government use. But placing government procurement under the WTO framework would imply a move towards opening this sector to international competition. Thus before agreeing to negotiate a multilateral agreement that goes beyond transparency, or negotiating accession to the GPA, developing countries need to carefully assess the implications for human development—for employment, for income distribution and for the growth and sustainability of small-scale industry.

NOTE

1. However, even in the European Union, a regional market bloc with harmonized policies and procedures, suppliers from outside a country rarely win government contracts. The Economic Commission green paper on procurement issued in 1996 reported that among all eligible transactions, only 3 per cent of awards were made to firms located outside the buying country (EC, 2002 as cited in ITC, 2002).

REFERENCES

Choi, I. 1999. 'Long and Winding Road to the Government Procurement Agreement: Korea's Accession Experience'. Paper presented at the World Bank and Pacific Economic Cooperation Council Trade Policy Forum, Manila, 19–20 July.

Das, B. L. 2002. 'The New WTO Work Program'. Third World Network, Penang, Malaysia.

EC (European Commission). 1996. 'Green Paper on Public Procurement'. http://europa.eu.int/comm/internal_market/en/publproc/green/index.htm

Hoekman, B. 1998. 'Using International Institutions to Improve Public Procurement'. *World Bank Research Observer* 13 (2): 249–69.

ITC (International Trade Centre). 2000. 'Improving SME Access to Public Procurement'. Geneva.

———. 2002. International Trade Center Presentation at the Inter-Secretariat Meeting on Technical Cooperation and Capacity Building Relating to Transparency in Government Procurement sponsored by the World Trade Organization, 27–28 March, held at Inter-American Development Bank Headquarters, Washington, D.C.

Khor, Martin. 1996. 'Government Procurement: The Real Aim of the Majors'. Third World Network, Penang, Malaysia.

———. 2002. 'The WTO, Post-Doha Agenda and the Future of the Trade System: A Development Perspective'. Paper presented at the Asian Development Bank's annual meeting, Shanghai, 10 May.

Srivastava, V. 1999. 'India's Accession to the GPA: Identifying Costs and Benefits'. Paper presented at the World Bank, National Council of Applied Economic Research and World Trade Organization South Asia Workshop, New Delhi, 20–21 December.

Wittig, W. 2002. 'Public Procurement and the Development Agenda'. International Trade Centre, Geneva.

WTO (World Trade Organization). 2001. 'Doha 4th Ministerial, Ministerial Declaration'. http://www.wto.org/english/tratop_e/dda_e/dda_e.htm#dohadeclaration

———. 2002. Presentation on procurement at the Inter-Secretariat Meeting on Technical Cooperation and Capacity Building Relating to Transparency in Government Procurement sponsored by the World Trade Organization, 27–28 March, held at Inter-American Development Bank Headquarters, Washington, DC.

CHAPTER 16
TRADE FACILITATION

The World Trade Organization (WTO, 2002a) defines trade facilitation as 'the simplification and harmonization of international trade procedures'. And it defines these procedures as the 'activities, practices and formalities involved in collecting, presenting, communicating and processing data required for the movement of goods in international trade' (WTO, 2002a). This definition covers a wide range of activities, such as transport formalities, import and export procedures (for example, customs or licensing procedures) and payments, insurance and other financial requirements. Trade facilitation has not historically been a subject of discussion for negotiation in the multilateral trade regime, as a brief history shows (box 16.1).

Of all the issues proposed for new negotiations, trade facilitation is perhaps the least contentious. Many of the implied reforms, such as modernizing facilities and building institutional capacity, are viewed as advantageous by both industrial and developing countries. But implementing trade facilitation reforms can be complex, time consuming and expensive for developing countries. If the trade facilitation agenda is implemented under binding WTO agreements, without taking into consideration the special needs of developing countries and especially those of the least developed among them, it could increase the vulnerability of these countries. It could also impose high implementation and opportunity costs in developing countries, which could be detrimental to human development given the countries' scarce financial and human resources and multiple competing priorities.

POTENTIAL FOR INCREASED VULNERABILITY

Introducing new trade facilitation systems could increase vulnerability and lead to unexpected costs for developing countries if the systems are adopted without full recognition of their institutional, management and other complexities. Pakistan illustrates the potential problems faced by many developing countries, not only the least developed ones. Its switch to preshipment inspections in 1995–97 in the absence of a well-developed information system and full documentation on the Pakistani economy led to substantial under- and overvaluation by traders. With the problems remaining unchecked, revenue collection fell significantly, forcing the

Box 16.1 TRADE FACILITATION: A BRIEF HISTORY

Trade facilitation issues have traditionally been addressed in forums outside the General Agreement on Tariffs and Trade (GATT) and the trading regime. Historically, the most important forum has been the World Customs Organization (WCO). The International Convention on the Simplification and Harmonizing of Customs Procedures (Kyoto Convention), held in 1973 by the WCO, set out best practice in customs procedures and established the concept that such procedures should be internationally standardized and harmonized. The WCO's harmonized system, adopted at the International Convention on the Harmonized Commodity Description and Coding System in 1988, is an international product naming system that today probably represents the most widely adopted common standards on customs. The WCO Declaration of the Customs Cooperation Council Concerning Integrity in Customs (Arusha Convention) of 1993 is the reference point for addressing issues of corruption in customs as well as in other procedures. The United Nations Conference on Trade and Development (UNCTAD), in its 1994 Columbus Declaration, adopted 19 WCO conventions.

While the 1947 GATT referred to the basic guidelines for trade facilitation, all work in this area until 1996 was carried out by such organizations as the WCO, UNCTAD and the United Nations Economic Commission for Europe. But in December 1996, at the insistence of industrial countries, the World Trade Organization (WTO) ministerial meeting in Singapore included in its declaration a direction to the Council for Trade in Goods 'to undertake exploratory and analytical work, drawing on the work of other relevant organizations, on the simplification of trade procedures in order to assess the scope for WTO rules in this area' (WTO, 2002a). International business, the principal proponent of these measures, cites new realities of global economic integration to justify the need for rapid progress in this area. It argues that with the now much lower tariffs after the Uruguay Round, the losses that businesses suffer as a result of delays at borders, opaque and often redundant documentation requirements and the lack of automation of government-mandated trade procedures often exceed their costs from tariffs.

The Council for Trade in Goods has been working on these issues since 1996 despite concern and even opposition from many developing countries. It is framing issues for discussion with a view to adding them to the future trade negotiation agenda. At the WTO Ministerial Conference in Doha in 2001 many industrial countries called for 'immediate binding rules' to advance trade facilitation issues. This call faced stiff resistance. An intense dialogue led to a compromise clause in the ministerial declaration (article 27, p 10) stating that

> 'negotiations will take place after the Fifth Session of the Ministerial Conference on the basis of a decision to be taken, by explicit consensus, at that Session on modalities of negotiations. In the period until the Fifth Session, the Council for Trade in Goods shall review and as appropriate, clarify and improve relevant aspects of articles V, VIII and X of the GATT 1994 and identify the trade facilitation needs and priorities of Members, in particular developing and least-developed countries. We commit ourselves to ensuring adequate technical assistance and support for capacity building in this area'.

country to abandon the experiment. A big part of the problem was Pakistan's lack of capacity to quickly establish the automated control and information systems needed to support the new trade facilitation system. The result was less effective physical and administrative controls and regulation and a smaller revenue base, increasing the strain on Pakistan's budgetary resources (Pirzada, 2002). The potential for such vulnerability is particularly great in the current trade regime because of the elimination of non-tariff barriers and the reduction in tariffs. These changes leave countries with far fewer policy instruments to deal with such situations.

IMPLEMENTATION AND OPPORTUNITY COSTS

Minimizing the incidence and complexity of import and export formalities and simplifying documentation requirements are widely expected to increase efficiency and lead to absolute gains. Yet there is little hard evidence on the economic benefits of trade facilitation for business or government or on the cost of implementing such measures in low-income developing countries.

Existing data on implementation costs are drawn largely from country experience and donor project costs. Among developing countries, most trade facilitation initiatives have taken place (or commenced) in relatively advanced economies, and no estimates exist for the costs of sustaining these initiatives. Projects to implement the WTO Agreement on Customs Valuation, which also includes broader customs reform, have been estimated to cost between US$1.6 million and US$16.2 million. For example, a six-year programme in Tunisia to computerize and simplify procedures cost an estimated US$16.2 million (Finger and Schuler, 2000). However, Bolivia implemented a broad customs reform programme that cost US$38.5 million (Gutiérrez, 2001).

But cost estimates for specific trade facilitation projects do not tell the whole story. To be effective, such projects need to be implemented as part of a much broader process of reform and innovation in managing trade, both in private enterprise and at the administrative level. Taken together, the trade facilitation measures and the range of prior reforms needed to make them effective can involve significant expenditures.

Given the scarce resources and competing claims on them in developing countries, implementing trade facilitation measures often can also lead to high opportunity costs, since they can be undertaken only at the expense of development projects with more direct human development benefits. This is likely to be particularly true for the poorest and least developed countries, especially in the context of limited aid and technical assistance.[1]

Moreover, the reported gains have been mixed, and WTO data on the experiences of low-income economies—such as Chile, Costa Rica and Hong Kong, China (SAR)—typically do not capture the development dilemmas faced by these economies nor, especially, the least developed ones (WTO, 1998b, 2000a, 2000c). Singapore implemented an electronic declaration system for traders that generated savings estimated at 1 per cent of GDP or 0.4 per cent of external trade, with an expectation that it would cover its costs in three years (Woo and Wilson, 2000). And Bolivia found that revenue collection rose by 25 per cent after it reformed its customs system (Bolivia, 2001). But the Philippines reported that its new trade facilitation system led to an initial increase in revenue collection of only 2 per cent, and the cost of sustaining the new system led to an immediate budget crisis and a cessation of funding for the system (Jereos, 2001). Thus the gains and other impacts will clearly differ among countries.

Both the evidence and the historical experience suggest that demand for trade facilitation measures will increase with economic growth and greater trade integration. This is only logical, because as countries grow richer they are able to voluntarily undertake trade facilitation measures and sustain them.

A WAY FORWARD

Trade facilitation measures can play an important role in streamlining administrative procedures, increasing transparency and reducing delays and unnecessary paperwork. But future discussions on trade facilitation need to take into account developing countries' limited resources and capacity and their potential vulnerabilities. They also need to acknowledge the potentially significant opportunity costs for human development that can arise if such measures are implemented prematurely, without the institutional and other prerequisites in place.

The evidence and historical experience suggest that it would be best if the mandate for trade facilitation issues remains in the World Customs Organization (WCO), where it has historically been. Not only does the WCO have the experience needed, but the agreements reached in that forum will be voluntary and non-sanctionable, preserving the ability of governments to make policy choices most appropriate to their circumstances and resource constraints. This approach will make it possible to gradually streamline trade facilitation procedures without the risk of increasing developing country vulnerabilities or compromising human development priorities.

NOTE

1. For example, the European Union's total budget for customs modernization in ten Central and Eastern European countries between 1990–97 was only US$108 million, or roughly US$1.5 million a year. And customs modernization is only one part of trade facilitation.

REFERENCES

Gutiérrez, José Eduardo (Bolivian National Customs). 2001. 'Customs Reform and Modernization Program'. Paper presented at the World Trade Organization Workshop on Technical Assistance and Capacity Building in Trade Facilitation, 10–11 May, Geneva. [www.wto.org/english/tratop_e/tradfa_e/tradfac_workshop_presentations_e.htm]

Clarke, John (European Commission). 2001. Paper presented at the World Trade Organization Workshop on Technical Assistance and Capacity Building in Trade Facilitation, 10–11 May, Geneva. [www.wto.org/english/tratop_e/tradfa_e/ tradfac_workshop_presentations_e.htm]

European Commission. 2000. 'EC Approach to Trade Facilitation'. [europa.eu.int/ comm/trade/index_en.htm and www.unece.org].

Finger, J. Michael, and P. Schuler. 2000. 'Implementation of Uruguay Round Commitments: The Development Challenge'. World Bank, Development Research Group, Washington, DC.

Gurunlian, Jean (United Nations Conference on Trade and Development). 2001. 'Technical Assistance in Trade Facilitation'. Paper presented at the World Trade Organization Workshop on Technical Assistance and Capacity Building in Trade Facilitation, 10–11 May, Geneva. [www.wto.org/english/tratop_e/tradfa_e/ tradfac_workshop_presentations_e.htm]

Jereos, Georges M. (Philippine Bureau of Customs). 2001. Paper presented at the World Trade Organization Workshop on Technical Assistance and Capacity Building in Trade Facilitation, 10–11 May, Geneva. [www.wto.org/english/tratop_e/ tradfa_e/tradfac_workshop_presentations_e.htm]

Lozbenko, Leonid (World Customs Organization). 2001. 'The WCO Experience in T&TA and Capacity Building'. Paper presented at the World Trade Organization Workshop on Technical Assistance and Capacity Building in Trade Facilitation, 10–11 May, Geneva. [www.wto.org/english/tratop_e/tradfa_e/ tradfac_workshop_presentations_e.htm]

Pirzada, Moeed. 2002. 'Pakistan's Experience with New Trade Facilitation Measures'. Background note for Trade and Sustainable Human Development Project. United Nations Development Programme, New York.

Rodrik, Dani. 2001. 'The Global Governance of Trade As If Development Really Mattered'. Background paper for Trade and Sustainable Human Development Project. United Nations Development Programme, New York.

South Centre. 1998. 'WTO Multilateral Trade Agenda and the South'. Geneva.

UNCTAD (United Nations Conference on Trade and Development). 1999. 'The Challenge of Integrating LDCs into the Multilateral System: Coordinating Workshop for Senior Advisors to Ministers of Trade in LDCs in Preparation for the 3rd WTO Ministerial Conference'. UNCTAD/LDC/106. Geneva.

Walsh, James T. (International Monetary Fund). 2001. 'Customs Administration Modernization: The Role of IMF Technical Assistance'. Paper presented at the World Trade Organization Workshop on Technical Assistance and Capacity Building in Trade Facilitation, 10–11 May, Geneva. [www.wto.org/english/tratop_e/ tradfa_e/tradfac_workshop_presentations_e.htm]

Wilson, John S. (World Bank). 2000. 'Trade Facilitation Lending by the World Bank: Recent Experience, Research, and Capacity Building Initiatives'. Draft paper prepared for the World Trade Organization Workshop on Technical Assistance and Capacity Building in Trade Facilitation, 10–11 May, Geneva. [www.wto.org/ english/tratop_e/tradfa_e/tradfac_workshop_presentations_e.htm]

Woo, T. Y., and J. Wilson. 2000. 'Cutting through Red Tape: New Directions for APEC's Trade Facilitation Agenda'. Asia Pacific Foundation of Canada, Vancouver.

WTO (World Trade Organization). 1998a. 'Checklist of Issues Raised during the WTO Trade Facilitation Symposium'. Council for Trade in Goods. G/C/W/113.c. Geneva.

————. 1998b. 'Trade Facilitation: National Experience with Paper-Import and Export Procedures and Requirements'. Communication by Hong Kong, China (SAR). 28 September. G/C/W125. Geneva.

————. 1999a. 'Trade Facilitation in Relation to Development: Communication from the European Communities'. 10 March. G/C/W143_ WT/COMD/W/60. Geneva.

————. 1999b. 'Trade Facilitation: Status Report by the Council for Trade in Goods'. 18 October. G/L/333. Geneva.

————. 2000a. 'Costa Rica's Position on Trade Facilitation'. 31 October. G/C/W/240. Geneva.

————. 2000b. 'Council for Trade in Goods: Chairman's Progress Report on Trade Facilitation'. 5 December. G/L/425. Geneva.

————. 2000c. 'Trade Facilitation: Chile's Experience with Modernisation of Customs Administrations (Based on the Use of Information Technology)'. 31 October. G/C/W239. Geneva.

————. 2000d. 'Trade Facilitation: Technical Assistance and Capacity Building in Relation to Trade Facilitation'. European Communities submission to the Council for Trade in Goods. 24 October. G/C/W/235. Geneva.

————. 2001a. 'Doha Ministerial Declaration'. [www.wto.org/english/thewto_e/minist_e/min01_e/mindecl_e.htm].

————. 2001b. Trade Facilitation Experience Paper by Costa Rica. 17 May. G/C/W265. Geneva.

————. 2002a. 'Trade Facilitation'. [www.wto.org/english/thewto_e/whatis_e/eol/e/wto02/wto2_69.htm#note2].

————. 2002b. 'Trade Facilitation: Article X of GATT on the Publication and Administration of Trade Regulations'. European Communities submission to the Council for Trade in Goods. 12 April. G/C/W/363. Geneva.

CHAPTER 17
STANDARDS

Two related agreements, the Agreement on Technical Barriers to Trade (TBT) and the Agreement on Sanitary and Phytosanitary Standards (SPS), together cover the issues relating to standards in the World Trade Organization (WTO). The TBT Agreement aims to ensure that regulations, standards, testing and certification procedures, which vary from country to country, do not create unnecessary obstacles to trade. The SPS Agreement aims to prevent domestic sanitary and phytosanitary standards from being trade restrictive and protectionist. It focuses on protecting human, animal and plant life and the importing country from risks arising from the entry of pests, toxins, diseases and additives (box 17.1). Under the TBT and SPS Agreements, countries are encouraged to adopt international standards, though they are given flexibility in introducing more rigid or more lax regulations. Scientific justification is required for more rigid regulations.

Standards are important for human development for three main reasons. They protect public health by specifying safety standards. They facilitate trade by clarifying requirements and procedures. But they can be (and often are) used as protectionist barriers to trade by prohibiting the entry of imports that fail to meet the safety regulations of the importing country.[1]

There are three types of standards:

- Product standards, referring to characteristics that goods must possess, such as performance requirements, minimum nutritional content, maximum toxicity or noxious emissions or interoperability with component systems or networks.

- Production standards, referring to conditions under which products are made.

- Labelling requirements, enabling consumers to be informed about a product's characteristics or its conditions of production (Maskus and Wilson, 2000).

The WTO agreements encourage countries to use international standards issued by international standard-setting organizations—such as the International Organization for Standardization (ISO) for product and production standards for the manufacturing of goods, the Codex Alimentarius Commission for food safety,

---

Box 17.1 Multilateral agreements on standards: A brief history

The 1947 General Agreement on Tariffs and Trade (GATT) specified that countries could take measures to protect human, animal or plant life or health as long as these did not unjustifiably discriminate between countries where the same conditions prevailed or were not a disguised restriction on trade (article XX (b)). This concept eventually formed the basis of the Agreement on Sanitary and Phytosanitary Standards (SPS).

By the time the Uruguay Round was launched in 1986, there was a general consensus on the need to reform agricultural trade, and elements of the SPS Agreement were brought into the trade negotiations. At the start of the Uruguay Round the US and the European Community proposed measures, endorsed by the Cairns Group and Japan, for harmonizing standards based on those of international organizations. Developing countries proposed removing sanitary and phytosanitary standards that acted as non-tariff barriers to trade and supported the international harmonization of such standards so that industrial countries would be unable to impose arbitrarily strict ones. These positions were incorporated during the mid-term review of the Uruguay Round, which identified harmonizing international standards, developing an effective process for World Trade Organization members to notify other members about standards, having members provide scientific expertise and judgements to the multilateral trade regime and creating an effective dispute settlement mechanism as priorities.

The Agreement on Technical Barriers to Trade was initially negotiated during the Tokyo Round (1974–79). It was later revised during the Uruguay Round and included in the final act of that round.

Source: Zarilli, 2000b.

---

the International Office of Epizootics for animal health and the Secretariat of the International Plant Protection Convention for plant protection. Countries can introduce stricter measures but should justify these measures on the basis of a risk assessment. The agreements also allow countries to adopt standards lower than those set internationally.

Issues for developing countries

Standards have both direct and indirect links with human development. They have implications for human safety and public health. They can be used as protectionist devices. And they can have substantial implementation costs. Moreover, they may be inappropriate for the situation of developing countries.

Human safety

Governments need to ensure that goods and services in an economy, whether imported or domestically produced, adhere to basic minimum standards of safety relating to toxins, additives, disease-causing organisms and the like. In determining standards at the domestic level, it is important to take into account the country's industrial and resource capabilities. Also important, though more difficult, is to balance domestic public health concerns with differing levels of acceptable standards internationally.

Public health

Developing countries have been required to provide scientific justification for their sanitary and phytosanitary standards since 1999. But many lack the laboratories and technical personnel to conduct proper scientific tests. This affects their ability to set and defend their own standards as well as to meet the proof burdens of importing countries. It also limits their ability to negotiate mutual recognition agreements. These bilaterally negotiated agreements can improve market access by reducing duplicative testing, discrimination of products and the delays involved in both time-consuming processes. Because of the lack of confidence in the laboratory testing of developing countries, few mutual recognition agreements include these states (Zarilli, 2000b). As Zarilli explains (2000a, p. 40),

> 'As importers, developing countries are facing a different risk in the biotechnology field—that of importing and utilizing products which may prove to be harmful for human health or the environment. The limited capacity of developing countries to check products at the border and make their own assessment of the risks and benefits involved, and the lack of domestic legislation in this field, make their concern serious'.

Standards considered important for public health in one country are sometimes seen as protectionist measures in another (box 17.2). For example, the response to bovine spongiform encephalopathy (BSE), or mad cow disease, led to serious trade conflicts. In 2001 Canada banned the import of beef from Brazil not because of scientific evidence that infected cattle were present in Brazil but because of a lack of documentation proving conclusively that the country's cattle were BSE free. Pursuant to rules under the North American Free Trade Agreement, Mexico and the US followed suit, affecting more than US$85 million of Brazilian processed beef exports. The ban, the latest in a series of trade disputes, led to concerns that the issue was less about health and more about trade. Less than a month later, after a Brazilian, Canadian and US technical team conducted on-site validation tests and Brazilian officials supplied extensive documentation, the ban was revoked.

Standards as non-tariff barriers

Developing countries worry that increasingly restrictive sanitary and phytosanitary standards can also act as a non-tariff trade barrier. The decision by the European Union to apply restrictions going beyond international standards on the level of aflatoxins (highly toxic substances produced by certain moulds) in imports of nuts, cereals and dried fruits, for example, will have a significant impact on exports from Africa and Latin America. Otsuki, Wilson and Sewadeh (2001) estimate that African exports of these products to Europe will fall by 64 per cent (US$670 million a year) relative to sales under current international aflatoxin standards. The US groundnut industry, which will also be affected, estimates that complying with the EU sampling

---

BOX 17.2 THE MEAT HORMONE DISPUTE

Since 1989 the European Union (EU) has banned the import of meat and meat products from cattle treated with six growth hormones prohibited in its territory because they are seen as threatening human health. Canada and the US, believing that the use of these hormones is safe, considered the EU measure scientifically baseless and designed to protect EU producers from import competition. In 1996–97 the US challenged the ban in the dispute settlement body of the World Trade Organization (WTO), claiming that it violated the WTO's Agreement on Sanitary and Phytosanitary Standards (SPS).

The WTO dispute and appellate panels ruled in August 1997 that the ban was not based on scientific evidence nor justified by a risk assessment. The European Union had the option of conducting a risk assessment of the hormone-treated meat, and the WTO arbitration panel later gave it 15 months to bring its ban into compliance with rules on sanitary and phytosanitary standards. The appellate body upheld the panel's ruling but also ruled that the EU ban did not result in discrimination and was not a disguised restriction on trade. In addition, the appellate body disagreed with the panel's ruling that the ban was not based on international standards.

After conducting the risk assessment, the European Union decided to continue the ban after the WTO deadline of 13 May 1999. The European Commission offered evidence showing that one of the US-approved hormones was carcinogenic. US trade and health officials dismissed the evidence based on other scientific studies, and the WTO ruled in their favour, allowing the US to retaliate with tariffs on US$116.8 million of EU agricultural imports. Since then the European Union has offered to compensate by liberalizing imports of non-hormone-treated beef but has refused to remove the ban on one of the hormones and has lifted the ban on others only provisionally. US beef producers worry that this leaves the European Union with the option of asking the WTO to stop US retaliation without completely removing the ban.

The dispute highlights the tensions between multilateral rules and domestic policy concerns. From the US perspective it vindicated the SPS Agreement's aim of preventing the misuse of standards as protectionist tools. At the same time the WTO decision attracted widespread criticism from consumer associations and food safety organizations for giving trade priority over health and food safety concerns and for impinging on domestic policy issues.

Source: Zarilli, 2000a; Hanrahan, 2001.

---

method will increase the costs per lot (16 tonnes) by US$150. The cost is likely to be higher for Africa because of a higher expected rejection rate.

In another case the European Commission banned the import of frozen shrimp from Bangladesh from August to December 1997, citing hygiene concerns. The ban cost Bangladesh US$14.6 million in lost revenue, while upgrading sanitary conditions in the shrimp industry cost US$17.6 million (Henson and others, 1999).

Participation in setting standards

Developing countries have had little if any role in designing international standards. The SPS Agreement, for example, was developed outside the WTO, based largely on existing standards and regulations in industrial countries, and then brought in as a companion to the Agreement on Agriculture during the Uruguay Round. When developing countries have participated in developing standards, those standards were often adopted by a simple majority vote, without amendments to reflect the concerns of those in the minority (Zarilli, 2000b). Although developing countries now have greater opportunities to voice their opinions, full participation is often beyond the financial and technical means of even middle-income countries. Take the example of the Philippines. As a member of the 24 ISO Technical Committees, it participates only through correspondence. And it lacks the expertise to provide technical inputs or to gather information from industry and present its position effectively (WTO, 2001).

The attempt to harmonize international standards based on those of industrial countries has led to severe problems in implementation because of countries' varying circumstances and, for many, inadequate capacity. In October 2001, recognizing the need to respect the principle of equivalence, WTO members developed guidelines allowing countries to set standards based on their own capacity and requirements while providing adequate information to permit equivalence in standards to be measured.

Implementation costs

Once standards are in place, developing countries have little option but to comply with them—or risk being excluded from international trade opportunities. Compliance can require extensive investments. A five-year World Bank project to aid Argentina in declaring some agricultural zones free of pests and diseases cost US$82.7 million. And Hungary spent more than US$40 million to improve sanitary conditions in its slaughterhouses (Finger and Schuler, 1999).

Beyond concerns about market access, the SPS and TBT agreements also raise issues relevant to the newer debate over international trade in genetically modified organisms. There is still relatively little information about the potential health and environmental effects of many genetically modified products. Developing countries in particular lack the capacity to completely assess the safety implications of such products, and many are hesitant to allow their import.

Article 5.7 of the SPS Agreement allows countries to provisionally adopt a sanitary and phytosanitary standard affecting the import of a product if it is imposed when relevant scientific information is insufficient or on the basis of pertinent information available. The measure needs to be temporary unless the country seeks to obtain additional information necessary for a more objective risk assessment or reviews the measure within a reasonable time (Zarilli, 2000a). While reaffirming the need to base such measures on scientific evidence, the article does not prevent countries from temporarily restricting imports perceived to be harmful.

The TBT Agreement is more ambiguous: if genetically modified products are classified as 'like products' to conventional products, the agreement provides no grounds for treating them differently. This has important consequences for labelling requirements and thus for public health measures. Since 1998 several EU environment ministers have maintained a de facto moratorium on the authorization of genetically modified organisms for planting or use based on public concerns about their long-term effects on the environment. The US argues that the moratorium is a trade barrier, leading to losses of more than US$200 million a year for US corn farmers. It also argues that mandatory labelling and traceability requirements are inconsistent with WTO rules because they are excessively trade restrictive. The clash between the US and the European Union over the safety of genetically modified foods continues despite efforts to reach an agreement in October 2002. And even though new rules came into force in October that the European Commission hopes will help restart the approvals process, some EU member states are still refusing to lift the ban.

While the issue remains unresolved, there is clearly a thin line between protecting public health and preventing the misuse of standards as protectionist tools, especially where new technologies are concerned. From a human development perspective, public health concerns deserve priority.

A WAY FORWARD

Sanitary and technical standards are important for protecting public health and safety in developing countries, but they need to be developed and implemented at the national level. The SPS and TBT agreements create problems for developing countries: they establish standards that were set without consulting most developing countries, they impose huge implementation costs, and when used as tools of protection, they can drag countries into protracted disputes involving substantial legal and administrative costs.

International standards must be renegotiated to reflect more equitably the policy concerns of developing countries. Moreover, developing countries should be given sufficient financial and technical assistance to participate in setting international standards and to comply with them, enabling them to take greater part in international trade. Financial assistance to train scientific personnel and establish laboratories, perhaps at the regional level, would allow developing countries to better negotiate mutual recognition agreements. The laboratories could also provide technical assistance to industries to facilitate their upgrading. And both developing and industrial countries need adequate capacity to deal with the challenges of new technologies.

The WTO agreements' fundamental principle, requiring scientific evidence as the basis for restricting imports, is a sound one. But it is inadequate for technologies for which the scientific evidence is missing. In cases such as these, the agreements need to give public health concerns priority over trade expansion.

NOTE

1. Theoretically, standards have public good properties. Individual firms are unlikely to absorb the costs of investing in standards unless required to do so, since that may lead other firms to free ride on their efforts (Maskus and Wilson, 2000). In addition, standards may increase trade, since conformity makes goods more substitutable. For example, users may mix and match components within a system if the system is subject

to a certain standard. Under this scenario standardization leads to a more elastic increase in the demand for imported goods than under non-standardization (Baldwin, 2000).

REFERENCES

Baldwin, Richard E. 2000. 'Regulatory Protectionism, Developing Nations, and a Two-Tier World Trade System'. Graduate Institute of International Studies, Geneva.

Finger, J. Michael, and Philip Schuler. 1999. 'Implementation of Uruguay Round Commitments: The Development Challenge'. Policy Research Working Paper 2215. World Bank, Washington, DC.

Griffin, R. 2000. 'History of the Development of the SPS Agreement'. In Food and Agriculture Organization, *Multilateral Trade Negotiations on Agriculture: A Resource Manual*. Rome.

Hanrahan, Charles E. 2001. 'US-European Agricultural Trade: Food Safety and Biotechnology Issues'. Congressional Research Service Report 98-861. Library of Congress, Washington, DC.

Henson, Spencer, Rupert Loader, Alan Swinbank and Maury Bredahl. 1999. 'The Impact of Sanitary and Phytosanitary Measures on Developing Country Exports of Agricultural and Food Products'. Paper presented at the World Bank and World Trade Organization conference on Agriculture and the New Trade Agenda in the WTO 2000 Negotiations, Geneva, 1–2 October.

Macario, Carla. 1998. 'Why and How Do Manufacturing Firms Export? Evidence from Successful Exporting Firms in Chile, Colombia and Mexico'. Ph.D. dissertation. University of Missouri, Columbia.

Maskus, Keith, and John Wilson. 2000. 'Quantifying the Impact of Technical Barriers to Trade: A Review of Past Attempts and the New Policy Context'. Paper presented at the World Bank workshop Quantifying the Trade Effect of Standards and Technical Barriers: Is It Possible?, Washington, DC, 27 April.

Otsuki, Tsunehiro, John Wilson and Mirvat Sewadeh. 2001. 'A Race to the Top? A Case Study of Food Safety Standards and African Exports'. Policy Research Working Paper 2563. World Bank, Development Research Group, Washington, DC.

TWN (Third World Network). 2001. 'The Multilateral Trading System: A Development Perspective'. Background paper for Trade and Sustainable Human Development Project. United Nations Development Programme, New York.

WTO (World Trade Organization). 2001. 'Philippines Experience in the Implementation of the TBT Agreement'. Report to the Committee on Technical Barriers to Trade. G/TBT/W/166. Geneva.

Zarilli, Simonetta. 2000a. 'International Trade in Genetically Modified Organisms and Multilateral Negotiations: A New Dilemma for Developing Countries'. United Nations Conference on Trade and Development, Geneva.

———. 2000b. 'WTO Sanitary and Phytosanitary Agreement: Issues for Developing Countries'. In United Nations Conference on Trade and Development, *Positive Agenda and Future Trade Negotiations*. Geneva and New York: United Nations.

CHAPTER 18
TRADE AND ENVIRONMENTAL POLICY

The health and economic well-being of people living in poverty depends on a wide range of environmental resources: fresh water for drinking, sanitation and agriculture; fertile soil and healthy fisheries for the production of food; and the diverse products of forest and marine ecosystems. Moreover, the diversity of nature—its aesthetic, nutritional and pharmacological variety—greatly enriches people's physical and spiritual experience. But when natural resources are depleted, or when air, soil and water are polluted, poor and economically vulnerable people suffer the most.

The natural environment is thus clearly linked with human development. And sustaining environmental resources becomes critical for human development through the dimension of intergenerational equity. The present generation must ensure that its policies do not diminish the development potential of future generations. Human development today must not be at the cost of human development tomorrow. Thus the links between economic liberalization, environmental protection and human development lie at the core of the debate on sustainable development.

It is difficult to draw definitive conclusions about whether the overall impact of economic liberalization on a country's natural environment will be positive or negative. Properly managed, economic liberalization can contribute to human development. But it can also place added stress on the scarce natural resources on which present and future generations depend. As a result governments often intervene in markets to regulate access to scarce natural resources and to protect their country's environment and citizens from risks associated with particular products and activities. When these environmental measures directly or indirectly affect market access or the competitiveness of imported products, they can give rise to conflicts with international trade rules.

Globalization has increased the interaction between environmental measures and trade rules. As trade grows and spreads, domestic regulators can become more sensitive to risks associated with imported products. For example, many countries have put in place trade regulations aimed at banning or controlling imports of hazardous wastes or of genetically modified organisms. And with the expansion of our understanding of what is meant by the environment, environmental regulators are increasingly designing measures aimed at protecting not just the domestic environment but also environmental assets of shared global concern, such as the ozone layer, the climate system and biological diversity. While some of these measures are supported by multilateral environmental agreements, others have been imposed unilaterally, raising questions about their legitimacy and fairness.

Both industrial and developing countries use trade-related measures to achieve environmental and human health objectives (WTO, 2002). But industrial country governments, which hold the keys to the most important markets, have applied these measures more often and with a greater impact on international trade. Trade-related environmental measures have sometimes been used as a form of trade protectionism, choking off markets to products from countries with lower or merely different environmental standards. Producers in developing countries often find it difficult or impossible to meet these environmental standards. When designed unilaterally, the standards tend to be based on technologies, perceptions of risk and other cultural biases that favour, intentionally or unintentionally, the products of industrial country producers. Developing country governments and producers have had little choice but to adjust their own standards to meet these demands—or lose market share.

This tension between environmental policy and free trade has been further complicated by the role of the General Agreement on Tariffs and Trade (GATT) and its successor, the World Trade Organization (WTO; box 18.1). While not an environmental organization, the WTO has jurisdiction over any measure that has an impact on trade in products between its members, including environmental measures. Discussion within and around the WTO has rarely moved beyond polarized extremes of industrial and developing countries—or dipped below the level of international politics to assess the issues from a human development perspective. But participants in the 2001 WTO Ministerial Conference in Doha agreed to place environmental issues back on the substantive agenda of multilateral trade negotiations. Negotiations will focus on the relationship between the WTO and multilateral environmental agreements, on the liberalization of trade in environmental goods and services and on the reduction of subsidies in the fisheries sector.

This chapter seeks to lay the groundwork for an analysis of the links between environmental policy and free trade from a human development perspective by raising the following questions:

- Why do environmental standards and the measures used to achieve them matter to human development?

- Do societies face trade-offs between maintaining high environmental standards and attracting the trade and investment flows necessary for economic development?

- When trade-offs between environmental and trade policies must be managed, what principles should guide those trade-offs so as to foster human development?

- Which procedures and institutions should be entrusted with managing trade-offs between environmental and trade policies?

Box 18.1 Environmental policy and GATT/WTO: A history of implicit policy-making

The links between trade and the environment have been recognized implicitly in the multilateral trading regime since the design of the General Agreement on Tariffs and Trade (GATT) in 1947. But neither the contracting parties to the GATT nor the members of the World Trade Organization (WTO) have agreed on a specific set of principles and approaches for managing these links. The original GATT included, among the policy objectives that a country could invoke to justify a measure that might otherwise violate its rules, the protection of human, animal or plant life or health and the conservation of exhaustible natural resources. In the years that followed, a growing awareness of environmental and health concerns led to higher product-related standards in industrial countries, with a consequent impact on market access and trade.

The need to strike a balance between trade and environmental concerns was recognized at the Stockholm Conference on the Human Environment, the predecessor of the 1992 United Nations Conference on Environment and Development, held in Rio de Janeiro (the Rio Earth Summit), and the 2002 World Summit for Sustainable Development, held in Johannesburg. Studies by the GATT secretariat on these links led to the establishment in 1971 of the GATT Working Group on Environmental Measures and International Trade. But the working group did not meet until 1991, when several European countries requested that the group be convened to address environmental issues in preparation for the Rio Earth Summit.

Nevertheless, the expanding system of trade rules began to extend into areas of environmental policy. Concerned that environmental and other technical standards might erode progress made in opening markets through tariff reductions, the GATT contracting parties called for additional trade disciplines aimed at regulating this growth in technical barriers. During the Tokyo Round of GATT trade negotiations (1973–79) agreement was reached on the Standards Code, which among other things called for non-discrimination and transparency in the preparation, adoption and application of technical regulations and standards. It did not deal specifically with trade and its environmental links.

During the Uruguay Round (1986–94), which led to the establishment of the WTO, the scope of international trade rules expanded dramatically, including into areas of concern to environmental regulators. Under the WTO, global trade rules now explicitly govern the design of measures aimed at protecting human, animal and plant life or health (the Agreement on Sanitary and Phytosanitary Measures), environment-related technical standards (the Agreement on Technical Barriers to Trade), subsidies related to agriculture and the environment (the Agreement on Agriculture) and restrictions on the patentability of inventions necessary to protect the environment (the Agreement on Trade-Related Aspects of Intellectual Property Rights). In addition, the WTO charter generally endorses the need for trade rules to allow the 'optimal use of the world's resources in accordance with the objective of sustainable development'. The Uruguay Round did not, however, result in any specific guidance on how the WTO system would reconcile conflicting trade and environmental objectives.

Since the Uruguay Round, trade negotiators have struggled and failed to produce any generally applicable solutions. The WTO Committee on Trade and Environment was established in 1995 to study the interaction between trade and environmental policy. It has held dozens of meetings and produced general recommendations calling on WTO members to design trade and environmental policies in a 'mutually supportive' manner. In the interim,

(Box continues on next page.)

however, the GATT and now the WTO dispute settlement systems have processed a series of cases dealing with challenges to environmental and health measures designed to promote clean air, to protect endangered species, to restrict imports of foodstuffs carrying health risks and to ban trade in asbestos. These decisions have produced a patchwork of principles and interpretations that are relevant to the relationship between trade and the environment, but from which it is often difficult to draw general lessons.

Source: UNDP, 1998b; UNDP, 2002b.

WHY DO ENVIRONMENTAL STANDARDS AND THE MEASURES USED TO ACHIEVE THEM MATTER TO HUMAN DEVELOPMENT?

The development and implementation of effective environmental standards can have enormous significance for human development. Whether in industrial or developing countries, environmental damage almost always hits poor people hardest (box 18.2). Ironically, though the poor generally bear the brunt of environmental damage, they are seldom the principal cause. The rich tend to pollute more, contributing more heavily to consumption-driven phenomena such as global warming. The rich also tend to generate more waste, increasing the stress on nature's ability to recover its balance. Environmental standards help conserve natural resources and help prevent and reverse environmental degradation. Both these aspects are crucial for enhancing human capabilities: a secure natural resource base provides economic opportunities, and clean air and water promote good health and nutrition and longer lives.

Environmental standards can also bring indirect benefits to poor people. Compliance with environmental requirements can translate into clean production processes, better working conditions and fewer workplace hazards. All these can enhance labour productivity and improve efficiency, increasing both growth and income. Of course, it can also be argued that higher environmental standards often increase costs, nullifying some of their benefits. But empirical studies show that environmental control costs generally amount to a very small fraction of production costs (Walter, 1973; Robinson, 1988; Grossman and Krueger, 1993). Moreover, by promoting efficient use of energy and materials, environment-friendly production and consumption can release resources for alternative uses. They also generate less waste, reducing the resources required for waste disposal.

Environmental standards, by minimizing environmental harm, can also have a positive gender dimension. Sustainable management of forest and water resources can reduce the time women must devote to collecting drinking water and firewood. And because a lack of appropriate fuel can cause poorer households to slip further down the energy ladder, environmental policies promoting cleaner fuels not only protect forests but also reduce indoor pollution from fuel and firewood—and thus health problems and even deaths among women and girls, the main victims of this pollution.

Box 18.2 EFFECTS OF ENVIRONMENTAL DEGRADATION IN THE DEVELOPING WORLD

- Water-related diseases, such as diarrhoea and cholera, kill an estimated 3 million people in developing countries, most of whom are children under age five.

- Vector-borne diseases such as malaria cause 2.5 million deaths a year. Such diseases are linked to a wide range of environmental conditions or factors related to water contamination and inadequate sanitation.

- Nearly 3 million people die every year from air pollution—more than 2 million from indoor pollution. More than 80 per cent of these deaths are of women and girls.

- As many as 25 million agricultural workers—11 million of them in Africa—may be poisoned each year by fertilizers.

- Soil erosion and other land degradation affect more than 1 billion people, and some 250 million are at risk from falling crop yields.

- Desertification costs the world US$42 billion a year in lost income.

- Over the past decade 154 million hectares of tropical forests have been lost—almost three times the land area of France.

- About 650 million poor people live on marginal and ecologically fragile lands in the developing world.

Source: Jahan, 1998b; UNDP, 2000.

DO SOCIETIES FACE TRADE-OFFS BETWEEN HIGH ENVIRONMENTAL STANDARDS AND TRADE AND INVESTMENT FLOWS?

Do greater trade and capital flows adversely affect the environment—and do high environmental standards discourage trade and investment flows? Given the highly polarized debate about the links between trade and the environment, it is not surprising that these empirical questions have been raised so starkly, and have often been answered simplistically.

Do trade and capital flows harm the environment? Examining the channels through which environmental impacts are transmitted produces no conclusive answer, though it suggests that the net outcome depends on the objective conditions. The few empirical studies that have examined the trade-environment relationship are also inconclusive (see, for example, Smith and Espinosa, 1996). Private capital flows, such as foreign direct investment or portfolio investment, can have a positive or negative net effect on the environment. But in the absence of data, estimating the net effect empirically is difficult.

Do environmental standards matter for trade and capital flows? Environmental control standards can affect trade patterns by raising production costs, if higher costs reduce a country's trade competitiveness. But this does not usually happen, especially since environmental control costs are an insignificant part of production costs. The comparative advantage created by lax environmental standards is generally overwhelmed by other sources of comparative advantage, such

---

BOX 18.3 ECONOMIC LIBERALIZATION AND THE ENVIRONMENT

Case studies reveal that economic liberalization can have positive as well as negative effects on the environment. In China, liberalizing cotton imports has reduced the land under cotton cultivation by more than 1 per cent (about 92,000 hectares). That reduced the application of chemical pesticides and fertilizers, with positive effects on the environment. But as textile production based on cotton imports grew, so did water pollution and consumption. Thus the increase in export revenues from textiles may be offset by the cost of resource use and environmental damage.

In Argentina, liberalizing the marine fishery sector had serious adverse effects on the sustainability of the most exploited species. Growth in unregulated fishing activity during the 1990s pushed fish stocks beyond their maximum sustainable yield, leading to a direct cost of about US$500 million. If expansion of the sector had been properly managed, the net economic gains from the same species could have amounted to US$5 billion over the same ten-year period.

The liberalization of shrimp aquaculture in Bangladesh led to a 70 per cent increase in the sector's exports between 1980 and 1998. But even a partial cost-benefit analysis shows that it also led to significant costs through land degradation, mangrove destruction and human health impacts. The cumulative costs of these adverse effects have been estimated to be 20–30 per cent of the revenues from shrimp production.

Source: UNEP, 2002.

---

as differences in infrastructure, technologies, resource endowments, the macroeconomic policy framework and human and physical capital. So, higher environmental standards do not reduce comparative advantage and thus do not undermine trade competitiveness.

WHAT PRINCIPLES SHOULD GUIDE THE MANAGEMENT OF TRADE-OFFS BETWEEN ENVIRONMENTAL AND TRADE POLICIES?

In general, protecting the environment and promoting trade and investment flows should not be characterized as mutually exclusive policy objectives. Nevertheless, in some circumstances environmental measures can adversely affect trade, and trade and investment liberalization can adversely affect the environment. Links between economic liberalization and environmental protection can result in either synergy or conflict, depending on how the relationship is managed (box 18.3).

Trade-related environmental measures designed to manage this relationship can take a variety of forms (UNDP, 2002b):

- *Environmental taxes.* To internalize the costs of environmentally harmful products and to encourage consumers to purchase environmentally preferable alternatives, taxes could be levied on product content (such as the carbon content of a fuel) or on production processes (the energy intensity of production). If an environmental tax is linked to a production process and is levied on an imported product, it can raise trade concerns if it is seen as seeking to regulate behaviour in the exporting state.

- *Environmental subsidies and procurement policies.* To encourage environment-friendly economic activities, governments can provide direct or indirect payments to producers who meet environmental standards and government agencies can use their purchasing power to support environment-friendly products. Where such payments or purchasing policies directly or indirectly favour domestically produced goods, they may run counter to free trade rules.

- *Environmental technical standards.* Governments can protect consumers and the environment by supporting the use of environmental technical standards, such as content requirements or energy efficiency standards. These can be mandatory standards that must be met before the product can be imported or marketed, or they can become part of voluntary schemes designed to promote best practice.

- *Trade bans and quarantines.* Governments can take the extreme step of banning the import and sale of products. Such bans most often take the form of sanitary or phytosanitary measures designed to protect human, animal or plant life or human health from pests or diseases carried by a product or to prevent the import of such dangerous materials as asbestos and hazardous waste. Some governments have gone further, banning the import of products that do not in themselves pose a risk to the environment but whose production may have harmed the environment.

- *Environmental labelling.* Governments may use labelling schemes to alert consumers to the hazards or benefits associated with certain products. Such schemes can be mandatory or voluntary. Those that seek to distinguish between otherwise identical products on the basis of how environment-friendly their production process is have been criticized as advocating measures that run counter to free trade disciplines.

When deciding whether to apply such measures, governments may assess the potential costs and benefits of market intervention, including potential welfare gains and losses like those described above. Governments of WTO member countries also need to take into account the compatibility of any such measures with their trade obligations. Moreover, any trade-offs that need to be made between environmental and trade policies must be guided by principles that serve—or at least do not undermine—the interests of poor people. At present, however, national and international institutions with the authority to manage such trade-offs appear ill equipped to effectively incorporate the human development dimension.

While the disciplines of the WTO vary from agreement to agreement, trade rules generally assess the legitimacy of trade-related environmental measures on the basis of whether they limit market access to imported products or otherwise directly or indirectly discriminate against 'like' imported products. If a trade-related environmental measure is challenged in the WTO system, any restrictions that it places on trade will be tested to see whether they are necessary to achieve a legitimate environmental objective. Global trade rules are designed to weed out trade-related environmental measures that restrict trade more than necessary to achieve such an objective, that are arbitrarily or unjustifiably discriminatory or that

---

BOX 18.4 THE SHRIMP-TURTLE DISPUTE

India, Malaysia, Pakistan and Thailand used the WTO dispute settlement system to challenge US restrictions on the import of shrimp caught with nets known to drown endangered sea turtles. The US ban affected all countries that did not require shrimping boats in their jurisdiction to use essentially the same 'turtle excluder devices' US shrimping boats had to use. Developing countries' main objection to the ban was that it distinguished between otherwise identical shrimp on the basis of how they had been caught. By conditioning access to its huge consumer market, the US was in effect using its economic clout to coerce other countries into changing their environmental standards.

The WTO dispute settlement process found that this trade-related environmental measure was arbitrary and unjustifiable, because it required exporters to use essentially the same environmental technology used in the US in order to gain market access. The WTO process required the US to redraft the measure so that it would allow exporters to demonstrate that other, equally effective but more locally appropriate techniques for protecting turtles were in use. It also encouraged the US to make greater efforts to engage its trading partners in bilateral negotiations and to provide financial and technical assistance to countries wishing to comply with the US requirements.

The outcome angered many developing countries, since it allowed the US to continue its import restrictions. Still, WTO disciplines led to the redesign of the measure to take better account of development concerns.

Source: UNDP, 2002b.

---

amount to disguised protectionism. Scientific risk assessments and internationally agreed standards often provide the main reference points for determining the legitimacy of trade-related environmental measures.

For developing countries the WTO disciplines can act as both a sword and a shield when applied to trade-related environmental measures. WTO disciplines can provide a basis for challenging measures put in place for the illegitimate purpose of protecting markets from competition, helping to moderate the potential harm of one country's trade policies on another's development choices (box 18.4). But WTO disciplines can also provide a means for challenging trade-related environmental measures put in place by developing countries.

For example, a number of developing countries, including China and Sri Lanka, have sought to restrict imports of genetically modified crops, citing health, environmental and socio-economic concerns. Many developing countries fear that introducing genetically modified crops could undermine traditional farming practices and increase the economic dependency of poor farmers on the patented technologies of multinational seed suppliers. Industrial country exporters have pressured these countries to suspend their trade restrictions, by invoking WTO trade disciplines and the need to justify concerns about the risks of genetically modified organisms with 'sound science'. Although no formal dispute relating to genetically modified organisms has arisen at the WTO, there can be little doubt that the threat of potential WTO-backed sanctions has helped pry open markets to these products.

From a human development perspective, the issue is not simple. Some have argued that genetically modified seeds can enhance food security in developing countries by incorporating genetic traits that increase crops' productivity, nutritional value and resistance to drought and diseases. At the heart of the debate is a question about how much freedom each country should have to balance trade and domestic concerns in the way it deems best, given its human development objectives.

By relying on scientific disciplines and internationally agreed standards to test the legitimacy of trade measures, the WTO system may disadvantage countries that lack technical capacity and are marginalized from international standard setting. When developing countries have played a more forceful role in shaping international trade policy outside the WTO system, they have helped design trade rules more sensitive to development concerns. For example, under the Basel Convention on the Control of Transboundary Movements of Hazardous Wastes and Their Disposal, exporters are required to seek the prior informed consent of an importer before any shipment can take place. Under the Cartagena Protocol on Biosafety, which will govern international trade in genetically modified seeds and other products, a developing country has the right to demand that the potential exporter of a covered product pay for a scientific risk assessment before deciding whether to allow its import.

In the WTO negotiations, however, many developing countries see support for trade-related environmental measures as driven largely by environmental interests in high-income countries. Many developing country trade negotiators argue, at least implicitly, that environmental quality is a luxury good matching consumer preferences in industrial countries. Environmental standards to meet legitimate environmental and health concerns of a country's own population are broadly acceptable. But controversy arises when those standards appear to be arbitrarily high or designed to force changes in the environmental standards of the exporting country. Developing countries see such standards as *green imperialism* or *eco-imperialism*, arguing that if the trading system continues to develop in this way, it will endanger their growth and development in the long run.

Moreover, trade restrictions in the name of environmental standards seem to run counter to the trade liberalization reforms that developing countries have been encouraged to pursue in recent years. And complying with environmental standards imposed by industrial countries could increase dependency for many developing countries, because it may require acquiring clean production technology and environmental quality certifications. These have price tags. And the technology may be available from only a few firms, allowing them to charge monopoly rents for its use and licensing.

Industrial country governments and consumers increasingly support the use of eco-labels showing that such products as fish, timber and agricultural commodities have been produced in an environment-friendly way. Most of these schemes are voluntary, but the political and commercial pressure to display eco-labels is growing in many sectors important to developing countries. Such schemes require assessing the ecological impact of goods during their life cycle, from production through consumption and disposal. Developing country producers not only have to pay for eco-labels but sometimes feel compelled to obtain multiple eco-labels for the same product if they intend to export it to different markets. And many have difficulty obtaining appropriate and timely information on eco-labelling schemes as well as import regulations.

For all these reasons many developing country trade negotiators have a negative, even hostile, view of the trade and environment debate. They have resisted the opportunity to propose their own principles for managing trade-offs between trade and environmental objectives in ways that could help distinguish legitimate environmental policy from disguised protectionism. But outside the WTO the international community has endorsed a number of broad principles applicable to the trade, environment and development interface (box 18.5).

From a human development perspective, these general principles can be distilled into three central insights relating to trade-related environmental measures:

- Each country should be free to manage its domestic environmental problems consistent with its human development priorities. Trade measures designed to protect a country's consumers and its national environment from hazardous products are a legitimate part of its human development strategy. But trade measures designed to coerce the harmonization of domestic environmental standards by another country are fundamentally protectionist. It is inappropriate to use trade policy to negate a legitimate source of comparative advantage conferred by differences in environmental endowments, pollution assimilation capacities or social preferences relating to environmental outcomes. Such trade measures, by imposing specific environmental standards that may not be appropriate, may conflict with the development priorities and policies of the exporting country. Coercive measures, unilaterally designed and imposed, are inherently undemocratic and run counter to the principles of human development.

- Trade measures targeted at global or transboundary environmental problems, if designed unilaterally and without consultation with the trading partners affected, are likely to be inefficient and inequitable instruments for correcting market failures. Multilaterally negotiated standards and policies based on the assignment of property rights, the creation of markets and production or consumption interventions are economically more efficient and more equitable. Such standards should reflect the principle of common but differentiated responsibility: domestic environmental standards aimed at achieving global environmental objectives must take into account differences between countries in economic development levels and financial and technical capacity.

- Trade measures nonetheless have a useful role to play in securing participation in and compliance with internationally agreed standards such as multilateral environmental agreements. The threat of trade sanctions may be enough to alter the behaviour of would-be free-riders.

BOX 18.5 RIO PRINCIPLES FOR MANAGING TRADE-OFFS BETWEEN TRADE AND THE ENVIRONMENT

At the 1992 United Nations Conference on Environment and Development, held in Rio de Janeiro, more than 100 heads of state and delegations from 178 countries adopted the Rio Declaration on Environment and Development. This declaration sets forth principles that reflect an international consensus on how to balance trade-offs between environmental and trade objectives and that have guided the negotiations of environmental treaties and trade disputes. Following are four of those principles:

- States should co-operate to promote a supportive and open international economic system that would lead to economic growth and sustainable development in all countries to better address the problems of environmental degradation. Trade policy measures for environmental purposes should not constitute a means of arbitrary or unjustifiable discrimination or a disguised restriction on international trade. Unilateral actions to deal with environmental challenges outside the jurisdiction of the importing country should be avoided. Environmental measures addressing transboundary or global environmental problems should, as far as possible, be based on an international consensus. (Principle 12)

- States should effectively co-operate to discourage or prevent the relocation and transfer to other States of any activities and substances that cause severe environmental degradation or are found to be harmful to human health. (Principle 14)

- States shall enact effective environmental legislation. Environmental standards, management objectives and priorities should reflect the environmental and developmental context to which they apply. Standards applied by some countries may be inappropriate and of unwarranted economic and social cost to other countries, in particular developing countries. (Principle 11)

- In order to protect the environment, the precautionary approach shall be widely applied by States according to their capabilities. Where there are threats of serious or irreversible damage, lack of full scientific certainty shall not be used as a reason for postponing cost-effective measures to prevent environmental degradation. (Principle 15)

In general, using trade-restrictive measures for environmental purposes is more legitimate when the aim is to enlist participation and compliance for addressing widely recognized global environmental problems.

These general principles can take shape only when applied to specific trade-offs. Thus the legitimacy of trade-related environmental measures must be tested case by case.

WHICH PROCEDURES AND INSTITUTIONS SHOULD BE ENTRUSTED WITH MANAGING TRADE-OFFS BETWEEN ENVIRONMENTAL AND TRADE POLICIES?

Reaching an international consensus on how to manage trade-offs between environmental and trade policies, beyond a set of general principles, has proved difficult. The WTO Committee on Trade and Environment (CTE) has missed an important opportunity. Rather than seeking synergies between environment

---

Box 18.6 Proposals in the 1990s on Environment and Trade

- Introduce a new general exception under GATT/WTO to supplement the existing exceptions for measures designed to protect human, animal and plant life or health and to conserve natural resources. Debates have focused on the appropriate scope for the exception. A loosely worded exception would allow wide-ranging departures from existing GATT/WTO disciplines, while a tightly worded and constrained exception would be both hard to draft and difficult to enforce.

- Encourage the use of case-by-case, negotiated waivers that would exclude from WTO jurisdiction certain categories of trade-related measures, such as those authorized under multilateral environmental agreements. But waivers require unanimity in the WTO, and there has been no consensus on how to proceed.

- Negotiate environmental revisions to existing WTO articles, perhaps in a special trade and environment mini-round. Many problems may arise here. One is that it could potentially be argued that nearly every WTO article requires rewriting on environmental grounds.

- Take more targeted approaches to trade and environment, such as revising relevant WTO articles to clarify their environmental content. The problem here is that in the past WTO articles have been clarified through the route of dispute settlement and panel reports, and while this might appear to be the obvious approach, the outcomes have come under severe attack.

Source: UNDP, 2002a.

---

and trade as equally legitimate policy objectives, the CTE has explored how to fit environmental concerns within the framework of existing trade regimes (Ewing and Tarasofsky, 1996). It has focused narrowly on two issues: whether eco-labelling schemes constitute non-tariff trade barriers and whether there should be a 'safe harbour' within the WTO for the trade-related measures included in the many multilateral environmental agreements. While failing to produce any concrete outcomes, the CTE process has covered analytical issues, institutional concerns and political questions. And from observers of and participants in the environment-trade debate, several suggestions emerged in the 1990s on what could be done to promote the global interest and what developing countries could do (box 18.6).

The work programme of the WTO agreed at the Doha ministerial meeting, and scheduled to run from 2002 to January 2005, gives the CTE a renewed and more focused mandate. The Doha agenda reflects a strange mix resulting from a tough set of horse trades. It has essentially been divided between issues that will be the subject of negotiations and those that will be the subject of further analysis and debate. Negotiations will move ahead on the relationship between WTO rules and specific trade obligations in multilateral environmental agreements and on the reduction or elimination of tariff and non-tariff barriers to environmental goods and services. In both cases, defining the scope of the mandate will be crucial. Which multilateral environmental agreements can be considered to have 'specific trade obligations'? Will the negotiations conclude by privileging measures taken under some multilateral environmental agreements over measures taken under others?

As discussed, some developing countries have championed the strong human development dimension of some multilateral environmental agreements. For example, some developing countries want progress in ensuring that the interface between the Agreement on Trade-Related Aspects of Intellectual Property Rights (TRIPS) and the Convention on Biological Diversity will respect traditional knowledge. Others wish to ensure that the Cartagena Protocol on Biosafety, the Basel Convention on Hazardous Wastes, the Rotterdam Convention on Prior Informed Consent and the Stockholm Convention on Persistent Organic Pollutants protect the ability of developing country governments to use trade measures to protect their citizens and domestic environment. But many developing countries are also concerned that these negotiations will allow multilateral environmental agreements to become a blanket exception for protectionist measures.

The Doha work programme on environmental goods and services carries both opportunities and risks for developing countries. Liberalizing trade in environmental products could promote developing country access to environment-friendly technologies and know-how. And it could open industrial country markets to environmentally preferable products from developing countries, including organic agricultural products and sustainable forest products (UNCTAD, 2002). But developing country negotiators must be careful to ensure that privileging certain environmental goods in market access negotiations does not lead to trade barriers based on process and production methods. They also need to take care in the negotiations on the liberalization of environmental services. Concerns have been raised that these negotiations could be used to pry open to foreign investors such environmentally and developmentally sensitive sectors as forestry, fisheries and water services delivery.

Under the Doha agenda, negotiations will also move ahead on fisheries subsidies. Many developing countries and environmentalists have found common ground in calling for reducing these subsidies, which are distorting international markets and pushing some species towards extinction. The world spends about US$14–21 billion—equivalent to 20–25 per cent of global fisheries revenues—each year to shore up inefficient fisheries operations. The subsidies create overcapacity among the producers they benefit, encouraging them to overfish and endangering species.

Other areas for substantive negotiations related to the environment and human development are on the Doha agenda of WTO bodies other than the CTE. These include the relationship between the TRIPS Agreement and the Convention on Biological Diversity in the context of the protection of traditional knowledge and folklore, and negotiations on the reform of agricultural subsidies, including those designed to protect the rural environment and promote sustainable rural livelihoods.

Relegated to further analysis in the CTE are several issues of critical concern to developing countries. The Doha agenda calls for the CTE to continue its analytical work on the effects of environmental measures on market access, especially for developing countries. This work will focus on environmental labelling requirements, relevant provisions of the TRIPS Agreement and situations in which eliminating or reducing trade restrictions and distortions would benefit trade, the environment and development ('win-win-win' scenarios). The work will continue to look at unresolved issues relating to the internalization of environmental costs; process and production methods, where WTO rules have increasingly come into conflict with global product life-cycle perspectives; and the gradual removal of domestic energy, chemical and water subsidies that distort trade and damage the environment.

Finally, during the Doha-mandated negotiations the CTE and its sister organ, the Committee on Trade and Development, are each expected to act as a forum to identify and debate the developmental and environmental aspects of the negotiations, to help ensure that sustainable development is appropriately reflected. This could open a new opportunity for developing country governments and civil society to assess the potential environmental and development impact of international trade rules as they are negotiated.

Without significant new efforts by developing countries and their negotiating partners, the treatment of environmental issues in the multilateral trade regime is likely to remain unsatisfactory from a human development perspective. Institutions that might have asserted jurisdiction over such issues in a manner better reflecting a human development perspective, such as the Commission on Sustainable Development, have been unable or unwilling to intervene. Nor did the process leading up to the September 2002 World Summit on Sustainable Development contribute much.

The summit's plan of implementation usefully re-emphasizes that trade policy should be seen as a means to achieving sustainable development and eradicating poverty. It highlights the need to reform subsidies that damage the environment and to support domestic and international markets for environment-friendly goods and services. It recalls the Rio principles for managing the links between trade and the environment by discouraging unilateral trade measures and encouraging international consensus on measures to address transboundary or global environmental problems. And it stresses the need for more technical assistance and capacity building to promote effective participation of developing countries in trade and environmental policy-making. But most of the text was drawn from existing agreements, including the Doha agenda, and it provides little concrete guidance on how to resolve any conflicts between trade, the environment and development.

A WAY FORWARD

The trade and environment debate remains polarized and heated, with developing countries playing a largely defensive role. Many developing countries fear protectionism and a 'green capture' of policies by environmental lobbyists in industrial countries. And they feel as if they are often bypassed by multilateral policy discussions. For these reasons the post-Doha work programme points to the need to ensure that developing countries participate effectively in setting standards and have greater access to legal, scientific and economic advice.

Empowered and informed developing countries can promote a positive, human development–based agenda in a new round of negotiations on trade and the environment. Such an agenda could seek to ensure:

- That trade policy allows countries to pursue locally appropriate solutions to their domestic environmental challenges without fear of facing trade sanctions by countries with different environmental priorities. This flexibility should include the ability to impose import restrictions to protect against health and environmental risks associated with specific products.

- That the evolving relationship between global trade rules and multilateral environmental agreements respects the principle of common but differentiated responsibilities. Domestic environmental standards aimed at achieving global environmental objectives must take into account differences between countries in economic development levels and financial and technical capacity.

- That efforts to liberalize trade in environmental goods and services help identify products and sectors that will open new opportunities for developing country exporters, rather than constructing new conditions for market access.

- That developing country policy-makers and civil society participate fully and effectively in assessing the potential environmental and development impact of any new trade rules negotiated.

- That negotiations on environment-related issues of agricultural reform and intellectual property rights reform take into account the human development dimension. As discussed in greater detail in other chapters, initiatives in this area should allow developing countries to retain trade policies that support food security and rural livelihoods (chapter 5) and ensure respect for traditional knowledge (chapter 11).

All these issues must be addressed in the context of human development rather than purely from the perspective of market liberalization or environmental protection. The ultimate aim should be to coordinate trade and environmental measures so that they help enhance human capabilities and expand human choices. All countries, developing and industrial, should work towards this goal.

REFERENCES

Ewing, K. P., and R. G. Tarasofsky. 1996. 'The Trade and Environment Agenda: Survey of Major Issues and Proposals—From Marrakesh to Singapore'. IUCN–World Conservation Union, Environmental Law Centre, Bonn.

Grossman, A. M., and A. B. Krueger. 1993. 'Environmental Impacts of the North American Free Trade Agreement'. In P Garber, ed, *The US-Mexico Free Trade Agreement*. Cambridge, Mass: MIT Press.

Jahan, Selim. 1998a. 'Consumption, Natural Resource Use and Environment: Impact for Human Development'. United Nations Development Programme, Human Development Report Office, New York.

———. 1998b. 'Environmental Damage: Unequal Human Impacts'. United Nations Development Programme, Human Development Report Office, New York.

Low, Patrick. 1992. 'Trade and Environment: A Survey of Literature'. In Patrick Low, ed, *International Trade and the Environment*. World Bank Discussion Paper 159. Washington, DC.

Panayotou, Theodore. 1999. 'Globalization and Environment'. In United Nations Development Programme, 'Background Papers for the Human Development Report 1999'. Vol. 1. Human Development Report Office, New York.

Rapetto, R. 1993. 'Trade and Environment Policies: Achieving Complementarities and Avoiding Conflicts'. World Resources Institute, Washington, DC.

———. 1995. 'Jobs, Competitiveness, and Environmental Regulations: What Are the Real Issues?' World Resources Institute, Washington, DC.

Robinson, H. D. 1988. 'Industrial Pollution Abatement: The Impact on the Balance of Trade'. *Canadian Journal of Economics* 21 (1): 187–99.

Smith, K., and J. S. Espinosa. 1996. 'Environmental and Trade Policies: Some Methodological Lessons'. *Environment and Development Economics* 1 (1): 19–40.

South Asian Watch on Trade, Economics and Environment. 2000. 'Trade, Environment and Sustainable Development in South Asia'. Briefing Paper 2. Kathmandu.

Strutt, A., and K. Anderson. 1998. 'Will Trade Liberalization Harm the Environment? The Case of Indonesia to 2020'. Seminar Paper 98-04. University of Adelaide, Centre for International Economic Studies.

UNCTAD (United Nations Conference on Trade and Development). 2002. *Trade and Development Report*. Geneva.

UNDP (United Nations Development Programme). 1998a. *Human Development Report 1998*. New York: Oxford University Press.

———. 1998b. *Trade and Environment: Capacity Building for Sustainable Development.* New York.

———. 1999. *Human Development Report 1999*. New York: Oxford University Press.

———. 2000. *Human Development Report 2000*. New York: Oxford University Press.

———. 2002a. 'Environmental Standards and Trade Policy'. Background note for Trade and Sustainable Human Development Project. United Nations Development Programme, New York.

———. 2002b. 'Trade and Environmental Policy'. Background note for Trade and Sustainable Human Development Project. United Nations Development Programme, New York.

UNDP (United Nations Development Programme) and European Commission. 2000. *Attacking Poverty while Improving the Environment: Towards Win-Win Policy Options*. New York: UNDP.

UNEP (United Nations Environment Programme). 2002. UNEP Brief on Economics, Trade and Sustainable Development. Geneva.

Walter, I. 1973. 'The Pollution Content of American Trade'. *Western Economic Journal* 11: 61–70.

Whalley, John. 1996. 'Trade and Environment, WTO, and the Developing Countries'. In Robert Z. Lawrence, Dani Rodrik and John Whalley, eds, *Emerging Agenda for Global Trade: High Stakes for Developing Countries*. Policy Essay 20. Washington, DC: Overseas Development Council.

———. 1999. 'Developing Countries in the Global Economy: A Forward-Looking View'. In United Nations Development Programme, 'Background Papers for the Human Development Report 1999'. Vol. 1. Human Development Report Office, New York.

Wheeler, David, and Ashoka Mody. 1992. 'International Investment Decisions: The Case of US Firms'. *Journal of International Economics* 33: 57–76.

WTO (World Trade Organization). 2002. 'Environmental Database for 2001'. Note by the Secretariat on environment-related trade measures or provisions notified to the WTO Secretariat in 2001. WT/CTE/EDB/1. Geneva.

CHAPTER 19
STRENGTHENING CAPACITIES

A global trading system based on a negotiating framework cannot deliver fair outcomes unless its members have the capacity to both negotiate international trade agreements and extract benefits from them that are in their interest. None of the reforms proposed in this book will bring the hoped-for results unless developing countries gain the capacity to use the reforms effectively in achieving their development goals. Strengthening the capacities of developing countries, especially the least developed countries, is therefore a crucial part of a human development–oriented multilateral trading regime.

Most developing countries lack the capacity to set the agenda for and the pace of negotiations in the multilateral trading system, to negotiate effectively on issues of greatest concern to them or to fulfil their commitments to the trading regime. Many of the reforms proposed in this book include measures to develop such capacities.

Many developing countries lack adequate or effective policy research capacity. This is especially true of sub-Saharan African countries, which remain severely handicapped by their inadequate understanding of the complex issues being negotiated. Until recently they had defined goals in general terms, and they have lacked resources for the policy research and analysis necessary to assess how different agreements might affect their interests (Ohiorhenuan, 1998). But in more recent years their capacity to define goals and articulate their interests has improved. This has been evident in the stances taken by the Like-Minded Group, the African Group, the group of least developed countries and the African, Caribbean and Pacific group in the lead-up to and at the World Trade Organization (WTO) Ministerial Conference in Doha in 2001. Nevertheless, there is an urgent need to further strengthen the capacities of developing countries.

Probably in part because of differing interests on a range of trade issues, developing countries as a bloc have not devoted financial or technical resources to creating an independent research programme on trade issues equivalent to the Washington, DC–based Group of 24 (G-24) research programme on international monetary and financial issues.[1] The G-24 programme, a useful model for research on trade and development themes, is already studying some of the new issues, such as investment and competition policy. The United Nations Conference on Trade and Development (UNCTAD) through its 'Positive Agenda', the South Centre through its trade programme, and some non-governmental organizations have provided policy research and analysis of this kind. To be sustainable, however, such a programme needs to be genuinely independent of both the UN system and non-governmental organizations and clearly owned and led by developing countries. The South Centre trade programme, given its mandate and existing work in the area, could potentially play this role if strengthened and enhanced.

TECHNICAL ASSISTANCE WITHIN THE FRAMEWORK OF THE WORLD TRADE ORGANIZATION

This section focuses on capacity development and assistance measures in the context of WTO agreements and through WTO-partnered initiatives outside the agreements—the Joint Integrated Technical Assistance Programme to Selected Least Developed and Other African Countries and the Integrated Framework for Trade-Related Technical Assistance. An analysis of the measures in the WTO agreements shows that they are limited in scope, aiming primarily at compliance with WTO provisions. The WTO-partnered initiatives have had mixed results.

World Trade Organization agreements

Within the WTO, efforts are made to address the gap in capacity by providing technical assistance under WTO agreements. This assistance emphasizes workshops, seminars, technical missions, briefing sessions and documentation to assist developing countries in adjusting to WTO rules, implementing their WTO commitments and exercising their rights as members.

Each agreement has specific clauses on technical assistance (box 19.1). Although many of these provisions are binding, they tend to be difficult to implement because they require mutual agreement on the terms of the assistance provided.

The technical assistance provisions are comprehensive, span the range of agreements and are aimed at assisting developing countries as they integrate into the global trading system. But most technical assistance in this framework has failed to address the real needs of developing countries on two counts; in assisting them to participate effectively at the international level and in helping to build capacity on their terms and tailored to their needs. Part of the reason is that such technical assistance is limited primarily to helping developing countries become compliant with WTO provisions rather than helping them build the capacity to trade more, negotiate better or adjust internally to the demands of increased integration. The measures suffer from four main shortcomings:

- *Compliance focused.* Although the technical assistance has been aimed at assisting developing countries in complying with WTO agreements and commitments, there has been little work done to estimate the

---

BOX 19.1 TECHNICAL ASSISTANCE IN WORLD TRADE ORGANIZATION AGREEMENTS

- The General Agreement on Trade in Services refers to technical assistance from the WTO secretariat and the need for members to encourage and support participation in the field of telecommunications services.

- The Agreement on Trade-Related Aspects of Intellectual Property Rights requires that members provide, on request and on mutually agreed terms and conditions, technical and financial cooperation for developing and least developed countries (article 67).

- The Agreement on Sanitary and Phytosanitary Standards requires that members agree to facilitate technical assistance, bilaterally or through international organizations. And where meeting sanitary and phytosanitary standards requires substantial investment, the agreement obligates members to provide assistance to allow developing countries to expand market access opportunities for the product affected (articles 9.1 and 9.2).

- The Agreement on Technical Barriers to Trade requires that, if requested, members advise developing country members on regulations and grant technical assistance on mutually acceptable terms in a way that does not create unnecessary obstacles to developing country exports (articles 11 and 12).

- The Agreement on Customs Valuations requires industrial country members to furnish technical assistance on request and on mutually agreed terms.

- Under the rules for dispute settlement the WTO secretariat agrees to make available a qualified legal expert to any developing country member (article 27.2).

---

costs of compliance and factor them into the technical assistance efforts. These costs can be significant, with compliance often involving substantial administrative requirements, changes in legislation and new institutions and enforcement mechanisms. Moreover, the technical assistance provisions are narrowly defined and often have little relevance to the development process of countries. And many have little relevance for countries at low levels of economic and industrial development.

- *Donor driven.* Technical assistance has remained primarily a top-down process with little ownership by developing countries. But donor-driven technical assistance has historically not worked: it undermines local capacity, distorts priorities, increases administrative burdens and is driven by donor priorities and needs rather than local requirements. More important, it focuses on 'development as displacement rather than development as transformation' (UNDP, 2002, p. 8).

- *Open ended.* The provisions for technical assistance are largely open ended. They are contingent on future negotiations, with most requiring that technical assistance be provided 'on mutually agreed terms' or 'if requested'. Much of the technical assistance has been intended as a quid pro quo for an expanded negotiation agenda and has been used as a political tool to promote a negotiation mandate (Tandon, 2002). While the terms of the technical assistance provisions are reasonable, they are hard to implement and often require yet more negotiating capacity in developing countries. Moreover, even though the provisions are technically binding, there are few mechanisms to ensure that they are actually implemented.

- *Inadequate and inappropriate provisions.* The provisions for technical assistance are inadequate for addressing the needs of developing countries. Technical assistance fails to recognize the diversity among developing countries and their needs, rarely going beyond categorizing countries as least developed or not. Moreover, the WTO has limited personnel and other resources for meeting the demands and requests of developing countries.

Joint Integrated Technical Assistance Programme to Selected Least Developed and Other African Countries

By contrast, the Joint Integrated Technical Assistance Programme to Selected Least Developed and Other African Countries (JITAP) appears to have played an important and useful role in developing recipient countries' capacity to understand the international trading system. JITAP emerged in 1994 as a result of a call by African trade ministers to strengthen their capacity to participate in the WTO, to enable their countries to integrate effectively into the international trading system and take advantage of new trade opportunities through greater export readiness. Formalized in March 1998, the programme is jointly sponsored by the International Trade Centre, UNCTAD and WTO. It provided initial assistance to eight African countries: four least developed countries (Benin, Burkina Faso, the United Republic of Tanzania and Uganda) and four others (Côte d'Ivoire, Kenya, Ghana and Tunisia).

One of the most effective roles of JITAP has been in building human resource capabilities. Another has been in fostering participation beyond a country's government on the issues and debates relating to the multilateral trading system—involving business and even civil society organizations. It has also played a useful role in bringing together country-level experience for the negotiators in Geneva, to support a better articulation of their interests.

Still, JITAP could be much more effective. It has suffered from several organizational and administrative problems (Pallangyo, 2002). A key concern is JITAP's continued focus on market access and marketing issues rather than on strengthening the supply side of developing country economies, essential for export expansion. JITAP could also be linked more explicitly with poverty reduction and human development strategies.

Integrated Framework for Trade-Related Technical Assistance

Along with the technical assistance provisions in the WTO agreements, the ministerial conference in 1996 set the agenda for assisting and promoting the integration of the least developed countries into the global economy and the multilateral trading system. The programme for doing so is the Integrated Framework for Trade-Related Technical Assistance, a joint initiative of the WTO, the International Trade Centre, UNCTAD, the World Bank, the International Monetary Fund and UNDP.

It was widely agreed that the Integrated Framework achieved little in its first three-year phase, getting off the ground only in 2000, revamped and with a mandate to integrate ('mainstream') trade and trade-related endeavours of least developed countries into their national development strategies through the instrument of the poverty reduction strategy paper (PRSP).

The Integrated Framework, as remodelled, seeks to identify key constraints to a country's ability to successfully mainstream trade priorities into national development strategies. Based on findings of a diagnostic study, a programme of trade and trade-related technical assistance is then planned for strengthening the economy's competitiveness, including by building human and institutional capacity.

But the Integrated Framework has so far failed to effectively link trade and poverty reduction strategies, in part because poverty reduction strategies give priority to public expenditure policies rather than to enhancing economic productivity and supply-side capacity (Luke, 2002). The Integrated Framework pilots in Cambodia, Madagascar and Mauritania have brought to the fore the challenge of linking trade and poverty reduction strategies. The pilot exercise led to an extension to 11 other least developed countries by the end of 2002, with accompanying demands for enhancements, adaptation and flexibility to suit their differing circumstances.

The Integrated Framework is still in an early stage, and its focus is still on the initial diagnostic studies rather than follow-up capacity building. As a result, assessing its development impact remains difficult. But while it is clear that the Integrated Framework is potentially an important initiative, integrating pro-poor trade strategy into national development strategies continues to represent a major challenge.

TECHNICAL ASSISTANCE AFTER DOHA

Growing criticism from developing countries and civil society organizations has renewed attention to the issue of technical assistance. The fourth WTO ministerial conference, held in Doha in 2001, emphasized the need to increase technical assistance to least developed countries and small and transition economies as a priority, as well as the need to support domestic efforts aimed at mainstreaming trade into national plans. For least developed countries, it directed the WTO Sub-Committee on LDCs to design a work programme to:

- Incorporate trade-related elements of the 2001 Brussels LDC Programme of Action.
- Review the Integrated Framework and the appraisal of the ongoing pilot scheme in selected least developed countries.
- Facilitate and accelerate the negotiations with least developed countries acceding to the WTO.

As a result of the Doha ministerial conference, the WTO general council decided to establish a regular fund for WTO trade-related technical assistance, with the aim of initially raising 15 million Swiss francs. Contributions to the Doha

Development Agenda Global Trust Fund have totalled more than twice that amount, with industrial country governments pledging more than 32 million Swiss francs to boost technical assistance in the context of WTO agreements.

The fund is an encouraging step in recognizing the importance of technical assistance and providing sufficient resources for this assistance. But new technical assistance programmes in the context of WTO agreements do not appear to differ significantly from the old ones in their underlying assumptions or in their purpose. Only when the structure and content of such technical assistance change will it effectively meet the needs of developing and least developed countries. A starting point would be to have the needs of developing countries, not donors, shape the design of the capacity building efforts. An important part of the framework for capacity development should be an independent policy research and analysis programme on trade, located in Geneva and driven by developing country needs. This framework could build on the South Centre's trade programme or be established separately.

Finally, assistance to developing countries needs to be linked to the costs they face in implementing the WTO agreements. Technical assistance has been focused on compliance, driven by donor interests and negotiated in the context of further concessions by developing countries. To ensure that technical assistance is directly relevant to developing countries, the implementation costs of all existing and future WTO agreements should be estimated, and the technical assistance provided should be commensurate with those costs.

For the trading system to benefit its poorest and most vulnerable members, capacity development in the context of the WTO is crucial. A multi-pronged strategy is required, aimed at making compliance with WTO provisions less onerous and helping to develop supply-side capacities to take advantage of new trade opportunities. Ideally, the strategy should also be aimed at enabling all countries to participate in the world trading system with equal opportunities to benefit from it.

NOTE

1. Despite the many challenges that prevent the G-24 from exerting a substantive influence in global debates on international monetary and financial reform, it has had some achievements in recent years. One has been to better integrate its research programme into G-24 operations through the creation of a technical group meeting in 1995, with the membership taking partial responsibility for funding the research programme (Mohammed, 2001).

REFERENCES

ICTSD (International Centre for Trade and Sustainable Development). 2002. 'Reference Table: Special and Differential Treatment under WTO Agreements'. Geneva.

Luke, David. 2002. 'Rethinking the Poverty Reduction Strategy Paper (PRSP) as an Instrument for Mainstreaming Trade Capacity Development'. Paper presented at the Organisation for Economic Co-operation and Development Regional Workshop on Trade Capacity Building, Mombasa, Kenya, 26–27 August. [www.oecd.org/EN/document/0,,EN-document-70-nodirectorate-no-20-33840-24,00.html#title4].

Mohammed, Azizali. 2001. 'Governance Issues in Inter-Governmental Groupings of Developing Countries'. Background paper. Global Financial Governance Initiative, Working Group on Institutional Reform, Oxford University. [users.ox.ca.uk/~ntwoods/wg3.htm].

Ohiorhenuan, John. 1998. 'Capacity Building Implications of Enhanced African Participation in Global Trade Rules-Making and Arrangements'. WTO Working Paper CRC-3-11. World Trade Organization, Geneva; African Economic Research Consortium, Nairobi.

Pallangyo, Abraham. 2002. 'Integrated Approaches to Trade Capacity Building: Lessons from the JITAP'. Paper presented at the Organisation for Economic Co-operation and Development Regional Workshop on Trade Capacity Building, 26–27 August, Mombasa, Kenya. [www.oecd.org/EN/document/0,,EN-document-70-nodirectorate-no-20-33840-24,00.html#title4].

Tandon, Yash. 2002. 'Evaluation of the WTO and Other Forms of Technical Assistance to Developing Countries in the Context of the Uruguay Round of Agreements'. Southern and Eastern African Trade, Information and Negotiations Initiative, Harare, Zimbabwe.

UNDP (United Nations Development Programme). 2002. *Capacity for Development: New Solutions to Old Problems.* London: Earthscan.